Emerging Technologies
for Healthcare

Scrivener Publishing
100 Cummings Center, Suite 541J
Beverly, MA 01915-6106

Publishers at Scrivener
Martin Scrivener (martin@scrivenerpublishing.com)
Phillip Carmical (pcarmical@scrivenerpublishing.com)

Emerging Technologies for Healthcare

Internet of Things and Deep Learning Models

Edited by

**Monika Mangla, Nonita Sharma,
Poonam Mittal,
Vaishali Mehta Wadhwa,
Thirunavukkarasu K.
and Shahnawaz Khan**

Scrivener
Publishing

WILEY

Wiley Global Headquarters
111 River Street, Hoboken, NJ 07030, USA

For details of our global editorial offices, customer services, and more information about Wiley prod-ucts visit us at www.wiley.com.

Limit of Liability/Disclaimer of Warranty
While the publisher and authors have used their best efforts in preparing this work, they make no rep-resentations or warranties with respect to the accuracy or completeness of the contents of this work and specifically disclaim all warranties, including without limitation any implied warranties of merchant-ability or fitness for a particular purpose. No warranty may be created or extended by sales representa-tives, written sales materials, or promotional statements for this work. The fact that an organization, website, or product is referred to in this work as a citation and/or potential source of further informa-tion does not mean that the publisher and authors endorse the information or services the organiza-tion, website, or product may provide or recommendations it may make. This work is sold with the understanding that the publisher is not engaged in rendering professional services. The advice and strategies contained herein may not be suitable for your situation. You should consult with a specialist where appropriate. Neither the publisher nor authors shall be liable for any loss of profit or any other commercial damages, including but not limited to special, incidental, consequential, or other damages. Further, readers should be aware that websites listed in this work may have changed or disappeared between when this work was written and when it is read.

Library of Congress Cataloging-in-Publication Data

ISBN 978-1-119-79172-0

Cover image: Pixabay.Com
Cover design by Russell Richardson

Set in size of 11pt and Minion Pro by Manila Typesetting Company, Makati, Philippines

10 9 8 7 6 5 4 3 2 1

Contents

Preface   xvii

Part I: Basics of Smart Healthcare   1

1 **An Overview of IoT in Health Sectors**   3
   Sheeba P. S.
   1.1   Introduction   3
   1.2   Influence of IoT in Healthcare Systems   6
         1.2.1   Health Monitoring   6
         1.2.2   Smart Hospitals   7
         1.2.3   Tracking Patients   7
         1.2.4   Transparent Insurance Claims   8
         1.2.5   Healthier Cities   8
         1.2.6   Research in Health Sector   8
   1.3   Popular IoT Healthcare Devices   9
         1.3.1   Hearables   9
         1.3.2   Moodables   9
         1.3.3   Ingestible Sensors   9
         1.3.4   Computer Vision   10
         1.3.5   Charting in Healthcare   10
   1.4   Benefits of IoT   10
         1.4.1   Reduction in Cost   10
         1.4.2   Quick Diagnosis and Improved Treatment   10
         1.4.3   Management of Equipment and Medicines   11
         1.4.4   Error Reduction   11
         1.4.5   Data Assortment and Analysis   11
         1.4.6   Tracking and Alerts   11
         1.4.7   Remote Medical Assistance   11
   1.5   Challenges of IoT   12
         1.5.1   Privacy and Data Security   12
         1.5.2   Multiple Devices and Protocols Integration   12

	1.5.3	Huge Data and Accuracy	12
	1.5.4	Underdeveloped	12
	1.5.5	Updating the Software Regularly	12
	1.5.6	Global Healthcare Regulations	13
	1.5.7	Cost	13
1.6	Disadvantages of IoT		13
	1.6.1	Privacy	13
	1.6.2	Access by Unauthorized Persons	13
1.7	Applications of IoT		13
	1.7.1	Monitoring of Patients Remotely	13
	1.7.2	Management of Hospital Operations	14
	1.7.3	Monitoring of Glucose	14
	1.7.4	Sensor Connected Inhaler	15
	1.7.5	Interoperability	15
	1.7.6	Connected Contact Lens	15
	1.7.7	Hearing Aid	16
	1.7.8	Coagulation of Blood	16
	1.7.9	Depression Detection	16
	1.7.10	Detection of Cancer	17
	1.7.11	Monitoring Parkinson Patient	17
	1.7.12	Ingestible Sensors	18
	1.7.13	Surgery by Robotic Devices	18
	1.7.14	Hand Sanitizing	18
	1.7.15	Efficient Drug Management	19
	1.7.16	Smart Sole	19
	1.7.17	Body Scanning	19
	1.7.18	Medical Waste Management	20
	1.7.19	Monitoring the Heart Rate	20
	1.7.20	Robot Nurse	20
1.8	Global Smart Healthcare Market		21
1.9	Recent Trends and Discussions		22
1.10	Conclusion		23
	References		23
2	**IoT-Based Solutions for Smart Healthcare**		**25**

2 IoT-Based Solutions for Smart Healthcare — **25**
*Pankaj Jain, Sonia F Panesar, Bableen Flora Talwar
and Mahesh Kumar Sah*

2.1	Introduction		26
	2.1.1	Process Flow of Smart Healthcare System	26
		2.1.1.1 Data Source	26
		2.1.1.2 Data Acquisition	27

		2.1.1.3	Data Pre-Processing	27
		2.1.1.4	Data Segmentation	28
		2.1.1.5	Feature Extraction	28
		2.1.1.6	Data Analytics	28

2.2   IoT Smart Healthcare System   29
    2.2.1   System Architecture   30
        2.2.1.1   Stage 1: Perception Layer   30
        2.2.1.2   Stage 2: Network Layer   32
        2.2.1.3   Stage 3: Data Processing Layer   32
        2.2.1.4   Stage 4: Application Layer   33
2.3   Locally and Cloud-Based IoT Architecture   33
    2.3.1   System Architecture   33
        2.3.1.1   Body Area Network (BAN)   34
        2.3.1.2   Smart Server   34
        2.3.1.3   Care Unit   35
2.4   Cloud Computing   35
    2.4.1   Infrastructure as a Service (IaaS)   37
    2.4.2   Platform as a Service (PaaS)   37
    2.4.3   Software as a Service (SaaS)   37
    2.4.4   Types of Cloud Computing   37
        2.4.4.1   Public Cloud   37
        2.4.4.2   Private Cloud   38
        2.4.4.3   Hybrid Cloud   38
        2.4.4.4   Community Cloud   38
2.5   Outbreak of Arduino Board   38
2.6   Applications of Smart Healthcare System   39
    2.6.1   Disease Diagnosis and Treatment   41
    2.6.2   Health Risk Monitoring   42
    2.6.3   Voice Assistants   42
    2.6.4   Smart Hospital   42
    2.6.5   Assist in Research and Development   43
2.7   Smart Wearables and Apps   43
2.8   Deep Learning in Biomedical   44
    2.8.1   Deep Learning   46
    2.8.2   Deep Neural Network Architecture   47
    2.8.3   Deep Learning in Bioinformatic   49
    2.8.4   Deep Learning in Bioimaging   49
    2.8.5   Deep Learning in Medical Imaging   50
    2.8.6   Deep Learning in Human-Machine Interface   53
    2.8.7   Deep Learning in Health Service Management   53

2.9 Conclusion   55
     References   55

3 QLattice Environment and Feyn QGraph Models—A New Perspective Toward Deep Learning   **69**
Vinayak Bharadi
3.1 Introduction   70
     3.1.1 Machine Learning Models   70
3.2 Machine Learning Model Lifecycle   71
     3.2.1 Steps in Machine Learning Lifecycle   71
         3.2.1.1 Data Preparation   72
         3.2.1.2 Building the Machine Learning Model   72
         3.2.1.3 Model Training   72
         3.2.1.4 Parameter Selection   72
         3.2.1.5 Transfer Learning   73
         3.2.1.6 Model Verification   73
         3.2.1.7 Model Deployment   74
         3.2.1.8 Monitoring   74
3.3 A Model Deployment in Keras   75
     3.3.1 Pima Indian Diabetes Dataset   75
     3.3.2 Multi-Layered Perceptron Implementation in Keras   76
     3.3.3 Multi-Layered Perceptron Implementation With Dropout and Added Noise   77
3.4 QLattice Environment   80
     3.4.1 Feyn Models   80
         3.4.1.1 Semantic Types   82
         3.4.1.2 Interactions   83
         3.4.1.3 Generating QLattice   83
     3.4.2 QLattice Workflow   83
         3.4.2.1 Preparing the Data   84
         3.4.2.2 Connecting to QLattice   84
         3.4.2.3 Generating QGraphs   84
         3.4.2.4 Fitting, Sorting, and Updating QGraphs   85
         3.4.2.5 Model Evaluation   86
3.5 Using QLattice Environment and QGraph Models for COVID-19 Impact Prediction   87
     References   91

**4   Sensitive Healthcare Data: Privacy and Security Issues
and Proposed Solutions**   **93**
Abhishek Vyas, Satheesh Abimannan and Ren-Hung Hwang
4.1   Introduction   94
    4.1.1   Types of Technologies Used in Healthcare Industry   94
    4.1.2   Technical Differences Between Security and Privacy   95
    4.1.3   HIPAA Compliance   95
4.2   Medical Sensor Networks/Medical Internet
    of Things/Body Area Networks/WBANs   97
    4.2.1   Security and Privacy Issues in WBANs/WMSNs/
        WMIOTs   101
4.3   Cloud Storage and Computing on Sensitive Healthcare Data   112
    4.3.1   Security and Privacy in Cloud Computing
        and Storage for Sensitive Healthcare Data   114
4.4   Blockchain for Security and Privacy Enhancement
    in Sensitive Healthcare Data   119
4.5   Artificial Intelligence, Machine Learning, and Big Data
    in Healthcare and Its Efficacy in Security and Privacy
    of Sensitive Healthcare Data   122
    4.5.1   Differential Privacy for Preserving Privacy of
        Big Medical Healthcare Data and for Its Analytics   124
4.6   Conclusion   124
    References   125

**Part II: Employment of Machine Learning
in Disease Detection**   **129**

5   Diabetes Prediction Model Based on Machine Learning   **131**
*Ayush Kumar Gupta, Sourabh Yadav, Priyanka Bhartiya
and Divesh Gupta*
5.1   Introduction   131
5.2   Literature Review   133
5.3   Proposed Methodology   135
    5.3.1   Data Accommodation   135
        5.3.1.1   Data Collection   135
        5.3.1.2   Data Preparation   136
    5.3.2   Model Training   138
        5.3.2.1   K Nearest Neighbor Classification Technique   139

5.3.2.2   Support Vector Machine   140
5.3.2.3   Random Forest Algorithm   142
5.3.2.4   Logistic Regression   144
5.3.3   Model Evaluation   145
5.3.4   User Interaction   145
5.3.4.1   User Inputs   146
5.3.4.2   Validation Using Classifier Model   146
5.3.4.3   Truth Probability   146
5.4   System Implementation   147
5.5   Conclusion   153
References   153

6   **Lung Cancer Detection Using 3D CNN Based
on Deep Learning**   **157**
*Siddhant Panda, Vasudha Chhetri, Vikas Kumar Jaiswal
and Sourabh Yadav*
6.1   Introduction   157
6.2   Literature Review   159
6.3   Proposed Methodology   161
6.3.1   Data Handling   161
6.3.1.1   Data Gathering   161
6.3.1.2   Data Pre-Processing   162
6.3.2   Data Visualization and Data Split   162
6.3.2.1   Data Visualization   162
6.3.2.2   Data Split   162
6.3.3   Model Training   163
6.3.3.1   Training Neural Network   163
6.3.3.2   Model Optimization   166
6.4   Results and Discussion   168
6.4.1   Gathering and Pre-Processing of Data   169
6.4.1.1   Gathering and Handling Data   169
6.4.1.2   Pre-Processing of Data   170
6.4.2   Data Visualization   171
6.4.2.1   Resampling   173
6.4.2.2   3D Plotting Scan   173
6.4.2.3   Lung Segmentation   173
6.4.3   Training and Testing of Data in 3D Architecture   175
6.5   Conclusion   178
References   178

7   Pneumonia Detection Using CNN and ANN Based
    on Deep Learning Approach   181
    Priyanka Bhartiya, Sourabh Yadav, Ayush Gupta
    and Divesh Gupta
    7.1   Introduction   182
    7.2   Literature Review   183
    7.3   Proposed Methodology   185
          7.3.1   Data Gathering   185
                  7.3.1.1   Data Collection   185
                  7.3.1.2   Data Pre-Processing   186
                  7.3.1.3   Data Split   186
          7.3.2   Model Training   187
                  7.3.2.1   Training of Convolutional Neural Network   189
                  7.3.2.2   Training of Artificial Neural Network   191
          7.3.3   Model Fitting   193
                  7.3.3.1   Fit Generator   193
                  7.3.3.2   Validation of Accuracy and Loss Plot 193
                  7.3.3.3   Testing and Prediction   193
    7.4   System Implementation   194
          7.4.1   Data Gathering, Pre-Processing, and Split   194
                  7.4.1.1   Data Gathering   194
                  7.4.1.2   Data Pre-Processing   195
                  7.4.1.3   Data Split   196
          7.4.2   Model Building   196
          7.4.3   Model Fitting   197
                  7.4.3.1   Fit Generator   197
                  7.4.3.2   Validation of Accuracy and Loss Plot 197
                  7.4.3.3   Testing and Prediction   198
    7.5   Conclusion   199
          References   199

8   Personality Prediction and Handwriting Recognition
    Using Machine Learning   203
    Vishal Patil and Harsh Mathur
    8.1   Introduction to the System   204
          8.1.1   Assumptions and Limitations   206
                  8.1.1.1   Assumptions   206
                  8.1.1.2   Limitations   206
          8.1.2   Practical Needs   206

8.1.3	Non-Functional Needs	206
8.1.4	Specifications for Hardware	207
8.1.5	Specifications for Applications	207
8.1.6	Targets	207
8.1.7	Outcomes	207
8.2	Literature Survey	208
8.2.1	Computerized Human Behavior Identification Through Handwriting Samples	208
8.2.2	Behavior Prediction Through Handwriting Analysis	209
8.2.3	Handwriting Sample Analysis for a Finding of Personality Using Machine Learning Algorithms	209
8.2.4	Personality Detection Using Handwriting Analysis	210
8.2.5	Automatic Predict Personality Based on Structure of Handwriting	210
8.2.6	Personality Identification Through Handwriting Analysis: A Review	210
8.2.7	Text Independent Writer Identification Using Convolutional Neural Network	210
8.2.8	Writer Identification Using Machine Learning Approaches	211
8.2.9	Writer Identification from Handwritten Text Lines	211
8.3	Theory	212
8.3.1	Pre-Processing	212
8.3.2	Personality Analysis	215
8.3.3	Personality Characteristics	216
8.3.4	Writer Identification	217
8.3.5	Features Used	219
8.4	Algorithm To Be Used	220
8.5	Proposed Methodology	224
8.5.1	System Flow	225
8.6	Algorithms *vs.* Accuracy	226
8.6.1	Implementation	228
8.7	Experimental Results	231
8.8	Conclusion	232
8.9	Conclusion and Future Scope	232
	Acknowledgment	232
	References	233

9   **Risk Mitigation in Children With Autism Spectrum Disorder Using Brain Source Localization**   237
    Joy Karan Singh, Deepti Kakkar and Tanu Wadhera
    9.1   Introduction   238
    9.2   Risk Factors Related to Autism   239
          9.2.1   Assistive Technologies for Autism   240
          9.2.2   Functional Connectivity as a Biomarker for Autism   241
          9.2.3   Early Intervention and Diagnosis   242
    9.3   Materials and Methodology   243
          9.3.1   Subjects   243
          9.3.2   Methods   243
          9.3.3   Data Acquisition and Processing   243
          9.3.4   sLORETA as a Diagnostic Tool   244
    9.4   Results and Discussion   245
    9.5   Conclusion and Future Scope   247
          References   247

10 **Predicting Chronic Kidney Disease Using Machine Learning**   251
    Monika Gupta and Parul Gupta
    10.1   Introduction   252
    10.2   Machine Learning Techniques for Prediction
           of Kidney Failure   253
           10.2.1   Analysis and Empirical Learning   254
           10.2.2   Supervised Learning   255
           10.2.3   Unsupervised Learning   256
                    10.2.3.1   Understanding and Visualization   257
                    10.2.3.2   Odd Detection   257
                    10.2.3.3   Object Completion   258
                    10.2.3.4   Information Acquisition   258
                    10.2.3.5   Data Compression   258
                    10.2.3.6   Capital Market   258
           10.2.4   Classification   259
                    10.2.4.1   Training Process   260
                    10.2.4.2   Testing Process   260
           10.2.5   Decision Tree   261
           10.2.6   Regression Analysis   263
                    10.2.6.1   Logistic Regression   263
                    10.2.6.2   Ordinal Logistic Regression   265
                    10.2.6.3   Estimating Parameters   266
                    10.2.6.4   Multivariate Regression   268
    10.3   Data Sources   269

10.4	Data Analysis	272
10.5	Conclusion	274
10.6	Future Scope	274
	References	274

Part III: Advanced Applications of Machine Learning in Healthcare 279

11 Behavioral Modeling Using Deep Neural Network Framework for ASD Diagnosis and Prognosis 281
Tanu Wadhera, Deepti Kakkar and Rajneesh Rani

11.1	Introduction	282
11.2	Automated Diagnosis of ASD	284
	11.2.1 Deep Learning	289
	11.2.2 Deep Learning in ASD	290
	11.2.3 Transfer Learning Approach	290
11.3	Purpose of the Chapter	292
11.4	Proposed Diagnosis System	293
11.5	Conclusion	294
	References	295

12 Random Forest Application of Twitter Data Sentiment Analysis in Online Social Network Prediction 299
Arnav Munshi, M. Arvindhan and Thirunavukkarasu K.

12.1	Introduction	300
	12.1.1 Motivation	300
	12.1.2 Domain Introduction	300
12.2	Literature Survey	302
12.3	Proposed Methodology	304
12.4	Implementation	311
12.5	Conclusion	311
	References	311

13 Remedy to COVID-19: Social Distancing Analyzer 315
Sourabh Yadav

13.1	Introduction	315
13.2	Literature Review	318
13.3	Proposed Methodology	321
	13.3.1 Person Detection	321
	13.3.1.1 Frame Creation	324
	13.3.1.2 Contour Detection	325

13.3.1.3   Matching with COCO Model   326

13.3.2   Distance Calculation   326

13.3.2.1   Calculation of Centroid   326

13.3.2.2   Distance Among Adjacent Centroids   327

13.4   System Implementation   328

13.5   Conclusion   333

References   334

14 IoT-Enabled Vehicle Assistance System of Highway Resourcing for Smart Healthcare and Sustainability   **337**

Shubham Joshi and Radha Krishna Rambola

14.1   Introduction   338

14.2   Related Work   340

14.2.1   Adoption of IoT in Vehicle to Ensure Driver Safety   341

14.2.2   IoT in Healthcare System   341

14.2.3   The Technology Used in Assistance Systems   343

14.2.3.1   Adaptive Cruise Control (ACC)   343

14.2.3.2   Lane Departure Warning   343

14.2.3.3   Parking Assistance   343

14.2.3.4   Collision Avoidance System   343

14.2.3.5   Driver Drowsiness Detection   344

14.2.3.6   Automotive Night Vision   344

14.3   Objectives, Context, and Ethical Approval   344

14.4   Technical Background   345

14.4.1   IoT With Health   345

14.4.2   Machine-to-Machine (M2M) Communication   345

14.4.3   Device-to-Device (D2D) Communication   345

14.4.4   Wireless Sensor Network   346

14.4.5   Crowdsensing   346

14.5   IoT Infrastructural Components for Vehicle Assistance System   346

14.5.1   Communication Technology   346

14.5.2   Sensor Network   347

14.5.3   Infrastructural Component   348

14.5.4   Human Health Detection by Sensors   348

14.6   IoT-Enabled Vehicle Assistance System of Highway Resourcing for Smart Healthcare and Sustainability   349

14.7   Challenges in Implementation   353

14.8   Conclusion   353

References   354

15 Aids of Machine Learning for Additively Manufactured Bone Scaffold   **359**

Nimisha Rahul Shirbhate and Sanjay Bokade

15.1   Introduction   360
     15.1.1   Bone Scaffold   360
     15.1.2   Bone Grafting   362
     15.1.3   Comparison Bone Grafting and Bone Scaffold   363
15.2   Research Background   364
15.3   Statement of Problem   364
15.4   Research Gap   365
15.5   Significance of Research   366
15.6   Outline of Research Methodology   366
     15.6.1   Customized Design of Bone Scaffold   366
     15.6.2   Manufacturing Methods and Biocompatible Material   367
         15.6.2.1   Conventional Scaffold Fabrication   368
         15.6.2.2   Additive Manufacturing   369
         15.6.2.3   Application of Additive Manufacturing/ 3D Printing in Healthcare   370
         15.6.2.4   Automated Process Monitoring in 3D Printing Using Supervised Machine Learning   376
15.7   Conclusion   377
     References   377

Index   **381**

Preface

The use of computing technologies in the healthcare domain has been creating new avenues for facilitating the work of healthcare professionals. Several computing technologies, such as machine learning and virtual reality, have been flourishing and in turn creating new possibilities. Computing algorithms, methodologies and approaches are being used to provide accurate, stable and prompt results. Moreover, deep learning, an advanced learning technique, is striving to enable computing models to mimic the behavior of the human brain; and the Internet-of-Things (IoT), the computer network consisting of "things" or physical objects in addition to sensors, software or methods, is connecting to and exchanging data with other devices. Therefore, the primary focus of this book, *Emerging Technologies for Healthcare*, is to discuss the use and applications of these IoT and deep learning approaches for providing automated healthcare solutions.

Our motivation behind writing this book was to provide insight gained by analyzing data and information, and in the end provide feasible solutions through various machine learning approaches and apply them to disease analysis and prediction. An example of this is employing a three-dimensional matrix approach for treating chronic kidney disease, the diagnosis and prognostication of acquired demyelinating syndrome (ADS) and autism spectrum disorder, and the detection of pneumonia. In addition to this, providing healthcare solutions for post COVID-19 outbreaks through various suitable approaches is also highlighted. Furthermore, a detailed detection mechanism is discussed which is used to come up with solutions for predicting personality through handwriting recognition; and novel approaches for sentiment analysis are also discussed with sufficient data and its dimensions.

This book not only covers theoretical approaches and algorithms, but also contains the sequence of steps used to analyze problems with data, processes, reports, and optimization techniques. It will serve as a single source for solving various problems via machine learning algorithms.

In brief, this book starts with an IoT-based solution for the automated healthcare sector and extends to providing solutions with advanced deep learning techniques.

Here, we would like to take the opportunity to acknowledge the assistance and contributions of all those engaged in this project. We especially would like to thank our authors for contributing their valuable work, without which it would have been impossible to complete this book. We express our special and most sincere thanks to the reviewers involved in the review process who contributed their time and expertise to improving the quality, consistency, and arrangement of the chapters. We also would like to take the opportunity to express our thanks to the team at Scrivener Publishing for giving the book its final shape and introducing it to the public.

Editors
Monika Mangla, Nonita Sharma,
Poonam Mittal, Vaishali Mehta Wadhwa,
Thirunavukkarasu K. and Shahnawaz Khan

Part I

BASICS OF SMART HEALTHCARE

An Overview of IoT in Health Sectors

Sheeba P. S.

Department of Electronics Engineering, Lokmanya Tilak College of Engineering, Navi Mumbai, India

Abstract

In the recent past, several technological developments have happened owing to the growing demand for connected devices. Applications of Internet of Things (IoT) are vast, and it is used in several fields including home-automation, automated machines, agriculture, finance sectors, and smart cities. Life style diseases are increasing among urban population and lot of money is spent for the diagnosis and treatment of diseases. Adaption of IoTs in health sectors enables real-time monitoring of the patients and alerts the patients for health checkups whenever required and communicate the information from time to time. During pandemic situations like Covid-19 which we are facing today, the need for IoT-enabled services in health sector is essential as the doctors have to treat the patients from remote locations. The connected devices can help in surveillance and disease control, keep track of nutritional needs, mental health, stress management, emergency services, etc., which will lead to an efficient health management system. This article gives an overview of applications of IoT in health sectors and how it can be used for sustainable development and also addresses various challenges involved in it. Efficient use of IoT in health sectors can benefit healthcare professionals, patients, insurance companies, etc.

Keywords: IoT, healthcare, smart gadgets, health monitoring

1.1 Introduction

Due to the increase in awareness of a healthy life style, the number of people depending on smart devices for monitoring their health is increasing day

Email: sheebaps@gmail.com

Monika Mangla, Nonita Sharma, Poonam Mittal, Vaishali Mehta Wadhwa, Thirunavukkarasu K. and Shahnawaz Khan (eds.) Emerging Technologies for Healthcare: Internet of Things and Deep Learning Models, (3–24) © 2021 Scrivener Publishing LLC

by day. IoT devices have become very essential to be the part of daily life in this technological advanced world. Various advancements are happening in the healthcare sectors from the recent past. With the advancement in technology in the use of IoTs integrated with Artificial Intelligence, a major digital transformation is happening in the healthcare sector. Various research is going on in this area which will add new dimensions to the healthcare system.

Wireless Body Area Networks (WBANs) have also been used extensively in healthcare services due to the advancement in technology. A survey on healthcare application based on WBAN is discussed in [1]. The paper also analyses the privacy and security features that arises by the use of IoTs in healthcare systems.

Use of RFID has become very common owing to the extensive applications of IoTs. A survey on RFID applications for gathering information about the living environment and body centric systems is discussed in [2]. The challenges and open research opportunities are also discussed in the article.

Various research is ongoing on to find the methods to improve the monitoring and tracking of the patients in an efficient manner. In [3], a novel IoT-aware smart architecture is proposed to monitor and track the patients. A smart hospital system is proposed which can collect real-time data and environmental factors by making use of ultra-low power hybrid sensing network.

A secure IoT-based healthcare system which operates with body sensor network architecture is introduced in [4]. Two communication mechanisms for authenticity and secured communication is addressed. The proposed method was implemented and tested using a Raspberry Pi platform.

In [5], authors address a survey paper on the IoT research and the discusses about the challenges, strengths and suitability of IoT healthcare devices and mentions about the future research directions.

One of the challenges faced by the IoT systems is regarding the security and privacy of data. In [6], the authors proposed a hybrid model for securing the medical images data. This model aims to hide the confidential patient data from the image while transmitting it.

Wireless body networks are becoming popular with the increased use of IoT smart devices. In [7], a solar energy powered wearable sensor node is addressed. At various positions of the body multiple sensors are deployed and a web-based application is used for displaying sensor data.

Experiment results achieved good results for autonomous operation for 24 hours.

Body sensor networks is the one of the significant technologies used to monitor the patients by means of tiny wireless sensor nodes in the body. Security of such IoT devices poses a major issue in privacy of the patients. A secure system for healthcare called BSN-care is addressed in [8].

Securing the privacy of patients is of utmost importance for IoT-based healthcare systems. Various research is going on this area. In [9], a big data storage system to secure the privacy of the patients is addressed. The medical data generated is encrypted before it is transferred to the data storage. This system is designed as a self-adaptive one where it can operate on emergency and normal conditions.

Various systems are developed to take care of the personal needs while traveling which can aid in travel and tourism. An intelligent travel recommender system called ProTrip is developed in [10]. This system helps travelers who are on strict diet and having long-term diseases in getting proper nutritional value foods according to the climatic conditions. This system supports the IoT healthcare system for food recommendation.

The issues in the security and privacy of IoT-based healthcare system are a major concern. Most of the system is based on cloud computing for IoT solutions which has certain limitations based on economic aspects, storage of data, geographical architecture, etc. To overcome this limitation, a Fog computing approach is addressed in [11] and authors explores the integration of traditional cloud-based structure and Cloud Fog services in interoperable healthcare solutions.

For IoT-based healthcare system efficient authorization and authentication is required for securing the data. Such a system is addressed in [12]. It was found that the proposed model is more secure than the centralized delegation-based architecture as it uses a secure key management between the smart gateway and sensor nodes.

Recent security attacks for the private data and integrity of data is a matter of concern for the IoT healthcare systems. Conventional methods of security solutions are for the protection of data during patient communication but it does not offer the security protection during the data conversion into the cipher. A secure data collection scheme for IoT healthcare system called SecureData scheme is proposed in [13], and the experimental results showed that this scheme is efficient in protecting security risks.

Life style diseases like diabetes are common nowadays. It is very important for such patients to follow a strict diet and most of the time it is difficult for the healthcare professionals to get the precise physiological parameter of the patients. Without the knowledge of the current condition of the patients, it is difficult for the ontologies to recommend a proper diet for such patients. A fuzzy-based ontology recommendation system is proposed in [14] which can determine patient's conditions and risk factors by means of wearable sensors and accordingly can suggest the diet. The experimental results proved that the system is efficient for diabetes patients.

The data generated through IoT devices are prone to security threats. Maintaining the privacy of the patient data is of utmost importance. Traditional encryption schemes cannot be applied on healthcare data due to the limitations in the properties of digital data. A chaos-based encryption cryptosystem to preserve the privacy of patients is proposed in [15]. Random images are generated by the cryptosystem which ensures highest security level for the patient data. The performance of this model was found to be better than other encryption schemes.

The trends of IoT in healthcare sectors and the future scope for research is discussed in [16]. A sensor-based communication architecture and authentication scheme for IoT-based healthcare systems is addressed in [17]. Various research articles on big data analytics, and IoT in healthcare is addressed in [18].

With the enormous research happening in the field of IoT applications in healthcare sectors, new dimensions to the healthcare treatments and hospital services can be expected in the coming years.

1.2   Influence of IoT in Healthcare Systems

Due to the awareness about the importance of healthy life, people have become more health conscious nowadays. Humans are finding new ways to improve and track their health. Due to the implementation of emerging technologies like IoTs and Artificial Intelligence (AI), the healthcare systems have evolved as an entirely new system replacing the old system. Various stages of IoT system is shown in Figure 1.1.

Various developments have occurred in the healthcare systems in the recent past. Some of the advancements are discussed in this section.

1.2.1   Health Monitoring

Health monitoring on real-time basis became possible due to the invention of wearable smart gadgets. These devices continuously monitor various

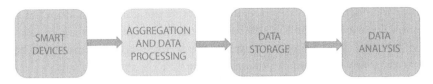

Figure 1.1 Stages of IoT.

parameters like blood pressure, heart rate, oxygen level, and calories burnt. Fitness bands helps individuals to maintain their body healthy and fit by regularly alerting them about the steps taken per day and how much calories needs to be burnt to stay healthy.

These devices can be interconnected by IoT devices so that the healthcare workers and immediate family members can monitor the parameters and they will be alerted for any emergency situation. Such devices are very helpful for elderly persons who are living alone as they get immediate medical attention if there are variations in their body parameters.

1.2.2   Smart Hospitals

Smart hospitals mean all the equipment in the hospitals are connected through IoTs in addition to real-time monitoring system for the patients. Managing the assets in the hospitals can be made in a smarter way by means of IoTs. The equipment like oxygen cylinders, wheelchairs, and nebulizers can be tracked on real-time basis and made available when in need.

Now, in the current Covid-19 scenario, we have observed how the hospitals were managing the resources in a smarter way. The number of occupied beds and available bed status is updated on real-time basis, and the data is made available in various digital platforms.

Cleanliness and hygiene also can be maintained in an efficient manner. Environmental conditions like humidity and temperature can be monitored continuously and the spread of diseases can be prevented efficiently.

1.2.3   Tracking Patients

Due to the advancement of technology, hospitals have become more patient friendly. The duration of hospital stay can be reduced due to the online real-time monitoring of the patient data through IoT devices. It is easier for doctors to track the patient data at the comfort of sitting at a remote location. As the IoT devices are attached to the patients, continuous monitoring of the vital parameters is possible, and the doctors will be alerted for any variations in the parameters.

These smart devices not only track the patient's health parameters but also alert the patients for their consultation schedules. It also keeps the records of previous medications or medical history which aids the doctors in right diagnosis and treatments.

The availability of patient's data on IoT devices helps the hospitals to track the patients and provide quick medical attention in an efficient manner.

1.2.4   Transparent Insurance Claims

Healthcare insurance policy holders are increasing on a yearly basis. Due to the large number of policy holders who aims to get maximum profits by claiming the insurance, false claims are also increasing. Due to the presence of IoT devices which tracks the patient data, insurance companies can easily detect any fraud in the claims.

These devices not only help the patients to manage their insurance policies but also help the insurance companies to track the health of patients, underwriting, risk assessments, etc. Due to the IoT-enabled devices, the insurance claims became transparent and benefitting the genuine policy claims.

1.2.5   Healthier Cities

Population in cities are more compared to the rural areas as people prefer to have better quality and standards of living in cities with better facilities and infrastructures. Most of the cities are crowded and majority of the population use public and private transport for commuting. Vehicle densities in cities are more compared to villages which lead to more air pollution which, in turn, affect the health of the individuals and the environment.

Due to the advancement in technology in terms of usage of IoT devices, continuous real-time monitoring of the air quality is possible. The tracking of the air quality patterns helps the authorities to take appropriate actions to improve the air quality which, in turn, help to maintain a healthier city.

1.2.6   Research in Health Sector

Research in medical field is a continuous process which requires lot of time in gathering the patient data and analyzing it. Connected devices through IoTs generate large amount of real-time data which can be used for research purposes in an efficient manner as data collection becomes much easier with less amount of time and money. Statistical and comparative study analysis is possible as these devices can be connected anywhere in the world and data can be generated which will aid in medical research.

Innovative methods of treatments can be introduced by doing proper research in an efficient and quick manner due to the presence of IoT devices. This also helps to improve the healthcare services.

Smart monitoring devices will monitor all the parameters inside a medical laboratory and alerts if there is an abnormality so that immediate action can be taken. Based on the data available, various research studies can be done with much ease.

1.3   Popular IoT Healthcare Devices

New devices are invented to match with the technological advancements. These new devices aim to make the life easier for humans. Some of the popular IoT devices for healthcare are as follows:

1.3.1   Hearables

Hearables are one of the popular IoT devices which are used by the people for hearing aid. With these devices, people who have difficulty in hearing or those who are hearing impaired can interact with the outside world. This device can be connected with other smart devices like mobile phones and data can be synchronized. Various types of filters and equalizers are used for better user experience to match with the real sounds.

1.3.2   Moodables

Moodables are devices which enhances the mood of a person by sending triggering signals to the brain. These devices must be worn on head which has inbuilt sensors to elevate the mood.

1.3.3   Ingestible Sensors

These are like small pills which can be ingested to monitor our body from inside and can give warning signals to the doctors in case of any abnormalities. This device is made up with sensors of pill size which can give warning for any underlying diseases. These sensors can detect whether the prescribed medicines are taken properly and also can help in drug management.

1.3.4   Computer Vision

Computer vision technology mimics the human vision by making use of Artificial Intelligence. This technology has been implemented in drones which help them to navigate and detect obstacles. Visually impaired people can make use of this technology to navigate easily.

1.3.5   Charting in Healthcare

IoT devices helps doctors to maintain the patient data in an efficient manner. Doctors can easily get the charting of various parameters like blood pressure and sugar level from the connected devices and it can be immediately reviewed and shared with the patient's devices. This saves huge amount of time that doctors spend in creating manual charts for individual patients.

1.4   Benefits of IoT

Various benefits of IoTs are discussed in this section.

1.4.1   Reduction in Cost

As the doctors can remotely monitor the patients using IoT-enabled devices, the cost in visiting the healthcare facilities and consultation can be drastically reduced. Since the real-time monitoring of the patients is possible with IoT devices, hospital admissions can also be reduced by providing timely treatments.

1.4.2   Quick Diagnosis and Improved Treatment

Doctors can easily diagnose the diseases as real-time monitoring is possible with IoT devices and can give appropriate treatment on time at an early stage. Patients can also be fully aware about their health conditions and the treatments provided. Hence, the transparency in treatment can also be maintained. Doctors can provide proactive treatment to the patients based on the real-time data collected.

The continuous monitoring of patients helps to save many lives during emergency medical situations which arise due to heart attacks, asthma attacks, high blood pressure, etc.

1.4.3   Management of Equipment and Medicines

It is very important for the hospitals to manage the healthcare equipment as the utilization of those equipment should be optimized. Through IoT connected devices, it will be easier to manage the equipment as the utilization of the equipment is properly monitored on real-time basis and the equipment which are available for use at a particular time can be easily identified with the location of the equipment. Similarly, the medicine stocks can also be properly monitored using IoT devices.

1.4.4   Error Reduction

As the real-time data is continuously collected through IoT devices, decision-making becomes much easier which helps in the smooth functioning of the healthcare systems. This not only saves the time but also reduces the cost of operation.

1.4.5   Data Assortment and Analysis

Huge amount of data is collected by IoT devices. These data can be used for analysis purposes. As IoT devices collect and analyse the data, storing of manual records is not required. The data is available on real time and stored in cloud and can be made available to the healthcare professionals or patients. The error in analysis can be eliminated compared to the manual analysis.

1.4.6   Tracking and Alerts

The patients are connected to IoT devices so that the doctors can keep track of their health on real-time basis. Doctors get alerts on life threatening emergency situations which enables them to take proper decisions and provide right treatments with better accuracy.

1.4.7   Remote Medical Assistance

In an emergency, patients can contact doctors through connected devices irrespective of the location which enables them to avoid the hospital visits and un-necessary expenses. Doctors will be able to check the patients online and prescribe the medicines. In future, delivery chains are aiming to provide machines which can distribute medicines to the patients based on their data available through the connected devices.

1.5   Challenges of IoT

Various challenges faced by the IoT devices are discussed in this section.

1.5.1   Privacy and Data Security

Data security and privacy are the most crucial challenges of IoT devices. As huge amount of data is generated through the connected devices, it is highly susceptible to cybercrimes. Without proper data security and protocols, personal data of patients as well as doctors can be hacked and misused. Fake IDs may be created by cyber criminals which can be used for fake insurance claims and businesses.

1.5.2   Multiple Devices and Protocols Integration

Various devices of different manufacturers must be interconnected for the implementation of IoT. As there are no standardized communication protocols to be followed by the manufacturers, integration of multiple protocols becomes difficult and it will hinder the operation of these devices. Also, the system may become more complicated. This may result in an inefficient system if standardized communication protocols are not in place.

1.5.3   Huge Data and Accuracy

A huge amount of data is generated by the IoT devices. As the number of devices increases, the data generated also will increase. If huge amount of data is generated, it will be difficult for the doctors to analyse the data and take proper decisions which, in turn, may affect the accuracy.

1.5.4   Underdeveloped

Even though the use of IoT devices in health sector is increasing day by day, still the development is not up to the mark. It is still in development stage only. It has to progress in a faster pace for better results.

1.5.5   Updating the Software Regularly

With the implementation of hardware for IoT devices, software also becomes part of the system. It has to be regularly updated for better performance and added security features. Regularly monitoring and updating the software is required which may not be possible easy at times.

1.5.6   Global Healthcare Regulations

For every new technology implementation, proper approval from healthcare regulating bodies is required. But formulations of new regulations are not done very frequently and is a time-consuming process which may cause difficulty in implementation of new technologies and innovations.

1.5.7   Cost

The cost of healthcare facilities in developed countries is high compared to the developing countries. With the use of IoT devices, cost is not reduced for using the healthcare facilities. It must be made cost effective then only it can benefit the common man.

1.6   Disadvantages of IoT

Disadvantages of IoT is discussed in this section.

1.6.1   Privacy

As IoT devices operates hugely on personal data, serious security issues can happen due to hacking which may result in data theft. So, there should be proper security and firewalls in place which may require additional expenses.

1.6.2   Access by Unauthorized Persons

As the real-time sensitive data is available in connected devices, the access to those data needs to be protected. Proper care should be taken to ensure that the data is accessed by authorized persons only. Unauthorized access may create data leaking and misuse of the data.

1.7   Applications of IoT

Various applications of IoT devices are discussed in this section.

1.7.1   Monitoring of Patients Remotely

Patient monitoring from remote locations is possible with the help of IoT devices. This reduces the number of cases of hospital admissions which, in turn, reduces the expenses. After a major illness or surgery, when the patients are discharged from the hospitals, doctors can keep track of the health of the patients and reduce re-admissions.

In rural areas where the healthcare facilities are poor, doctors can monitor the patients sitting at a remote location and can reduce the death rates.

The expenses incurred for traveling long distance for consultations, hospitalizations, etc., can be reduced. Even IoT devices can alert the healthcare professionals if the patients are not taking medicines regularly or taking wrong medications. With the continuous monitoring of the patients, health risks can be reduced drastically.

1.7.2   Management of Hospital Operations

Hospital operations involves management of various equipment and drugs. It is difficult to manage this equipment in an optimal way as the doctors are always busy with their patients. By means of IoT devices, management of equipment becomes much easier. As the equipment are regularly monitored, fault in that equipment can be easily detected and rectified. Also, IoT devices can alert the authorities about any outdated equipment which needs replacement.

Most of the time, it is difficult to track how many available equipment are for use and the exact location of the equipment. IoT devices keep track of the available equipment and their locations which helps the healthcare professional to locate the equipment quickly which can save many lives.

IoT devices also alert the hospital authorities about the cleanliness and hygiene of the surrounding environment which can lead to maintenance of a healthy environment which, in turn, prevent the spread of the diseases.

1.7.3   Monitoring of Glucose

Glucose monitoring on a daily basis is very essential nowadays due to the rise in life style diseases like diabetes. Diabetes is a high-risk disease which can lead to high blood pressure, heart attacks, etc. This life style disease is due to the abnormal functioning of the pancreas gland.

There may be variations in sugar level due to the abnormal functioning of the pancreas gland. These variations can lead to organ damages if not properly detected. Hence, continuous monitoring of the sugar level is essential for a healthy life style.

With the advancement in technology several wearable connected devices and sensors are available in the market which can monitor glucose levels on real-time basis and update it on the connected devices.

As the sugar levels are monitored on regular basis, any rise in sugar levels can be detected early and proper action can be taken at the right time before it affects the overall health.

Hence, by the use of IoT devices, many lives can be saved and also can save hospital expenses.

1.7.4   Sensor Connected Inhaler

Air pollution is increasing day by day due to the increase in the number of vehicles on road. Increase in air pollution leads to increase in lung diseases. One of the most common lung diseases which is on rise is asthma. These lung diseases are controlled by inhalers.

Usually, symptoms of an asthma attack appear few hours before the peak. If the sensor connected inhalers are used by the patients, then it can detect triggering factors and alert the patients as well as the doctors about the possibility of an asthma attack through IoT connected devices.

IoT devices not only can alert the patients about the possible asthma attacks but also can help doctors in instructing the patients when to stop inhalers there by optimizing the medication and reducing the expenses for medical bills.

1.7.5   Interoperability

Data collected through IoT devices is huge. These data play a major role in healthcare system as doctors can always look into the historical data of the patients.

Most of the time when a new patient consults a doctor, it is difficult for the doctors to diagnose the diseases without proper testing. But if the historical data is available with the doctors, diagnosis of the chronic diseases becomes much easier. The data can be made available at multiple locations, wherein interoperability becomes much easier and patient care can be optimized. The historical data can also be used for medical research and development.

1.7.6   Connected Contact Lens

Eye is the most important part of human organ. Diagnosis of some of the diseases can be made through by observing the changes that occur in the eyes.

Contact lens is commonly used nowadays for eye sight problems and for enhancing the appearance of the eyes. With IoT-based contact lens, it can do wonders for humans. It not only aids in enhancement of eye sight it also monitors the changes that occurs in the eyes which can lead to early diagnosis of diseases.

By monitoring the variations in the eye ball size, it can diagnose glaucoma at an early stage, any delay in detection of abnormalities may result in loss of eye sight.

Even the eye medications can be directly administered to the eyes with the aid of contact lens which, in turn, gets rid of the inconvenience of administering the eye drops.

In future, such technologies will add new dimensions to the eyecare system.

1.7.7   Hearing Aid

Hearing aid has been used by many people around the world who have hearing issues and wants to enhance hearing. But due to the invention of IoT devices, hearing aids became smarter. It not only aids in hearing but also assist in other activities too.

People even can hear their door bells ringing from a far place if it is connected by IoT devices. It can detect smoke if the smoke sensor is attached to it. These devices can filter out the noise effectively so people can enjoy music or personal conversations in a noisy environment without any disturbances. Also, several conversations can be listened simultaneously.

1.7.8   Coagulation of Blood

Clotting of blood plays a very important role in human body. To avoid serious medical conditions which may result in strokes, regular monitoring of blood clot level is essential.

With IoT-enabled devices, it is possible to monitor the blood clot level on a regular basis. With the regular monitoring of clot levels, bleeding in the brain, strokes, heart attacks, etc., can be minimized by seeking medical attention at the right time. This can avoid unnecessary medications, hospital admissions, surgeries, etc., which, in turn, can save the medical expenses.

This IoT devices for monitoring blood clot level helps the anticoagulated blood patients to lead a normal life as the devices alert them to check the blood clot levels.

1.7.9   Depression Detection

Depression is one of the common health conditions faced by the current generation individuals. With the advent of smart devices like wearable smart watches, it is easy to track depression levels. These smart devices monitor the depression levels and provides suggestions about the type of treatments available.

As the data is continuously monitored by the connected devices, it will be available for reference to the mental healthcare professionals. Psychiatrists or psychologists can study about the mental conditions of the patients by observing their historical data of depression levels and can provide right treatments.

With the invention of such smart devices, depression can be easily treated by studying the sleep patterns and depression levels of the patients.

1.7.10   Detection of Cancer

Early detection of cancer is very important to save the life of an individual. Due to the advancement in technology, sensors are attached to the connected wearable devices which can sense any abnormalities in the cell.

The most common and dangerous cancers seen among women is breast cancer, and if it is not detected at an early stage, it leads to fatal condition.

With the advancement in new technologies, sensor-enabled bras are developed which makes use of Artificial Intelligence which, when worn, can detect abnormalities in breast tissues. These bras need not be worn throughout for detection; women can wear this bra for 2 to 12 hours per month. This wearable sensor embedded cloth does not produce any radiations or side effects. This can detect breast cancers at an early stage so that the treatment can start at an early stage for which complete cure is possible.

These wearable devices reduce the cancer risk among women and can reduce the treatment expenses as the doctors and patients will be alerted about the abnormalities in the tissues.

1.7.11   Monitoring Parkinson Patient

Parkinson is a health condition in which brain behaves abnormally which leads to difficulty in movement and coordination. Parkinson affects the central nervous system so the patients may feel stiffness and loss balance in movement.

It is very important to monitor the Parkinson patients on real time. With IoT devices, regular monitoring of Parkinson's patients is possible. Patients may suddenly face lack of movement which is very common in Parkinson disease called Freezing of Gait (FOG). This FOG stage can be detected by means of IoT devices and alerts can be given to doctors and patients. Even early detection of symptoms of this disease is also possible by the use of IoT devices.

In future, such devices will help the Parkinson's patients to lead a better life without risking their lives.

1.7.12   Ingestible Sensors

Sensors are embedded into the pills which can be ingested by the patients. These sensors will monitor whether the patient has taken prescribed medicines at the right time. If the medicines are not taken properly, it will be alerting through the connected devices.

Most of the times patients does not follow doctor's prescription, they either miss to take medicines on time or they may take overdose of the medicines. They may not follow the proper time gap for each medicine. All these issues may lead to serious medical conditions and result in expensive medical treatments.

These situations can be avoided by ingestible sensors which regularly monitors the patients and alerts them to take medicines on time. Taking care of the patients also becomes much easier with the support of such smart devices.

1.7.13   Surgery by Robotic Devices

Robotic surgeries are becoming common nowadays, owing to the precision, it gives compared to the normal surgeries performed by the doctors.

Robots connected to IoT devices can perform complex surgeries with more precision and control by the supervision of doctors. Doctors even can instruct robots to perform surgeries sitting at a remote location. This can save many lives as quick action is possible even at a remote location.

Many of the surgeries lasts for hours to complete which is a tiresome job for the doctors. In such situation, robots can perform the surgeries with much better precision. Complicated surgeries can be done successfully with the help of robotic devices connected to IoTs. This gives new dimensions to the classical surgery procedures.

1.7.14   Hand Sanitizing

Due to the current Covid-19 pandemic situation, the awareness about the importance of hand hygiene is increased among the common public. Proper care should be taken to prevent the spread of diseases especially in healthcare facilities. IoT-enabled devices play a major role in maintaining the hygiene of healthcare workers and patients.

With sensor-enabled hand sanitizing machines, monitoring of hand hygiene becomes easier. The sensor sets a threshold value of cleanliness and, if any staff fails to maintain the threshold value, will be alerted about sanitizing their hands. Even the sensors can track the time of sanitization done and alert them to sanitize their hands.

Since real-time monitoring of the hand hygiene is possible by the IoT connected devices, everyone will be more aware and alerted about the cleanliness and importance of the hygiene hands which leads to a healthy environment and helps to control the spread of viruses.

1.7.15   Efficient Drug Management

Using IoT-enabled devices management of drugs can be done in an efficient manner starting from the production to the supply chain management.

Radio Frequency Identification (RFID) tags are used for distribution purpose which also records a real-time record of the availability of the drugs and whether distribution is correctly done. The temperature during production process is also monitored to detect any variations.

With the proper supply chain management, production cost can be reduced and patients will get good quality drugs at a reduced rate.

1.7.16   Smart Sole

Alzheimer is a dreaded disease for elderly people and their loved ones as handling such patients is a difficult task. The patients tend to forget their daily activities and many of them loss their way back home and it creates difficulty in locating them.

IoT-enabled devices with smart GPS sole embedded system will provide a solution for this problem. It tracks the patient's location and updates it into the connected devices. It is a waterproof system so even if the patient enters water bodies, it will be working and sending signals to the connected devices. It will alert the loved ones about the location of the patients if they are wandering anywhere. This device is easy to wear as it is embedded into the sole and patients will never forget to wear footwear while going out.

Such smart devices will help Alzheimer patients to lead a healthy and normal life.

1.7.17   Body Scanning

To lead a healthy life, regular body checkups are required but most of the time people ignore the checkups on regular basis. To overcome this, a smart body scanner which scans the body and updates about the variations in body parameters can be used.

The scanner is basically a full-length mirror with a 3D camera and a weigh scale which scans the entire body and stores the images and the data will be used for processing the results in a mobile application. This application will create a graphical chart about the variations in body dimensions and parameters which will be helpful in maintaining fitness.

1.7.18 Medical Waste Management

Hospital waste management is a difficult problem faced by the healthcare facilities throughout the world. If these bio medical wastes are not disposed properly, it may lead to spread of infectious diseases. IoT-enabled waste management system will provide a smart solution to this problem.

Sensor-enabled dustbins may be used which is connected through IoT devices. The sensors detect the amount of trash present and automated messages will be generated to dispose the waste when the garbage bin is full. Through the connected devices, autonomous robots can fetch the garbage and dispose it in a smart way.

As robots are involved in disposing medical wastes, this may reduce the risk of spreading of the diseases through housekeeping staff who generally deals with disposal of garbage. This smart way of waste disposal will keep the hospital environment clean and safe.

1.7.19 Monitoring the Heart Rate

There is an increase in the number of heart patients throughout the world due to the unhealthy lifestyle. Most of the time delay in getting medical attention results in the loss of life of the patients.

With the advancement in technology, regular monitoring of the heartbeat and pulse rate is possible by means of sensor-enabled IoT devices. Since it is a real-time monitoring, any variations in the heart rate or pulse rate will be alerted to the patients as well as doctors through connected devices. Immediate medical attention is possible which can save many lives.

1.7.20 Robot Nurse

Workload of the nurses in hospitals are more which makes them exhausted and less efficient. Artificial Intelligence–enabled robots can assist the nurses in their day-to-day activities. The robots may be connected to IoT devices so that the activity of the robots can be scheduled and monitored by the nurses.

Robots can assist the nurses in picking and placing the medicines and alerting the patients to take medicines on time. They can give personal care for the patients and also can clean the rooms and beds. Nurses can assign the tasks to robots and monitor it. These robots may be controlled by the patients and nurses by means of mobile devices.

With these assistant robots, nurses can manage their workload in an efficient manner and provide better service to the patients.

These are some of the IoT applications in healthcare system which can give a new dimension to the patient treatment and healthcare services.

1.8   Global Smart Healthcare Market

It has been found that the four factors which demand the growth of smart healthcare operations are the following:

- Remote health monitoring for aged people
- Awareness about the importance of health and staying fit
- Increased use of wearable smart gadgets for monitoring health
- New business models based on smart healthcare systems

The global market growth is as shown in Figure 1.2. It has been estimated that the remote health monitoring will increase the global healthcare market by 24.55% by 2020. Increase in the use of ingestible smart pills will drive the market to 6.93 billion dollars by 2020 with a market growth of 23.62%. It has been estimated that the total market value of smart healthcare will be169.32 billion dollars by 2020.

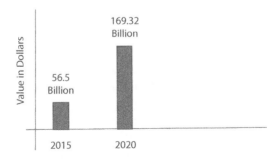

Figure 1.2 Global market growth.

It has also been estimated that the use of robots along with IoTs will increase by 50% in the near future to assist in the healthcare daily activities. Globally, about 60% of the healthcare organizations have implemented IoT devices for their services and facility. This is a digital transformation era for the healthcare services.

1.9   Recent Trends and Discussions

We have discussed about the various applications, advantages, and challenges of IoT in health sectors in the previous sections. The combination of AI and ML along with IoT devices can open up new opportunities in the field of health sectors especially in prediction, detection, risk assessment, treatments, etc. Cloud services can easily be utilized to overcome the limited resources and computational capacity required for the implementation of AI and ML.

The quality of the internet connectivity also needs to be improved, owing to the huge amount of data generated as for real-time data generation, response time, and performance plays a major role. Healthcare professionals should be able to take proactive decisions based on the real-time data to prevent the degradation of health conditions.

Remote diagnostics can be made possible by means of combining big data analytics along with ML techniques and AI by analyzing the vast number of images stored in the database.

Human errors can be reduced due to the advancements in telerobotic surgeries, and hence, the Internet of Robotics will play a major role in future healthcare sectors.

Due to the evolutions of these technologies, more research will happen in biomedical sector and modern healthcare systems which may provide personalized drugs and targeted drug delivery systems.

With the promising research going on in the healthcare sectors, more innovative smart wearables and gadgets can be expected in future. Also, due to the increased use of IoT in healthcare sectors, countries around the globe are formulating new policies and rules for the usage of IoT in medical practices.

More research is happening to overcome the security challenges faced by the usage of IoT devices in healthcare sectors, the future of applications of IoT in healthcare services is very bright, and it will give an unprecedented transformation to the healthcare industry services.

In the coming decade, Internet of Healthcare things (IoHT) will lead to improved efficiency and effectiveness in terms of systems, process and service delivery in treatment, diagnosis and patient care standards.

1.10   Conclusion

IoT in health sectors is a major revolution that has happened in the recent past. With the advancement in technology, the awareness of the smart gadgets is also increasing among individuals. The increase in awareness of leading a healthy life style made the common people to depend on smart wearables to monitor their health and daily activities.

The ease at which the connected devices reduces the workload of healthcare facilities motivated majority of the healthcare services to implement IoT devices for healthcare system. With the increase in use of IoT devices, the security and privacy concerns of the patient private data also increased. Continuous research is happening in this field to protect the privacy data from security threats. With the proper care in implementation, securing the privacy data, and maintaining the IoT devices by timely updating it, these devices can bring a new dimension to the healthcare field.

References

1. Dhanvijay, M.M. and Patil, S.C., Internet of Things: A survey of enabling technologies in healthcare and its applications. *Comput. Networks*, 153, 113–131, 2019.
2. Amendola, S., Lodato, R., Manzari, S., Occhiuzzi, C., Marrocco, G., RFID Technology for IoT-Based Personal Healthcare in Smart Spaces. *IEEE Internet Things J.*, 1, 2, 144–152, 2014.
3. Catarinucci, L., de Donno, D., Mainetti, L., Palano, L., Patrono, L., Stefanizzi, M.L., Tarricone, L., An IoT-Aware Architecture for Smart Healthcare Systems. *IEEE Internet Things J.*, 2, 6, 515–526, 2015.
4. Yeh, K.-H., A Secure IoT-Based Healthcare system with Body Sensor Networks. *IEEE Access*, 4, 10288–10299, 2016.
5. Baker, S.B., Xiang, W., Atkinson, I., Internet of Things for Smart Healthcare: Technologies, Challenges and Opportunities. *IEEE Access*, 5, 26521–26544, 2017.
6. Elhoseny, M., Ramirez-Gonzalez, G., Abu-Elnasr, O.M., Shawkat, S.A., Arunkumar, N., Farouk, A., Secure Medical Data Transmission Model for IoT-Based Healthcare Systems. *IEEE Access*, 6, 20596–20608, 2018.
7. Wu, T., Wu, F., Redoute, J.-M., Yuce, M.R., An Autonomous Wireless Body Area Network Implementation Towards IoT Connected Healthcare Applications. *IEEE Access*, 5, 11413–11422, 2017.
8. Gope, P. and Hwang, T., BSN-Care: A Secure IoT-Based Modern Healthcare System using Body Sensor Network. *IEEE Sens. J.*, 16, 5, 1368–1376, 2015.
9. Yang, Y., Zheng, X., Guo, W., Liu, X., Chang, V., Privacy-preserving smart IoT-based healthcare big data storage and self-adaptive access control system. *Inf. Sci.*, 479, 567–592, 2019.

10. Subramaniyaswamy, V., Manogaran, G., Logesh, R., Vijayakumar, V., Chilamkurt, N., Maathi, D., Senthilselvan, N., An Ontology-driven personalized food recommendation in IoT-based healthcare system. *J. Supercomput.*, 75, 3184–3216, 2019.

11. Mahmud, R., Koch, F.L., Buyya, R., Cloud-Fog Interoperability in IoT-enabled Healthcare Solutions. *Proceedings of the 19th International Conference on Distributed Computing and Networking*, Article No. 32, pp. 1–10, 2018.

12. Sanaz, R.M., Tuan, N.G., Mohammad, R.A., SEA: A Secure and Efficient Authentication and Authorization for IoT-Based Healthcare Using Smart Gateways. *Proc. Comput. Sci.*, 52, 452–459, 2015.

13. Tao, H., Bhuiyan, Md Z. A., Abdalla, A.N., Hassan, M.M., Zain, J.M., Hayajneh, T., Secured Data Collection with Hardware-Based Ciphers for IoT-Based Healthcare. *IEEE Internet Things J.*, 6, 1, 410–420, 2019.

14. Ali, F., Riazul Islam, S.M., Kwak, D., Khan, P., Ullah, N., Yoo, S.-j., Kwak, K.S., Type 2 Fuzzy ontology-aided recommendation systems for IoT-based healthcare. *Comput. Commun.*, 119, 138–155, 2018.

15. Hamza, R., Yan, Z., Muhammad, K., Bellavista, P., Titouna, F., A privacy-preserving cryptosystem for IoT E-healthcare. *Inf. Sci.*, 527, 493–510, 2020.

16. Yin, Y., Zeng, Y., Chen, X., Fan, Y., The Internet of Things in Healthcare: An overview. *J. Ind. Inf. Integr.*, 1, 3–13, 2016.

17. Hou, J.-L. and Yeh, K.-H., Novel Authentication Schemes for IoT Based Healthcare Systems. *Int. J. Distrib. Sens. Netw.*, 4, 1–9, 2015.

18. Bhatt, C., Dey, N., Ashour, A.S., *Internet of Things and Big Data Technologies for Next Generation Healthcare*, Springer, Cham, 2017.

IoT-Based Solutions for Smart Healthcare

Pankaj Jain[1], Sonia F Panesar[2], Bableen Flora Talwar[3]
and Mahesh Kumar Sah[4*]

[1]*Department of Biomedical, National Institute of Technology, Raipur, India*
[2]*Department of Computer Engineering, Babaria Institute of Technology,*
BITS Edu Campus, Varnama, Gujarat, India
[3]*Department of Biotechnology, Lovely Professional University, Jalandhar - Delhi*
G.T. Road, Phagwara, Punjab, India
[4]*Department of Biotechnology, Dr. B. R. Ambedkar National Institute of Technology,*
Jalandhar, Punjab, India

Abstract

Globalization has taken over the healthcare system for efficient and faster facilities at the site or out of site. The diagnosis and monitoring of various diseases through the Internet of Things (IoT) that set up a web of wireless connectivity and repository of electronically maintained data through software, sensors, devices, and actuators have revolutionized the intelligent medical diagnosis and therapy. A wide range of diseases are being successfully monitored and treated using IoT that enhances the efficacy and reduces the cost by collecting and interpreting big data. IoT devices acquired data through sensors and can be utilized to monitor the real-time location of medical devices such as wheelchairs, heart monitors, and ventilators. The diagnosis and monitoring of various diseases through the IoT and deep learning models has set up a web of wireless connectivity and repository of electronically maintained data through software, sensors, devices, and actuators. In this chapter, the Cognitive Internet of Medical Things (CIoMT) and deep learning for the internet of medical things will be emphasized with the elaboration of basic associated technologies and strategies.

Corresponding author: sahmk@nitj.ac.in

Monika Mangla, Nonita Sharma, Poonam Mittal, Vaishali Mehta Wadhwa, Thirunavukkarasu K. and Shahnawaz Khan (eds.) Emerging Technologies for Healthcare: Internet of Things and Deep Learning Models, (25–68) © 2021 Scrivener Publishing LLC

Keywords: Internet of Things (IoT), wireless system, deep learning, healthcare system, biosensors, data acquisition

2.1   Introduction

Technological evolutions in the healthcare system have brought together to services confined to medical facilities with user-friendly, IoT-based healthcare devices. People who are busy in their schedule or due to some other reason like pandemic could not visit the hospital, and such IoT-based healthcare devices can help the patient to early diagnosis and prognosis of the disease and it alerts the patient as well as doctor for the invisible warning signs [1]. Technology plays a prominent impact on the healthcare process including patient records to data tracking, from laboratory tests to self-treatment instruments [2]. Cognitive IoT is the use of cognitive computing technologies like artificial intelligence (AI) and the Internet of Things (IoT) in combination with data generated by sensors and actuators [3]. An IoT device is a piece of hardware which has a sensor as input that detects movement and sends this data to the microcontroller, analyses the data and sends instructions telling the sensor to turn on or off as output called an actuator. Actuators are like Buzzer/Bell and Bulb IoT device sensors can measure the patient's body parameters in real time and transfer that data to microcontroller for further action [4].

2.1.1   Process Flow of Smart Healthcare System

The smart city is a contemporary concept that uses state-of-the-art technologies to increase operational efficiency, information gathering in various disciplines, and improve government welfare services [5]. IoT is the backbone of the smart cities concept. It incorporates smart home–enabled home appliances, smart automobiles with smart and wearable devices, smart healthcare devices featuring heartbeat, number of steps, audio/video smart devices, and other safety systems [187]. The flow chart in Figure 2.1 shows the process to create smart Healthcare applications using IoT and deep learning. The smart healthcare process can be witnessed in various steps that include data source, data acquisition, data pre-processing, and others [6].

2.1.1.1   Data Source

Smart healthcare band or application needs to have access to data to examine. Data source defines where the data resides whether it is available in

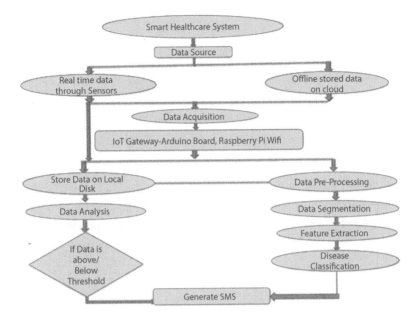

Figure 2.1 Process flow of smart healthcare application.

real time through sensors or it is stored on a hard disk on local computer or cloud [7].

2.1.1.2 Data Acquisition

Data acquisition is just the technique for remotely acquiring sample signals which have measured physiological parameters in real time depending mostly on sensors which are appropriate for detecting some parameters like temperature sensor for measuring body temperature, accelerometer sensor for sensing motion, and transforming the corresponding observations into electronic numerical values using an analog to digital converter, further that can be analyzed by a server [8] (Figure 2.1).

2.1.1.3 Data Pre-Processing

When the signal data is acquired through the sensors, some noise can also be instigated into another sensed output that can detrimentally reduce the performance of diagnosis. Hence, pre-processing of the raw signal is mandatory, it is a process for transforming the raw sensed signal into a signal which is free from noise and more suitable for any type of analysis—descriptive, predictive, or prescriptive analysis [9].

2.1.1.4   Data Segmentation

It is the procedure of splitting the sensed signal data into smaller parts and grouped into a similar scale of statistical characterizations such as the amplitude and frequency. This step is more significant for the efficient analysis of signals during automation [9].

2.1.1.5   Feature Extraction

This is a process for extracting only crucial information mostly from sensed data-signal which is required for the particular analysis. Signal samples acquired at the specified timestamp are useful instead of samples between the timestamps that are just not observed. In ML, this is considered as Dimensionality Reduction Technique [9].

2.1.1.6   Data Analytics

Healthcare data analytics is the special systematic approach of data analytics which allows healthcare professionals to find opportunities for improvement in the healthcare management system and patient engagement [10]. Healthcare data analytics includes four types of analytics as follows.

2.1.1.6.1   Descriptive Analytics
It focuses on the general observation of the parameters. It performs the comparison with the threshold value of the parameters set by the user and generate message accordingly. This type of analytics can be easily performed on the operational data (real-time data).

2.1.1.6.2   Diagnostic Analytics
It would explore the data until its root cause and find the correlation between different parameters. It includes the answer to Why? It performs the extensive analysis and exploration of the existing data using various OLAP operations in data mining—drill down, drill up, Slice, Dice, and Pivot to discover the root cause.

2.1.1.6.3   Predictive Analytics
This deals with the machine learning branch. The prediction will be made by machine learning model which is trained with the historical data and identify trends in data and predict future behaviors. This model can help to

predict future scenarios in conjunction with healthcare professionals and expertise by considering past and current medical data of patients [11].

2.1.1.6.4   Prescriptive Analytics

It includes the predictive analysis results of likely outcome and continues to demonstrate suggested actions and advises to make healthcare providers more successful and responsive in-patient needs.

2.2   IoT Smart Healthcare System

The IoT is really a ground-breaking paradigm of communication which focuses on building the invisible and inventive structure for linking wealth to electronic devices through the internet [12]. Exchanging data from tiny home appliances to huge industrial devices, the idea behind IoT has reduced the breach between the physical and the digital world. In other words, IoT which is a network of interconnected devices than sense, accumulate, and transfer data over the internet can interactively perform the task with the help of real world entities [13]. There is a variety of data available on the internet which can further be used as an offline data source for training different deep learning or machine learning applications. But to turn the city into a smart city and to automate various other applications like smart healthcare, there is a need to capture the real-time data, gathered that data and process it and take the immediate required action or reduce the loss and this is what "Internet of Things" [14]. This has given birth to many other terms like IOHT, IOCT, and so on as its major application. It is therefore designed to allow the internet with extra accessible and pervasive [15]. Sensors in IoT devices have a vast significance which inevitably increases the direct integration between both the wearable devices as well as the physical environment. Contemporary smart devices are designed with such a variety of sensors like accelerometer, gyroscope, headset, and photodetector that can detect environmental changes and perform the required action for efficient results [16]. The potential of sensors which determines the changes in its surrounding and connecting the digital world with the physical world more efficiently by taking autonomous decisions, which further extends its scope in other areas of use like healthcare monitoring systems, household gadgets, large industrialized devices, and smart cities, IoT systems are available in several necessary application areas. IoT systems are capable of integrated sensors, controllers, actuators, and transmitter, and the growing trend and usefulness of IoT system in diverse application areas have made the state-of-the-art technologies to grow at a gigantic rate [17]. IoT is not really a fixed entity; however, it is an integration of different technologies operating together in collaboration. The data acquired from the sensing device is transferred to a local edge computing device. The processing and storage of data can be done on the local edge computer. Usually, the stored information is sent through the remote (cloud) server [18]. The device computational and storage capabilities are constrained to its available resources, like size, power, control, and capacity limitation. As a consequence, acquiring information to its maximum accuracy becomes the primary research task. In addition to the difficulties of accurately data collecting and data analysing, some communication challenges are also there. Wireless communication protocols primarily transmit data among IoT systems and the cloud, since they are normally located at various distributed geographically areas [12].

2.2.1   System Architecture

An IoT device is a piece of hardware which has a sensor as input that detects movement and sends this data to the microcontroller, analyses the data, and sends instructions back to the sensor to turn on or off as output called an actuator. Actuators are like Buzzer/Bell and Bulb. Sensors can measure the patient's body parameters in real-time transfers, process the data, and send that information to the concerned person or signalled the warning through SMS and hold the mishap [19]. The architecture of IoT is a framework inclusive of hardware, software, network connectivity, and sensors so it comprised four different stages, and the function of each stage is described as follows (Figure 2.2).

2.2.1.1   Stage 1: Perception Layer

The perception layer validates the sensor in the devices' and gathers the real-time data. It is consisting of sensors and actuators like light sensors, temperature sensors, motion sensors, and pressure sensors [21]. It can emit, accept, and process signals. The design of the sensor plays an important role because it needs to be small, lightweight, compatible with body mass which requires very little power to operate properly like implantable sensors besides a surgeon to implant it correctly [22]. To get to transfer processed data between sensor and cloud intelligently, sensors are commonly incorporated via a middleware known as sensor hubs in the IoT-based applications [23]. For the flow of data between both sensors and devices in the IoT, a range of transport systems (Inter-Integrated Circuit

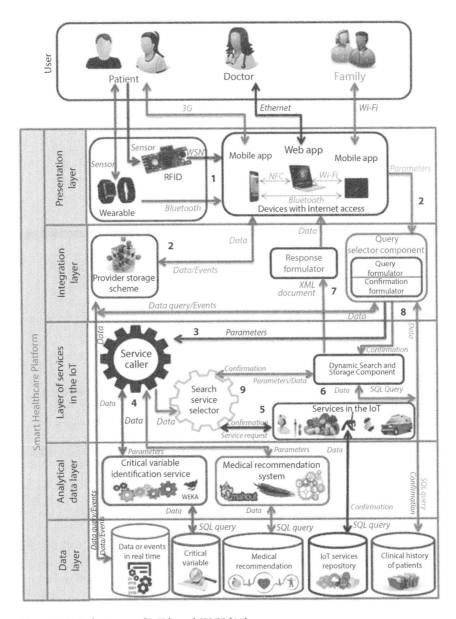

Figure 2.2 Architecture of IoT-based SHCS [20].

or Serial Peripheral Interface) have been used and to collect sensor data through these transport systems, a communication channel has been formed between both the sensors as well as the applications. Three wide categories of sensors in IoT devices are described below:

Sensors: A sensor is a transducer device that transforms a physical quantity into a specific electrical signal. Signal conditioning may be required if the signal from the transducer is not up to the mark for the DAQ hardware being used. In most cases, the signals may be needed to be screened, formed, or enhanced.

Motion Detectors (Sensors): Motion sensors are the electronic component which detects the interruption in the beam of infrared ray. The types of motion detectors are active motion detectors and passive motion detectors. These sensors calculate both motion change and system orientation in two ways as linear motions and angular motions [6].

Environmental Sensors: As it is clear from the name, it detects the change in the environment. It includes the temperature sensor, heart rate sensor, audio sensor light sensor, CCTV sensors, and pressure sensor so on. Such sensors are generally used in home automation systems, smart watches, etc. [12].

Position Sensors: These sensors help to detect the device's physical location, which includes magnetic position sensors and sensors of the Global Positioning System [12].

Biosensors: Biosensors are devices that are composed of biological and physicochemical components. Easily available and commonly used biosensors are rapid parturiency tests and diabetes tests; however, new biosensors are still needed for a wide variety of applications [24].

2.2.1.2   Stage 2: Network Layer

The network layer creates a communication link between IoT devices. It handles web services using HTTP and REST principles. The network layer includes various standards like Ipv4 and Ipv6 for communication technologies (such as Wi-Fi, Bluetooth, and cellular network) to ease the flow of data among other devices within the same network [7].

2.2.1.3   Stage 3: Data Processing Layer

This layer takes collected data from the sensing layer and processes it, to generate output that can be user friendly. This layer also saves the previous data in many IoT systems like a smart home hub, and smart watch that can improvise the user experience. This layer assists the network sharing of data processing with other connected devices [12].

2.2.1.4 Stage 4: Application Layer

This layer is a user-centred layer that contains a framework that can be used by users to track and manage different aspects of the IoT system. To fulfil the task of the IoT system, this layer actualizes the results data from the previous layer. Several IoT devices are available, like smart-transport, smart-home, and smart-healthcare [25] (Figure 2.3).

2.3 Locally and Cloud-Based IoT Architecture

For IoT implementation, we can use any microcontroller like 8051 microcontrollers, Arduino UNO, Raspberry Pie, or Arm 7. Following is the description of the Arduino Uno board.

2.3.1 System Architecture

The architecture of the smart healthcare system has the main objective to provide an encrypted smart and effective health application. The following are the basic parts of the system architecture (Figure 2.4).

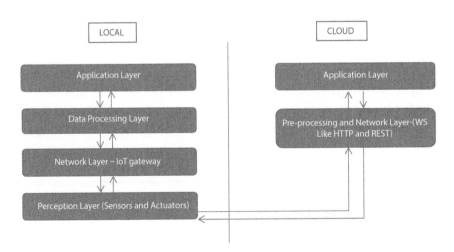

Figure 2.3 Layers of IoT on local server and on cloud server.

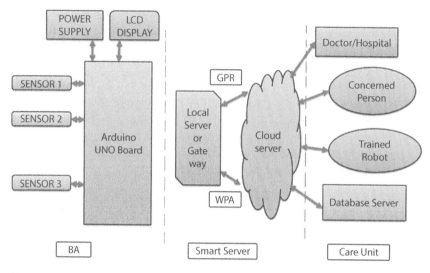

Figure 2.4 System architect of smart healthcare system.

2.3.1.1 Body Area Network (BAN)

These are a network of various miniaturized body sensor units which can be implanted to the body or superficially-mounted on the body, or humans can wear as in smart watch or smart band or carry in clothes pockets or by hand. The data generated through these sensor units can be managed with smart devices that function as a gateway and provide an interface for viewing and managing BAN applications [26], alternatively, named as Wireless Body Area Network (WBAN) or the Body Sensor Network (BSN) or the Medical Body Area Network (MBAN). The data are sensed through specific protocols like Wi-Fi, Bluetooth, and ZigBee and then transferred to the cloud network for further analysis. For long ranges, the WBAN system uses WPAN wireless technologies as gateways [27]. The wearable devices is designed to be internet connected through local gateways that help in the transfer of data on the cloud server and the doctor can easily access patient data online irrespective of the patient's location [28].

2.3.1.2 Smart Server

This part plays significant role in making the application smart way. It receives information from the BAN. The received raw data is regularly stored on both local and cloud servers and can be further scrutinized and interpreted statistically and graphically maintained at the server. The server is capable of learning the patient's specific thresholds of various parameters measured by sensors.

According to these threshold values, it decides whether or not a patient will be in a critical state [29]. In an emergency, the data shall be transmitted to the concerned person in the hospital for immediately enforcing emergency solutions, otherwise, the server simply stores the data. This stored data in the smart server is accessible to the hospital staff through a web page and android application [30]. Even the patient can also access this information and also some additional features have been added like specialized doctor appointments, suggestions from the patient, registration for the singles and families, health information access from everywhere, etc. [31, 32]. Smart server assists the medical experts to have the latest reports as well as medical history about the patients that help in the prevention of fatal diseases.

2.3.1.3   Care Unit

This part is associated with a hospital or concerned person or an emergency number. The access of data is given to a patient, doctor, and hospital supporting staff in case of an emergency. Depending on the report generated by the cloud server, hospital staff will take preventive or corrective measures for the patient, respectively [33].

2.4   Cloud Computing

Cloud computing provides on-demand services over the internet from applications to store, manage, and process. A web service is a collection of open protocols and standards required for transferring data between applications or systems [34]. Cloud computing provides various web services in its basic three standard services—Infrastructure as a Service (IaaS), Platform as a Service (PaaS), and Software as a Service (SaaS). Web services use HTTP (Hypertext Transfer Protocol)/SOAP (Simple Object Access Protocol) protocol and XML/JSON as a backend to run over the network [35].

This is also called "pay-as-you-go" services because this service helps the company to avoid buying and maintaining all its infrastructure, instead, keep paying with what and when they really need it. The five key characteristics for cloud computing recognized by the National Institute of Standards and Technology are as follows [36].

1. On-demand self-service available anytime without a need of service provider over the internet.
2. Broad Network Access as it can be accessed through any smart device such as smartphone and laptop.

3. Resource Pooling or Multitenancy means resources can be accessed by multiple consumers (tenants) simultaneously such that each is unaware of the other using multitenancy architecture that relies on virtualization technologies.
4. Measured service means pay as per the usage of service. It maintains the transparency between the user and the service provider.
5. Rapid elasticity is the ability to provide scalable services that our resources are accessible to users in unlimited quantity at any time.

High costs, conflicting quality, and poor online maintenance of data are found to some of the setbacks of the existing smart healthcare system. It is a complete wastage of time while patients had to go through the same health history each time whenever they visit the doctor. Prescriptions, medications, and emergency details can be easily be accessed through the internet, making ease for caregivers [37]. In order to improvise the smart healthcare system, cloud computing is playing a significant role in healthcare, and major benefits include the following:

1. Maintaining patient health record,
2. Smart treatment by taking the opinion of experts,
3. Prompt reply to patients using machine learning models, and
4. Safe and secured.

Cloud computing helps in increasing the efficiency of the medical system by many folds in lesser costs and also helping the medical professionals in reaching out to a wider public which was otherwise a challenge due to lack of medical personnel. The healthcare sector needs speedy and smooth access to medical resources such as patient medical reports, the prompt reply of ambulance available, and so on from the cloud server [11] have proposed a model to install the proxy server in between or near the location of a patient and cloud server. If any patient wants to access its information from any smart applications, then the information will be stored on a proxy instead of a cloud server. This is a simple way of getting rid of traffic on a network. Cloud computing architecture is based on a stack of a layer of services that is "Everything as a service" concept. Depends on the type of requirement, it provides the service [36]. The three standard services provided by cloud computing are as follows.

2.4.1   Infrastructure as a Service (IaaS)

IaaS provides the base infrastructure and complete control (it may be a virtual machine, software, and storage attached) over the internet. The resources can be available as a service and it can be immediately generated, modified, reformatted, and eliminated when any task requires them. The price varies depending on the choice of services and pays as per usage basis. Examples: Microsoft Azure and Amazon Elastic Compute Cloud [38].

2.4.2   Platform as a Service (PaaS)

PaaS provides a software development platform to facilitate testing, deployment, and hosting of software applications over the internet. Generally, developers work on the PaaS platform to build applications of software without worrying about resources. Several users can use the same development application. Examples: Google App Engine, Cloud Foundry, Heroku, and AWS (Beanstalk).

2.4.3   Software as a Service (SaaS)

SaaS, the most common software for cloud computing, is often called as "on-demand software". The software is hosted on a remote server by a service provider and available through a web browser over the internet at any time. The consumer need not worry about hardware-software firmware and its updates. Salesforce, Google Apps, DropBox, NetFlix, Gmail, WebEx, and GoToMeeting are the services found to be the best instance where only a browser is required by users [39].

2.4.4   Types of Cloud Computing

There are four types of cloud computing according to NIST.

2.4.4.1   Public Cloud

This type provides cloud computing service over the public internet to everyone such as storage, applications, and other resources. In this type, users pay as per their subscription plan that is for the time duration they have used the service. Nevertheless, being so reliable, public clouds are considered less secure. Examples: AWS Direct Connect, Microsoft Azure, Google App Engine, and IBM smart cloud [40, 41].

2.4.4.2   Private Cloud

This type provides cloud computing services such as storage, applications, and other resources to singular organizations, and those services are confined to users who are part of that particular organization. The organization has the right to customize the service. This is considered as more secure than Public cloud [41, 42] Examples: Amazon PVC and Ubuntu Enterprise Cloud.

2.4.4.3   Hybrid Cloud

This type is the combination of a private cloud with one or more than a public cloud. It is opted by an organization who wanted to store critical data on both private and public clouds where data security is challenged. These are considered as the most powerful and secured cloud service as it gives great control over Private data [42, 43]. Examples: EMC Hybrid Cloud and HP.

2.4.4.4   Community Cloud

This kind of cloud makes it possible for several organizations to work on the same platform, providing they have similar needs and concerns. This has many benefits including high security and lower cost than private cloud because the costs are shared across organizations [40]. Example: "Gov. Cloud" by Google.

2.5   Outbreak of Arduino Board

Arduino Board is a microcontroller board which was originated in Italy in 2005. While it is an inexpensive and open-source that helps in data acquisition and communication. Arduino is a platform-independent tool and runs on all platforms like Windows, Linux, and Macintosh. It has a development environment both in C and C++ [44]. The Arduino Integrated Development Environment (IDE) or Arduino Software consists of a text editor for writing code, a message area displays the saving file information and error information, a text console displays output or error message, and a toolbar including common functions. The Arduino systems are currently consisting of 19 board prototypes—one for each system. Arduino boards are the heart of the projects [45]. It accepts inputs through sensors signals and affects their surroundings by actuators. The Anatomy of the Arduino

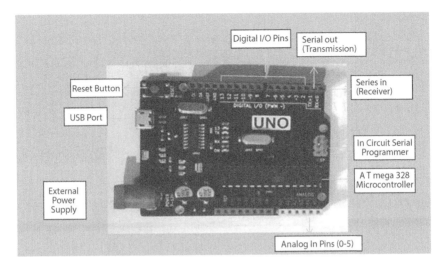

Figure 2.5 Arduino UNO model [44].

Uno board is shown in Figure 2.5. The UNO consists of ATMEL microcontroller, the ATmega-328P, with a permanent memory for storing both program and data, and internal memory for storing temporary data. Digital pins are used for digitalRead(), digitalWrite(), and analogWrite(). Analogs are used for analogRead(). The functioning and activity of the UNO have shown great flexibility with low power consumption as an essential feature since they are operated with a simple 9V cell.

2.6 Applications of Smart Healthcare System

In this world of digitization, almost every sector can be easily visualized through wireless technologies. With the advancements in technologies as the IoT, AI, and cloud computing, the smart healthcare system has been improvised to a new level from each perspective (Figure 2.6). The ease of communication, exchanging, and processing of data with little human involvement made a benchmark in this era. Smart homes, hospitals, smart devices, gadgets, and software are the live models of computer-assisted technological progress [46]. The healthcare sector contributes a major share of revenue and also generates huge employment leads to the development of a country. Earlier, diseases can be detected through comprehensive physical and pathological examination by the experts on the appearance of related symptoms, but nowadays, a smartwatch marks the

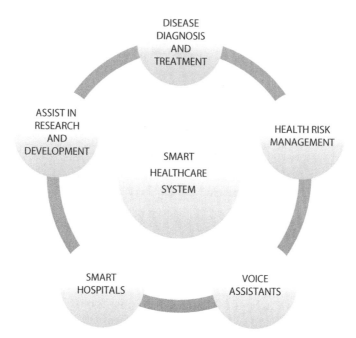

Figure 2.6 Smart healthcare system with its dimensions.

ease of detecting the aberrations in our health. For instance, the heart rate can easily be noticed through the smartwatch [47]. The rapid spread of epidemic diseases as Ebola, SARS, and COVID has been prevented by taking major steps in controlling the contact or the source of its evolution. In addition, the remote diagnosis and testing have been successfully achieved through telecommunication and data as a service (DaaS) technology. IoT also enabled global communication through which the pandemic cause, its spread, and preventive can be easily shared. In a divergent view, these improved communication skills also helped the patients to easily be connected with other family members, caretakers, and doctors even in the conditions of emergency [48].

In this tech-savvy world, the wireless network is a new paradigm that takes over almost every sector. Smart Healthcare system diverges its applications from Virtual assistant and diagnosis along with the treatment of diseases to the electronic medical record. Smart healthcare along with AI and cloud computing elevated the functioning of the overall healthcare sector. Nowadays, a large number of computerized devices and apps based on IoT deep learning and AI are available at finger touch [49]. With the increasing population, the need for advanced health facilities became a challenge and extensive research seemed going to develop a better health-care system. Cardiovascular disease is still found to be the most fatal disease that contributes to high mortality rates in the world. The need for heart monitoring becomes a vital approach toward prevention of the heart disease. Advanced technologies inclusive of Information and Communication Technology (ICT) assisted the ease of access, transfer, interpret, and gather the same from different signals—both permanent and remote. IoT built up an intelligent system along with the other technologies inclusive of sensor technologies, wireless communications, nanoelectronics, and others. Another technology of nanomaterials boosted up the healthcare system by removing the cons of conventional materials and improvising the overall system functioning [16]. These potential devices allowed flexible communication between human beings or coordination between machines and interconnection between the patient and the machine [50].

2.6.1   Disease Diagnosis and Treatment

A smart healthcare system rooted its branches in the diagnosis of a disease and appropriate treatment as per the necessity. Earlier, the disease can be detected through intensive laboratory testing and physical examination later summarized by expert opinion. But nowadays, ease of pathological testing and diagnosis of disease blossom up the early cure and treatment of disease. In addition, cloud computing and AI improvised pathological issues. Ease of online appointments for testing in labs and getting the reports through the internet reduced the stress of waiting long hours. In addition, several apps and sites are available inclusive of Diagnosis and Lab Values Pro that assist the patients to understand the reports and the standard normal values of a particular examination. Amin and co-workers proposed a cognitive model for EEG pathological diversification and detection [51]. EEG diagnosis tools have been successfully used in the detection of various disorders inclusive of epilepsy, stroke, Alzheimer's [52], and brain injuries [53]. A new program field-programmable gate array (FPGA) analysis system along with mobile application has been reported that updates the pathological data of a patient to its wearable device to monitor the abrupt changes further and finally controlling the fatal impact of a disease. Further, another system has been developed to sense the data of the patient and uploaded the data once it hits the threshold values which further transferred to an analysis system named FPGA system. The data has been analyzed through FPGA system and can be viewed on wearable IoT device of the patient [54].

2.6.2   Health Risk Monitoring

Numerous approaches have been reported in monitoring health on daily basis. Earlier the disease can only be detected once symptoms appeared but this limitation has been overcome by the smart healthcare system. Big data analysis and deep learning made this possible to monitor health issues and manage the risk developed for a particular disease. Additionally, various gadgets and wearables have been reported that helps in monitoring health. For instance, smartwatches, smart bracelets, smart headsets, smart clothing [55], and wearable sensor patches serve as a platform for monitoring temperature, heart rate, blood pressure, and others [56]. In addition, pillboxes are found to be another accomplice that reminds the patient of their daily dosages. Adhere to Tech's smart pillbox, iMedipac, MedMinder, and smart pillboxes are some of the examples of pillboxes. Not confined to pill bottles but ingestible biosensors have also been reported that monitors drinking of water and pill pickups ultimately promotes medication adherence. RFID and computer vision technologies also assist dosage patterns [57]. Voice disorder became prevalent among lawyers, teachers and singer's these days which can be now be monitored through computed linear prediction (LP) analysis that interprets the irregularities in vocal fold vibrations [58]. An IoT-based ECG wearable node along three electrodes have been proposed eliminating the need for mobile application [4].

2.6.3   Voice Assistants

In this tech-savvy world, voice technology has defeated the stress and loneliness of elderly and loner patients. Alexa, Apple Siri found to act like virtual assistants that not only remind the patients for their dosage but also monitors the health. Chatbots were found to be another emerging field that has been designed to communicate with people through texting and empowered with AI [59]. Another proposed virtual assistant reported "MoSHcA" that has developed the ability to make decisions on clinical considerations about a patient as per the input with or without human interventions [60].

2.6.4   Smart Hospital

Another demonstration of a smart healthcare system can be witnessed through smart hospitals. Smart hospitals ease the processes from the patient as well as doctor perspectives. Remote patient monitoring allows patient-doctor interactions that limit the need of hospitals whereas device monitoring is linked with IoT improving the efficiency of the device and lowers the problem by early monitoring and hence reduces rescheduling and botheration of doctors [61]. Nevertheless, the intravenous drug infusion and the rate of delivery has been reported to be monitored through narrowband IoT (NB-IoT) successfully in smart hospitals [188]. Another IoT-based monitoring under Incentive Care Unit (ICU) has been reported by using INTEL GALILEO second-generation development board that not only enhances the communication between the patient and the medical professions but also record blood pressure, heart rate, temperature, and ECG. Under emergency conditions, the system sends the generated to the patient's doctor with medical conditions of the patient [62].

2.6.5   Assist in Research and Development

For drug discovery and ongoing research for various diseases, health monitoring devices play a vital role. Patients bioanalysis can be analyzed through wearable devices. These devices monitor a number of essential biometrics inclusive of step count, calorie burnt, heart rate, and sleep, and specific wearables also detect glucose levels, sweat analysis, pressure sensors, and even some the patches have also been reported that can be used for cardiovascular disease, respiratory and stress disorders. The outcome pattern of the specific patients helps in clinical trials as well as reduce the cost of drug development. Commonly used wearable includes Empatica used for Epilepsy monitoring, Fitbit, epidermal iontophoretic biosensors sweat pattern detections, and many more [63].

2.7   Smart Wearables and Apps

The culture of mart life is taking over the world. Although the trend of wearable was found to be still low in some of the developing countries most of the nations, smart healthcare has been diversified. Numerous proposed systems and devices have been scrutinized that helps in monitoring the biometric of a person health. Enlisted are some of the FDA approved devices and commercially available. Wearables have different forms starting from wristwatches, bands, skin patches, or sensors to the textiles monitoring the life of a patient. From sweat analysis to the electrocardiogram ECG monitoring, every analysis has been made easy and on track. This reduces the fatality of a disease leading to diminishing mortality rates. In addition, various mobile applications improvise mobile health technology and online platforms that help the patient to understand the various terminology and aspects of health issues or updates medicine information. Table 2.1 and Table 2.2 shows some mobile applications and online sites for smart healthcare system and wearables commercially available for health monitoring, respectively. Online sites or applications not only ease the purchase of drugs but also improve patient-doctor interactions through online communication.

2.8   Deep Learning in Biomedical

The domain of biomedical sustains a very rich area of research, with expert medical applications and related pathologies. With the advancement of technologies, biomedical information is very well utilized by clinical experts in different domains [74]. In a broader context, deep learning poses a huge potential to help doctors, biologists, and medical experts, to enhance and improves clinical information investigation, with less probability of medical error and also to produce standardized protocols for diagnosis and prognosis [75].

Table 2.1 List of mobile apps and online sites for smart healthcare system.

S. no.	Apps/Sites	Application	References
1	Dropbox	Cloud storage and file-sharing	[64]
2	DailyRounds	Drug guide	[65]
3	Medscape	Online drug purchase	[30]
4	Medpage Today	Medical updates	[30]
5	Youper-Anxiety and Depression	Online consultation	[50]
6	Visual DX	Reference for skin diseases	[66]
7	Doximity	Social networking site	[30]
8	Skyscape/Omnio	Drug reference	[30]
9	Diagnosaurus App	Medical diagnosis list	[30]
10	Lab Values Pro	Medical Lab values, Abbrevations references	[30]

Table 2.2 List of wearables commercially available for health monitoring.

S. no.	Wearables	Wearable platform	Applications	References
1	K'Watch	Watch	Glucose monitoring	[67]
2	Abilify MyCite	Ingestible sensor	Schizophrenia, bipolar, and stress disorders	[68]
3	AliveCor KardiaBand	Watch/Band	ECG monitoring watch	[69]
4	Empatics Embrace 2	Skin patch	Epilepsy tracking	[67]
5	Siren Smart Sock	Smart clothing	Monitors foot ulcers and inflammation in diabetic patients	[67]
6	Viatom Checkme O2	Wrist band	Wrist pulse oximeter	[67]
7	VivaLNK	Skin patch	ECG and heart rate monitoring	[67]
8	SugarBEAT patch- Nemaura	Skin patch	Oxygen depletion and glucose monitoring	[67]
9	sKan	Portable device	Skin cancer and contains thermistors to detect heat released from cancer cells	[70]
10	GlucoTrack	Finger clip	Blood glucose monitoring	[71]
11	Eversense	Small stick implant to subcutaneous skin	Glucose monitoring	[72]
12	TermoTelll bracelet	Band wearable	Sweat patterns and temperature variations	[73]

Nowadays, deep learning is the dominant machine learning technique in different medical domains, like computer vision, image processing, and anomaly detection. Everything in deep learning starts, with a huge amount of informational data [76]. This huge amount of information is vast but highly interdependent, from organic compounds to bioinformatic data, bioimaging and medical data, and electronic health information records. The biomedical deep learning applications cover all medical fields from bioinformatics to health service management [77].

The utilization of deep learning in the biomedical application is organized in some directions such as computer-aided diagnosis for accurate and effective early diagnosis, customized medical treatments of the patient to strengthen medical treatment, and human-machine interface to improve human health being [78]. To achieve these utilizations of deep learning, we divide the biomedical domains into different sub-areas like bioinformatics, bioimaging, medical imaging, human-machine interface, and health service management.

2.8.1 Deep Learning

In the 1960s, ANN was motivated by the biological neural system, with some feedforward interconnected neurons. A deep neural network or deep learning is a branch of ANN that utilizes multiple layers to learn how to fit and extract nonlinear information from highly complex data [79, 80] (Figure 2.7).

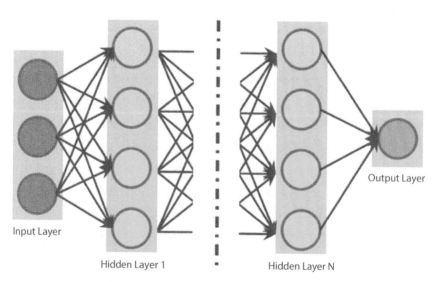

Figure 2.7 Activation model for deep learning.

A deep neural network contains artificial neurons, which are arranged in a series of layers where every neuron is interconnected with some weight during the process of learning [81]. The first layer is structured to obtain different types of information from the network named as input and output layer as the final layer with an expected outcome that responds to the learned information. In between the input and output layer, there are multiple layers known as hidden layers, where almost all processing occurs through weights and biases. Each neuron evaluates the weighted sum of obtained inputs with biases and then introduces an activation function to compute output performance. The most frequently used activation function is rectified linear unit (ReLU), softmax, sigmoid, and hyperbolic tangent [11, 81, 82].

2.8.2   Deep Neural Network Architecture

The principal applications of deep neural networks are classification and regression. The classification is aimed to structure a given input data into different classes through supervised or unsupervised learning. The regression is aimed mainly to predict an unidentified output mainly through supervised learning [83]. In a supervised technique, the predicted output for the current set of models is compared with the actual input labeled data for calculating the error loss. In deep neural networks, the error loss gradually decreases through the layers, leading to small modifications of the weights to the previous layer. Relu and softmax activation function are used to solve the problem with fast learning [84]. The well-known unsupervised methods are autoencoder (AE) and restricted Boltzmann machine (RBM), mainly used to solve the problem related to random weight initialization [83, 84] (Figure 2.8).

Some other commonly used deep neural networks inclusive of applications are recurrent neural networks (RNN-LSTM), deep perceptron network (DMLP), deep autoencoder (DAE), RBM, deep belief network (DBN), and convolutional neural network (CNN) (Figure 2.8). In RNN, the output of the previous phase is feed to the current phase as an input. RNN transforms the exponential random activations into responsive activations by supplying the same biases and weights for all layers, thus minimizing the difficulty of increasing parameters [85]. RNN is simply a typical neural network by providing edges to feed into previous layer instead of next layer. RNN is normally fed with input training data having a relevant description of what occurred in the preceding layer. RNNs utilize two categories of layers, input and hidden, and provide the new data output [86, 87]. DMLP is a feedforward ANN type. An MLP consist of approximately three layers:

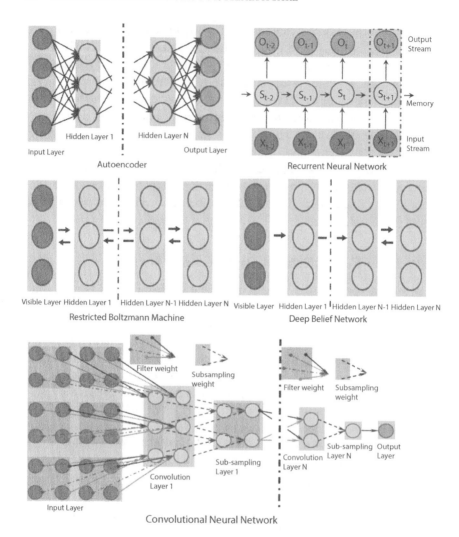

Figure 2.8 Different deep neural network architectures for biomedical engineering.

the first layer as an input, the last layer as an output, and a hidden layer in between. MLP supports the technique of the backpropagation method for its various layers with nonlinear activation functions [82, 87, 88]. AE is a hidden layer multilayer perceptron unsupervised learning. The AE's objective is just to reduce the error function between outputs and inputs. DAEs are achieved by integrating various auto-encoders. DAEs are composed of two deep beliefs one for encoding and another for decoding network [89, 90]. A DBN is presented as a series of RBM where each preceding RBM hidden states are used to train the next RBM [91, 92]. An RBM is a conceptual probabilistic two-layered artificial neural network with [93–95] the ability to understand a probability distribution across its input network and consists only of two layers visible and hidden layer [96, 97]. CNN has been introduced for the study of image data, where a convolution filter is used to perform complicated operations. A CNN is a model of a multi-layer neural network, influenced by visual cortex neurobiology, consisting of convolution layers accompanied by fully-connected layers [98]. A CNN usually comprised of many convolution and pooling layers that enables so many abstract features in the hidden layers to be learned [61]. The most common CNNs used are GoogleNet, AlexNet, Clarifai, and VGG [93–95].

2.8.3   Deep Learning in Bioinformatic

Bioinformatics involves all research from genome analysis, sequencing, expression, protein structure, and also its ability to interact with many other drugs. Bioinformatics means genomics and proteomics study, i.e., DNA/RNA structure prediction and interactions between the protein molecules [100, 101]. The bioinformatics includes genetic information and (gen/protein/transcript/multi/metabol/epigene/pharmacogen) and sought to scrutinize and recognize various biological mechanisms at molecular and cellular level to analyze and avoid disease conditions by including the patient in the implementation of effective and personalized healthcare [85, 101].

RNN is ideal for dealing with DNA array and genomics series, due to its structural properties [102]. Also, BRNN is used for secondary protein structure prediction [74], and LSTM is used for histone modifications and gene expression prediction [103]. Deep-Chrome (CNN architecture) is used for predicting gene expression by extracting features from histone change. Sparse and denoising autoencoder (i.e., SAE and DAE) are used for the prediction of protein secondary structure [104]. Many deep learning models for bioinformatics are also shown in Table 2.3.

2.8.4   Deep Learning in Bioimaging

After research in DNA and protein, the next phase is research in cytopathology and histopathology, i.e., research in cells and tissues. In bioimaging, the examination of biological tissues and cell are through cytopathology and histopathology images [115]. Generally, histopathology and cytopathology are widely used to detect many contagious diseases inclusive of cancer, diabetes thyroid, and other inflammatory disorders.

Digital pathology is the system through which histology slides were transcribed to create images of high resolution. These digitalized slides

Table 2.3 Deep learning models for bioinformatics.

S. no.	Bioinformatic	Deep learning models	References
1	Identifying the splicing junction at the DNA level	DBN	[105]
2	Identifying profiling GE on the RNA-seq	DBN	[106]
3	Pre-processing CHIP-seq data	CNN	[107]
4	Predicting RNA and DNA-binding protein	Deep CNN	[102]
5	Predicting RBP binding and interaction, predicting RNAs motifs	CNN-DBN	[108]
6	Interpreting noncoding genome	CNN	[109]
7	Predicting binding between DNA and protein	CNN	[110]
8	Identifying noncoding GV	CNN	[111]
9	Predicting miRNA precursor	LSTM-RNN	[112, 113]
10	Predicting human cells response against particular stimuli focusing on rat cells response.	DBN	[114, p.]

create the feasibility of implementing image processing techniques for segmentation, detection, and classification [116].

In bioimaging, deep learning architectures are tuned to a biological pixel-level image for training neural network [101]. Mostly DBNs, DAEs, and CNN architectures are used for bioimaging applications. Some of them are shown in Table 2.4.

2.8.5   Deep Learning in Medical Imaging

The human tissue and organs in biomedical imaging are analyzed by evaluating various clinical and medical imaging [129]. Magnetic resonance imaging (MRI scan), computed tomography with multiple slice (CT scan), ultrasonic technology (US), positron emission tomography (PETscan), and X-ray are some of the high-resolution medical imaging technologies

Table 2.4 Deep learning models for bioimaging.

S. no.	Bioimaging area	Deep learning models	References
1	Segmentation of images of cellular components using electron microscope image	CNN	[117]
2	Identifying mitosis in histology images	Deep CNN	[118, 119]
3	A search of neuronal membranes and segmentation of neuronal structures in EMI automatically	Deep CNN	[119]
4	Cancer nuclei identification from histopathology images	DAE	[120]
5	Label free and multilevel cell classification.	DAE, CNN	[121, 122]
6	Detection of fluorescent protein automatically using microscopic pictures of yeast	CNN	[123]
7	For counting of bacterial colonies in agar plates	CNN	[124]
8	Single-cell flow analyzation using cytometry images	DBN-CNN	[125]
9	For scrutinizing the bright-field microscopic images of neural stem cells	CNN	[126]
10	For analyzing gold immunochromatographic strip	DBN	[127]
11	The study of breast cancer samples by electron microscopy	MDRNN	[128]

available for biomedical imaging to denoising, segmentation, classification, and anomalies detection from these images [88]. The accuracy of the diagnosis of a disease in biomedical imaging depends on image interpretation and image acquisition. Most of the deep learning in biomedical imaging is about segmenting, locating, and classifying the lesion and biological targets (such as organs, markers, and other elements) [85, 87]. Deep learning architectures for biomedical imaging area are as shown in Table 2.5.

Table 2.5 Deep learning models for biomedical imaging area.

S. no.	Biomedical imaging area	Deep learning models	References
1	Segmentize the lesions in multichannel MRI	CNN, DBN	[132]
2	Compartmented structures of the brain from MRI and 3-D EMI	RNN	[133]
3	Neck-head region volume sectioning through CT scan	Deep CNN	[134]
4	Cardiac MRI was separated for left heart's ventricle and many more.	DBN and CNN	[135]
5	Segmentation of anterior visual pathway from MRI sequences	Sparse autoencoder	[136]
6	A denoising technique to validating it along with mammograms and dental radiography	Autoencoder and CNN	[137]
7	Image denoising, confirmed through CT scan of the head	Sparse autoencoder	[138]
8	Cognitive impairment detection and Alzheimer's detection through MRI and PET scans	autoencoder, DBM, RBM	[139–141]
9	To differentiate breast masses obtained from mammograms, analysis of neuroimages, rheumatoid arthritis from hand radiographs	CNN	[89, 142–145]
10	Detection of anatomical structure for cancer detection. Interstitial lung disease through MRI and for brain tumors extracts the deep diffusion tensor images through MRI	CNN	[146–151]
11	To recognize attention deficit hyperactivity disorder, schizophrenia, Huntington detection, and fetal abdominal standard plane detection	DBN	[152–154]

(Continued)

Table 2.5 Deep learning models for biomedical imaging area. (*Continued*)

S. no.	Biomedical imaging area	Deep learning models	References
12	Neuroendocrine carcinoma detection; identify haemorrhages and digestive diseases detection and validating oesophageal carcinoma and neoadjuvant chemotherapy	CNN	[148, 155–158]

2.8.6 Deep Learning in Human-Machine Interface

In the human-machine interface, a relation between human and decoding machine interface is established and analysis is done by using various bio-signals such as EEG and EPG by using appropriate sensors. An amplifier, a sensor, a filter, and a control mechanism are the main components of the human-machine interface system [159]. Various measuring instruments for the human-machine interface are electroencephalogram, functional magnetic resonance imaging, magnetoencephalography, electrocorticography, and near-infrared spectroscopy [159, 160].

Deep learning is applied to the human-machine interface for abnormalities detection and to diagnose diseases such as coronary artery disease, myocardial infarction, and Alzheimer's disease [161]. Various deep learning architectures used in the human-machine interface are represented as Table 2.6.

2.8.7 Deep Learning in Health Service Management

In the health management system (HMS), the large medical data are analyzed to make better medical decisions for human welfare. Patient health information is the major source of medical data that comes from electronic health records, which include details of all the clinical information and medical history [176]. Effective exploitation of these large datasets would certainly render useful information on health management. Deep learning methods with highly distributed data have been considered the best choice. The success of deep neural network success is attributed to the capability to understand and learn the data models with new features. Deep neural networks have also proved effective in managing multimodal details because they can combine multiple architectural designs [177, 178] (Table 2.7).

Table 2.6 Deep learning models for human-machine interface area.

S. no.	Human-machine interface area	Deep learning models	References
1	Motor Imagery decoding	CNN, autoencoder	[162, 163]
2	To differentiate signal frequency information as features and to classify single channels in EEG signals	DBN	[164, 165]
3	Low dimensional latent features Critical channel selection	DBN	[126] [166]
4	Emotion detection with DEAP and MAHNOB-HCI data set using EEG signals	CNN, LSTM-RNN	[167, 168]
5	Driver's cognitive estimation in EEG	CNN-RBM, sparse DBN	[169, 170]
6	Anomaly detection in diverse scenarios detect and predict seizures	DBN, CNN, RNN	[171–173]
7	EMG signals can be decoded for hand movements	CNN	[112, 174]
8	ECG arrhythmias detection, to distinguish ECG signals accomplished with two leads	DBN	[175]

Table 2.7 Deep learning models for HMS and public care.

S. no.	HMS and public care	Deep learning models	References
1	To predict diseases of lifestyle	DBN	[179, 180]
2	To predict air pollutants	RNN, DNN	[181–183]
3	To predict geographic health info	Deep autoencoder	[184]
4	To predict epidemic diseases	CNN	[185]
5	Temporal pattern discovery	DBN	[186]

2.9   Conclusion

The technological interventions in healthcare system have revolutionized the medical facilities by bringing services at door step with more user-friendly features. The IoT-based healthcare devices can help the patient to early diagnosis and prognosis of the disease and it alerts the patient as well as doctor for the invisible warning signs even when the patient is unable to visit hospital due to unavoidable circumstances such as ongoing pandemic condition. Cognitive IoT technologies like AI, IoT, and deep learning models can be utilized to set up a web of wireless connectivity and repository of electronically maintained data through software, sensors, devices, and actuators. The strategies associated with these technologies have been shown promising for medical hospitality and management and expected to contribute to the most advanced therapeutic strategies for disorder management.

References

1. Pires, I.M., Marques, G., Garcia, N.M., Flórez-Revuelta, F., Ponciano, V., Oniani, S., A Research on the Classification and Applicability of the Mobile Health Applications. *J. Pers. Med.*, 10, 1, 11, 2020.

2. Council, N.R., *The role of human factors in home healthcare: Workshop summary*, National Academies Press, Washington, 2010.

3. Pramanik, P.K.D., Pal, S., Choudhury, P., Beyond automation: the cognitive IoT. artificial intelligence brings sense to the Internet of Things, in: *Cognitive Computing for Big Data Systems Over IoT*, pp. 1–37, Springer, Cham, Switzerland, 2018.

4. Yang, Z., Zhou, Q., Lei, L., Zheng, K., Xiang, W., An IoT-cloud Based Wearable ECG Monitoring System for Smart Healthcare. *J. Med. Syst.*, 40, 12, 286, Dec. 2016.

5. Albino, V., Berardi, U., Dangelico, R.M., Smart cities: Definitions, dimensions, performance, and initiatives. *J. Urban Technol.*, 22, 1, 3–21, 2015.

6. Sikder, A.K., Petracca, G., Aksu, H., Jaeger, T., Uluagac, A.S., A Survey on Sensor-based Threats to Internet-of-Things (IoT) Devices and Applications, *arXiv preprint arXiv:1802.02041*. http://arxiv.org/abs/1802.02041.

7. Ray, P.P., A survey on Internet of Things architectures. *J. King Saud Univ.-Comp. Info. Sci.*, 30, 3, 291–319, 2018.

8. Dias, D. and Paulo Silva Cunha, J., Wearable health devices—vital sign monitoring, systems and technologies. *Sensors*, 18, 8, 2414, 2018.

9. Zhang, W., Peng, G., Li, C., Chen, Y., Zhang, Z., A new deep learning model for fault diagnosis with good anti-noise and domain adaptation ability on raw vibration signals. *Sensors*, 17, 2, 425, 2017.

10. Raghupathi, W. and Raghupathi, V., Big data analytics in healthcare: promise and potential. *Health Inf. Sci. Syst.*, 2, 1, 3, 2014.

11. Liu, W., Wang, Z., Liu, X., Zeng, N., Liu, Y., Alsaadi, F.E. A survey of deep neural network architectures and their applications. *Neurocomputing*, 19, 234, 11–26, 2017.

12. Sethi, P. and Sarangi, S.R., Internet of Things: Architectures, Protocols, and Applications. *J. Electr. Comput. Eng.*, Jan. 26, 2017, https://www.hindawi.com/journals/jece/2017/9324035/ (accessed Sep. 20, 2020).

13. Lee, H.J. and Kim, M., The Internet of Things in a smart connected world, in: *Internet of Things-Technology, Applications and Standardization*, p. 91, 2018.

14. Rodrigues, J.J. *et al.*, Enabling technologies for the internet of health things. *IEEE Access*, 6, 13129–13141, 2018.

15. Mehmood, Y., Ahmad, F., Yaqoob, I., Adnane, A., Imran, M., Guizani, S., Internet-of-Things-Based Smart Cities: Recent Advances and Challenges. *IEEE Commun. Mag.*, 55, 9, 16–24, 2017.

16. Masoud, M., Jaradat, Y., Manasrah, A., Jannoud, I., Sensors of Smart Devices in the Internet of Everything (IoE) Era: Big Opportunities and Massive Doubts. *J. Sens.*, 2019, 2019.

17. Bansal, S. and Kumar, D., IoT Ecosystem: A Survey on Devices, Gateways, Operating Systems, Middleware and Communication. *Int. J. Wireless Inf. Networks*, 27, 1–25, 2020.

18. Medagliani, P. *et al.*, *Internet of things applications-from research and innovation to market deployment*, River Publisher, Denmark, 2014.

19. Saura, J.R., Using Data Sciences in Digital Marketing: Framework, methods, and performance metrics. *J. Innovation Knowledge*, 2020.

20. Machorro-Cano, I. *et al.*, An IoT-based architecture to develop a healthcare smart platform, in: *International Conference on Technologies and Innovation*, pp. 133–145, 2017.

21. de Morais, C.M., Sadok, D., Kelner, J., An IoT sensor and scenario survey for data researchers. *J. Braz. Comput. Soc.*, 25, 1, 4, 2019.

22. Bhalla, N., Jolly, P., Formisano, N., Estrela, P., Introduction to biosensors. *Essays Biochem.*, 60, 1, 1–8, Jun. 2016.

23. Perera, C., Jayaraman, P., Zaslavsky, A., Christen, P., Georgakopoulos, D., Dynamic configuration of sensors using mobile sensor hub in internet of things paradigm, in: *2013 IEEE Eighth International Conference on Intelligent Sensors, Sensor Networks and Information Processing*, Melbourne, VIC, pp. 473–478, 2013.

24. Mehrotra, P., Biosensors and their applications–A review. *J. Oral. Biol. Craniofac. Res.*, 6, 2, 153–159, 2016.

25. Zahariadis, T., *et al.*, FIWARE lab: managing resources and services in a cloud federation supporting future internet applications, IEEE/ACM 7th International Conference on Utility and Cloud Computing. IEEE, 729–299, 2014.

26. Schmidt, R., Norgall, T., Mörsdorf, J., Bernhard, J., von der Grün, T., Body Area Network BAN–a key infrastructure element for patient-centered medical applications. *Biomed. Tech. (Berl)*, 47, Suppl 1 Pt 1, 365–368, 2002.

27. Ullah, S. *et al.*, A comprehensive survey of wireless body area networks. *J. Med. Syst.*, 36, 3, 1065–1094, 2012.

28. Dang, L.M., Piran, M., Han, D., Min, K., Moon, H., A survey on internet of things and cloud computing for healthcare. *Electronics*, 8, 7, 768, 2019.

29. Fernando, N., Loke, S.W., Rahayu, W., Mobile cloud computing: A survey. *Future Gener. Comput. Syst.*, 29, 1, 84–106, 2013.

30. Ventola, C.L., Mobile Devices and Apps for Healthcare Professionals: Uses and Benefits. *Inf. Manage.*, 9, 39, 5, 356, 2014.

31. Budida, D.A.M. and Mangrulkar, R.S., Design and implementation of smart HealthCare system using IoT. *2017 International Conference on Innovations in Information, Embedded and Communication Systems (ICIIECS)*, 2017.

32. Gelogo, Internet of Things (IoT) Framework for u-healthcare System | Request PDF, ResearchGate. *Int. J. Smart Home*, 9, 11, 323–330, 2015. https://www.researchgate.net/publication/298213267_Internet_of_Things_IoT_Framework_for_u-healthcare_System (accessed Sep. 20, 2020).

33. Vitabile, S. *et al.*, Medical data processing and analysis for remote health and activities monitoring, in: *High-Performance Modelling and Simulation for Big Data Applications*, pp. 186–220, Springer, Cham, 2019.

34. Mohammadinejad, *et al.*, Recent Advances in Natural Gum-Based Biomaterials for Tissue Engineering and Regenerative Medicine: A Review. *Polymers*, 12, 1, Art. no. 1, Jan. 2020.

35. Metheny, M., *Federal cloud computing: The definitive guide for cloud service providers*, Syngress, USA, 2017.

36. Mell, P. and Grance, T., The NIST Definition of Cloud Computing. Institute of Science and Technology, Special Publication 800, 145, 2011.

37. Knebel, E. and Greiner, A.C., *Health professions education: A bridge to quality*, National Academies Press, Washington, 2003.

38. Moura, J. and Hutchison, D., Review and analysis of networking challenges in cloud computing. *J. Netw. Comput. Appl.*, 60, 113–129, 2016.

39. Ahmad, M.O. and Khan, D.R.Z., The Cloud Computing: A Systematic Review. 3, 5, 10, 2007.AU: Please provide journal title.

40. Jadeja, Y. and Modi, K., Cloud computing - concepts, architecture and challenges, in: *2012 International Conference on Computing, Electronics and Electrical Technologies (ICCEET)*, Nagercoil, Tamil Nadu, India, Mar. 2012, pp. 877–880.

41. Mattess, M., Vecchiola, C., Kumar Garg, S., Buyya, R., Cloud Bursting: Managing Peak Loads by Leasing Public Cloud Services, in: *Cloud Computing*, 1st ed., L. Wang, R. Ranjan, J. Chen, B. Benatallah (Eds.), pp. 343–367, CRC Press, Australia, 2017.

42. Khurana, S. and Verma, A.G., Comparison of Cloud Computing Service Models: SaaS, PaaS, IaaS. *Int. J. Electron. Commun. Tech.*, 4, 3, 29–32, 2013.

43. Narayana, K.E., Kumar, S., Jayashree, D.K., A Review on Different types of Deployment Models in Cloud Computing. *Int. J. Innov. Res. Comput. Commun. Eng.,* 5, 2, 7, 2007.

44. Lin, Y.-W., Lin, Y.-B., Yang, M.-T., Lin, J.-H., ArduTalk: An Arduino network application development platform based on IoTtalk. *IEEE Syst. J.,* 13, 1, 468–476, 2017.

45. Kim, S.-M., Choi, Y., Suh, J., Applications of the Open-Source Hardware Arduino Platform in the Mining Industry: A Review. *Appl. Sci.,* 10, 14, 5018, 2020.

46. Al-Fuqaha, A., Guizani, M., Mohammadi, M., Aledhari, M., Ayyash, M., Internet of things: A survey on enabling technologies, protocols, and applications. *IEEE Commun. Surv. Tut.,* 17, 4, 2347–2376, 2015.

47. Lu, T.-C., Fu, C.-M., Ma, M.H.-M., Fang, C.-C., Turner, A.M., Healthcare applications of smart watches: a systematic review. *Appl. Clin. Inform.,* 7, 3, 850, 2016.

48. Caswell, G., Pollock, K., Harwood, R., Porock, D., Communication between family carers and health professionals about end-of-life care for older people in the acute hospital setting: a qualitative study. *BMC Palliat. Care,* 14, 1, 1–14, 2015.

49. Bansal, M. and Gandhi, B., IoT based smart healthcare system using CNT electrodes (for continuous ECG monitoring), in: *2017 International Conference on Computing, Communication and Automation (ICCCA),* Greater Noida, May 2017, pp. 1324–1329.

50. Albesher, A.A., IoT in Healthcare: Recent Advances in the Development of Smart Cyber-Physical Ubiquitous Environments. *IJCSNS,* 19, 2, 181, 2019. 2019.

51. Amin, S.U., Hossain, M.S., Muhammad, G., Alhussein, M., Md., A., Rahman, Cognitive Smart Healthcare for Pathology Detection and Monitoring. *IEEE Access,* 7, 10745–10753, 2019.

52. Sarraf, S. and Tofighi, G., Classification of Alzheimer's Disease using fMRI Data and Deep Learning Convolutional Neural Networks, *arXiv:1603.08631 [cs],* Mar. 2016.

53. Zhang, B., *Automatic EEG Processing for the Early Diagnosis of Traumatic Brain Injury,* ResearchGate, *20th International Conference on Knowledge Based and Intelligent Information and Engineering Systems, KES2016,* pp. 5–7, September 2016, York, United Kingdom, 2016.

54. Satpathy, S., Mohan, P., Das, S., Debbarma, S., A new healthcare diagnosis system using an IoT-based fuzzy classifier with FPGA. *J. Supercomput.,* 76, 8, 5849–5861, Aug. 2020.

55. Chen, M., Ma, Y., Li, Y., Wu, D., Zhang, Y., Youn, C.-H., Wearable 2.0: Enabling Human-Cloud Integration in Next Generation Healthcare Systems. *IEEE Commun. Mag.,* 55, 1, 54–61, Jan. 2017.

56. Chakraborty, C., Banerjee, A., Kolekar, M.H., Garg, L., Chakraborty, B. (Eds.), *Internet of Things for Healthcare Technologies*, vol. 73, Springer Singapore, Singapore, 2021.

57. Aldeer, M., Javanmard, M., Martin, R., A Review of Medication Adherence Monitoring Technologies. *ASI*, 1, 2, 14, May 2018.

58. Ali, Z., Muhammad, G., Alhamid, M.F., An Automatic Health Monitoring System for Patients Suffering From Voice Complications in Smart Cities. *IEEE Access*, 5, 3900–3908, 2017.

59. Bates, M., Healthcare Chatbots Are Here to Help. *IEEE Pulse*, 10, 3, 12–14, May 2019.

60. Hommersom, A. *et al.*, MoSHCA - my mobile and smart healthcare assistant, in: *2013 IEEE 15th International Conference on e-Health Networking, Applications and Services (Healthcom 2013)*, Lisbon, Portugal, Oct. 2013, pp. 188–192.

61. Pandharkame, H.P. and Mudholkar, P., Smart Hospitals using Internet of Things (IoT). *Int. Res. J. Eng. Tech. (IRJET)*, 8, 5, 4, 2017.

62. Gupta, P., Agrawal, D., Chhabra, J., Dhir, P.K., IoT based smart healthcare kit, in: *2016 International Conference on Computational Techniques in Information and Communication Technologies (ICCTICT)*, New Delhi, India, Mar. 2016, pp. 237–242.

63. Kim, J., Campbell, A.S., de Ávila, B.E.-F., Wang, J., Wearable biosensors for healthcare monitoring. *Nat. Biotechnol.*, 37, 4, 389–406, Apr. 2019.

64. Eisenmann, T. R., Pao, M., Barley, L., Dropbox: "It Just Works". President and Fellows of Harvard College, US, 2014.

65. DailyRounds, https://dailyrounds.org/.

66. VisualDx, Visual Clinical Decision Support System (CDSS), https://www.visualdx.com/.

67. Wearable Technology in Healthcare - Thematic Research. https://store.globaldata.com/report/gdhcht026–wearable-technology-in-healthcare-thematic-research/.

68. FDA Approves Antipsychotic Agent With Sensor to Track Ingestion - MPR. https://www.empr.com/home/news/fda-approves-antipsychotic-agent-with-sensor-to-track-ingestion/.

69. 510(k) Vs CE Mark - EMMA International. https://emmainternational.com/510k-vs-ce-mark/.

70. Ianculescu, M., Alexandru, A., Coardo, D., Coman, O.A., Smart Wearable Medical Devices-The Next Step in Providing Affordable Support for Dermatology Practice, *Dermatovenerologie-J. Rom. Soc. Dermatol.,*, 63, 295–306, 2018.

71. GlucoTrack, Your track to health!.™, http://www.glucotrack.com/.

72. Eversense Continuous Glucose Monitoring | Long-term Continuous Glucose Monitor. https://www.eversensediabetes.com/.

73. Guk, K. *et al.*, Evolution of Wearable Devices with Real-Time Disease Monitoring for Personalized Healthcare. *Nanomaterials*, 9, 6, 813, May 2019.

74. Baldi, P., Brunak, S., Frasconi, P., Soda, G., Pollastri, G., Exploiting the past and the future in protein secondary structure prediction. *Bioinformatics*, 15, 11, 937–946, Nov. 1999.

75. Ky, N. and Iw, K., Big data and machine learning algorithms for healthcare delivery. *Lancet Oncol.*, 20, 5, e262–e273, May 2019.

76. Suzuki, K., Overview of deep learning in medical imaging. *Radiol. Phys. Technol.*, 2017, DeepDyve, https://www.deepdyve.com/lp/springer-journal/overview-of-deep-learning-in-medical-imaging-Gs2bpwO6Pe (accessed Sep. 19, 2020).

77. Lundervold, A.S. and Lundervold, A., An overview of deep learning in medical imaging focusing on MRI. *Z. Med. Phys.*, 29, 2, 102–127, May 2019.

78. Ahuja, A.S., The impact of artificial intelligence in medicine on the future role of the physician. *PeerJ*, 7, e7702, Oct. 2019.

79. Abiodun, O., II, Jantan, A., Omolara, A.E., Dada, K.V., Mohamed, N.A., Arshad, H., State-of-the-art in artificial neural network applications: A survey. *Heliyon*, 4, 11, Nov. 2018.

80. Shahid, N., Rappon, T., Berta, W., Applications of artificial neural networks in healthcare organizational decision-making: A scoping review. *PloS One*, 14, 2, e0212356, Feb. 2019.

81. Montavon, G., Samek, W., Müller, K.-R., Methods for interpreting and understanding deep neural networks. *Digital Signal Process.*, 73, 1–15, Feb. 2018.

82. Schmidhuber, J., Deep Learning in Neural Networks: An Overview. *Neural Networks*, 61, 85–117, Jan. 2015.

83. Zemouri, Applied Sciences | Free Full-Text | Deep Learning in the Biomedical Applications: Recent and Future Status. *Appl. Sci.*, 9, 8, 1526, 2019.

84. Alom, M.Z. *et al.*, A State-of-the-Art Survey on Deep Learning Theory and Architectures. *Electronics*, 8, 3, 292, Mar. 2019.

85. Ravi, Deep Learning for Health Informatics. *IEEE J. Biomed. Health Inform.*, 21, 1, 4–21, 2017.

86. Lyu, C., Chen, B., Ren, Y., Ji, D., Long short-term memory RNN for biomedical named entity recognition. *BMC Bioinf.*, 18, 1, 462, Oct. 2017.

87. LeCun, Y., Bengio, Y., Hinton, G., Deep learning. *Nature*, 521, 7553, 436–444, May 2015.

88. Rumelhart, D.E., Hinton, G.E., Williams, R.J., Learning representations by back-propagating errors. *Nature*, 323, 533–536, Oct. 1986.

89. Hosseini, A., Deep Learning of Part-Based Representation of Data Using Sparse Autoencoders With Nonnegativity Constraints. *IEEE Trans. Neural Netw. Learn. Syst.*, 27, 12, 2015.

90. Vincent, P., Larochelle, H., Bengio, Y., Manzagol, P.-A., Extracting and composing robust features with denoising autoencoders, in: *Proceedings of the 25th international conference on Machine learning*, New York, NY, USA, Jul. 2008, pp. 1096–1103.

91. Hinton, G.E., Deep belief networks. *Scholarpedia*, 4, 5, 5947, May 2009.

92. Hinton, G.E., Reducing the Dimensionality of Data with Neural Networks. *Science*, 313, 5786, 504–507, Jul. 2006.

93. Krizhevsky, A., Sutskever, I., Hinton, G.E., ImageNet Classification with Deep Convolutional Neural Networks, in: *Advances in Neural Information Processing Systems 25*, F. Pereira, C.J.C. Burges, L. Bottou, K.Q. Weinberger (Eds.), pp. 1097–1105, Curran Associates, Inc., US, 2012.

94. Zeiler, M.D. and Fergus, R., Visualizing and Understanding Convolutional Networks. In: *Computer Vision – ECCV 2014. ECCV 2014*, D. Fleet, T. Pajdla, B. Schiele, T. Tuytelaars (Eds.), vol. 8689. ECCV 2014. Lecture Notes in Computer Science, Springer, Cham. https://doi.org/10.1007/978-3-319-10590-1_53.

95. Szegedy, M.D., Going deeper with convolutions. *IEEE Conference Publication*, 2015, https://ieeexplore.ieee.org/document/7298594 (accessed Sep. 19, 2020).

96. Zhang, N., Ding, S., Zhang, J., Xue, Y., An overview on Restricted Boltzmann Machines. *Neurocomput.*, 275, C, 1186–1199, Jan. 2018.

97. Fischer, A., Training restricted Boltzmann machines: An introduction. *Pattern Recognit.*, 47, 25–39, 2014.

98. Hubel, D.H. and Wiesel, T.N., Receptive fields, binocular interaction and functional architecture in the cat's visual cortex. *J. Physiol.*, 160, 1, 106–154, 1962.

99. Wiatowski, T. and Bölcskei, H., A Mathematical Theory of Deep Convolutional Neural Networks for Feature Extraction, Cornell University, US, *arXiv:1512.06293*.

100. Min, S., Lee, B., Yoon, S., Deep learning in bioinformatics. *Brief. Bioinf.*, 18, 5, 851–869, 01 2017.

101. Mahmud, M., Kaiser, M.S., Hussain, A., Vassanelli, S., Applications of Deep Learning and Reinforcement Learning to Biological Data. *IEEE Trans. Neural. Netw. Learn. Syst.*, 29, 6, 2063–2079, 2018.

102. Alipanahi, B., Delong, A., Weirauch, M.T., Frey, B.J., Predicting the sequence specificities of DNA- and RNA-binding proteins by deep learning. *Nat. Biotechnol.*, 33, 8, 831–838, Aug. 2015.

103. Sekhon, A., Singh, R., Qi, Y., DeepDiff: DEEP-learning for predicting DIFFerential gene expression from histone modifications. *Bioinformatics*, 34, 17, i891–i900, Sep. 2018.

104. Meng, Research of stacked denoising sparse autoencoder. *Neural Comput. Appl.*, 30, 2083–2100, 2018.

105. Lee, T. and Yoon, S., Boosted Categorical Restricted Boltzmann Machine for Computational Prediction of Splice Junctions, in: *International Conference on Machine Learning*, Jun. 2015, pp. 2483–2492, Accessed: Sep. 19, 2020, [Online]. Available: http://proceedings.mlr.press/v37/leeb15.html.

106. Chen, Y., Li, Y., Narayan, R., Subramanian, A., Xie, X., Gene expression inference with deep learning. *Bioinformatics*, 32, 12, 1832–1839, Jun. 2016.

107. Denas, O. and Taylor, J., Deep modeling of gene expression regulation in an Erythropoiesis model. Representation Learning, ICML Workshop. New York, USA: ACM, 2013.

108. Pan, X. and Shen, H.-B., RNA-protein binding motifs mining with a new hybrid deep learning based cross-domain knowledge integration approach. *BMC Bioinf.*, 18, 1, 136, Feb. 2017.

109. Kelley, D.R., Snoek, J., Rinn, J.L., Basset: learning the regulatory code of the accessible genome with deep convolutional neural networks. *Genome Res.*, 26, 7, 990–999, Jul. 2016.

110. Zeng, H., Edwards, M.D., Liu, G., Gifford, D.K., Convolutional neural network architectures for predicting DNA-protein binding. *Bioinformatics*, 32, 12, i121–i127, 15 2016.

111. Zhou, J. and Troyanskaya, O.G., Predicting effects of noncoding variants with deep learning-based sequence model. *Nat. Methods*, 12, 10, 931–934, Oct. 2015.

112. Park, K.-H. and Lee, S.-W., Movement intention decoding based on deep learning for multiuser myoelectric interfaces, in: *2016 4th International Winter Conference on Brain-Computer Interface (BCI)*, Feb. 2016, pp. 1–2.

113. Lee, B., Baek, J., Park, S., Yoon, S., deepTarget: End-to-end Learning Framework for microRNA Target Prediction using Deep Recurrent Neural Networks, *Proceedings of the 7th ACM International Conference on Bioinformatics, Computational Biology, and Health Informatics - BCB '16*, 2016.

114. Chen, L., Cai, C., Chen, V., Lu, X., Trans-species learning of cellular signaling systems with bimodal deep belief networks. *Bioinformatics*, 31, 18, 3008–3015, 2015.

115. Chandrasekhar, K., Kumar, R.P., Bharathi, P., Triveni, K.V., HISTOPATHOLOGIC CANCER DETECTION. *Int. Res. J. Comput. Sci.*, 6, 04, 23, 2019.

116. Nam, S. *et al.*, Introduction to digital pathology and computer-aided pathology. *J. Pathol. Transl. Med.*, 54, 2, 125–134, Mar. 2020.

117. Xing, F. and Yang, L., Robust Nucleus/Cell Detection and Segmentation in Digital Pathology and Microscopy Images: A Comprehensive Review. *IEEE Rev. Biomed. Eng.*, 9, 234–263, 2016.

118. Wang, H. *et al.*, Mitosis detection in breast cancer pathology images by combining handcrafted and convolutional neural network features. *J. Med. Imaging (Bellingham)*, 1, 3, 034003, Oct. 2014.

119. Ciresan, D., Giusti, A., Gambardella, L.M., Schmidhuber, J., Deep Neural Networks Segment Neuronal Membranes in Electron Microscopy Images, in: *Advances in Neural Information Processing Systems 25*, F. Pereira, C.J.C. Burges, L. Bottou, K.Q. Weinberger (Eds.), pp. 2843–2851, Curran Associates, Inc., US, 2012.

120. Xu, J. *et al.*, Stacked Sparse Autoencoder (SSAE) for Nuclei Detection on Breast Cancer Histopathology Images. *IEEE Trans. Med. Imaging*, 35, 1, 119–130, Jan. 2016.

121. Chen, C.L. *et al.*, Deep Learning in Label-free Cell Classification. *Sci. Rep.*, 6, 1, 21471, Mar. 2016.

122. Meng, Large-Scale Multi-Class Image-Based Cell Classification With Deep Learning - PubMed, 2017, https://pubmed.ncbi.nlm.nih.gov/30387753/ (accessed Sep. 20, 2020).

123. Parnamaa, Accurate Classification of Protein Subcellular Localization from High-Throughput Microscopy Images Using Deep Learning. *G3 (Bethesda)*, 7, 5, 1385–1392, 2017.

124. Ferrari, A., Lombardi, S., Signoroni, A., Bacterial colony counting with Convolutional Neural Networks in Digital Microbiology Imaging. *Pattern Recognit.*, 2017.

125. Eulenberg, P. *et al.*, Reconstructing cell cycle and disease progression using deep learning. *Nat. Commun.*, 8.1, 1–6, 2017.

126. Jiang, B., Wang, X., Luo, J., Zhang, X., Xiong, Y., Pang, H., Convolutional Neural Networks in Automatic Recognition of Trans-differentiated Neural Progenitor Cells under Bright-Field Microscopy. *2015 Fifth International Conference on Instrumentation and Measurement, Computer, Communication and Control (IMCCC)*, 2015.

127. Zeng, N., Wang, Z., Zhang, H., Liu, W., Alsaadi, F.E., Deep Belief Networks for Quantitative Analysis of a Gold Immunochromatographic Strip. *Cogn. Comput.*, 8, 4, 684–692, Aug. 2016.

128. Aslan, Z., On the use of deep learning methods on medical images. *Int. J. Energy Eng. Sci.*, 3, 2, 1–15, 2019.

129. Haque, I.R., II and Neubert, J., Deep learning approaches to biomedical image segmentation. *Inform. Med. Unlocked*, 18, 100297, 2020.

130. Bercovich, E. and Javitt, M.C., Medical Imaging: From Roentgen to the Digital Revolution, and Beyond. *Rambam Maimonides Med. J.*, 9, 4, Oct. 2018.

131. Hosny, A., Parmar, C., Quackenbush, J., Schwartz, L.H., Aerts, H.J.W.L., Artificial intelligence in radiology. *Nat. Rev. Cancer*, 18, 8, 500–510, Aug. 2018.

132. Kamnitsas, K. *et al.*, Efficient multi-scale 3D CNN with fully connected CRF for accurate brain lesion segmentation. *Med. Image Anal.*, 36, 61–78, Feb. 2017.

133. Stollenga, *Parallel Multi-Dimensional LSTM, With Application to Fast Biomedical Volumetric Image Segmentation*, NY, 2015, https://arxiv.org/abs/1506.07452

134. Fritscher, K., Raudaschl, P., Zaffino, P., Spadea, M.F., Sharp, G.C., Schubert, R., Deep Neural Networks for Fast Segmentation of 3D Medical Images, in: *Medical Image Computing and Computer-Assisted Intervention - MICCAI 2016*, Oct. 2016, pp. 158–165.

135. Dou, Q. *et al.*, 3D deeply supervised network for automated segmentation of volumetric medical images. *Med. Image Anal.*, 41, 40–54, Oct. 2017.

136. Gondara, L., Medical Image Denoising Using Convolutional Denoising Autoencoders. *2016 IEEE 16th International Conference on Data Mining Workshops (ICDMW)*, 2016.

137. Mansoor, A. *et al.*, Deep Learning Guided Partitioned Shape Model for Anterior Visual Pathway Segmentation. *IEEE Trans. Med. Imaging*, 35, 8, 1856–1865, 2016.

138. Agostinelli, 27 nips-2013-Adaptive Multi-Column Deep Neural Networks with Application to Robust Image Denoising. *NIPS'13: Proc. 26th Int. Conf. Neural Inf. Process. Syst.*, 1, 1493–1501, 2013.

139. Suk, H.-I. and Shen, D., Deep Learning-Based Feature Representation for AD/MCI Classification, in: *Medical Image Computing and Computer-Assisted Intervention – MICCAI 2013*, Springer, Berlin, Heidelberg, pp. 583–590, 2013.

140. Suk, H.-I., Lee, S.-W., Shen, D., Hierarchical Feature Representation and Multimodal Fusion with Deep Learning for AD/MCI Diagnosis. *Neuroimage*, 101, 569–582, Nov. 2014.

141. Li, F., Tran, L., Thung, K.-H., Ji, S., Shen, D., Li, J., A Robust Deep Model for Improved Classification of AD/MCI Patients. *IEEE J. Biomed. Health Inform.*, 19, 5, 1610–1616, Sep. 2015.

142. Lee, S., Choi, M., Choi, H., Park, M.S., Yoon, S., FingerNet: Deep learning-based robust finger joint detection from radiographs, in: *2015 IEEE Biomedical Circuits and Systems Conference (BioCAS)*, Oct. 2015, pp. 1–4.

143. Gao, *Classification of CT brain images based on deep learning networks. Comput. Methods Programs Biomed.*, 138, 2017.

144. Jiao, Z., Gao, X., Wang, Y., Li, J., A deep feature based framework for breast masses classification. *Neurocomputing*, 197, 221–231, Jul. 2016.

145. Arevalo, J., González, F.A., Ramos-Pollán, R., Oliveira, J.L., Guevara Lopez, M.A., Representation learning for mammography mass lesion classification with convolutional neural networks. *Comput. Methods Programs Biomed.*, 127, 248–257, Apr. 2016.

146. N.D., Z.H., A.E., L.L., S.D., 3D Deep Learning for Multi-modal Imaging-Guided Survival Time Prediction of Brain Tumor Patients. *Medical image computing and computer-assisted intervention : MICCAI ... International Conference on Medical Image Computing and Computer-Assisted Intervention*, Oct. 2016, https://pubmed.ncbi.nlm.nih.gov/28149967/ (accessed Sep. 20, 2020).

147. Shen, W. *et al.*, Multi-crop Convolutional Neural Networks for lung nodule malignancy suspiciousness classification. *Pattern Recognit.*, 61, 663–673, Jan. 2017.

148. Cheng, J.-Z. *et al.*, Computer-Aided Diagnosis with Deep Learning Architecture: Applications to Breast Lesions in US Images and Pulmonary Nodules in CT Scans. *Sci. Rep.*, 6, Apr. 2016.

149. Shin, Deep Convolutional Neural Networks for Computer-Aided Detection: CNN Architectures, Dataset Characteristics and Transfer Learning. *IEEE Trans. Med. Imaging*, 35, 5, 1285–1298, Feb. 2016.

150. Roth, Improving Computer-aided Detection using Convolutional Neural Networks and Random View Aggregation. *IEEE Trans. Med. Imaging*, 35, 5, 1170–1181, 2015.

151. Cho, J., Lee, K., Shin, E., Choy, G., Do, S., *Medical Image Deep Learning with Hospital PACS Dataset*, undefined, arXiv preprint arXiv:1511.06348, 2015.

152. Chen, H. *et al.*, Standard Plane Localization in Fetal Ultrasound via Domain Transferred Deep Neural Networks. *IEEE J. Biomed. Health Inform.*, 19, 5, 1627–1636, Sep. 2015.

153. Plis, Sergey M., *et al.*, Deep learning for neuroimaging: a validation study. *Front. Neurosci.*, 8, 229, 2014.

154. Kuang, D. and He, L., Classification on ADHD with Deep Learning, in: *2014 International Conference on Cloud Computing and Big Data*, Nov. 2014, pp. 27–32.

155. Ypsilantis, P.-P. *et al.*, Predicting Response to Neoadjuvant Chemotherapy with PET Imaging Using Convolutional Neural Networks. *PloS One*, 10, 9, e0137036, Sep. 2015.

156. Yu, J., Chen, J., Xiang, Z.Q., Zou, Y.-X., A hybrid convolutional neural networks with extreme learning machine for WCE image classification, in: *2015 IEEE International Conference on Robotics and Biomimetics (ROBIO)*, Dec. 2015, pp. 1822–1827.

157. van Grinsven, M.J.J.P., van Ginneken, B., Hoyng, C.B., Theelen, T., Sanchez, C., II, Fast Convolutional Neural Network Training Using Selective Data Sampling: Application to Hemorrhage Detection in Color Fundus Images. *IEEE Trans. Med. Imaging*, 35, 5, 1273–1284, 2016.

158. Kleesiek, J. *et al.*, Deep MRI brain extraction: A 3D convolutional neural network for skull stripping. *Neuroimage*, 129, 460–469, 2016.

159. Shih, J.J., Krusienski, D.J., Wolpaw, J.R., Brain-Computer Interfaces in Medicine. *Mayo Clin. Proc.*, 87, 3, 268–279, Mar. 2012.

160. Ferreira, A., Celeste, W.C., Cheein, F.A., Bastos-Filho, T.F., Sarcinelli-Filho, M., Carelli, R., Human-machine interfaces based on EMG and EEG applied to robotic systems. *J. NeuroEng. Rehabil.*, 5, 1, 10, Mar. 2008.

161. Jiang, F. *et al.*, Artificial intelligence in healthcare: past, present and future. *Stroke Vasc. Neurol.*, 2, 4, 230–243, Jun. 2017.

162. Yang, On the use of convolutional neural networks and augmented CSP features for multi-class motor imagery of EEG signals classification. *IEEE Conference Publication*, 2015, https://ieeexplore.ieee.org/document/7318929 (accessed Sep. 21, 2020).

163. Tabar, Y.R. and Halici, U., A novel deep learning approach for classification of EEG motor imagery signals. *J. Neural. Eng.*, 14, 1, 016003, 2017.

164. Lu, N., Li, T., Ren, X., Miao, H., A Deep Learning Scheme for Motor Imagery Classification based on Restricted Boltzmann Machines. *IEEE Trans. Neural Syst. Rehabil. Eng.*, 25, 6, 566–576, 2017.

165. An, X., Kuang, D., Guo, X., Zhao, Y., He, L., A Deep Learning Method for Classification of EEG Data Based on Motor Imagery, in: *Intelligent Computing in Bioinformatics*, Springer, Cham, pp. 203–210, 2014.

166. Li, K., Li, X., Zhang, Y., Zhang, A., Affective state recognition from EEG with deep belief networks, in: *2013 IEEE International Conference on Bioinformatics and Biomedicine*, Dec. 2013, pp. 305–310.

167. Li, J., Zhang, Z., He, H., Hierarchical Convolutional Neural Networks for EEG-Based Emotion Recognition. *Cogn. Comput.*, 10, 2, 368–380, Apr. 2018.

168. Soleymani, M., Asghari-Esfeden, S., Pantic, M., Fu, Y., Continuous emotion detection using EEG signals and facial expressions, in: *2014 IEEE International Conference on Multimedia and Expo (ICME)*, Jul. 2014, pp. 1–6.

169. Hajinoroozi, M., Mao, Z., Huang, Y., Prediction of driver's drowsy and alert states from EEG signals with deep learning, in: *2015 IEEE 6th International Workshop on Computational Advances in Multi-Sensor Adaptive Processing (CAMSAP)*, Dec. 2015, pp. 493–496.

170. Chai, R. *et al.*, Improving EEG-Based Driver Fatigue Classification Using Sparse-Deep Belief Networks. *Front. Neurosci.*, 11, 2017.

171. Petrosian, A., Prokhorov, D., Homan, R., Dasheiff, R., Wunsch, D., Recurrent Neural Network Based Prediction of Epileptic Seizures in Intra- and Extracranial EEG. *Neurocomputing*, 30, 201–218, Jan. 2000.

172. Mirowski, P., Madhavan, D., LeCun, Y., Kuzniecky, R., Classification of patterns of EEG synchronization for seizure prediction. *Clin. Neurophysiol.*, 120, 11, 1927–1940, Nov. 2009.

173. Wulsin, D.F., Gupta, J.R., Mani, R., Blanco, J.A., Litt, B., Modeling electroencephalography waveforms with semi-supervised deep belief nets: fast classification and anomaly measurement. *J. Neural Eng.*, 8, 3, 036015, Jun. 2011.

174. Atzori, M., Cognolato, M., Müller, H., Deep Learning with Convolutional Neural Networks Applied to Electromyography Data: A Resource for the Classification of Movements for Prosthetic Hands. *Front. Neurorobot.*, 10, 2016.

175. Yan, Y., Qin, X., Wu, Y., Zhang, N., Fan, J., Wang, L., A restricted Boltzmann machine based two-lead electrocardiography classification, in: *2015 IEEE 12th International Conference on Wearable and Implantable Body Sensor Networks (BSN)*, Jun. 2015, pp. 1–9.

176. Dash, S., Shakyawar, S.K., Sharma, M., Kaushik, S., Big data in healthcare: management, analysis and future prospects. *J. Big Data*, 6, 1, 54, Jun. 2019.

177. Miotto, R., Wang, F., Wang, S., Jiang, X., Dudley, J.T., Deep learning for healthcare: review, opportunities and challenges. *Brief. Bioinf.*, 19, 6, 1236–1246, 27 2018.

178. Obermeyer, Z. and Emanuel, E.J., Predicting the Future - Big Data, Machine Learning, and Clinical Medicine. *N. Engl. J. Med.*, 375, 13, 1216–1219, Sep. 2016.

179. Ali, S.A. *et al.*, An Optimally Configured and Improved Deep Belief Network (OCI-DBN) Approach for Heart Disease Prediction Based on Ruzzo–Tompa and Stacked Genetic Algorithm. *IEEE Access*, 8, 65947–65958, 2020.

180. Phan, *presented at the 2012 IEEE/ACM International Conference on Advances in Social Network Analysis and Mining*, Istanbul, Aug. 2012.

181. Zou, B., Lampos, V., Gorton, R., Cox, I.J., On Infectious Intestinal Disease Surveillance using Social Media Content, in: *Proceedings of the 6th International Conference on Digital Health Conference*, New York, NY, USA, Apr. 2016, pp. 157–161.

182. Garimella, V.R.K., Alfayad, A., Weber, I., Social Media Image Analysis for Public Health, in: *Proceedings of the 2016 CHI Conference on Human Factors in Computing Systems*, New York, NY, USA, May 2016, pp. 5543–5547.

183. Zhao, L., Chen, J., Chen, F., Wang, W., Lu, C.-T., Ramakrishnan, N., SimNest: Social Media Nested Epidemic Simulation via Online Semi-Supervised Deep Learning, in: *2015 IEEE International Conference on Data Mining*, Nov. 2015, pp. 639–648.

184. Ong, B.T., Sugiura, K., Zettsu, K., Dynamically pre-trained deep recurrent neural networks using environmental monitoring data for predicting PM2.5. *Neural Comput. Appl.*, 27, 1553–1566, 2016.

185. Felbo, Using Deep Learning to Predict Demographics from Mobile Phone Metadata, ICLR 2016 workshop submission, arXiv: 1511.06660v4, Cornell University, US, 2016.

186. Mehrabi, S. *et al.*, Temporal Pattern and Association Discovery of Diagnosis Codes Using Deep Learning, in: *2015 International Conference on Healthcare Informatics*, Oct. 2015, pp. 408–416.

187. Din, Ikram Ud, *et al.*, The Internet of Things: A review of enabled technologies and future challenges. *Ieee Access*, 7, 7606–7640, 2018.

188. Zhang, H. *et al*, Connecting intelligent things in smart hospitals using NB-IoT. *IEEE Internet of Things J.*, 5, 3, 1550–1560, 2018.

QLattice Environment and Feyn QGraph Models—A New Perspective Toward Deep Learning

Vinayak Bharadi

Department of Information Technology, Finolex Academy of Management and Technology, Mirjole, Ratnagiri, Maharashtra, India

Abstract

Artificial neural networks (ANNs) have been with us for quite a time, and with the advancement in the technology, the availability of graphical processing unit (GPU) and tensor processing unit (TPU) advanced architectures has been in the reach of the common person. Deep neural networks are now playing a major role in pattern recognition. In this chapter, a new type of deep learning model is discussed, and they are called Feyn models under the QLattice environment. These are inspired by quantum mechanics; they extend the concept of photon movement to evaluate the best possible model for a given deep learning problem. It is based on the Feyn framework, which evaluates maximum possible models for a given type of problem, and then, the best model can be further selected and tested.

The world is suffering from the COVID-19 outbreak, and daily, the COVID-19 impact data is released, and this data is used to train the QLattice models as a regression problem and predict the next impact estimate of the COVID-19 outbreak over the world. Further, the models are tested for binary classification problem for the prediction of a person is diabetic or not. The results show that the QLattice framework has a future in deep learning research.

Keywords: QLattice, deep learning, quantum mechanics, pattern recognition, statistics, COVID-19

Email: vinayak.bharadi@famt.ac.in; vinayak.bharadi@outlook.com

Monika Mangla, Nonita Sharma, Poonam Mittal, Vaishali Mehta Wadhwa, Thirunavukkarasu K. and Shahnawaz Khan (eds.) Emerging Technologies for Healthcare: Internet of Things and Deep Learning Models, (69–92) © 2021 Scrivener Publishing LLC

3.1   Introduction

Machine learning (ML) enables compute machines or the computer the capability to learn without explicitly programming them. This comes under the artificial intelligence (AI) that enables software programs or applications to precisely predict the outcome. In deep learning, the patterns in the data are modeled as complex multi-layered networks, and this is the most general way to model a problem. This makes deep learning capable of solving difficult problems, which are otherwise not addressable by modular programming logic [1, 2].

In general, deep learning indicates ML using deep (artificial) neural networks. There exist a couple of algorithms which implement deep learning using hidden layers other than conventional neural networks [3]. The concept of "artificial" neural networks dates back to the 1940s. It consists of a network of artificial neurons programmed out of interconnected threshold switches. This network is referred as artificial neural network and it can learn to recognize patterns like the human brain does [4].

The best example could be computer vision and natural language processing. These domains outstrip both conventional ML as well as programming techniques. In conclusion, ML and deep learning are both forms of AI. As the experts have predicted, the AI and ML are all set to change the way humans interacts with machines and vice versa in the coming days.

3.1.1   Machine Learning Models

In the domain of AI/ML a model is referred as an entity that is created by the training process. These models are simply derived from the ML algorithms, such as the decision tree model and random forest. A real-world process can be represented mathematically as a ML model [5].

The learning algorithm discovers the patterns in the training data and is responsible for the mapping of the inputs to the outputs from the available dataset. The training process results in a ML model which can be used for predictions [6]. These learning methods are dependent on the task and are further classified as given as follows:

1. Classification models
2. Regression models
3. Clustering
4. Dimensionality reductions
5. Principal component analysis

Algorithms are the procedures or methods followed for the completion of a task or solve a problem. Models are, in contrast, homogenous functions consisting of the well-defined computations resulting out of an algorithm that receives particular set of values or data as input and generates some value or set of values as output. The ML models are homogenous functions.

In order to generate the ML model, the following things are required:

1. The training data with demarcation of target attributes.
2. The algorithm selected as per the nature of target attribute.

The process to generate ML models:

- Read the training dataset and feed it to the ANN.
- Execute the ML algorithm on the data.
- Tune the parameters to control the learning of the algorithm.
- As the algorithm is finished with the learning the model is built.

As the new dataset comes in for prediction, it is given as input to the model. The model that is built by learning the past sample data thus predicts the output [7].

3.2   Machine Learning Model Lifecycle

The ML cycle consists of three phases, namely, the pipeline development, training phase, and inference phase. This ML lifecycle is followed by the data scientist and engineers to develop, train, and serve the models using the large scales of data that is related to various applications. This model can be used for predictions related to a particular problem and the organization can leverage the AI and ML algorithms for business growth [8, 9].

3.2.1   Steps in Machine Learning Lifecycle

As the ML Model performance depends completely on the input data and the training process, and there is a need for continuous experimentation with new datasets, models, software libraries, and tuning parameters to optimize and improve the accuracy of the model. The following section describes the seven steps in the lifecycle of a typical ML model.

3.2.1.1   Data Preparation

For a particular problem, the data is specific and has its own source of generation or extraction. Various types of data can be used as input. As discussed earlier, this data can be sourced from a business management information systems, social networks, Pharma companies, IoT devices, enterprises, banks, hospitals, etc. Considerably high amount of data is required for the leaning or the training stage. This allows faster convergence toward desired results and better performance of the ML model. The output and the model state and parameters are used for analysis and fed to other systems or ML applications as a seed.

3.2.1.2   Building the Machine Learning Model

In this step, the model is scripted by detailing the algorithm or encoding it in a feasible programming language or the frameworks like Pytorch, Keras, TensorFlow, and Theano.

Various types of ML models are possible such as the classification models, regression models, clustering models, supervised model, unsupervised model, and reinforcement learning models.

3.2.1.3   Model Training

This stage has main focus on creating the model from the data fed to it; in this stage, training data and testing data are separated out of the input data. The training data is used to estimate the model parameters like the polynomial coefficients or weights of the ANN used in the model, such that the error is minimized. A particular training mechanism such as backpropagation is used for training. Then, the model is tested on the test data. This process is iterated over a number of epochs to improve the performance of the model. A ML model has a number of parameters that need to be learned from the data. The model training with existing data results in fitting of the model parameters [10].

3.2.1.4   Parameter Selection

The fourth step involves the selection of the parameters associated with the training which are also called the hyperparameters. Besides regular parameters of a ML model, there is a separate set of parameters referred as the hyperparameters. These parameters differ from the regular parameters as they cannot be directly learned from the regular training process.

The hyperparameters are generally fixed before the start of actual training process. The hyperparameters express important properties of the ML model such as the complexity or the learning speed. The hyperparameters control the effectiveness of the training process and, in turn, the performance of the model. The hyperparameters are the crucial aspect for the successful production of the ML model.

3.2.1.5   Transfer Learning

In transfer learning a model developed for a particular task is reused as the initial point for a model on a different task. This enables the transfer of knowledge acquired from training on one particular problem and applying it in learning a separate one.

In deep learning, this is a quite popular approach where the pre-trained models are used as the initial point on a particular set of tasks in computer vision, text and natural language processing, and digital signal processing. The design and training of ML models for these problems require an enormous compute and time resources. Transfer learning provides the huge jumps in skill on related problems. There are a lot of benefits in reusing ML models across various domains.

The research shows that a model cannot be transferred between different domains directly; hence, transfer learning is used for providing a starting material for beginning the training of a next stage model. This results in significant reduction of the training time [11].

3.2.1.6   Model Verification

The trained model is analyzed in this stage and the output is a verified model that provides sufficient information for estimating whether the model is suitable for its intended application. The unseen data is given to the model and the performance of the model is evaluated in this stage. ML models are more susceptible to overfitting and underfitting (the bias-variance dilemma) than the conventionally developed predictive models. An overfitted model might be performing well on the in-sample data but will give poor prediction performance on the unseen data. The overfitting of model results from the complex nonlinear and nonparametric methods which are part of the ML algorithms and the utilization of compute power. An underfitted model has poor performance, in general, and this results from simplified model algorithm that poorly interprets the insights of the training data.

To detect and prevent the fitting or "generalization capability" issues in ML, a common technique known as cross-validation is quite popular.

The training data is partitioned into K subsets in K-Fold cross-validation. Then, the ML model is trained on all the training data except the Kth subset, and later on, the Kth subset is used to validate the performance. It can be estimated that model's generalization capability is low if the accuracy ratios are consistently low this indicates underfitted model or higher on the training set but lower on the validation set indicating overfitted one. To benchmark performance, the conventional models such as regression analysis can be used [12].

3.2.1.7   Model Deployment

The ML model is integrated with processes and applications in this stage. The decisive goal of this stage is the proper functionality of the model post deployment. The deployment is done in such a way that the models can be used for inference as well regular updates are possible. The deployment stage enables the ML model into production so that it can start adding value by making predictions [11, 12].

3.2.1.8   Monitoring

As the ML model is deployed to production, it rapidly becomes apparent that the work is not over and it is actually beginning as new production related issues do emerge. Monitoring should be designed to provide early warnings to the myriad of things that can go wrong with a production ML model. The monitoring refers the ways the model's performance is tracked, understood, and analyzed in production environment from both a data science and operational perspective. Insufficient monitoring may result in incorrect models left unchecked in production, obsolete models that no more add any business value, or subtle bugs in models that surface over time and are difficult to locate. When the ML model play critical role in the business, a failure to address these issues and bugs can be a catastrophic event—particularly, if the company operates in a regulated environment.

Figure 3.1 shows this process in a diagram contain depiction of continuous delivery mode. As the data generated as well as involved in variety of application is increasing rabidly due to cloud evolution, the ML systems are becoming more important. The AI ML-based techniques are situated in core components of smart devices, household appliances, and cloud services. The victory of ML applications is further spanning to data management, safety-critical systems, high-performance computing, etc.; these applications cover a larger domain of IT applications and services.

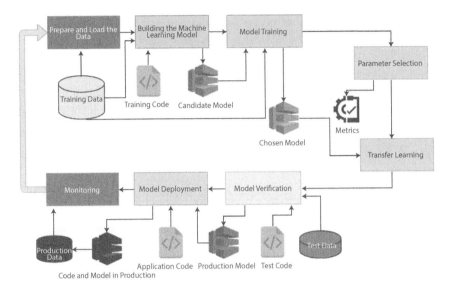

Figure 3.1 Machine learning end-to-end process for continuous delivery of ML models.

3.3   A Model Deployment in Keras

In this research, a binary classification problem is considered, and this is going to be addressed with conventional multi-layered Perceptron (MLP) model deployed in Keras and the QLattice model. The diabetes prediction over the Pima Indians Diabetes Database is the problem under consideration. Following the ML lifecycle as discussed, two MLP models are implemented. One with simple architecture and other with added layers such as dropout and the Gaussian noise addition layer [13–15].

3.3.1   Pima Indian Diabetes Dataset

The National Institute of Diabetes and Digestive and Kidney Diseases has originally released the dataset. The goal of the Pima dataset is to clinically diagnose and, based on certain diagnostic measurements included in the dataset, to predict the existence of diabetes condition in a patient. This database was created by filtering out various cases after placing a number of constraints on a larger database [16]. The database is created from health conditions related data of females' under age of 21 of Pima Indian heritage. The dataset has several medical predictor (independent) variables and one target (dependent) variable, outcome. Independent variable set consists of the number of pregnancies of the person has had in the past, their BMI, insulin level, age, etc. The dataset has total eight attributes, one outcome, and total 768 records [17].

This database is split in to 80:20 ratio for training and testing of the MLP models in the Keras framework. Keras is one of the most recently developed libraries to facilitate neural network training. Keras and its use in ANN research started in early 2015, and now, it has evolved into one of the most popular and widely used libraries that are built on top of Theano and allows us to utilize our GPU to accelerate neural network training. Keras has very intuitive API, which allows us to implement neural networks in only a few lines of code [14, 15].

3.3.2   Multi-Layered Perceptron Implementation in Keras

The first MLP model has two hidden layers: one input layer and one output layer. This is defined as a sequential model in Keras. All the layers are fully connected dense layers. The input layer takes eight parameters of the dataset as input and the output layer gives a single target as in the database, and it tells whether a person in diabetic (1) or not (0). The model is summarized as follows:

```
Model: "sequential"
```

Layer (type)	Output Shape	Param #
dense (Dense)	(None, 12)	108
dense_1 (Dense)	(None, 12)	156
dense_2 (Dense)	(None, 12)	156
dense_3 (Dense)	(None, 1)	13

```
Total params: 433
Trainable params: 433
Non-trainable params: 0
```

The model is trained with the training data as discussed above. Once the model is trained it was tested for the performance on the test dataset. Figure 3.2 shows the model visualization plot and the confusion matrix generated using the test data. The model has given 71.43% accuracy for the prediction.

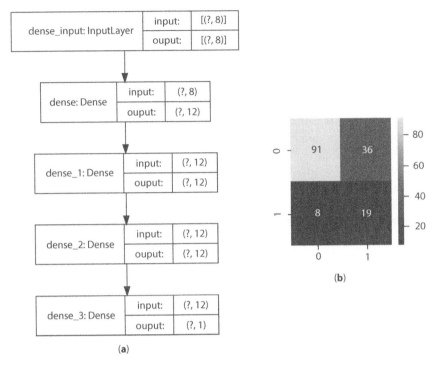

Figure 3.2 (a) The model visualization plot. (b) Confusion matrix after evaluation.

3.3.3   Multi-Layered Perceptron Implementation With Dropout and Added Noise

All real-life data has some noisy content and it is practically impossible to remove noise completely from a dataset. For this reason, probability and statistics-based algorithms for pre-processing of the data are used in ML models. Probability enables quantification of uncertainty caused due to noise in a prediction [17, 18]. Overfitting is a key concern as far as any ML algorithm is studied, this is a phenomenon when a model is actually remembering all the training data due to huge size of network and its weights, and it performs well on test data but on the training data the performance degrades. Further, research shows that adding noise can regularize and reduce overfitting to a certain level [19].

Keras allows the addition of Gaussian noise through a separate layer referred as the Gaussian noise layer. The Gaussian noise layer will add noise to the inputs with given shape and the output will also have the same shape. The noise has a zero mean and additionally requires that a standard deviation (SD) of the noise be specified as a parameter. In the current model, the SD is 0.1.

Another simple and powerful ANN regularization technique is dropout. An ANN model can be used to simulate having a large number of different network architectures by randomly dropping out nodes during training. This is referred as dropout and offers a computationally lightweight and efficient regularization method to address overfitting and improve generalization error in ANNs. This is implemented by adding a dropout layer with rate as a specified parameter [20].

Another layer added in this model is ReLU activation layer. ReLU is the abbreviation for rectified linear activation unit and this activation function is referred as one of the few milestones in the deep learning revolution. Though it is a simple function, it is far better than its predecessor activation functions such as sigmoid or tanh. ReLU function and its derivative both are monotonic. The function returns 0 for any negative input, and for any positive value x as input, the same value is returned back. Hence, ReLU has an output that has a range from 0 to infinity. This is a computationally simple, linear, and a function capable of returning a true zero value [21].

Then, final MLP model has three dense hidden layers, but with addition of two ReLU activation layers, one dropout and one Gaussian noise layer. This overall design is a step for regularization of the model.

In the current implementation, the dropout rate is 0.25. The final model summary is as follows.

```
Model: "sequential_1"
```

Layer (type)	Output Shape	Param #
dense_4 (Dense)	(None, 100)	900
activation (Activation)	(None, 100)	0
dropout (Dropout)	(None, 100)	0
dense_5 (Dense)	(None, 100)	10100
activation_1 (Activation)	(None, 100)	0
gaussian_noise (GaussianNois)	(None, 100)	0
dense_6 (Dense)	(None, 1)	101
activation_2 (Activation)	(None, 1)	0

```
Total params: 11,101
Trainable params: 11,101
Non-trainable params: 0
```

Figure 3.3 shows the model visualization plot, and this gives a better idea of the model. Then, model was trained for the same dataset. The dropout and noise addition has made the model robust and given a marginal increase in the performance, the accuracy achieved by the model is 75.32%.

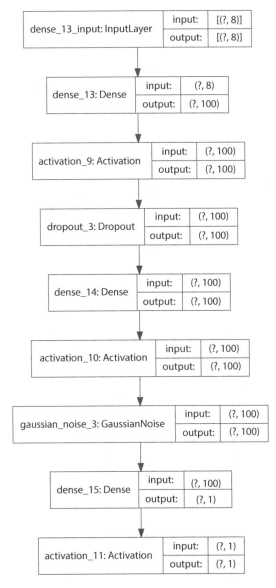

Figure 3.3 The model visualization plot showing dropout and gaussian noise layer.

In this section, two sequential MLP models are discussed with and without regularization technique. The next section will discuss the new approach to the deep learning models called as the QLattice.

3.4 QLattice Environment

QLattice is as short for of Quantum Lattice. These models are part of the Feyn library by www.abzu.ai. Feyn is a Python library and this introduces a new horizon for the deep learning by taking inspiration from the quantum physics. The path integral formulation of quantum physics originally proposed by American physicist Richard P. Feynman is the driving impetus to the Feyn models [22].

Path integrals are inferred from the sum over all paths between the source and the destination. These paths satisfy some boundary conditions and can be defined as extensions to an infinite number of integration variables of usual multi-dimensional integrals. Path integrals are very significant tools for the study of quantum mechanics. Further, they generalize the action principle of classical mechanics. It replaces the classical notion of a single, unique classical trajectory or path for a system with a sum, or functional integral, over an infinity of quantum-mechanically possible trajectories or paths to evaluate a quantum amplitude.

In simple words, consider an object moving from point A to Point B in a quantum space. The classical mechanics will consider the straight line path for the calculations for all the calculations and will give a definite answer.

However, in case of path integrals, there are infinite possible paths to reach point B from point A, and Figure 3.4b shows six of such infinite paths. This basic idea is used in Feyn models while solving a classification problem.

3.4.1 Feyn Models

Feyn models are quite similar to neural network (or deep learning) models in many aspects. Feyn model introduces a new way to work with the data together with an innovative way to accumulate and transfer learnings. To work with the Feyn model access to the QLattice, short for Quantum Lattice is required. QLattice is inspired from the path integral framework. QLattice provides and environment that considers all possible models of a dataset and finds the model with optimum accuracy and least loss. In other words, it finds the model that fits the problem the best or the "path of least resistance".

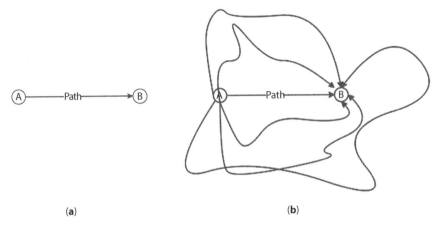

(a)   (b)

Figure 3.4 Path integrals (a) classical mechanics case. (b) Path integrals showing six of infinite possible paths.

QLattices produce QGraphs which is actually an unbounded list of models. A model looks a little bit like a standard neural network. It is analogous to an ANN in following ways:

1. These model takes input from the features.
2. It consists of nodes with arbitrary functions associated with them.
3. These models are trained with backpropagation.

As compared to ANN models, these QGraphs are different in a way that:

1. QGraph models have fewer nodes and connections.
2. They have kind of processing functions like Gaussian, sine, and multiply, which are not used as activation function in ANN.
3. One hot encoding is not required in case of multiclass clarification. In case a feature takes only categorical values, the Feyn library automatically detects and encodes them.
4. The QLattice is a high-performance quantum simulator and it runs on a dedicated hardware, hosted on a cluster. The results are sent back to the calling program through API calls.

One regression sample that only takes four categorical features is shown in Figure 3.5. This model is one of the other possible models for the above-mentioned diabetes prediction problem.

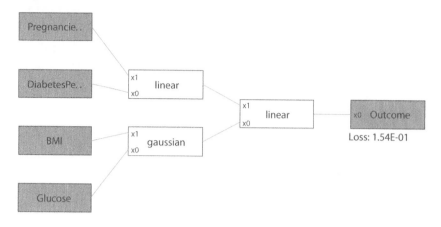

Fitting 5: 100% completed. Best loss so far: 0.154302

Figure 3.5 A Sample QLattice QGraph model for diabetes prediction.

Essentially in the QLattice environment, a complete set of possible QGraphs is explored and search for the best one is performed.

3.4.1.1 Semantic Types

Before QGraph is produced it is required to finalize the type of data which the inputs and output are belonging to. In this way, the model is informed about what type of data it should expect and deal with it. They are referred as semantic types. Two semantic types are identified they are numerical and categorical. When the deep learning models are explored with QLattice the input data variables or the attributes need to be assigned to either of the semantic types.

1. Continuous value type inputs are categorized into **Numerical** Semantic type. Examples include height, age, and weight. Inputs are automatically normalized to $[-1;1]$ range.
2. Inputs having discrete nature are categorized as **Categorical** Semantic type. Examples include nationality, gender, and skin color. These inputs are automatically encoded with weights also into a $[-1;1]$ range

If no type is assigned to a feature, then QLattice automatically assigns the numerical semantic type to it as default.

3.4.1.2   Interactions

In the conventional deep learning models, the neurons have the activation functions which process and generate the synapse and pass it on to further connections. In the Feyn models, similar functionality is done by the interaction functions. Each Feyn model has basic computation units called as interactions. Excluding multiply, all other interactions have weights and biases that are optimized using the backpropagation algorithm. This is done when the Feyn models are fit to the input data.

3.4.1.3   Generating QLattice

The QLattice environment is a high performance quantum simulator, and it is accessed through API calls. The QLattice environment finds all possible QGraphs for the given set of semantic types and the target. This is a quite heavy computation task and needs high end hardware. Hence, the QLattice runs on a dedicated hardware cluster provided by www.abzu.ai. The QLattice has two main parts: registers and interactions. The registers are the entities used to interact with the QLattice. They are the input and output interface of a Feyn model, and essentially, they are the features of input data set. The basic computation units of QLattice are referred as the interactions. By holding their own state, they transform input data into output. They store the learning for the purpose of extraction of the QGraphs (Quantum Graphs). QGraphs represent all possible combinations (the path integrals) connecting the input registers to the output register. That means all possible explanations for the given output with the given inputs, generated by the QLattice. The QLattice explores thousands of potential models for the one graph with the right combinations set of features and interaction. Ultimately, it finds the perfectly tweaked model for the given problem.

3.4.2   QLattice Workflow

The QLattice graph is beyond the notion of a neural network or a decision tree-based model; rather it can be said that the QLattice unpacks the Blackbox neural network and provides the explanation of ability/interpretability like the decision tree.

Earlier, the implementation of Keras MLP models for the prediction of diabetes over Pima Indian dataset is discussed, and the same example will be considered here to explain the workflow of the QLattice environment and Feyn models.

3.4.2.1   Preparing the Data

The dataset is first read into memory, and all null values are removed. Further, the outcome column is separated and assigned to a target vector. Figure 3.3 shows the preprocessed dataset. As all the attributes are continuous numbers, they automatically assigned to default of numerical semantic types. The dataset is then split into training and testing data with a proportion of 60:40.

3.4.2.2   Connecting to QLattice

QLattice is supported by high-end infrastructure provided by www.abzu. ai. One has to register and obtain the API access token (currently free of cost) for the same. Once the necessary credentials are ready, the QLattice object can be invoked by the following commands.

```
from feyn import QLattice
qlattice = QLattice(url=" your_qlattice_url", api_token="
your_api_token")
```

Next, the semantic types need to be encoded, but as for the problem under consideration has all the numerical attributes, hence, they will be automatically set to default numerical semantic type.

3.4.2.3   Generating QGraphs

A QGraph is a collection of all possible models that connect the input to output. The QLattice explores virtually infinite possibilities in the QGraph but due to compute as well as memory limitations, the QGraph does not hold all possible models. In practice, the QGraph is a subset of the infinite list of models, generally a couple of thousands of models.

We need to inform QLattice about the inputs and output of the model.

```
target = 'Outcome'
qgraph = qlattice.get_qgraph(train.
columns,target, max_depth=5)
qgraph.head()
```

This will generate some random untrained models as shown in Figures 3.5 and 3.6.

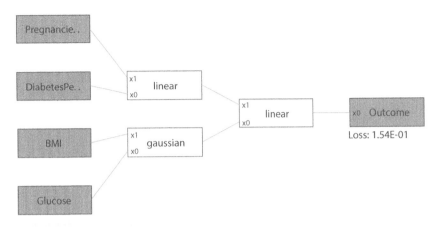

Fitting 5: 100% completed. Best loss so far: 0.154302

Figure 3.6 The best QGraph model extracted for the given diabetes prediction problem.

Two types of boxes can be seen in each model. The input and output are designated by the green once and the pink ones are the interactions as discussed earlier. The interaction function takes in a value, evaluates a function at that value, and passes it on to the next interaction.

The similarity of these models to a neural network is quite eminent. However, the QGraph models have fewer nodes, and the typical type of activation function on the node is absent rather the interactions can be found here. The control flows form from left to right for these models that is why each row of input dataset is fed to green box on the left and then it is evaluated at each pink box and then produces a prediction at far right output box.

3.4.2.4   Fitting, Sorting, and Updating QGraphs

The conventional ANN or any other ML technique needs to be trained; similarly, each of these QGraph models has to be trained. The random weights are assigned initially and they are further updated on every iteration. The QGraph fit method is given the training data and the loss function as the input parameters. As the problem under consideration is a typical regression problem, the standard mean squared error loss is used.

```
# Defining the number of loops/updates and epochs
nloops = 5
nepochs = 10
```

```
qgraph = qlattice.get_qgraph(train.columns,
target, max_depth=4) # (1)
# And training finally begins
for loop in range(nloops): # (5)
    qgraph.fit(train, n_samples=len(train)*nepochs,
loss_function='mean_squared_error', threads=4, show='graph')
# (2)
    best = qgraph.sort(train, loss_function='mean_squared_
error')[0] # (3)
    qlattice.update(best) # (4)
```

Each model in the subset QGraph is trained. While fitting is going on, the graph displayed is the model with the lowest MSE. The next step is to find the best ones, and this is achieved by sorting command. The models are sorted as per the MSE and the first graph is the best one, indicated by index [0].

The process of finding the best in the current iteration is over and this is informed to QLattice by the update command. This will push forward the best learnings to impact the next draw of graphs from the QGraph. The next iteration will try to find more similar graphs like this so that the MSE is minimized. The fit, sort, and update will run for given number of iterations (nloops). The final best graph is as shown in Figure 3.6.

3.4.2.5　Model Evaluation

The best model then can be used for prediction of the target vector based on the test data. The code is as follows:

```
best_graph = qgraph.sort(train)[0]
df_pred = valid.copy()
df_pred['predicted'] = best_graph.predict(valid)
threshold = 0.5
y_pred = np.where(df_pred predicted > threshold,
True, False)
y_true = df_pred[target].astype(bool)
```

The model performance is given by the accuracy. The best model has given overall training accuracy of 78.70%, and overall validation accuracy of 73.37%. The ROC curve, confusion matrix, and prediction probability distribution are shown in Figure 3.7.

The previous MLP models have given 71.43% and 75.32% accuracy for the ANN with and without regularization mechanism. The Feyn models discussed here have given training accuracy of 78.70%, and the overall validation accuracy is 73.37%. The performance is quite comparable.

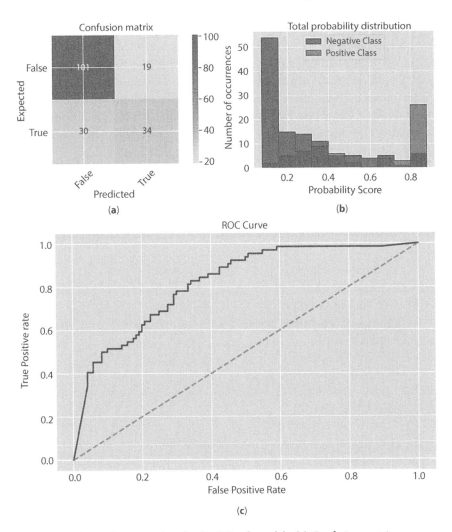

Figure 3.7 The performance plots for the QGraph models. (a) Confusion matrix; (b) Positive and negative class probability distribution; (c) Receiver operating characteristic (ROC) curve.

3.5 Using QLattice Environment and QGraph Models for COVID-19 Impact Prediction

Use of these models is further extended for a sequence prediction problem. In early 2020, a new virus began came in news all over the world because of the unparalled speed of its transmission and infection. This virus is believed to be originated in a food market in Wuhan, China, in December

2019. Since then, it has reached countries as distant as the USA and the Britain and gulf countries [22].

The virus is officially named as SARS-CoV-2 and has been the cause of 10.2 million of infections globally, causing 502 thousand deaths. The United States is the country which is the most affected one with 2.6 million infections and 128 thousand death as on July 2020.The SARS-CoV-2 infection causes the disease called as COVID-19, which stands for coronavirus disease 2019 [23–25].

In this work, the COVID-19 daily status used as the input, and this data is made avail-able by John Hopkins University. The data till 18 Aug 2020 is considered as input [26].

The input data has following counts available for 14k datapoints globally having following attributes.

1. Global Confirmed
2. Global Death
3. Global Recovered
4. India - Confirmed Cases
5. India - Death
6. India - Recovered
7. USA - Confirmed Cases
8. USA - Death
9. USA - Recovered

The plot for the data points can be seen in Figure 3.8.

For the given COVID-19 data, first eight attributes along with the country name are taken as input and the number of deaths is taken as the target variable. The death count will be predicted by the model. The QGraph is given with 167 days data for training remaining 42 days data was used for testing. The best model is shown in Figure 3.9.

This QGraph model has given excellent production with RMSE = 3470.58, the prediction is shown in Figures 3.10 and 3.11. It can be seen that it is a quite accurate prediction of the global deaths.

The implementation of all the Keras MLP and then QLattice-based Feyn QGraph models mentioned above along with the datasets used is available for download at https://doi.org/10.5281/ZENODO.3997056 [27].

It is quite clear that the COVID-19 impact prediction is a sequence prediction problem, and it is taken here to evaluate the possibility of QGraph models in such kind of problems. In this chapter, concepts of deep learning using sequential MLP models in Keras framework and a new type

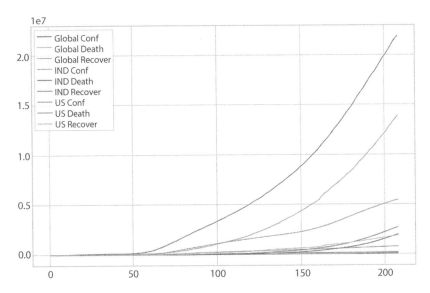

Figure 3.8 COVID-19 data plot (actual figures scaled by100,000 on Y-axis).

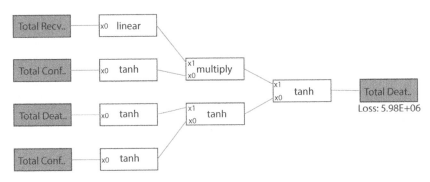

Fitting 5: 100% completed. Best loss so far: 5983838.978585

Figure 3.9 Best QGraph model for the COVID-19 global deaths prediction.

of Feyn QGraph models using QLattice environment are discussed. The new QGraph models are based on path integral formulation of Quantum Mechanics Theory. The vast possibilities of QGraph models are explored by the QLattice, and best models are given for the prediction. The QLattice runs on a dedicated hardware cluster and performs massive calculations to find the best model for the given problem. This is a promising approach and can be further explored in the study of deep learning.

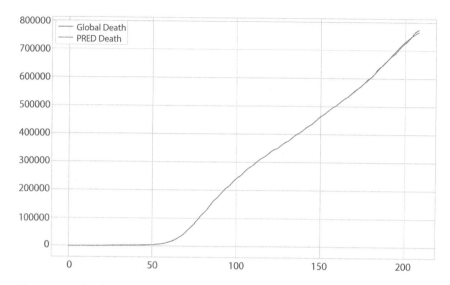

Figure 3.10 Plot for actual data of global deaths vs. predicted global deaths (red).

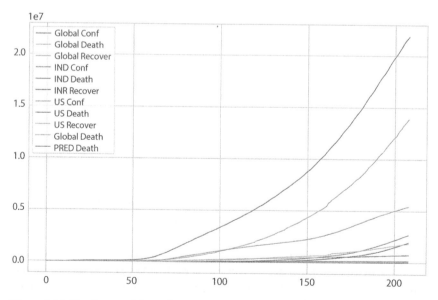

Figure 3.11 Plot for actual data of COVID-19 pandemic vs. predicted global deaths (red).

References

1. Rosenblatt, F., The Perceptron: A Probabilistic Model for Information Storage and Organization in The Brain. *Psychol. Rev.*, 65, 6, 386–408.

2. Mcculloch, W.S. and Pitts, W., A Logical Calculus of The Ideas Immanent in Nervous Activity. *Bull. Math. Biol.*, 52, 2, 3, 1990.

3. Krizhevsky, A. and Hinton, G.E., ImageNet Classification with Deep Convolutional Neural Networks. *Commun. ACM*, 60, 6, 1–9, 2017. https://doi.org/10.1145/3065386.

4. Pham, T., Tran, T., Phung, D., Venkatesh, S., Predicting healthcare trajectories from medical records: A deep learning approach. *J. Biomed. Inf.*, 69, 218–229, 2017, https://doi.org/10.1016/j.jbi.2017.04.001.

5. Ranzato, M. A., Boureau, Y.-L., Lecun, Y., Sparse Feature Learning for Deep Belief Networks. *Advances in Neural Information Processing Systems 20 - Proceedings of the 2007 Conference*, Vancouver, BC, Canada, 2009.

6. Xiao, C., Choi, E., Sun, J., Opportunities and challenges in developing deep learning models using electronic health records data: A systematic review. *J. Am. Med. Inf. Assoc.*, Oxford University Press, 25, 10, 1419–1428, 2018, October 1, https://doi.org/10.1093/jamia/ocy068.

7. Che, Z. and Liu, Y., Deep learning solutions to computational phenotyping in healthcare, in: *IEEE International Conference on Data Mining Workshops (ICDMW)*, pp. 1100–1109, New Orleans, LA, USA, 2017.

8. Zaharia, M., Chen, A., Davidson, A., Ghodsi, A., Hong, S.A., Konwinski, A., Zumar, C., Accelerating the Machine Learning Lifecycle with MLflow. *Bull. IEEE Comput. Soc Tech. Commun. Data Eng.*, 24, 4, 39–45, 2018.

9. Databricks, Standardizing the Machine Learning Lifecycle. E-Book. Retrieved from https://pages.databricks.com/EB-Standardizing-the-Machine-Learning-Lifecycle-LP.html, 2019.

10. Dong, Q. and Luo, G., Progress Indication for Deep Learning Model Training: A Feasibility Demonstration. *IEEE Access*, 8, 79811–79843, 2020, https://doi.org/10.1109/ACCESS.2020.2989684.

11. Weiss, K., Khoshgoftaar, T.M., Wang, D.D., A survey of transfer learning. *J. Big Data*, 3, 1, 1–40, 2016, https://doi.org/10.1186/s40537-016-0043-6.

12. Wong, T.T. and Yeh, P.Y., Reliable Accuracy Estimates from k-Fold Cross Validation. *IEEE Trans. Knowl. Data Eng.*, 32, 8, 1586–1594, 2020, https://doi.org/10.1109/TKDE.2019.2912815.

13. Rosebrock, A., Keras vs. tf.keras: What's the difference in TensorFlow 2.0? - PyImageSearch. https://www.pyimagesearch.com/2019/10/21/keras-vs-tf-keras-whats-the-difference-in-tensorflow-2-0/, 2019.

14. Chollet, F., The Sequential model. Https://Keras.Io/. https://keras.io/guides/sequential_model/, 2020, April 12.

15. Wang, Z., Liu, K., Li, J., Zhu, Y., Zhang, Y., Various Frameworks and Libraries of Machine Learning and Deep Learning: A Survey. *Arch. Comput. Methods Eng.*, 26, 4, 1–40, 2019, https://doi.org/10.1007/s11831-018-09312-w.

16. Kaur, H. and Kumari, V., Predictive modelling and analytics for diabetes using a machine learning approach. *Appl. Comput. Inf.*, 24, 12, 6558–6570, 2020, https://doi.org/10.1016/j.aci.2018.12.004.

17. Smith, J.W., Everhart, J.E., Dickson, W.C., Knowler, W.C., Johannes, R.S., Using the ADAP learning algorithm to forecast the onset of diabetes mellitus, in: *Proceedings of the Symposium on Computer Applications and Medical Care*, IEEE Computer Society Press, pp. 261–265, 1988.

18. Srivastava, N., Hinton, G., Krizhevsky, A., Sutskever, I., Salakhutdinov, R., Dropout: A simple way to prevent neural networks from overfitting. *J. Mach. Learn. Res.*, 15, 56, 1929–1958, 2014, https://jmlr.org/papers/v15/srivastava14a.html.

19. Bu, F., A High-Order Clustering Algorithm Based on Dropout Deep Learning for Heterogeneous Data in Cyber-Physical-Social Systems. *IEEE Access*, 6, 11687–11693, 2017, https://doi.org/10.1109/ACCESS.2017.2759509.

20. Bisong, E. and Bisong, E., Regularization for Deep Learning, in: *Building Machine Learning and Deep Learning Models on Google Cloud Platform*, pp. 415–421, Apress, USA, 2019, https://doi.org/10.1007/978-1-4842-4470-8_34.

21. Hanin, B., Universal Function Approximation by Deep Neural Nets with Bounded Width and ReLU Activations. *Mathematics*, 7, 10, 992, 2019, https://doi.org/10.3390/math7100992.

22. Caves, C.M., Quantum mechanics of measurements distributed in time. A path-integral formulation. *Phys. Rev. D*, 33, 6, 1643–1665, 1986, https://doi.org/10.1103/PhysRevD.33.1643.

23. Li, H., Liu, Z., Ge, J., Scientific research progress of COVID-19/ SARS-CoV-2 in the first five months. *J. Cell. Mol. Med.*, Blackwell Publishing Inc., 2020, June 1, https://doi.org/10.1111/jcmm.15364.

24. Sharma, N., Yadav, S., Mangla, M., Mohanty, A., Mohanty, S.N., Multivariate Analysis of COVID-19 on Stock, Commodity & Purchase Manager Indices: A Global Perspective, Researchsquare, 2020.

25. Mangla, M., Poonam, Sharma, N., Fuzzy Modelling of Clinical and Epidemiological Factors for COVID-19, 2020.

26. Dong, E., Du, H., Gardner, L., An interactive web-based dashboard to track COVID-19 in real time. *Lancet Infect. Dis.*, 20, 533–534, 2020, https://doi.org/10.1016/S1473-3099(20)30120-1.

27. Bharadi, V.A., QLattice Environment and Feyn QGraph Models - A new Perspective towards Deep Learning (1.0), 2020, https://doi.org/10.5281/ZENODO.3997056.

4

Sensitive Healthcare Data: Privacy and Security Issues and Proposed Solutions

Abhishek Vyas[1], Satheesh Abimannan[2]* and Ren-Hung Hwang[1]

[1]CSIE Department, National Chung Cheng University, Chiayi, Taiwan (R.O.C)
[2]School of Data Science, Symbiosis Skills and Professional University, Pune, India

Abstract

In today's day and age, there is a flood of data related to the patient's healthcare records. With the proliferation of such a vast volume of data on healthcare, it becomes clear that the confidentiality and safety of this kind of confidential data on healthcare is a topic of utmost importance. Computer scientists, engineers, medical doctors, and lawyers all are worried about the security and privacy issues related to healthcare data of patients. This chapter addresses the various acts and statues related to the healthcare data of patients. The chapter also gives a glimpse into how modern internet-connected healthcare devices, such as BANs, which include IoT wrist bands for a pulse, temperature and skin condition monitoring, pacemakers, EEG and ECG devices, and ICU medical devices, contribute to the enormous big healthcare data. Here, we also discuss how different computing paradigms, *viz.*, cloud computing, edge computing, big data analytics, and machine learning models, are making strides in managing this big healthcare data. Finally, this chapter discusses the various problems with the security and privacy of such big healthcare data in regard to its storage methodology, its computing methodology, and its communication modalities and methodology. The chapter primarily reflects on the prevention methods currently in use or being developed for healthcare data security and privacy. To sum up, all applicable techniques relating to the protection and privacy of broad healthcare data are discussed, and a conclusion is drawn based on this thorough review; potential changes and enhancements to the techniques are discussed.

Keywords: Security, privacy, big healthcare data, anonymization, blockchain, medical IoT, sensitive medical data, HIPAA

Corresponding author: satheesha23@gmail.com

Monika Mangla, Nonita Sharma, Poonam Mittal, Vaishali Mehta Wadhwa, Thirunavukkarasu K. and Shahnawaz Khan (eds.) Emerging Technologies for Healthcare: Internet of Things and Deep Learning Models, (93–128) © 2021 Scrivener Publishing LLC

4.1   Introduction

Computers and computing have become ubiquitous in the present times. All kinds of data are now being managed by computer systems. Big size databases are being maintained for all kinds of purposes using networked and distributed computing systems. Cloud computing, edge computing, and big data analytics are the buzz words in computing in this previous decade of computing. The aforementioned technologies plus the fact that internet of things, industrial internet of things, medical internet of things, big data storage and some analytics technologies are becoming necessary in most of the applications related to healthcare scenario. With all these interconnected technologies, there is threat perception that malicious actors can hack into these systems and devices using state-of-the art hacking techniques and can cause a lot of financial and psychological damage by exploiting the security and privacy of individuals and institutions.

Here, in this chapter, the main focus on the security and privacy issues plaguing the healthcare data of patients, which is sensitive in nature as a persons' health information, is not a public matter, it is a very personal matter. This chapter looks into these issues in detail and what are the steps that can be taken to mitigate these issues. The chapter will delve into many tools and techniques that are being used for mitigating the privacy and security issues in healthcare. This chapter will also discuss the laws enacted to protect the patients' health data form prying eyes of data hungry corporations like insurance agencies and big healthcare firms. The chapter will also look into some case studies regarding this issue.

4.1.1   Types of Technologies Used in Healthcare Industry

There are various types of technologies used in the medical/healthcare sector for the benefit of the patients and doctors as well. The following is a comprehensive list of technologies that are used in healthcare industry where there is a possibility that the information or data flow security and privacy is at a risk:

1. Medical Sensor Networks (MSNs)/Medical Internet of Things (MIoT)/Body Area Networks (BANs) or Wireless Body Area Networks (WBANs)
2. Artificial Intelligence (AI) for Medical Diagnosis and Medical Image Analysis
3. Cloud Computing for Medical Data Storage and Analysis

4. Big Data Analytics in Healthcare Industry
5. Blockchain Technology
6. Telemedicine Systems

If one can find a pattern in the aforementioned technologies, all of them use the internet to connect to each other or to a server or cloud server for data storage and processing. Anything connected to the internet and using internetworking as a medium of communication is suspectable to intrusion, manipulation, cyber espionage, data leaks, etc.

This chapter introduces and addresses the problems in security and privacy in these smart healthcare technologies. It also discusses the mitigations that can be taken for the given technology as per the current research and future directions of those researches.

4.1.2   Technical Differences Between Security and Privacy

Table 4.1 differentiates between security and privacy in terms of their applications to information technology systems.

Table 4.1 intends to make the technical differences between security and privacy clear in context of this chapter.

4.1.3   HIPAA Compliance

HIPAA stands for Healthcare Insurance Privacy and Accountability Act; it was enacted in 1996. It is one of the major acts in any nation of the world pertaining to the compliance of the security of patient's healthcare information and about the rights of use of the patient's healthcare information by medical and non-medical professional. It covers electronic health records as well as non-electronic health records of patients. Many nations of the world are now emulating this act to fit their nation's healthcare records security and privacy.

"The Health Insurance Portability and Accountability Act of 1996 (HIPAA) required the Secretary of the U.S. Department of Health and Human Services (HHS) to develop regulations protecting the privacy and security of certain health information. To fulfil this requirement, HHS published what are commonly known as the HIPAA Privacy Rule and the HIPAA Security Rule. The Privacy Rule, or Standards for Privacy of Individually Identifiable Health Information, establishes national standards for the protection of certain health information. The Security Standards for the Protection of Electronic Protected Health Information (the Security Rule) establish a national set of security standards for protecting certain health information that is held

Table 4.1 Differences between security and privacy [1].

Security	Privacy
The confidentiality, integrity, and availability of data is known as security.	The appropriate use of a user's information/data is known as privacy.
Techniques like encryption, hashing, network firewalls, antivirus software, and honeypots are used prevent data leakage and network intrusion from an organization's networked computer systems. This entails security.	The hospital/organization cannot sell or use the healthcare data of patient without his/her prior consent. This entails privacy.
Security techniques are used to protect the confidentiality of data and other resources of an enterprise or an organization.	Privacy is concerned with the patient's rights to make sure that their healthcare information is safe from other third parties.
With security, any organization or enterprise gains confidence that their business decisions and data are protected and respected by other third parties.	Privacy can also be defined as the ability of an individual to decide what information of theirs' go to which person/organization and where to, and also how much information that person or organization can access about that individual.

or transferred in electronic form. The Security Rule operationalizes the protections contained in the Privacy Rule by addressing the technical and non-technical safeguards that organizations called "covered entities" must put in place to secure individuals' "electronic protected health information" (e-PHI). Within HHS, the Office for Civil Rights (OCR) has responsibility for enforcing the Privacy and Security Rules with voluntary compliance activities and civil money penalties [2]."

"The HITECH Act of 2009 expanded the responsibilities of business associates under the HIPAA Security Rule. HHS developed regulations to implement and clarify these changes [2]."

HIPAA consists of various rules and regulations for all the parties involved in any manner in the exchange of healthcare information of patients for any purpose be it for research, medical concerns, law enforcement, health insurance, or any other medico-legal purpose.

4.2   Medical Sensor Networks/Medical Internet of Things/Body Area Networks/WBANs

Today, in healthcare industry, electronic devices are used to monitor patients, diagnose illnesses, treat illnesses, etc. With the advancement of microcontroller and microchip technology, advanced sensors are developed for specific purposes. These types of sensors can be used in a variety of applications such as monitoring of room temperature, body temperature, EEG monitoring, ECG monitoring, pulse monitoring, cardiovascular monitoring, pacemakers, defibrillators, etc.

With the advancement in the sensor technology, nowadays, sensors used in healthcare industry are essentially tiny computers controlled by a microcontroller, with embedded software and technologies to connect the sensors attached to various body parts of a patient to each other and the internet. These kinds of sensors are commonly known as wireless sensor networks (WSNs). BANs/WBANs, wireless medical sensor networks (WMSNs/MSNs), MIoT, and wireless biomedical sensor networks (WBSNs) are all synonyms. They are all based on the technologies derived from WSNs.

"Sensor is a device that is used to gather information about a physical process or a physical phenomenon and translate it into electrical signals that can be processed, measured, and analyzed. A Sensor Network is a structure consisting of sensors, computational units, and communication elements for the purpose of recording, observing and reacting to an event or a phenomenon [3]."

Whereas, a WBSN or MIOTs are sensor networks, that are connected externally and sometimes internally to various parts of a patient's body like eyes, brain, hands, heart, and mouth to continuously monitor the activity or correct the activity of a bodily function. Like for example, sensors placed externally on the left side of the chest of a patient can monitor the patient's heart rate, but if the same patient is having a heart disease, then a pacemaker can be installed surgically inside a heart to correct the heartbeat of a patient. These WBSNs not only monitor the vital signs of a patient and communicate it to the hospital or a care provider using the internet, but they also store the healthcare data in a central cloud database to further the medical diagnosis process using AI and machine learning (ML).

As shown in Figure 4.1, various sensors of the WBAN, communicate with each other with protocols like zigbee, low-power wan, and low power Bluetooth, but the sensors communicate via GPRS, low power radio telemetry, Bluetooth, etc., to communicate the sensor data with the base

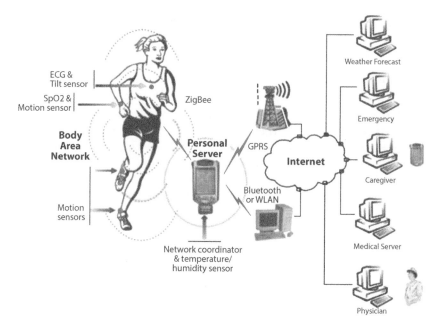

Figure 4.1 How WBSN/WMIOT/WBAN, etc., work? [4].

station (BS), i.e., the personal server/computer or database and then the personal server/computer communicates the sensor data using internet connectivity in the form of WAN, WLAN, etc., to the cloud database, from the cloud database, the medical data from the medical sensors can be accessed by the doctors, nurses, and other authorized personals and third parties for data analytics and processing.

Some salient features of WBANs or WMSNs or WMIOTs, etc., are the following:

> ➤ They are limited by the area and dimensions of the normal human body (m/cm).
> ➤ They have limited number of pervasive nodes.
> ➤ Single sensors for each task, nowadays, there are hybrid sensor being developed for coordinating multiple tasks and computations.
> ➤ Each sensor must measure the parameter it is designed to measure accurately.
> ➤ These sensors are exposed to a predictable environment only.
> ➤ The sensors are designed to detect early onset of some health abnormality.

➢ The sensors should be/are designed in such a manner that they should me compatible and robust enough to handle close proximity with human organs and tissue.

➢ The sensors should be equipped with some high-level data transfer security mechanism.

➢ The design of the sensors should be such that they are robust and can withstand biological and environmental variations and variability form patient to patient.

➢ Power supply mechanism should be very durable as for implantable devices like pacemaker and BCIs; the power supply should last for several years.

➢ The sensors should be designed in such a manner that they can do energy scavenging from body heat and motion of the patient's body.

➢ In case of failure, it is very tedious to replace implantable nodes like BCIs and pacemakers etc.

➢ Biodegradable and human body friendly material can be used to make implantable sensors failure problem less of a headache.

➢ These sensors require a low powered wireless technology like 6LOWPAN and low-powered Bluetooth.

➢ These sensors should be context aware based of the human physiology.

➢ During data transfer between various sensors and the BS, loss of data can be significant, so more Quality-of-Service (QoS) parameters should be used to ensure seamless data transfer.

➢ "There are standards for personal health devices the interoperability of such as scales, blood pressure monitors, and blood glucose monitors. This family of standards is based around a framework defined the IEEE 11073-20601-2008 standard ICBES 134-3 and its amendment, IEEE 11073-20601a-2010. The Personal, Home, and Hospital Care (PHHC) profile developed by the ZigBee Alliance relies on the on-going work being developed by IEEE 11073 to allow the interoperability with medical devices [5, 6]."

Some applications and projects where WBANs, WMSNs, or WMIOTs are used:

➢ Early cancer detection
➢ Glucose level monitoring

➤ For asthma care and monitoring of pulmonary activities in patients using pulse oximeter and other medical sensors.

➤ For detection of cardiovascular diseases and monitoring of heart rate

➤ Sensors can monitor body and brain activity of elderly to detect the onset of Alzheimer's, Parkinson's, and depression etc.

➤ Microsensors can be implanted in the eye to form an artificial retina.

➤ Brain Computer Interfaces are a new area where they have applications [5].

➤ CodeBlue: It uses ZIGBEE based radio transmissions to connect sensing medical devices within a WBAN to communicate with BS/device and access points (APs). The CodeBlue architecture is self-organizing and ad-hoc.

➤ AID-N: It is an application used to handle group casualty patients. It is also ad-hoc based self-organizing mechanism, in addition to this here in this application along with APs, wireless repeaters are used and GPS modules are used for localizations.

➤ CareNet: This project is about remote health monitoring and control, using a networking and web-based methods. It possesses a two-tier architecture, which makes it a scalable, secure, and reliable system.

➤ AlarmNet: It is project and application that combines WBAN and environmental sensor networks, it has a three-tier architecture: the first tier consists of WBAN, the second tier consists of environmental sensors, and the third tier has alarm-gate which works on internetworking and internet protocol (IP). The goal of AlarmNet is monitoring of patients in home environments.

➤ UbiMon: This is an ad-hoc network consisting of wearables and implantable medical sensors that creates a WBAN; the project's goals include the monitoring and capturing of psychological status of a patient and detection of any life-threatening symptoms in the patient.

➤ Many other MIoT/WBAN, application-based projects are Mobicare, MediSN, STAIRE, Vital-Jacket, Bike-Net, and eWatch [7, 8].

4.2.1   Security and Privacy Issues in WBANs/WMSNs/WMIOTs

As highlighted earlier, these sensors used in the medical care are nothing but mini-computers that are equipped with transceiver, microcontroller, memory, and a specific chipset for the task of the sensor. That is, they are nothing but WSNs. So, the security and privacy issues faced by them are the same as that faced by the WSNs.

WSNs and its extensions WBANs or WMSNs or WMIOTs are ad-hoc networks; they conduct their networking between the sensors and the BS and the cloud data using certain protocols. These protocols are very important; they also determine the security and privacy modalities for these sensors' communication with themselves and outside networks.

The following are the various routing protocols used by these sensor networks used in healthcare:

> ➢ Data-Centric Routing Protocol: Its purpose is to combine the data coming from various sensor nodes to a particular route. This protocol eliminates redundancies, and minimizes the total data transferred, before it reaches the BS. Example of this protocol is SPIN, i.e., "sensor protocol for information via negotiation" [9–11].
> ➢ Hierarchical Routing Protocol: "Hierarchical routing protocol classifies network nodes into hierarchical clusters. For each of the clusters, the protocol selects a node with high residual energy as the cluster head. The sensed data of each node in the cluster are transferred through the cluster heads of the clusters in the network. The cluster node aggregates the sensed data of all the nodes in the cluster before sending it to the sink. Hierarchical routing protocol reduces the energy consumption through multi-hop transmission mode [9, 11, 12]." "Some examples of hierarchical routing protocol are LEACH, i.e., low-energy adaptive clustering hierarchy, TEEN, i.e., threshold-sensitive energy-efficient sensor network protocol, APTEEN, i.e., adaptive threshold sensitive energy-efficient sensor network protocol, and SHEER, i.e., secure hierarchical energy-efficient routing [9]."
> ➢ Multipath-based Routing Protocol: This routing protocol was developed for effective and efficient delivery of data from the source to destination nodes. This protocol pre-forms a secondary path to the destination node if the

primary routing path fails. This routing protocol increases the fault tolerance, but it also makes sure that the energy and memory costs are increased, as the nodes now have to maintain and remember alternative routing paths [9].

➤ Location-based Routing Protocol: This routing protocol first calculates the distance between the source and the destination nodes and then it uses the best and the shortest distance to route data between the sensor nodes. This saves energy used by the nodes for routing purposes. The protocol used the signal strength of incoming signal to determine the distance. This protocol also saves the overall energy of the sensor network as it puts all non-active nodes in sleeping mode. Some examples of this routing protocol are location and geo forward protocol (LGF) and geographic adaptive fidelity protocol (GAF) are form MANETs but due to their energy saving nature are very suitable for WBANs/WMSNs, etc. Other examples include location-aided routing (LAR), greedy location-aided routing (GLAR), and energy-efficient location-aided routing (EELAR) [9].

➤ QoS-based Routing Protocol: QoS or quality of service-based routing protocol uses some pre-determined QoS metrics to achieve effective data delivery from the source node to the sink node. Some of the existing QoS based routing protocols are sequential assignment routing protocol (SAR), SPEED protocol uses stateless nonterminating geo forwarding (SNGF) algorithm to achieve its goal of keeling its neighbor information as parameter for routing and QHCR protocol, which stands for QoS aware and heterogeneously clustered routing [9].

➤ Mobility-based Routing Protocol: These types of protocols are lightweight routing protocols that used efficient data transfer techniques to send data from source to sink nodes. These protocols leverage the dynamism of the topology of the sensor node network. Some examples of these kind of protocols are tree-based efficient data-dissemination protocol (TEDD), scalable energy-efficient asynchronous dissemination (SEAD), two-tier data dissemination (TTDD), and data MULES [9].

Now, let us discuss some of the security and privacy issue that can plague these routing protocols and the WSN based WBANs, WMIOTs, etc.

Figure 4.2 below shows the need for security in medical sensor networks and what areas of WMSNs or WMIOTs or WBANs need to make security and privacy robust. The main goals of any security and privacy exercise are to achieve the following:

1. Confidentiality: To make sure that the data that is confidential remains confidential and it not accessed by any unwanted actor.

2. Availability: To make sure that the data that is required by any legitimate user of that data is available to the user at all the times.

3. Integrity: To make sure that the information/data is not corrupted in any way or form. This means that the information required is current, correct, and not corrupted by any malicious actor.

4. Non-repudiation: This is a very important principle in information security, it means that the data or information requested by a person say "A" from a person named "B" is exchanged between the two parties with each other's consent, and both "A" and "B" cannot later deny that information was exchanged between them or a transaction has occurred. A real-world example is a bank ATM machine transaction, a

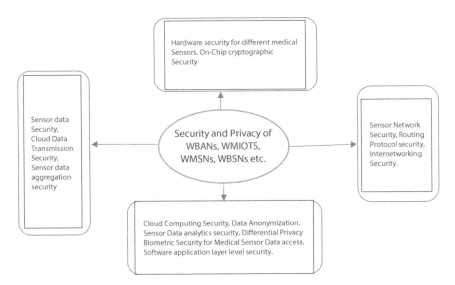

Figure 4.2 Various types of security and privacy needs for WBANs, WMSNs, WMIOTs, etc.

person withdraws $100 from his or her bank account using an ATM, this transaction is recorded by the bank's ATM server and is posted to the person's account, but then later, the person disputes the transaction, and this should not happen. For this using non-repudiation principle, the back keeps record of the person's identity, the date and time of the transaction, the location of the transaction, and other such details. That is why, non-repudiation principle is important in any security and privacy scenario, even in medical sensor networks.

5. Authentication: It means that the medical device use must also be allowed to authenticated users like patients, their relatives or their doctors. The devices authentication and authorization of use can be achieved through password-based security, biometric security, or location-based security [13].

6. Anonymization: It means that the healthcare data of a patient should remain anonymous to the third-party actors like insurance agents and healthcare researchers, when they use a patient's data for their business purposes. All the actors who use patient's data for research, insurance, clinical trials, etc., should do so by making sure the patients biographical and biometric information remains private and anonymized [13].

   Anonymization can be of different types as well:
   o Medical Device/Sensor Anonymization
   o Medical Data Anonymization
   o Communication Streams Anonymization
   o Unlikability, meaning that the adversary that is tracking the data communication between the sender sensor nodes and the medical device/BS should not be able to identify a relationship between the two.

Most of the routing protocols and the security and privacy solutions presently are redundant for the medical sensor networks and other types of medical devices networks talked about here. The adversary or the attacker can be a passive or an active one in case of the attacks that can happen on these devices. Types of attack vectors that can be used to damage the security and privacy of medical sensor networks, biomedical sensor networks, wireless body area networks, wireless medical devices internet, etc., are discussed below:

➢ Side channel analysis attack: These types of attacks are mainly deadly and very discerning in case of implantable medical devices like pacemakers, cochlear and ocular implants, and insulin pumps. Here, the attacker monitors the medical device in question, usually its power consumption cycle, and the faint electromagnetic signal that every electronic sensor or device generates. The attacker can use this monitoring information to repeat the same operation within the device multiple times and try to recover a secret key or perturb a perturbation used in embedded hardware a measure of security for the device. Different types of side channel analysis attacks that can happen are electromagnetic interference, differential power analysis, sensor spoofing, etc. [9, 13].

➤ Disclosure/knowledge of the identities of the source and destination nodes by the attacker using trust-based node tampering [9].

➤ Routing information manipulation: It is a passive attack and it is very hard to detect and identify. This attack manipulates the routing information between any two sensors nodes in a WMSN. It is launched through spoofing or replaying the routing information [9].

➤ Sybil attack: This attack compromises the WMSN, WBAN, etc., using fake identities in terms of sensor nodes, and it disrupts the network protocols used. It can lead to denial-of-service (DoS). It also affects mapping during routing due the fake identities created. It is very hard to detect and prevent due to the fact that these networks are ad-hoc and have very low energy and power availability [9].

➤ Sinkhole attack: This prevents the sink node form getting all the correct and error-free data/information for other sensors in the network; therefore, it prevents the flawless working of the higher layer applications which depend on this data, thus creating a potentially lethal situation for patients and medical care givers. Using this attack as a base, the attacker can then launch more sophisticated attacks like selective forwarding attack, modifying or dropping packets, etc. [9].

➤ Clone attack: Here, in this attack scenario, the attacker captures a valid device/sensor from the medical sensor network and then aggregates all the information and memory form the device/sensor and clones the device/sensor into several devices/sensors and plants the clones strategically in the medical sensor network again. Using the clones, the attacker can then launch other attacks [9].

➢ Wormhole attack: Here, an attacker captures the medical sensor networks traffic and some of its nodes, and the captured nodes tunnel all the information between themselves and also exhausts the energy of the network. This attack can lead to other attacks like energy exhaustion attack and blackhole attack [9, 14].

➢ Hello flood attack: This attack is based on the fact that whenever a sensor wants to communicate with other sensors in a WMSN or WBAN, it sends Hello packets to the receiving neighboring nodes. The attacker may use this fact to defraud the sensors receiving the Hello packets that they are within the radio range of the source sensor node or device [9].

➢ DoS attacks: This is a very common type of attack in any network-based communication system, be it ad-hoc networks, or TCP/IP-based networks. Here, the attacker uses the weakness of the sensor network to disrupt the networking capabilities. This attack can be implemented at the networking layer as well at the application layer where there are portals and software connected to the internet doing data analytics and interpretation on the medical device and sensor data. One of the ways to implement a DoS attack is to flood the network with messages to increase traffic and congestion, which ultimately brings the whole network down [9].

➢ Man-in-the-middle (MiTM) attack: This is a passive kind of attack; it can be implemented at various levels in the medical sensor network. It can be implemented when the medical devices and medical sensors are in communication. The attacker listens in to the network traffic and analyses the network traffic with some malicious intent to use that information for further damaging attacks in the future.

➢ Hardware manipulation attack: This type of attack is done with malicious intent at the device manufacturer's end. Here, a backdoor or trapdoor is set up within the medical implantable device and medical sensors, purposefully for some business intensive reasons or may be just pure malicious intent.

Above, we discussed the various types of attack vectors possible for the medical sensor networks or medical internet of things or body sensor networks. There are solutions for the mitigation and prevention of each of them; some solutions are implementable but some of them are in progress.

The following are some of the solutions or possible solutions and mitigations for the various security and privacy problems as discussed above:

> Solutions for the routing-based attacks: As discussed above, there are a lot of problems in the routing of WBANs/ WMIOTs/WMSNs, here are some of the solutions:
  • In MANET type ad-hoc sensor networks, a proposed solution is to use some light weight cryptographic algorithms and hashing algorithms embedded in the routing protocols for safe, secure, and robust routing. This kind of solution also prevents against network layer attacks like wormhole attack and blackhole attack [14].
  • Use of hierarchical key establishment scheme (HIKES), in routing, like used by the SHEER protocol.
  • Use of in trust-based routing scheme, like calculation of content trust, integrity trust, honesty trust, etc., between sensor nodes by using neighbor count, residual energy, transmission and receiving power, and residual memory [15].

> To prevent side channel analysis attacks, scalar blinding is usually used with some cryptographic based solution. "The scalar multiplication is blinded using integer j, where j is the order of the point $P \in E_q$ such that $mP = 0$. For example, instead of computing $Q=kP \bmod q$, $Q = (k+j) P \bmod q$ is computed [9]."

> Effective key management schemes: The use of asymmetric pre-distribution (AP) of keys gives better performance and security in the network [9].

> Use of effective Public Key Infrastructure (PKI): PKI can be used as a tool to ensure the authenticity of the sink node or BS. It has two phases, first is sink to node handshake, and second is to use the session keys to encrypt data. Here, a common key need to be agreed upon by the participating nodes in the network. To solve this, PKI can also be used for secure key exchange mechanisms. This approach thwarts

some types of DoS attacks and can be used in data authentication encryption [9].

➤ Effective grouping of nodes improves security in WMSNs, WMIOTs, WBANs, etc.:

➤ "Here, sensor nodes are grouped together into smaller clusters where each cell assigns a special sensor node to carry out all the burden of relaying multi-hop packets. Therefore, division of labor is possible in the network, which makes the scheme a low power consumption scheme [9]."

➤ Point-to-point security solution: "Olakanmi and Dada [9] proposed an effective point-to-point security scheme that engages point-to-point (PoP) mutual authentication scheme, perturbation, and pseudonym to overcome security and privacy issues in WMSNs, WBANs, etc. To reduce computational cost and energy consumption, they used elliptic curve cryptography, hash function, and exclusive OR operations to evolve an efficient security solution for a decentralized WMSNs, WBANs, etc. The PoP security scheme consists of the following phases—registration and key management phase, secure data exchange phase, perturb generation phase, signature and obfuscation phase, authentication and verification phase, and decryption phase [9]."

➤ Use of Intrusion Detection and Prevention Mechanisms: The use of algorithms like IDSHT (Intrusion detection using state context and hierarchical trust) and SHTIP (State context and hierarchical trust-based intrusion prevention) and many others to detect malicious and flawed nodes beforehand for better security and privacy of the WMSN or WBAN, or WMIOT, etc. [15].

➤ Access control lists for authorization and authentication: This scheme can be used to monitor and grant access to the operational medical devices and sensors to authenticated and authorized personal only. This list can be made for sensor and device network also, like who is allowed in the network who is not. One can make a list using ingress and egress filtering also. Some researchers have proposed a variety of access control lists for healthcare systems, which includes, proximity-based lists, identity-based lists, role-based lists, attribute-based lists, and risk-based access control lists [13].

- The use of hardware encryption, like on-chip (microcontroller here), embedded light weight encryption like light weight AES (Advanced Encryption Standard) with less rounds and small key size.
- Biometric-based authentication methods: As we know, nowadays, at application level, two or three factor authentication is often used for identity verification while logging into operating systems, mobile apps, desktop apps, web apps, etc. One of the factors of authentication is face of the user or the fingerprint of the user. Biometric authentication is always better than passwords as the user needs to be physically present near the device to identify himself/herself; it is the best type of authentication mechanism. There are a very few loopholes and vulnerabilities that can breach this authentication. Biometric behavioral traits, including signature, voice, gait, ECG, and keystrokes, can be used in WMSN, MIOT, WBAN, etc. There are two phases in biometric security and authentication: in the first phase, the subject registers the raw biometric samples into the biometric database, then processing is done on them for feature extraction, after that these processed samples are stored in another database. In the second phase, the subject is authenticated to use a medical device only if his/her biometric sample matches the database of feature extracted biometrics. Like a voice sample of Maya matches the feature extracted vector of the voice of Maya, to grant her access to the insulin pump [17]. Table 4.2 of the most common behavioral biometric traits that are/will be used for biometric authentication of medical devices and sensors.
- Use of AI-based and blockchain-based techniques to mitigate the adverse effects of various attacks on WMSNs/WMIOTs/WBSNs, etc. These techniques are based mainly at the application layer and transport layer level, which are discussed below.
- Use of SSL and TLS in the network data transfer between sensor nodes and transmission between the source and the BS. And the data transmission using TCP/IP, i.e., internet when the data is aggregated at the BS and transferred to the medical server/medical cloud for further analysis and processing.

Table 4.2 Common biometric traits [17].

Biometric trait	Strength	Weakness
Signature	Easily captured by a touchpad or a camera	Easily imitated, long term reliability in question
Voice	Low cost sensors like microphone are required	Voice can change due to emotions, sickness, etc., so not very reliable.
Gait	Easily accessible, can be captured via body sensors, or camera	Can change due to age, injury or due to impersonation and purposefulness. Lot of data extraction time is needed thus memory and computation intensive.
ECG	Easily accessible and captured by implantable or body-based sensors	Changes can happen due to cardiac abnormalities, physical activity and intense emotions. ECG can degrade the ECG based biometric systems
Keystrokes	No user intervention required to capture this	Keystroke software for recording keystrokes is required for different devices like laptop, mobiles, and desktops. Low recognition rate.
Fingerprint	Easily accessible and captured	Wet and wrinkled fingers can degrade performance, forgeries can happen and must be detected
Palmprint	Easily accessible and captured	Wet and wrinkled palms can degrade performance. Not suitable for laptops, mobiles and other small devices.

(Continued)

Table 4.2 Common biometric traits [17]. (*Continued*)

Biometric trait	Strength	Weakness
Face	Easily accessible and captured	It requires high-end high-resolution cameras. Variation in light and facial expression can cause degradation in performance. Making of face and other face clothing can also degrade performance.
Retina/iris	Easily accessible, blood vessel pattern within iris provides a wide variety of feature vectors.	High precision iris scanner required to capture the details, lenses, specs, and other eyewear can degrade the performance. Not suitable for mini-MIOT devices.
Hand Geometry	Easily accessible and very adequate number of features available.	Requires specialized hardware and software for capture. Not applicable for mini-MIOTs.
Ear Shape	Very easily accessible	Can be covered up by hair, head gear etc. effecting the performance.
Body Odor	Easily accessible, can be easily captured by on-body sensor nodes in WBSNs	Deodorants, perfumes etc., can affect the natural body odor of a person thus degrading performance.
Vein Pattern	It provides a large number of features thus, high level of security.	It requires infrared-based special cameras, so not very reliable due to complexity in vein patterns.
DNA	It can be easily obtained via saliva, blood, hair, etc. Very high identification rate.	Sample processing is complex and expensive, like PCR based techniques. Not-applicable for mini-MIOTs

4.3   Cloud Storage and Computing on Sensitive Healthcare Data

Cloud computing is a ubiquitous in present day. If you are using services like Google drive, Microsoft one-drive, and Dropbox, you are using cloud computing for storage of your different type of files. In a way, nowadays, anyone using a smart phone or laptop or desktop for that matter is using cloud computing in one or other. Similarly, for storing sensitive healthcare data, medical institutions and government agencies use cloud computing services. So, considering the sensitive nature of healthcare data all the databases, applications and analytics software used over the cloud for storage and computing must be secure and private as per law (HIPAA Act, etc.) and basic scientific and humanist ethics.

According to Microsoft, "Simply put, cloud computing is the delivery of computing services, including servers, storage, databases, networking, software, analytics, and intelligence; over the Internet ('the cloud') to offer faster innovation, flexible resources, and economies of scale. You typically pay only for cloud services you use, helping you lower your operating costs, run your infrastructure more efficiently, and scale as your business needs change [18]."

Some benefits of cloud computing are the following:

➢ Cost: saves cost of expensive hardware and software, as these services are hosted by the cloud vendor and the client saves the costs.

➢ Global scale: "The benefits of cloud computing services include the ability to scale elastically. In cloud speak, that means delivering the right amount of IT resources for example, more or less computing power, storage, bandwidth right when they're needed, and from the right geographic location [18]."

➢ Performance: "The biggest cloud computing services run on a worldwide network of secure datacenters, which are regularly upgraded to the latest generation of fast and efficient computing hardware. This offers several benefits over a single corporate datacenter, including reduced network latency for applications and greater economies of scale [18]."

➢ Speed: Almost all of the cloud computing services are provided at the time of need and on-demand; and thanks to today's internetwork infrastructure, all these services are available within the blink of an eye form the cloud vender.

So, businesses and organizations can save important time by using these services [18].

➢ Productivity: "Onsite datacenters typically require a lot of 'racking & stacking' hardware setup, software patching, and other time-consuming IT management chores. Cloud computing removes the need for many of these tasks, so IT teams can spend time on achieving more important business goals [18]."

➢ Reliability: Cloud computing uses data backup, disaster recovery techniques, which makes business and organizations survival easier as the cloud provider can mirror the important data at several redundant sites in the cloud providers' network [18].

➢ Security: Almost all the market leaders in cloud computing provide state-of-the-art security features for its clients, like use of homographic encryption with ECC, differential privacy, anonymization etc. They use broad set of policies, technologies and controls like defence in depth approach etc., that helps mitigate any major security issues.

Types of cloud computing are public cloud, private cloud, and hybrid cloud. These names are self-explanatory.

Types of Cloud Services are:

➢ Infrastructure as a service (IaaS): It can be used to rent IT infrastructure like, virtual machines, operating systems, databases, networks, storage, and servers.

➢ Platform as a service (PaaS): "Platform as a service refers to cloud computing services that supply an on-demand environment for developing, testing, delivering, and managing software applications. PaaS is designed to make it easier for developers to quickly create web or mobile apps, without worrying about setting up or managing the underlying infrastructure of servers, storage, network, and databases needed for development [18]."

➢ Serverless computing: "In conjunction with PaaS, serverless computing focuses on building app functionality without spending time continually managing the servers and infrastructure required to do so. Serverless architectures are highly scalable and event-driven, only using resources when a specific function or trigger occurs [18]."

> ➤ Software as a service (SaaS): "SaaS is a method for deliver-
> ing software applications over the Internet, on demand and
> typically on a subscription basis. With SaaS, cloud providers
> host and manage the software application and underlying
> infrastructure, and handle any maintenance, like software
> upgrades and security patching. Users connect to the appli-
> cation over the Internet, usually with a web browser on their
> phone, tablet, or PC." IoT application and software for data
> analytics of medical devices and sensors comes under this
> service [18].

The widespread use and deployment of WBANs, WMSNs, etc., in
healthcare systems required new technologies like IoT and cloud computing. These technologies are able to meet the needs of healthcare systems in
terms of processing and storage of large amounts of data [19]. Thus, it is
imperative that the cloud computing technology is also secure and robust
for a strong a robust overall healthcare IT infrastructure.

4.3.1   Security and Privacy in Cloud Computing and Storage for Sensitive Healthcare Data

The following are the requirements of data security and privacy in cloud
storage:

> ➤ Data Confidentiality
> ➤ Data Integrity
> ➤ Data Availability
> ➤ Data anonymity
> ➤ Data authenticity
> ➤ Data accountability from the Cloud Service Providers
> ➤ Stored data should be collusion resistant
> ➤ Non-Repudiation
> ➤ Fine grained access control
> ➤ Secure data sharing in Dynamic Groups
> ➤ Leak resistance
> ➤ Complete data deletion from the cloud when the users
>   no-longer require the data
> ➤ Use of privacy protection policies to safeguard, name, iden-
>   tity, location, and sensitive data exposer for healthcare
>   industry and other sensitive businesses [19, 20]

Some of the mechanisms by which a Cloud Service Provider can implement security and privacy for the sensitive healthcare data are as follows:

- Data encryption technologies: As soon as the sensitive healthcare data is uploaded to the cloud, its security becomes vulnerable. Data encryption is a very effective way to protect data security. As known, in encryption, the plain interpretable data is transformed by some encryption technique to an unintelligible form to protect its integrity and confidentiality and privacy. They are two main types of encryption methodologies—symmetric and asymmetric encryption; these two differ in the use of number of keys and complexity of encryption process. Some encryption technologies widely used in cloud storage systems are as follows.
  - IBE (Identity-based encryption): It is based on PKI. In PKI, in process to confirm the identity of a user, the sender needs to authenticate the receiver's identity information with a trusted third-party CA (Certificate Authority) before encryption with a public key. This significantly increases the responsibility of the sender if he/she wants to share data with multiple sources. In order to solve this problem Shamir in 1984 proposed an identity-based cryptography. Here, the problem was solved by associating the user's identity information with the public key, so there is no need to verify the receivers' certificate before encryption of the information. "In such a system, Alice is a sender wants to send an encrypted message to Bob. Private Key Generator (PKG), a trusted third party, is required to generate the corresponding public key and private key. First, in order to encrypt the message, Alice utilizes the receiver's unique identity information (Bob's e-mail: Bob@g.com) to generate the public key from PKG. Then Alice sends the encrypted message to Bob. The receiver Bob contacts the PKG and authenticates to obtain the corresponding private key [20]."
  - ABE (attribute-based encryption): It replaces unique identity with a set of attributes in an attribute-based encryption and only the users whose attribute sets matches access control policy can access the encrypted data. The ABE algorithm is a four-part algorithm:

- o "Setup phase, also known as the system initialization phase, in which pertinent security parameters are input and corresponding public parameters (PK) and master key (MK) are generated [20];"
- o "KeyGen stage, namely the key generation stage, data owner submit their own attributes to the system to obtain the private key associated with the attributes [20];"
- o "Encryption phase, the data owner encrypts the data by his/her public key and get the ciphertext (CT) and sends it to the receiver or to the public cloud [20]."
- o "Decryption phase, decryption users get ciphertext, decryption with their own private key SK."

ABE looks very promising enough to provide fine grained access control encrypted files in data sharing applications, where the data owner can specify who can access the encrypted data. It is mainly divided into two–Key Policy ABE (KP-ABE) and Ciphertext Policy ABE (CP-ABE). Figure 4.3 shows the pictorial example of both schemes [20].

- Homomorphic encryption: "Homomorphic encryption is a public key encryption scheme which allows users to perform certain algebraic operations on ciphertext and still get the encrypted text, and the result after the ciphertext is decrypted is consistent with the result of the same operation on plaintext [20]." Basically, homomorphic encryption is a technique which is used to perform computing, analysis, updating and deletion tasks on encrypted data/text, while preserving the integrity, privacy, and confidentiality of the original data or information. It is used as a security and privacy preserving technique in cloud computing and storage. This can help in maintain the security and privacy of sensitive healthcare data migrated over cloud. Here, the "Data owner encrypt the file by homomorphic encryption and sends it to the cloud server. The authorized users can decrypt the ciphertext with the corresponding private keys. If the second user

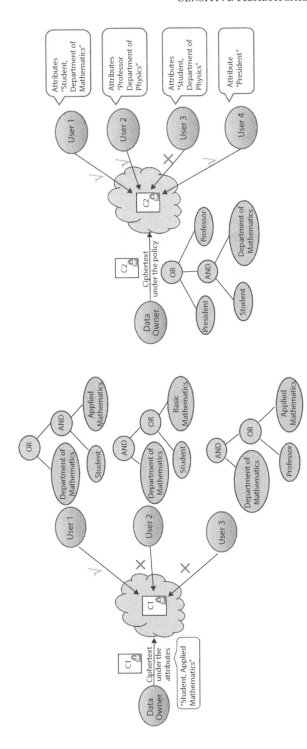

Figure 4.3 KP-ABE and CP-ABE schemes in cloud computing and storage [20].

wants to perform some specific operations on cipher-text, the only thing he needs to do is send the functions corresponding to the operations to the cloud server. The server gets operand and performs the operation without decrypt the ciphertext and return the encrypted result to user 2. Homomorphic encryption effectively protects the security of outsourced data [20]." Mathematically, homo-morphic encryption derives its origins form the concept of homomorphism, "Given a homomorphism f: $A \rightarrow A^*$ is a structure preserving map between sets A and A^* with the composition operations $\bigcirc$ and $\bullet$, respectively. Let a, b, c be elements of set A, with $c = a \bigcirc b$ and $a^* = f(a)$ and $b^* = f(b)$, $c^* = f(c)$ is an element of A^*. Based on the above assumptions, we can get $f(a \bigcirc b) = f(a) \bullet f(b)$. Consider that the homomorphism, $f(.)$ is a one-to-one mapping, and represents the encryption procedure, and D' is a data set consisting of the data stored in cloud; f^{-1}, the inverse of 'f', with $a = f^{-1}(a^*)$, $b = f^{-1}(b^*)$, $c = f^{-1}(c^*)$, is the decryption procedure, and the composition operations are the var-ious types of computations performed with ciphertext. As per the computing power of the cipher text, homo-morphic encryption can be divided into three catego-ries, partial homomorphic encryption (PHE), somewhat homomorphic encryption (SHE) and fully homomorphic encryption (FHE) [20]."

- Searchable encryption: Organizations and people store their sensitive data on the cloud due to the seemingly unlimited space available in the cloud, but before they store their data on the cloud, they use encryption and then store the data in the cloud. But now, the problem arises, if the users of the cloud want to search some infor-mation in the data stored in the cloud, it is impossible to search the information as the data is encrypted. Now, if the user wants to search the required information, they need to either download the entire dataset from cloud and then decrypt it and then search for the required infor-mation, which is a cumbersome process. Or the user can decrypt the data on the cloud itself and then try to search the required information, but this exposes the data to other third parties on the cloud. "Searchable encryption is a cryptography primitive that allows authorized users to retrieve ciphertext in the cloud by some means (such as keyword query). Its feature is to ensure that the cloud server returns encrypted data files of interest to users without knowing the ciphertext content. In terms of the way of encryption, searchable encryption can be divided into Searchable Symmetric Encryption (SSE) and Public Key Encryption with Keyword Search (PEKS) [20]."

➢ Privacy preserving ML in cloud storage: Some researchers are working on ML for cloud computing and cloud data security, ML with public auditing, ML training and classification scheme with homomorphic encryption, and homomorphic deep learning (DL) [20].

➢ Post quantum cryptography: With the advent of quantum computers, the classical methods of encryption will become obsolete, so quantum encryption technologies are being developed with cloud computing in mind. Basically, post quantum cryptography is a new generation of cryptography that can resist attacks on existing cryptography. This kind of cryptography uses advanced mathematical concepts from number theory and quantum mechanics to provide security and privacy of sensitive data like healthcare data [20].

4.4 Blockchain for Security and Privacy Enhancement in Sensitive Healthcare Data

Blockchain definition: "The blockchain is an incorruptible digital ledger of economic transactions that can be programmed to record not just financial transactions but virtually everything of value," Don & Alex Tapscott, authors of Blockchain Revolution (2016) [21, 23]."

"Basically, blockchain ledger is digital, distributed and decentralized. As per the blockchain definition; its records transactions across a global network of computers where the information is highly secure. As the name suggests, blockchain is nothing but a linear chain of blocks that holds information of transactions taking place over the web. Every block contains data in the form of coding that is organized in a chronological manner [21, 23]."

In simple terms, it is a digital ledger, where one can store whatever one wants and can later access it through the hash value received. Blockchain is an immutable ledger, where it stores all the transactions in a block. When a new transaction is made, a new block of that transaction is added to an existing set of blocks, in a systematic way which is authenticated by everyone in the transaction. Blockchain uses best cryptographic practices and algorithms, so it is difficult to hack, and it is best suited for the security and privacy of sensitive healthcare data. SHA-256 is used to keep hash value secured in blockchain. To get an idea about the security robustness of blockchain technology, it can be safely said that, to hack a blockchain system, a malicious hacker will need at least 50% of the computational capacity of all the supercomputing systems deployed in the world, plus the hacker will need to change the information in all the blocks as they are cryptographically linked to each other; other than this, all the block in the chain reside in distributed nodes, and each and every time each node checks with other nodes whether they possesses the same transaction details based on the consensus protocol. Blockchain works on these four salient features: consensus, security, provenance, and trust. Each and every block in a blockchain has the following four details—Data, Nonce, Previous Hash, and Present Hash. One needs to grasp the following concepts to completely understand blockchain technology—Hash Cryptography, Immutable Ledger, Distributed P2P network, Mining, Smart Contracts, and Consensus Protocol.

Liu *et al.* proposed a "Blockchain and Distributed Ledger Based-Improved Biomedical Security System (BDL-IBS)" to enhance privacy and security across all types of healthcare applications [22].

"The proposed BDL-IBS is designed to improve the trust- and privacy-related specifications of the electronic shareable healthcare records. The system is focused on maximizing the sharing rate of the secured records along with less adversarial impact. Here, blockchain technology is exploited by the medical server that tracks the trust privacy factors between the users and records. Figure 4.4 illustrates this system [22]."

"The components of the bio-medical system include storage and a medical server. The storage contains the health records of the end-users in a digital format. The medical server is responsible for processing user requests and responding to them with appropriate records. A common sharing platform such as cloud and associated infrastructures are responsible for sharing EHRs. The blockchain and distributed ledger are used in both the medical server and end-user applications. In the blockchain associated with the medical server, the trust and privacy factors are analyzed, whereas the privacy factors are alone assessed in the end-user blockchain. The trust factors include successful access and response to request ration, and privacy relies on convergence and complexity. In this bio-medical security system, malicious access due to man-in-middle and data tempering

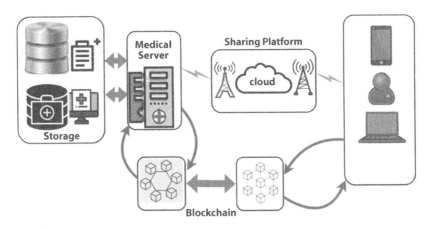

Figure 4.4 Biomedical security system with blockchain [22].

adversary models are considered. In a man-in-middle attack, the adversary overlaps the end user to gain access to the EHR. This results in sharing health information to an adversary and thus degrading the design of a secure biomedical system. In the case of a data tempering attack, the adversary breaches EHR from any node communicating with the biomedical system. It either modifies the actual data/tracks the communication through the EHR information. For defending the above attack, trust model and concentric authentication are introduced using blockchain technology; the blockchain process is differentiated in both the medical server and end-user applications. Here, the process of trust-based validation is performed using linear decision making and authentication is augmented through classification-based learning [22]."

"Zhao *et al.* developed a key management for healthcare blockchain. The efficient key management method is used as a privacy and security mechanism in the healthcare system. It is observed by embedding the sensor to analyze the blockchain. The proposed method is used to enhance the effectiveness and high security [22]."

"A blockchain is proposed for the medical records to access and permits the MedChain process, which is addressed by Daraghmi *et al.* Medchain is used for interoperating, secure, and effective access for patients' privacy. The security is time-based access that gives the degree of health providers. A blockchain is used for the Electronic Health Record system (EHRs) and is proposed by Guo *et al.* The authors implemented a secure attribute based on signature with multi authorities. The patients send the text according to the health as the attribute evidence to the healthcare center. The trust is given to the authorities to access the message, and both use the public and private keys to avoid the escrow problem. The medical service framework is designed to store the secure records of the patient by using the block-chain method and is introduced by Chen *et al.* The storage is done on the cloud for large data access. The records are shared by its aspect based on its service related to the authorized user. Griggs *et al.* observed a healthcare blockchain using smart contracts for patient monitoring. The smart contracts are used for secure analysis management for communication with the sensor. They are also used to monitor the patients and professionals to give notification regarding the health [22]."

From the above discussion, we can see that how the blockchain technology is used to secure the electronic healthcare system, and how using blockchain technology the security and privacy of sensitive healthcare data is protected.

4.5   Artificial Intelligence, Machine Learning, and Big Data in Healthcare and Its Efficacy in Security and Privacy of Sensitive Healthcare Data

AI is nowadays used in the area of medical image analysis and medical diagnosis. Medical imaging techniques like MRI, tomography, sonography, radiology, microscopy, and thermography are important tools for early stage illness detection and further treatment. AI agent–based systems, ML, and DL techniques are used in medical imaging–based medical diagnosis. Here, medical images like x-rays, sonograms, and MRIs are compared to a data set comprising of several images of which show disease related medical images, and other which are disease free. Now, using sophisticated ML and DL algorithms like CNNs, DNNs, and SVMs, the computer-aided disease detection and diagnosis is done. This process involves feature selection from medical images, choosing of the right model/classifier and the right algorithm, and then letting the machines train on the data, and the required result is acquired which is, of course, verified by a medical professional before making the final diagnosis [24].

These medical images constitute as a sensitive healthcare data. Some malicious actors can damage the content of these images if they are stored in a centralized database as these images when they are stored digitally are nothing but binary code. Using malwares, spyware, etc., hackers can modify the image database and corrupt the images. Hackers can also hack the servers of the medical database storing these medical images using ransomware, etc. Some of the methods to prevent these aforementioned things are as follows.

> Regular security upgradation of the hardware and software and operating system used in the medical database servers.
> Use of enhanced cryptography and encryption like RSA and ECC to store the medical images and other data.
> Use of anonymization and differential privacy in storing the medical data and protecting the privacy of the patient's healthcare information.
> Use of stare of the art anti-malware, anti-spyware software.
> Use of best firewalls, DMZs, and use of Honeypots and Honeynets to thwart attacks on the medical database server.

As, from the above comprehensive discussion, by now, it is known that medical healthcare databases are huge in size both laterally and vertically. They include medical images, EEG records, ECG records, implantable devices records, drug prescription records, etc. Here, big data technologies and software like HADOOP and NOSQL are used to manage these kinds of massive medical databases. But there is also an important factor of preserving the security and privacy of these massive medical databases, wherein comes some of the privacy and security preserving techniques for massive medical big data and its analysis.

There is a plethora of technologies that in use for the massive medical big data, and some of them are listed below:

> Authentication: The use of TLS or SSL at the transport layer of big data servers and protocols like HTTPS and FTPS in internal medical servers are helpful in authentication of client-servers to each other. The use of Kerberos protocol is also a helpful method for authentication of big data in medical servers [1].
> Various data encryption techniques already discussed above in the second and third section in detail [1].
> Data masking techniques can be quite helpful, when it comes to privacy preservation of medical big data. Masking uses a non-identifiable value to replace sensitive data elements in the big medical data. This technique reduces the cost of securing medical big data deployment [1].
> Access control mechanisms
> Use of data protection laws like HIPAA and HITECH Act 2009.

> ➤ De-identification techniques and algorithms like k-anonymity, l-diversity, t-closeness, and hybrid model of some of these techniques are also applicable [1].
> ➤ Differential privacy is the most important of these techniques and is discussed separately below.

4.5.1   Differential Privacy for Preserving Privacy of Big Medical Healthcare Data and for Its Analytics

Differential privacy is an important and state-of-the-art technique in big data analytics and ML. It allows the third party users, which is case of medical big data are health and medical insurance agencies, clinical researchers, medical professionals, big data analytics firms, cloud computing firms, medical software companies, etc., to use the medical big data in such a way that it is not in any way or form a breach of privacy of a patient and a medical doctor treating him/her. Using differential privacy these, third parties as described above can perform, data analysis, ML predications, and other analysis to improve their business or further their research without breaching the privacy, security, and trust of the sensitive medical data of various patients and remaining within HIPAA compliance.

"Dwork, first proposed ε- differential privacy, and established a Laplace transform mechanism perturb aggregated queries to guarantee differential privacy." Since then, various variations of the Dwork proposed differential privacy mechanisms have been proposed with relaxing criteria added to the mechanism. Like (ε, δ) probabilistic differential privacy achieves ε-differential privacy with the highest probability [26].

"Simply put, a mechanism is differentially private if its outcome is not significantly affected by the removal or addition of any user. An adversary thus learns approximately the same information about any individual, irrespective of his/her presence or absence in the original database [26]." Thus, differential privacy makes sure that the individual patient's data is safe and private in the medical big data. Thus, differential privacy is an important mechanism to protect and preserve user data in any big data breach.

4.6   Conclusion

This chapter discusses the security and privacy issues and problems with the sensitive healthcare data, and it also discusses its mitigations and proposed solution. The authors have given many examples of mechanisms, algorithms, techniques, etc., currently in use and proposed by various researchers in this area of preserving the security and privacy of sensitive healthcare data. With the advent of AI, ML, etc., there are various techniques involving automated protection of security and privacy of healthcare data are being developed. Medical and healthcare data is vast and varied, with many computing techniques and storage mechanisms used to analyze and preserve it. In future, highly technical and advanced techniques involving CNNs, DNNs, differential privacy, etc., will be developed that can make the privacy and security of sensitive healthcare data more robust and full proof. This is also an emerging research topic among engineering and medical researchers as almost all of our medical or other data is now online, on cloud or on edge. Future looks bright for the security and privacy of the sensitive medical healthcare data.

References

1. Karim, A., Abderrehim Beni, H., Hayat, K., Big healthcare data: preserving security and privacy. *J. Big Data*, 5, 1, 2018, https://doi.org/10.1186/s40537-017-0110-7.
2. Health Information Privacy, Summary of HIPAA Security Rule, https://www.hhs.gov/hipaa/for-professionals/security/laws-regulations/index.html, July 26 2013, Accessed: August 20, 2020.
3. Electronics Hub, Basics of Wireless Sensor Networks, https://www.electronicshub.org/wireless-sensor-networks-wsn/, March 25, 2019, Accessed: August 20, 2020.
4. WBAN image, https://www.waves.intec.ugent.be/files/images, Accessed: Aug 20. 2020.
5. Freitas, E. and Azevedo, A., Wireless Biomedical Sensor Networks: The Technology. *Proced. of 2nd World Congress of EECSS*, Budapest, Hungry, August 2016, Paper. ICBES 134.
6. Stankovic, J., Cao, Q., Doan, T., Fang, L., He, Z., Kiran, R., Lin, S., Son, S., Stoleru, R., Wood, A., Wireless Sensor Networks for In-Home Healthcare: Potential and Challenges, Department of Computer Science, University of Virginia, http://qosbox.cs.virginia.edu/~stankovic/psfiles/HCMDSS.pdf
7. Fatema, N. and Brad, R., Security Requirements, Counterattacks and Projects in Healthcare Applications Using WSNs- A Review. *Int. J. Comput. Netw. Commun.*, 2, 2, 1–9, May 2014.
8. Tewari, A. and Verma, P., Security and Privacy in E-Healthcare monitoring with WBAN: A Critical Review. *Int. J. Comput. Appl.*, 136, 11, 37–42, Feb. 2016.

9. Olakanmi, O.O. and Dada, A., *Wireless Sensor Networks (WSNs): Security and Privacy Issues and Solutions*, IntechOpen, London U.K., 2020, DOI: http://dx.doi.org/ 10.5772/intechopen.84989.

10. Jamil, I. and Imad, M., A secure hierarchical routing protocol for wireless sensor networks, in: *Paper Presented at the 10th IEEE Intl. Conf. on Comm. Systems*, Singapore, 2006.

11. Du, X., Xiao, Y., Chen, H.-H., Wu, Q., Secure cell relay routing protocol for sensor networks, Wirel. Commun. Mob. Comput. *Special Issue on Network Security*. Wiley InterScience, 6, Pt.3, 375–391, 2009.

12. Masruroh, S.U. and Sabran, K.U., Energy aware and QoS based routing protocol in wireless sensor network, 2014, in: *Paper Presented at IEEE Intl. Conf. on Intel. Auto. Agents Ntwrk & Syss.*

13. Newaz, I.A., Sikder, A.K., Rahman, A.M., Uluagac, A.S., A survey on security and privacy in modern healthcare systems: attacks and defences. *ACM Health*, 1, 1, 1–40, May 2020, https://doi.org/10.1145/1122445.1122456.

14. Vyas, A. and Satheesh, A., Implementing Security Features in MANET Routing Protocols. *Int. J. Comput. Netw. Inf. Secur. (IJCNIS)*, 10, 8, 51–57, 2018.

15. Vyas, A. and Satheesh, A., Intrusion Detection and Prevention Mechanism Implemented using NS-2 Based on State Context and Hierarchical trust in WSNs, in: *Advances in Intelligent Systems and Computing (AISC)*, vol. 1122, pp. 229–241, Springer Cham, Switzerland, Feb. 2020, https://doi.org/10.1007/978-3-030-39875-0_25.

16. Camara, C., Lopez-Periz, P., Tapiador, E.J., Security and Privacy issues in implantable medical devices: A comprehensive survey. *J. Biomed. Inf.*, 55, 272–289, 2015.

17. Sun, Y., Lo, P.-W.F., Lo, B., Security and Privacy for the Internet of Medical Things Enabled Healthcare Systems: A Survey. IEEE Access, 7, 183339–183355, Dec. 2019.

18. Microsoft Azure, What is cloud computing and its benefits? https://azure.microsoft.com/en-us/overview/what-is-cloud-computing/#benefits, August 2020.

19. Sajid, A. and Abbas, H., Data Privacy in Cloud-assisted Healthcare Systems: State of the Art and Future Challenges. *J. Med. Syst.*, 40, 155, 1–16, 2016.

20. Yang, P., Xiong, N., Ren, J., Data Security and Privacy Protection for Cloud Storage: A Survey, 8, 131723–131740, *IEEE Access*, July 2020.

21. Gururaj, H.L. *et al.*, Blockchain: A New Era of Technology, in: *Cryptocurrencies and Blockchain Technology and Applications*, G. Shrivastava, *et al.*, (Eds.), pp. 1–24, Scrivener Publishing, Wiley Online Library, USA, 2020.

22. Liu, H., Crespo, G.-R., Martinez, O.-S., Enhancing Privacy and Data Security across Healthcare Applications using Blockchain and Distributed Ledger Concepts. *Healthcare*, 8, 243, 1–17, J, MDPI, 2020.

23. What is Blockchain, https://intellipaat.com/blog/tutorial/blockchain-tutorial/what-is-blockchain/ July 6, 2020, Accessed: 23 August 2020.

24. Chakrabarti, A., *Demystifying Medical Image Analysis and Visualization using Machine Learning*, IEEE Computer Society Online Webinar Lecture Slides, June 2020.

25. Xin, X., Kong, L., Liu, Z. *et al.*, Machine Learning and Deep Learning Methods for Cyber Security. *IEEE Access*, 6, 35365–35381, July 2018.

26. Fan, L. and Jin, H., A Practical Framework for Privacy-Preserving Data Analytics. *IW3C2*, Florence Italy, WWW 2015, May 2015, ACM 978-1-4503-3469-3/15/05, http://dx.doi.org/10.1145/2736277.2741122.

27. Deokar, S., Mangla, M., Akhare, R.A., *Secure Fog Computing Architecture for Continuous Health Monitoring in Fog Computing for Healthcare 4.0 Environments*, Springer, Cham, pp. 269–290, August 2020.

Part II

EMPLOYMENT OF MACHINE LEARNING IN DISEASE DETECTION

5

Diabetes Prediction Model Based on Machine Learning

Ayush Kumar Gupta*, Sourabh Yadav, Priyanka Bhartiya and Divesh Gupta

Gautam Buddha University, Greater Noida, Uttar Pradesh, India

Abstract

Diabetes is one of the major health issues these days. Around 346 million people from the entire world are facing this disease. Diabetes is the disease in which glucose in the blood increases at an alarming rate. In this situation, insulin is not produced in an appropriate amount by the human body. Another condition is that body cannot respond to the produced insulin. The body is unable to utilize the insulin produced by the pancreas. Diabetes is incurable and therefore we can only take control measures. A diabetic person can develop perilous complications like respiratory failure, stroke, and kidney infection. In this venture, we will determine diabetes by the assistance of the Random Forest algorithm which is the most significant strategy of Machine Learning. Here, Random Forest is utilized on Pima Indian Diabetes Datasets. Accuracy gives us a thought regarding the performance of the classifier.

Keywords: Machine learning, diabetes, supervised learning, support vector machine, decision tree, random forest classifier

5.1 Introduction

Diabetes is chronic infection that happens when the glucose level in blood increases drastically. Blood glucose is the principal reservoir for the vitality of our body. Blood glucose is extracted from the food that we eat normally. The abnormality in the level of blood glucose is caused due to defective

*Corresponding author: akgayush059@gmail.com

Monika Mangla, Nonita Sharma, Poonam Mittal, Vaishali Mehta Wadhwa, Thirunavukkarasu K. and Shahnawaz Khan (eds.) Emerging Technologies for Healthcare: Internet of Things and Deep Learning Models, (131–156) © 2021 Scrivener Publishing LLC

insulin secretion. Diabetes can result in impairment, damage, and dysfunctions of several body parts like eyes, kidneys, heart, blood vessels, and nerves. Diabetes is classified into major categories, such as type 1 diabetes denoted by T1D, and type 2 diabetes denoted by T2D. Youths, mostly less 30 years old, falls in the type 1 category of diabetes. The clinical symptoms of this category are: often urination, high blood glucose levels. Type 1 diabetes cannot be cured effectively by medications and insulin therapy is required. Type 2 diabetes affects mostly adults and old people. People with type 2 diabetes mainly experiences obesity, hypertension, dyslipidemia, and other diseases.

With the rise in living standards, diabetes has also risen in people's day-to-day life. Therefore, there is a need to diagnose and analyze diabetes accurately as quickly as possible. In the United States, 30.2 million individuals who are over 18 years old are experiencing diabetes. Since diabetes is a ceaseless infection, therefore we can only anticipate. For that purpose, the earlier we detect diabetes, the much easier it will be to control. Machine Learning can provide an early prediction about diabetes according to their diagnosis data, and these predictions can be useful for doctors. Machine Learning modeling is based on steps of extraction of features, selection of valid features, and classification. The selection of important and valid feature and correct classifier for Machine Learning modeling are major problems.

A lot of work has been done to automate the detection of diabetes using Machine Learning techniques. In recent works, various algorithms were implemented to detect diabetes, which included Machine Learning methods in the classical form such as Support Vector Machine (SVM), Decision Tree, and Logistic Regression, and so on. To differentiate diabetes from normal people principle component analysis (PCA) and neuro-fuzzy inference were used. Former works used Linear Discriminant Analysis (LDA) to reduce dimensionality and extract features. Prediction models employed on Logistic Regression were used to analyze higher dimension data. To deal with multivariate regression problems support vector regression (SVR) was used to predict diabetes. In this endeavor, we have used the ensemble approach by using Random Forest to boost up accuracy. We have used an ensemble approach, namely, Random Forest, which combines various Machine Learning methods.

Machine Learning is most widely used to detect diabetes, and they give acceptable outcomes. Decision Tree is the most acknowledged method in the Machine Learning world and has great classification capability. Random Forest is the method that combines many Decision Trees, which gives better results in many aspects. So, in this venture, we used Random Forest to predict diabetes.

5.2   Literature Review

Machine Learning is considered to be a large utilization of Artificial Intelligence that assists the framework to learn automatically furthermore to improve encounters with being modified explicitly. Machine Learning intended to build projects on a framework that has the ability to get information and use this information to learn on their own. Mostly, Machine Learning is a blend of two unique fields that is computer science and mathematics. In this way, Machine Learning becomes quite handy to be depicted by utilizing linear variable-based maths and lattice polynomial maths. Also, its example or conduct can be portrayed by utilizing measurements and likelihood. One of the most beneficial pieces of Machine Learning is that it decreases the exertion of an individual. Machine Learning is divide into three categories: Supervised Learning, Unsupervised Learning, and Reinforcement Learning.

In this manuscript, Supervised Learning is used. In Supervised Learning, the framework for most of the part gets familiar with the target part. The target function is the outflow of the model that characterizes the information. The objective function predicts the estimations of yield variable from huge arrangements of free factors. The arrangement of information is called occasions. Every one of the classes is characterized by some arrangement of attributes. A subset of a considerable number of cases is known as preparation information. So as to get the best objective capacity, the framework gives a training set which is known as theory.

Many researchers from everywhere throughout the world are leading different sorts of inquiries about diabetes utilizing Machine Learning algorithms. A few algorithms that have been utilized are K-Nearest Neighbor (KNN), SVM, Decision Tree, and so on. Iancu *et al.* proposed method to diagnose diabetes using blood glucose (fasting), glucose tolerance, and random blood glucose levels [1]. Lee and Kim proposed a Machine Learning approach to detect diabetes and methods to extract valid features and correct classifiers [2]. As it is discovered that Machine Learning gives better results in diagnosing diabetes, combined data mining and Machine Learning increased immense fame as it can store tremendous informational indexes and can consolidate information from different sorts of assets which helps for study.

Diabetes prediction utilizing a Machine Learning algorithm implies the characterization of diabetes inside a human body by utilizing various kinds of calculations. There are several kinds of Machine Learning algorithms that resemble: Decision Tree, KNN, SVM, Naïve Bayes' Algorithm, Logistic Regression, and Random Forest. Kavakiotis used classical Machine

Learning models to predict diabetes [3]. Polat and Günes used principal component analysis and neuro-fuzzy inference to differentiate diabetes from normal people [4]. Yue used quantum particle swarm optimization and weighted least squares SVM for predicting type 2 diabetes [5]. Duygu and Esin proposed a methodology to detect diabetes using LDA, this work utilizes LDA to reduce dimension and to extract feature [6]. Linear Regression was used by Razavian to build a prediction model for diabetes [7]. Georga proposed a methodology to tackle the multivariate regression problem with the use of SVR, this work focused more on glucose [8]. Ozcift and Gulten proposed a new ensemble procedure that helped a lot boost the accuracy of models [9].

For anticipating diabetes we will be utilizing the Random Forest algorithm. In Random Forest, different sets of Decision Trees are constructed in order to isolate information from data mining, with different applied variable arrays. It randomly creates Decision Trees and merges them to form a "forest". The aim is not to depend on one learning model, but combinations of decision models to enhance accuracy. This technique offers four major advantages over Decision Tree: it can be used for both classification and regression, overfitting is less likely to happen as more Decision Trees are added to the forest, missing values are also easily handled and processed, and categorical values are also represented by the classifier.

Different sorts of Machine Learning algorithms are utilized to analyze the nearness of diabetes in a body. As diagnosis utilizing Machine Learning gives the progressively exact expectation of the ailment so, lately this Machine Learning algorithms have gigantic fame in the diagnosis of diabetes. AI algorithms are additionally used to foresee more sicknesses. For Random Forest calculation, we will actualize in this undertaking to foresee diabetes. Likewise, progressively such calculations can be utilized to foresee the malady. For training and evaluating the model, another thing that needs to be taken care of is dataset. Properly defined and cleaned dataset must be employed for efficient learning [10–13]. Moreover, playing with the dataset comes under machine learning. Depending upon the dataset, the accuracy of algorithms is improved and enhanced. But recent machine learning researches are more focused on enhancing the accuracy, whereas validating the dataset is ignored somewhere [14]. In the present scenario also, dataset importance is quite visible from the fact that every forecasting starts with prediction based on historical dataset [15–19]. Sentiment analysis is considered as widely acceptable branch of computer science, which always results in enhancement of efficiency of prediction model [20]. Moreover current ongoing research in field of computer vision is experiencing drastic changes and improved results quality due to introduction of machine and deep learning [21].

5.3   Proposed Methodology

Figure 5.1 illustrates the proposed methodology of our work.

5.3.1   Data Accommodation

Data accommodation is the initial and first step in the implementation of the Machine Learning model. In this step, data is grasped and cleaned to train the model. Datasets in its raw form are gibberish and do not contain any information. Sometimes, it may contain incorrect values that can harm the accuracy of the model. Datasets sometimes may also contain missing values, and that should be caught and treated before training of the model. Moreover, datasets should be collected from trustworthy sources otherwise it may harm the performance of the model.

Data is categorized into two categories:

- **Qualitative data**: Data which is defined in measurable terms like numbers, values, and quantity
- **Quantitative data**: Data which cannot be measured in numeric terms rather it can only be described.

Basically, this step is further bifurcated into two parts: data collection and data Preparation.

5.3.1.1   Data Collection

Data collection is an effective technique of gathering and inspecting explicit information to offer answers for requests and inspect the results.

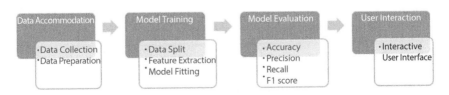

Figure 5.1 Proposed methodology.

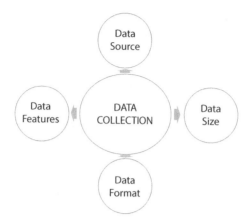

Figure 5.2 Data collection key points.

It generally means the quality and quantity of data, the quality and quantity generally say us the accuracy of the model. Representation of data is the outcome of data collection. In order to use collected data for developing Machine Learning solutions, it should be collected and kept in a way that makes sense for the framework at hand. There is an extent of result for which data is accommodated, for data specialists. Collecting data help us to view past records by which we can analyze data to trace recurring patterns. Such patterns help us to build Machine Learning models that can predict future changes in the trends. Predictive models rely on the data, using which they are trained, for their performance therefore predictive model as good as data from which they are trained. Data collection holds a significant role in modeling. A good collection of data is crucial for developing accurate and high-performance predictive models. Figure 5.2 portrays the key points that should be kept in mind while data collection. The data should be free from error, that is, it should have relevant data and no garbage values. Keeping these things in mind while the collection of data, a reliable model can be built that can utilize Machine Learning calculations to analyze the patterns and capture the nuance of the future.

5.3.1.2   Data Preparation

Data preparation is considered to be the most difficult and hectic task in Machine Learning modeling. The main reason behind that is every dataset is different from each other and specific to projects. This process provides a context in which we can consider the data preparation required for the project. The data is prepared for training in this phase of modeling. In this step, cleaning takes place, that is, error correction, removal of duplicates, normalization, etc. Figure 5.3 illustrates the problems resolved by data preparation. The next part takes place at this phase is the randomization of data. Randomization of data means deleting the order in which we collected the data. Then, visualization of data takes place where we can find out the relation between the variable and class imbalance, explore different kinds of analysis. Then, the dataset is divided into different evaluations and training parts.

The data preparation process can be complicated by issues such as follows:

- Missing records: It is not possible to retrieve all data point for every record. The missing values are represented by NULL or N/A, or sometimes by empty cells, or by special character as "?".
- Outliers: Unexpected values may be encountered while visualizing dataset. Such issues can be a typing error or it is due to unreliable source of dataset.
- Improperly formatted data: Sometimes, data is required in various format or location. To eradicate this issue, it is suggested to consult domain experts.
- Inconsistent values: When data is collected from various sources and lately combined into one dataset, then we can encounter a variation in values of a particular variable.

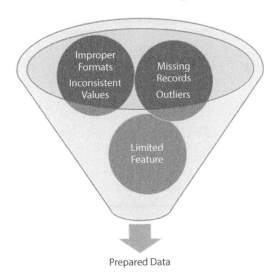

Prepared Data

Figure 5.3 Representation of issues resolved by data preparation.

- Limited or sparse features: Combining different dataset from different source is easy task when there exist a common feature in each dataset. But it becomes tricky when there is no common feature present in given datasets.
- Feature engineering: Sometimes, more data/attributes are required to achieve desired goal or to boost performance of the model. Such extra data/attributes are generated by method called feature engineering.

5.3.2   Model Training

After data collection and preparation, data is ready for analysis purposes. The fundamental motivation behind preparing is to make the training right, as it is important to do so. Figure 5.4 portrays the different classifiers used for training in our proposed work. For conducting training, first of all, we split the dataset into two parts mainly: a training set and a testing set. Often splitting is done in a 70–30 ratio. In which 70% of data is allotted to the training set and 30% of data is allotted to the testing set. Though these splitting ratios are not fixed, it can be adjusted according to the requirement.

Training Dataset
Training sets are the ones which are used to fit and tune the model. The model learns and adjusts their parameters/weights by using this data.

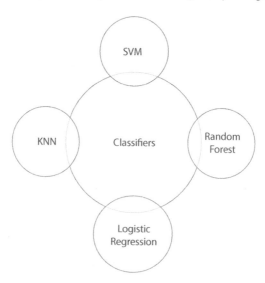

Figure 5.4 Different classifiers.

Testing Sets

This dataset is used to evaluate model performance. It is used only once after the model is completely trained. Purpose of this data is to see how the model will perform on unseen data.

After the split is performed successfully, the dataset is ready for model fitting. But before fitting the model, the target/classifying feature is extracted from the dataset and passed to the classifier. Different classifiers are deployed to perform analysis on the target feature. Some of the classifiers are discussed below.

5.3.2.1   *K Nearest Neighbor Classification Technique*

KNN is a method that is applied for relapse and characterization types issues. This KNN technique commonly stores available state and afterward orders of comparable measures as K (K = separation work). The separation can be estimated by Euclidean, Hamming, Minkowsky, and Manhattan separation for the clear cut worth. We can group an information point by utilizing the KNN separation estimate function. Figure 5.5 represents the pictorial view of KNN algorithm with two classes and new data point. At that point, normal will be utilized as opposed to casting a

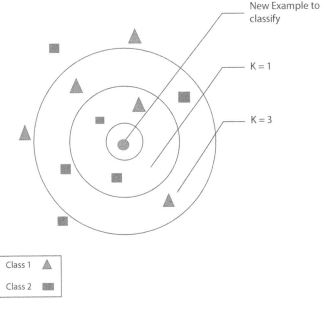

Figure 5.5 KNN algorithm.

vote from the closest neighbors. $(X = X_1, X_2,...,X_K)$ and $(Y = Y_1, Y_2,...,Y_K)$, the condition is given in Equation (5.1)

$$Euclidean = \sqrt{\sum_{i=1}^{k}(x_i - y_i)^2} \qquad (5.1)$$

Here, k = positive. Whole number (its worth can be speculated by watching the dataset).

This estimation of K will be isolated by the limits. This limit additionally separates the two unique classes with two distinct estimations of K. On the off chance that estimation of K = 1, at that point it has a place with the neighbor class which is closest. One of the most testing pieces of KNN strategy is picking the estimation of K. KNN gives exceptional outcomes for financial estimating and information pressure. In any case, the KNN procedure can be costly for the forecast in the ongoing application.

Features of KNN

- KNN uses labeled inputs to detect the outputs of the data points.
- It is based on feature similarity.
- It checks how much a data point is situated near to its neighbor and depending upon similarity with a class, data point is classified into that very class.

KNN Algorithm
STEP 1. #Calculate D(X, X_i)
  'D' - Euclidean distance between every data points.
STEP 2. #Sort Distances "D"
  In ascending order.
STEP 3. #Figure out K points
  For respective k Euclidean distances.
STEP 4. #Calculate K_i
  Data points belonging to the ith class.
STEP 5. If $K_i > K_j$ (where i not equal to j)
  Append X in class i

5.3.2.2 Support Vector Machine

SVMs have a special method of usage compared to other available classifier procedures. SVM method is appreciated much due to their tremendous capacity of dealing with different factors. Each data in SVM is considered as a point in space. When new data arrives, it is first mapped to space. The category of new data is decided by depicting on which side of the separating gap, the new data point will lie. In binary classification, the classification gap can be reckoned as a hyperplane. In case, if more than two classes are there then it can be viewed as a representation of the set of a hyperplane in multi-dimensions. SVM is utilized for grouping and regression of the model. Figure 5.6 represents the feature of SVM classifier.

Features of SVM

- Support Vector: These are the data points with least difference from hyperplane.
- Hyperplane: It is deciding surface, plane, or space which supports huge number of articles containing number of distinct classes.
- Margins: It is generally defined as the distance or difference among multiple linear developed upon the nearest information purposes of two distinct classes. It can also be determined as a perpendicular distance among support vector line.

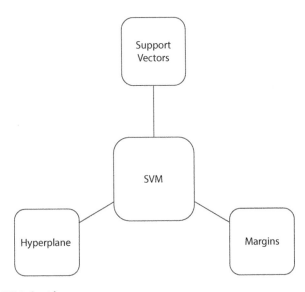

Figure 5.6 SVM classifier.

SVM Algorithm

STEP 1. #Import_packages
      Import Pandas package.

STEP 2. #Import_dataset
      Dataset imported using read.csv() command.

STEP 3. #Spliting_dataset
      Differentiating dataset into training and testing using sklearn.

STEP 4. #Import_SVM_classifier
      Import SVM classifier from predefined library sklearn.

STEP 5. #Model_fitting
      Fit SVM model by utilizing svc() function.

STEP 6. #Predict
      Call predict() using SVM algorithm.

5.3.2.3   Random Forest Algorithm

This technique is utilized for regression, classification issues. It very well may be additionally applied for building a huge number of Decision Tree at the preparation time. It is an asking strategy to enhance the net outcome by adding the irregularity to display. It does not part the hub as opposed to doing this it looks for the best component among the irregular subsets of the highlights.

As it is clearly understood that woods is contained trees and more trees infer forest areas. Random Forest uses the ensemble approach, many classifiers provide their respective expected value then Random Forest with help of weights, and these provided values produce the final output. So, that is how this algorithm works. Ensembling is defined as combining outputs of various classifiers, according to their assigned weighted, to produce one final output. Initially, Random Forest prepares Decision Trees using datasets and then extracts the expected value from every tree. Then, it combines these values according to the assigned weights of respective Decision Trees and produces output. Figure 5.7 visualizes the algorithm and flow of Random Forest classifier. The ensemble approach provides better performance and accuracy rather than a single Decision Tree. It was found with the help of recent work that Random Forest can overcome the problem of overfitting by averaging or consolidating the consequences of various classifiers.

Features of Random Forest:
- It beats up the issue of overfitting.
- It can handle missing data.
- It has less fluctuation than a Decision Tree.

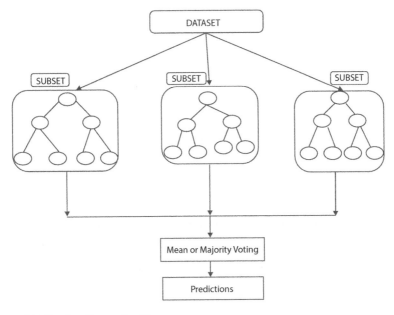

Figure 5.7 Random Forest classifier.

- Truly adaptable and have high precision.
- Scaling of data is not required for Random Forest calculation.

Random Forest utilizes Gini significance or means a diminishing in error values to figure the significance of each element. The Gini list can portray the general logical intensity of the factors. Random Forest is viewed as a particularly accurate and solid procedure taking into account the number of Decision Trees considering provoke at the same time. It does not encounter the impacts of the overfitting. The main reason is considered as it recognizes the normal of the considerable number of expectations, which counterbalances the predispositions.

Random Forest algorithm
STEP 1. #Import packages.
STEP 2. Read dataset using read.csv() command.
STEP 3. #Pre-processing
      Pre-processing of data.
STEP 4. Split the dataset into train dataset for model fitting and test dataset for testing.
STEP 5. #Model_fitting
      Build the Random Forest classifier model.

STEP 6. Prediction using model.
STEP 7. Accuracy check.

5.3.2.4   Logistic Regression

It is the most widely used supervised classification method in Machine Learning. It is a technique to analyze dependent variables and one or more independent variables present in the dataset to predict the outcomes. Independent variables are also called as predictors and dependent variables are called target. It is used to predict categorical values. In binary classification example, it will yield output as either 0 or 1. The Output in Logistic Regression can only predict discrete values for the given set of Inputs. Logistic Regression is commonly used for binary classification problems but it can also be modified for use in multiple classification problems. Logistic Regression predicts the probability of an event by using the sigmoid function. Figure 5.8 shows the sigmoid function graph. The sigmoid function is a scientific capacity that can take any genuine worth and guide it to 0 to 1. Prediction greater than 0.5 is considered to be 1 and lesser than 0.5 are to be 0.

When dealing with binary data, Logistic Regression is proved to be the best algorithm. This also can be used as a performance baseline. Figure 5.9 portrays the algorithm for Logistic Regression classifier. It is quite easy and simple to implement and efficient to train.

Logistic Regression Algorithm
STEP 1. Import module.
STEP 2. Read dataset using read.csv() command.
STEP 3. Train a classifier.

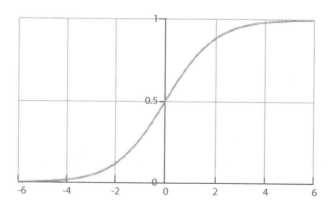

Figure 5.8 Graph of sigmoid function.

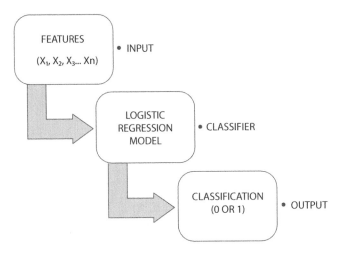

Figure 5.9 Logistic classifier.

STEP 4. Fit model.
STEP 5. Make a prediction using such classifier.

5.3.3 Model Evaluation

If the model performs well on the training set but performs poorly on the testing set, then it is overfitting. That means it can only perform well on the training set but cannot perform on unseen data or real-world data. If the model performs poorly on the training set as well as the testing set, then it is underfitting. The model needs to be trained in more data.

Some evaluation metrics are True Positive, False Positive, True Negative, and False Negative.

True Positive is when people groups who are analyzed as debilitated sick. False Positive is when healthy and fit people groups who are wrongly analyzed and distinguished as wiped out. True Negative is when healthy and fit people groups who are analyzed accurately and distinguished as sound. False Negative is when sick people groups who are wrongly analyzed and recognized as fit and sound.

5.3.4 User Interaction

The user interface of the proposed model is implemented by this module of the proposed methodology. Figure 5.10 illustrates User Interaction model of our work. This user interaction acts as a user interface and the above-stated modules work on the backend of the predictor model. The

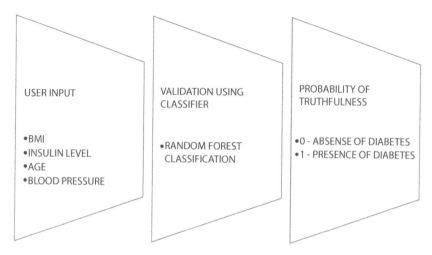

Figure 5.10 User interaction model.

user interface is classified into three subclasses, i.e., user input, validation of using a classifier, and lastly resulting in the output of the classifier.

5.3.4.1   User Inputs

User inputs are basically defined as the input for the classifier model. The performance of the classifier model is tuned and dependents upon user inputs. Therefore, it becomes very important to pass accurate and precise inputs to the model. These inputs should be grammatically correct and properly arranged.

5.3.4.2   Validation Using Classifier Model

Basically, a system with multiple classifier models (in this work, it is Decision Tree), one of the classifiers is selected at the end (in this work it is Random Forest), which acts as the main model for the forecasting or prediction. User input is passed to that model, depending upon its model parameters and hyper-parameters, it results as the degree of truthfulness.

5.3.4.3   Truth Probability

It is basically the output by classifier model. It evaluates the performance of the classifier and gives the result accordingly. For predictor, it tells the degree of truthfulness.

5.4 System Implementation

The aim of this research work is to prepare a predictor model, which can respond to user inputs such as concentration of plasma glucose, blood pressure, skinfold thickness, serum insulin, body mass index (BMI), and person's age, and to compute whether this particular individual is suffering from diabetes or not. For the evaluation purpose, the dataset is provided courtesy of the Pima Indians Diabetes Database which was retrieved from Kaggle.

Figure 5.11 portrays the basic implementation of the predictor model and tools used for implementing the predictor model in Python.

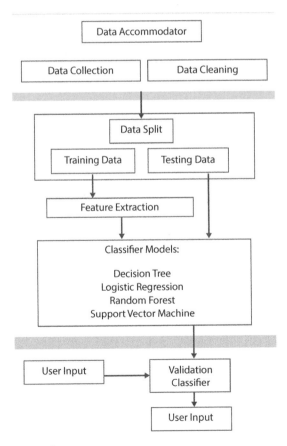

Figure 5.11 System implementation.

Stage 1 of the system comprises of data accommodation. During this phase, the dataset is prepared. Basically, the dataset carries two attributes that are medical predictor variables and target variables, i.e., outcome. Predictor variables are the one that includes the number of pregnancies the patient has had, their BMI, level of insulin they have, their age, and so on. These predictors are collected from trustworthy resources. The label attribute contains the labels whether a particular individual is suffering from diabetes or not. This label plays a vital role in depicting whether the user is suffering from diabetes or not, based on their diagnosis data present in the dataset. This model deals with binary classification problem and target variable are labeled as:

0 – Absence of Diabetes
1 – Presence of Diabetes

The data preparation phase has ensured that the dataset does not contain any null values in either of the attributes. Figure 5.12 shows that there are no null values present in the dataset. Moreover, data preparation procedures are followed to improve the quality of the dataset and enhance the performance of the classifiers by making the dataset in an understandable form for the classifiers.

It is quite visible from Figure 5.13 that there are two attributes, medical predictor variables, and target variable, i.e., outcome. The dataset has nine columns as shown in the figure. The label attribute carries binary values, i.e., 0 or 1.

Stage 2 comprises passing the dataset for model training. At this stage, the dataset is splitted into a training set and testing set. For this purpose,

```
In [20]:  #Check for missing values

          dataset.isnull().sum()

Out[20]:  Pregnancies                 0
          Glucose                     0
          BloodPressure               0
          SkinThickness               0
          Insulin                     0
          BMI                         0
          DiabetesPedigreeFunction    0
          Age                         0
          Outcome                     0
          dtype: int64
```

Figure 5.12 Dataset for model having no null values.

```
In [2]:  #Reading the dataset
         dataset = pd.read_csv('diabetes.csv')
         dataset.head(10)
```

Out[2]:

	Pregnancies	Glucose	BloodPressure	SkinThickness	Insulin	BMI	DiabetesPedigreeFunction	Age	Outcome
0	6	148	72	35	0	33.6	0.627	50	1
1	1	85	66	29	0	26.6	0.351	31	0
2	8	183	64	0	0	23.3	0.672	32	1
3	1	89	66	23	94	28.1	0.167	21	0
4	0	137	40	35	168	43.1	2.288	33	1
5	5	116	74	0	0	25.6	0.201	30	0
6	3	78	50	32	88	31.0	0.248	26	1
7	10	115	0	0	0	35.3	0.134	29	0
8	2	197	70	45	543	30.5	0.158	53	1
9	8	125	96	0	0	0.0	0.232	54	1

Figure 5.13 Dataset for model implementation.

data splitting module is deployed. It is a python code that will convert the main dataset into two CSV files, i.e., train.csv and test.csv.

Figure 5.14 portrays the function in data splitting code.

Once the dataset is bifurcated in training and testing parts, the dataset is ready to be passed to the different classifiers. Distinctive classifiers are employed for our research, such as the Random Forest classifier, SVM classifiers, and Decision Tree classifier. After the model fitting of all the classifiers, the confusion matrix is compared for all the classifiers. The "Accuracy" metric is used to evaluate models. Accuracy is defined as the ratio of correct estimations of records to the total number of records present in the dataset. In our research, Random Forest classifiers have performed extremely well among all. Figure 5.15 portrays there performances.

After building the model, the "accuracy score" of the model has been calculated. The accuracy score of the classifier helps to decide how good this classifier can perform in real-world data. The accuracy score is shown in Figure 5.16.

```
In [26]:  #Splitting dataset

          X = dataset.drop('Outcome', axis=1)
          y = dataset['Outcome']

In [27]:  from sklearn.model_selection import train_test_split

          X_train, X_test, y_train, y_test = train_test_split(X,y, test_size=0.30,
                                                              random_state=27)
```

Figure 5.14 Data splitter module.

```
In [30]:  #Builidng the model using RandomForest Classifier

          from sklearn.ensemble import RandomForestClassifier

          rf = RandomForestClassifier(n_estimators=200)
          rf.fit(X_train, y_train)

Out[30]:  RandomForestClassifier(bootstrap=True, class_weight=None, criterion='gini',
                     max_depth=None, max_features='auto', max_leaf_nodes=None,
                     min_impurity_decrease=0.0, min_impurity_split=None,
                     min_samples_leaf=1, min_samples_split=2,
                     min_weight_fraction_leaf=0.0, n_estimators=200, n_jobs=None,
                     oob_score=False, random_state=None, verbose=0,
                     warm_start=False)

In [31]:  predictions = rf.predict(X_test)
```

Figure 5.15 Building Random Forest model.

```
In [32]:  #Accuracy score for Random Forest Classifier

          from sklearn import metrics

          print("Accuracy_Score =", format(metrics.accuracy_score(y_test, predictions)))

          Accuracy_Score = 0.7559055118110236
```

Figure 5.16 Accuracy score of Random Forest classifier.

Random Forest gives an accuracy score of **0.7559**.

Precision, recall, and F1 score are the numbers used to evaluate the performance of the classifier. In Figure 5.17, the precision, recall, and F1 score for the Random Forest classifier are portrayed. This table is generated by importing the "classification_report" module in the code.

```
In [33]:  #Getting classification report and confusion matrix
          from sklearn.metrics import classification_report, confusion_matrix

          print(confusion_matrix(y_test, predictions))
          print(classification_report(y_test,predictions))

          [[132  30]
           [ 32  60]]
                          precision    recall  f1-score   support

                     0       0.80      0.81      0.81       162
                     1       0.67      0.65      0.66        92

          micro avg         0.76      0.76      0.76       254
          macro avg         0.74      0.73      0.73       254
       weighted avg         0.75      0.76      0.76       254
```

Figure 5.17 Evaluation metrics of Random Forest classifier.

After Random Forest, a Decision Tree model has been trained to perform classification. In python, there is no need to implement classifiers from scratch. Scikit-Learn Library in python provides a great level of abstraction while implementing these classifiers. Scikit-Learn is a great utility tool for building Machine Learning models in python. Figure 5.18 portrays the deployment of Decision Tree classifier and the evaluation of Decision Tree classifier.

After model fitting, evaluation of performance of the Decision Tree on the testing set has been done. Decision Tree gives an accuracy score of **0.7440**. The accuracy score of the Decision Tree classifier is slightly less than the Random Forest classifier. Figure 5.19 gives value precision, recall, and F1 score for a Decision Tree model. The intention of Machine Learning modeling is to build a model that can give precision and recall values as near as possible to 1. However, achieving precision and recall to such an extent is not possible; therefore, the main focus is to achieve optimum values of precision and recall which is measured by the F1 score.

SVM classifier has been deployed and evaluated its performance on test set. The accuracy metric tells the number of rightly classified records from the total number of records available in test data. The more accuracy model will have, the more it will have the capability to deal with real-world data. Figure 5.20 shows the accuracy of the SVM classifier.

SVM gives an accuracy score of **0.6378**. It was found that the SVM classifier was not able to perform well on the test set. Its performance was very

```
In [34]:  #Building the model using DecisionTree Classifier

          from sklearn.tree import DecisionTreeClassifier

          dt = DecisionTreeClassifier()
          dt.fit(X_train, y_train)

Out[34]:  DecisionTreeClassifier(class_weight=None, criterion='gini', max_depth=None,
                      max_features=None, max_leaf_nodes=None,
                      min_impurity_decrease=0.0, min_impurity_split=None,
                      min_samples_leaf=1, min_samples_split=2,
                      min_weight_fraction_leaf=0.0, presort=False, random_state=None,
                      splitter='best')

In [35]:  predictions = dt.predict(X_test)

In [36]:  #Getting the accuracy score for Decision Tree

          from sklearn import metrics

          print("Accuracy Score =", format(metrics.accuracy_score(y_test,predictions)))

          Accuracy Score = 0.7440944881889764
```

Figure 5.18 Performance of Decision Tree classifier.

```
In [37]:  ##Getting classification report and confusion matrix
          from sklearn.metrics import classification_report, confusion_matrix

          print(confusion_matrix(y_test, predictions))
          print(classification_report(y_test,predictions))

          [[128  34]
           [ 31  61]]
                        precision    recall  f1-score   support

                     0       0.81      0.79      0.80       162
                     1       0.64      0.66      0.65        92

             micro avg       0.74      0.74      0.74       254
             macro avg       0.72      0.73      0.72       254
          weighted avg       0.75      0.74      0.74       254
```

Figure 5.19 Evaluation metrics of Decision Tree classifier.

```
In [43]:  #Building the model using Support Vector Machine (SVM)

          from sklearn.svm import SVC

          svc = SVC()
          svc.fit(X_train, y_train)

Out[43]:  SVC(C=1.0, cache_size=200, class_weight=None, coef0=0.0,
              decision_function_shape='ovr', degree=3, gamma='auto_deprecated',
              kernel='rbf', max_iter=-1, probability=False, random_state=None,
              shrinking=True, tol=0.001, verbose=False)

In [44]:  #Predict
          svc_pred = svc.predict(X_test)

In [45]:  #Accuracy score for SVM
          from sklearn import metrics

          print("Accuracy Score =", format(metrics.accuracy_score(y_test, svc_pred)))

          Accuracy Score = 0.6377952755905512
```

Figure 5.20 Performance of SVM classifier.

low as compared to Random Forest. Figure 5.21 shows the evaluation score of the SVM classifier. The precision score tells us how many instances were predicted as 1 out of instances that were actually 1, whereas the recall score tells us out of actual 1's how many of them were predicted as 1. We focus on "precision" where we cannot afford to have "False Positives" in our model. On the other hand, we focus on "recall" where we cannot afford to have "False Negatives" in our model.

In this research, Random Forest classifier performs well among all and has been chosen as a final classifier model.

```
In [46]:  #Getting classification report and confusion matrix
          from sklearn.metrics import classification_report, confusion_matrix

          print(confusion_matrix(y_test, svc_pred))
          print(classification_report(y_test,svc_pred))
```

```
[[162    0]
 [ 92    0]]
                precision    recall  f1-score   support

            0       0.64      1.00      0.78       162
            1       0.00      0.00      0.00        92

   micro avg        0.64      0.64      0.64       254
   macro avg        0.32      0.50      0.39       254
weighted avg        0.41      0.64      0.50       254
```

Figure 5.21 Evaluation metrics of SVM classifier.

5.5   Conclusion

Diabetes is a perilous sickness, which causes many hazardous complications in the body. Hence, it is very crucial to detect as early as possible. How exactly diabetes is predicted by using state-of-the-art Machine Learning is worthy of studying. The health of the heart is affected by diabetes as it damages nerve tissues. In this manuscript, Machine Learning approaches are preferred to detect diabetes, based on certain diagnostic measurements. For this research, we implemented Machine Learning algorithms. The proposed manuscript gives the error-free, accurate, and precise prediction model for identifying the presence and the absence of diabetes. The software used for model development is Python and the tool used to do so is Jupyter Notebook. For the development of our prediction model, we started our endeavor with data accommodation which comprises a collection of data and preparation of data. Then, we performed model fitting which comprises dataset splitting and model training. Lastly, we evaluated three classifiers of Machine Learning based on their accuracy score and confusion matrix. In our research, Random Forest classifier fits best with our dataset.

References

1. Iancu, I., Mota, M., Iancu, E., Method for the analysing of blood glucose dynamics in diabetes mellitus patients, in: *Proceedings of the 2008 IEEE International Conference on Automation, Quality and Testing, Robotics*, Cluj-Napoca, 2008.

2. Lee, B.J. and Kim, J.Y., Identification of type 2 diabetes risk factors using phenotypes consisting of anthropometry and triglycerides based on Machine Learning. *IEEE J. Biomed. Health Inform.*, 20, 39–46, 2016.

3. Kavakiotis, I., Tsave, O., Salifoglou, A., Maglaveras, N., Vlahavas, I., Chouvarda, I., Machine learning and data mining methods in diabetes research. *Comput. Struct. Biotechnol. J.*, 15, 104–116, 2017.

4. Polat, K. and Günes, S., An expert system approach based on principal component analysis and adaptive neuro-fuzzy inference system to diagnosis of diabetes disease. *Digit. Signal Process.*, 17, 702–710, 2007.

5. Yue, C., Xin, L., Kewen, X., Chang, S., An intelligent diagnosis to type 2 diabetes based on QPSO algorithm and WLS-SVM, in: *Proceedings of the 2008 IEEE International Symposium on Intelligent Information Technology Application Workshops*, Washington, DC, 2008.

6. Çalişir, D. and Doğantekin, E., An automatic diabetes diagnosis system based on LDA-wavelet support vector machine classifier. *Expert Syst. Appl.*, 38, 8311–8315, 2011.

7. Razavian, N., Blecker, S., Schmidt, A.M., Smith-McLallen, A., Nigam, S., Sontag, D., Population-level prediction of type 2 diabetes from claims data and analysis of risk factors. *Big Data*, 3, 277–287, 2015.

8. Georga, E., II, Protopappas, V.C., Ardigo, D., Marina, M., Zavaroni, I., Polyzos, D. *et al.*, Multivariate prediction of subcutaneous glucose concentration in type 1 diabetes patients based on support vector regression. *IEEE J. Biomed. Health Inform.*, 17, 71–81, 2013.

9. Ozcift, A. and Gulten, A., Classifier ensemble construction with rotation forest to improve medical diagnosis performance of machine learning algorithms. *Comput. Methods Programs Biomed.*, 104, 443–451, 2011.

10. Yadav, S. and Sharma, N., Homogenous ensemble of time-series models for indian stock market, in: *International Conference on Big Data Analytics*, 2018, December, Springer, Cham, pp. 100–114.

11. Yadav, S. and Sharma, N., Forecasting of Indian stock market using time-series models, in: *Computing and Network Sustainability*, pp. 405–412, Springer, Singapore, 2019.

12. Yadav, S. and Sharma, K.P., Statistical analysis and forecasting models for stock market, in: *2018 First International Conference on Secure Cyber Computing and Communication (ICSCCC)*, 2018, December, IEEE, pp. 117–121.

13. Sultana, N. and Sharma, N., Statistical models for predicting swine flu incidences in India, in: *2018 First international conference on secure cyber computing and communication (ICSCCC)*, 2018, December, IEEE, pp. 134–138.

14. Chauhan, P., Sharma, N., Sikka, G., The emergence of social media data and sentiment analysis in election prediction. *J. Ambient Intell. Hum. Comput.*, 12, 1–27, 2021.

15. Singh, B., Kumar, P., Sharma, N., Sharma, K.P., Sales forecast for Amazon sales with time series modeling, in: *2020 First International Conference on*

Power, Control and Computing Technologies (ICPC2T), 2020, January, IEEE, pp. 38–43.

16. Mahajan, A., Rastogi, A., Sharma, N., Annual rainfall prediction using time series forecasting, in: *Soft Computing: Theories and Applications*, pp. 69–79, Springer, Singapore, 2020.

17. Verma, S. and Sharma, N., Statistical models for predicting chikungunya incidences in India, in: *2018 First International Conference on Secure Cyber Computing and Communication (ICSCCC)*, 2018, December, IEEE, pp. 139–142.

18. Verma, S., Sharma, N., Sharma, K.P., Comparative analysis of time series models for the prediction of conjunctivitis disease. *Proceedings of the International Conference on Advances in Electronics, Electrical & Computational Intelligence (ICAEEC) 2019*. Available at SSRN: https://ssrn.com/abstract=3572573 or http://dx.doi.org/10.2139/ssrn.3572573, 2020.

19. Sultana, N., Sharma, N., Sharma, K.P., Ensemble model based on NNAR and SVR for predicting influenza incidences. *Proceedings of the International Conference on Advances in Electronics, Electrical & Computational Intelligence (ICAEEC) 2019*. Available at SSRN: https://ssrn.com/abstract=3574620 or http://dx.doi.org/10.2139/ssrn.3574620, 2020.

20. Singh, N., Sharma, N., Sharma, A.K., Juneja, A., Sentiment score analysis and topic modelling for gst implementation in India, in: *Soft Computing for Problem Solving*, pp. 243–254, Springer, Singapore, 2019.

21. Sharma, S., Juneja, A., Sharma, N., Using deep convolutional neural network in computer vision for real-world scene classification, in: *2018 IEEE 8th International Advance Computing Conference (IACC)*, 2018, December, IEEE, pp. 284–289.

6

Lung Cancer Detection Using 3D CNN Based on Deep Learning

Siddhant Panda*, Vasudha Chhetri, Vikas Kumar Jaiswal
and Sourabh Yadav

Gautam Buddha University, Greater Noida, Uttar Pradesh, India

Abstract

Lung cancer is perhaps the most common cause of cancer death across the globe, responsible for about 25% of the overall deaths from cancer. According to stats, it accounts for 13% of all new cases of cancer and 19% of deaths worldwide diagnosed with cancer. Lung cancer cannot be completely avoided but via the early diagnosis, and its risk can be reduced which can enhance patients' survival rate. This paper proposes an approach from deep learning, especially 3D CNN, for detection of lung cancer on patient's lung CT scans data. The objective here is to extract the data from the dataset, consisting of low-dose CT scan information, and predict how possibly a patient is suffering from lung cancer using deep learning technique and 3D convolutional neural network. Hopefully, this research will provide all medical research communities with the expertise to understand the CNN concept to make use of it to enhance the overall human healthcare system.

Keywords: Lung cancer, computed tomography (CT) scan, lung nodule, DICOM, deep learning, neural network, convolutional neural network (CNN), 3D convolutional neural network (3D CNN)

6.1 Introduction

Cancer is becoming increasingly common yet hazardous disease out of which lung cancer has been categorized as the deadliest one. According to stats, it accounts for 13% of all new cases of cancer and 19% of deaths

Corresponding author: siddhantpanda786786@gmail.com

Monika Mangla, Nonita Sharma, Poonam Mittal, Vaishali Mehta Wadhwa, Thirunavukkarasu K. and Shahnawaz Khan (eds.) Emerging Technologies for Healthcare: Internet of Things and Deep Learning Models, (157–180) © 2021 Scrivener Publishing LLC

worldwide diagnosed with cancer [1]. According to a report by ICMR, tobacco-related cancers are expected to contribute 3.7 lakhs (27.1 %) of the overall cancer burden in 2020 [2]. In India, lung cancer is one of the six most common cancer types with approx. In addition, 68,000 cases were recorded annually [3]. Lung cancer contributes to 6.9% of all newly diagnosed cases of cancers and 9.3% of all deaths caused by cancer India [1]. In the year 2012, the estimated cumulative death rate for lung cancer was 63,759, making it India's third most common cause of cancer mortality [4].

What makes lung cancer such a deadly disease is its very low 5-year survival rate. With around 15% in developed countries and 5% in developing countries, the 5-year survival rate of lung cancer is quite disappointing. The possible reason behind this low 5-year survival rate is due to the late detection of the nodule. Early detection can improve the chances of survival. But unfortunately by the time lung nodules are detected, it is already late in the process of intervention and good treatment to happen. So, the idea is that if lung cancer is detected early or treated at an early stage, it could significantly increase the survival rate, thus decreasing the death rate from this deadly cancer.

The early diagnosis or detection of the lung nodule is done by various medical imaging techniques such as computed tomography (CT), sputum cytology, chest x-ray, and magnetic resonance imaging (MRI). These lung screening techniques play a major role in locating the lung nodules or pulmonary nodules which are the key indicator or symptoms of the early development of lung cancer.

A lung nodule is a round oval mass of tissues of diameter less than 30 mm (less than 10 mm in diameter for early-stage detection). These nodules can be cancerous or non-cancerous based on which they are classified as benign (non-cancerous) and malignant (cancerous). The benign nodules can show low growth which makes them less harmful whereas the malignant one grows rapidly and can affect other parts and are dangerous to health.

The sole methodology that the paper uses is to look into CT scan data of thousands of patients and predict the chances of them developing or already having lung cancer. To do so, the paper proposes to use deep learning methods more specifically 2D, 3D CNN to build a system technically a classifier which can accurately determine if a person is suffering from lung cancer or not.

So, the common question arises, while there have already been multiple medical techniques available to detect the cancer nodule, why following an automated method for detecting the cancer nodules using ML and DL algorithms? The response lies in the fact that while existing methods of diagnosis involve biopsies such as CT scan, the issue with CT scan is that CT scan data is very enormous. It has millions of pulmonary voxels, but as compared to the size of that CT scan, our nodule is very small. Secondly, the variance in the assessment of radiologists makes the automated process a safer solution. One radiologist may see the nodule and identify it as a benign one but it may be malignant for another. This variation can lead to erroneous cancer detection or late detection of cancer nodules. Therefore, for better accuracy or even comparable accuracy, the automated approach has to be adopted instead of manual interpretation by the radiologists.

Thus, in this paper, extensive use of deep learning techniques are taken into account to solve high-impact medical problems like lung cancer and, more precisely, to utilize 3D CNN when detecting lung cancer in this particular application.

6.2   Literature Review

Deep learning is regarded as a subset of machine learning which is used for the large and complex dataset and high data quality. It uses a neural network which is a processing device whose design was inspired by the design and functionality of the human brain. A neural network can learn from examples which make it different from others and which is very powerful. There is a wide range of deep learning in cognitive psychology, linguistics, philosophy, computer science neurobiology, artificial intelligence, mathematics (optimization, approximation theory), dynamic physics and statistical physics, economics (time series, data mining), and engineering (image/signal processing, robotics control theory).

In the present time, there is a lot of discussion going about the technique of deep learning. It has been considered the most in-demand technology. This high demand among the industry is due to its vast applications domain and its multidisciplinary nature. Even though there is consider to be many techniques that can handle an image data proficiently, CNN will remain the best player. When it comes to image recognition and classification, CNN has proven to be extremely effective. CNN operates on quite a simple methodology. In simple terms, it is just an image that has to be extracted and fed to the CNN architecture. It will classify the image into a certain class. CNN is widely used in the classification of medical images and the performance is also quite impressive. Hence, this research preferred to utilize CNN due to its precision and high performance in image recognition domain to develop a model for the detection and segmentation of lung nodules. CNN itself has variants some of those are AlexNet [5], LeNet [6],

GoogleNet [7], ResNet [8], and VGC Net [9] which further has variants like VGC-16 and VGC-19.

This may not be the first work to be performed in this area. Prior to this, extensive research has been carried out in this field of lung nodule detection using various other machine learning and deep learning approaches. Some previously carried out research include algorithms like ANN, ConvNet, U-Net, and many more. AlakWaa et al. proposed a model that utilizes the U-Net method for the detection of lung cancer on Kaggle data and used trained U-net on LUNA16 data. For several techniques such as watershed, a threshold has been applied in the same research [10]. This throws light on various other CNN architectures such as ResNet, U-Net, and VGG-16. Apart from U-Net, some other architectures of CNN were also there which were capable enough to perform image segmentation. These were SegNet, DenseNet, PixelNet, DecovNet [11–14], and many more. Sasikala et al. proposed a 2D lung nodule detection approach for CNN. This paper proposed an approach using CNN to classify lung tumors as malignant or benign. Extensive use of watershed segmentation can be observed in this work [15]. Tekade and Rajesari came up with a research that has utilised three dataset, LUNA 16, IDRI-DC, and DSB, to improve the efficiency of lung nodule detection and predicting the level of malignancy accurately. The lung segmentation is carried out via U-NET architecture and malignancy level prediction and lung nodule classification is carried out using 3D MULTIPATH VGG [16]. Monkam et al. proposed a CNN approach to detection and classification of pulmonary nodules. Paper provides a comprehensive study of various CNN approaches like 3D G-CNN, U-Net, and few more [17]. Song et al. explored the deep neural network (DNN). The research aims to classify the malignant and benign nodules using convolutional neural network (CNN), DNN, and stacked autoencoder (SAE) which is an unsupervised learning algorithm [18]. For training and evaluating the model, another thing that needs to be taken care of is dataset. Properly defined and cleaned dataset must be employed for efficient learning [19–22]. Moreover, playing with dataset comes under machine learning. Depending upon the dataset, the accuracy of algorithms is improved and enhanced. But recent machine learning researches are more focused on enhancing the accuracy, whereas validating the dataset is ignored somewhere [23]. In the present scenario also, dataset importance is quite visible from the fact that every forecasting starts with prediction based on historical dataset [24–28]. Sentiment analysis is considered a widely acceptable branch of computer science, which always results in the enhancement of the efficiency of prediction model [29]. Moreover, current ongoing research in the field of computer vision is experiencing drastic changes and improved results quality due to the introduction of the machine and deep learning [30].

6.3   Proposed Methodology

6.3.1   Data Handling

The first and foremost step in approaching toward implementing any model is data handling. It is regarded as a foundation in building any model. Here, in this step, the data is extracted from some source, and then, it is been cleaned to remove all form of errors and irregularities. This cleaned data is then fed to be trained on our model. When the data is crude or unprocessed it does not contain any kind of relevant information and hence is of no use. Such data might be erroneous, incomplete, i.e., contains a missing value, is inconsistent or might contain garbage values. Thus, it becomes essentially important to first process this data and then fed to the model for training purpose. Doing so will eventually increase models accuracy.

This phase is generally subdivided into two phases: data gathering and data pre-processing. Below cited Figure 6.1 gives the insight of proposed methodology.

6.3.1.1   Data Gathering

This is an extremely crucial phase before starting on the further process because hoe can things are taken to another level without having any data. This is a systematic process in which data has been collected from various trusted sources. While building a deep learning or any machine learning model, it is important to keep in mind that data collected should be from the trusted sources and the format in which it has been collected.

Figure 6.1 Proposed methodology.

A right way of data gathering or the correct gathered data can help in accessing the previous information which can promote in examining the recurrent trends. Data gatherings have a crucial role in developing high end and high-performance deep learning models which will be able to predict accurately and takes the precise decision.

6.3.1.2 Data Pre-Processing

Pre-processing of data is a method of preparing raw data and making it suitable for the model. While working on a model it is always important to use clean and formatted data. Thus, pre-processing step makes that data formatted for further use. The real data is generally not so organised. Most of the time it may contain bugs, garbage values, missing values, and numerous errors which make data unfit to be feed to the models. Thus, pre-processing step is required to make data on the point to be used in model, hence increasing efficiency. Most of the time pre-processing step works on finding missing value, inconsistent value, and duplicate values.

6.3.2 Data Visualization and Data Split

6.3.2.1 Data Visualization

Often heard concepts are easy to grasp when explained in visual format than in textual format. Data visualization works on the same ideology. Data visualization is presenting data in graphical format. It promotes understanding the significance of data via in simple and easy to understand format. It is nothing just depicting the whole dataset does not matter how humongous it is in a graphical format to find the trends in data and bring really interesting insights to the table.

Many IT and business firms use this technique to get the trends from the previous data generated by the company thus finding insight which can be beneficial for the growth. Many tools can be used for data visualization such as Microsoft Power Bi and Tableau. Many python libraries can be used to generate plots such as Matplotlib, ggplot, seaborn, and plotly.

6.3.2.2 Data Split

In data splitting, the available dataset is split into two portions for the sole purpose of doing cross-validation. While one part is used as a predictive model the other one is utilized to evaluate the performance of the model. Usually, the splitting ratio is 70:30, i.e., 70% for the training and 30% for testing. These splitting ratios can be changed based on the size of dataset and model been used.

- Training Dataset: In this, there is a set of examples used to match the model training parameter finished on the training dataset. It consists of the input vector corresponding to the output vector. Model is trained on the training dataset. Here, it learns and tries to adjust its parameters.
- Test Dataset: It is used to evaluate the model. This dataset is used to provide our model with an unbiased asset that works on the training dataset. Generally, this dataset is never used for training and cross-validating the dataset.

6.3.3   Model Training

6.3.3.1   Training Neural Network

After the pre-processing and normalizing, the dataset removing unnecessary noise apply the 3D CNN on the dataset and training of neural network is done. Here, neural network is trained using 5*5 feature detector in 3D CNN to classify CT scan data cancerously or non-cancerous.

Figure 6.2 gives the insight for preparing 3D CNN.

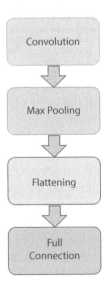

Figure 6.2 Flow chart for preparing 3D CNN.

- Convolution:

$$(f * g)(t) \overset{def}{=} \int_0^\infty f(T)g(t-T)d\tau$$

This feature is a convolution. The convolution is basically a combined integration of the two functions, and it shows you how another function modifies or changes the other's shape and widely used in signal processing or electrical engineering.

When it is about feature detector, it is not just a 3*3 feature detector, in CNN models like AlexNet, it is a 7*7 feature detector, and here we will use a 5*5 feature detector. The feature detector is also known as kernel/filter.

It multiplies each value of the input image with the value of the feature detector. Here, there is element-wise multiplication on these matrices, i.e., input image matrix element-wise multiplication with feature detector matrix.

Use of a feature detector will eventually lead to losing information of image because it will have less value of image and the resulting matrix. But at the same time, the object of the feature detector is to detect those features of the image that are integral. The highest number in the feature map is to fit the pattern.

That is what helps to put out and get rid of all the unnecessary information focusing mainly on main features. As a human, we do not process too much information going into our eyes, at any given time we process terabyte of information and still, we can process it fast as we get rid of unnecessary information and concentrate on exact features which is important to us and that is exactly what the feature map does.

In the image, feature map is looking for some essential features, and then, ultimately the network will determine through its training. It will determine which feature is essential for the types of certain types and certain categories by using different filters.

- Max Pooling:

Pooling in a convolution neural network reduces no parameter therefore avoiding the problem of overfitting in the model. The main advantage of the pooling layer in a CNN is that removing unnecessary information and so that the model could not be able to overfit that information. Even for humans, it is important to see and process necessary features rather than other noise. Same for neural networks, redundant information is discarded, and henceforth, over fitting is avoided. Figure 6.3 gives the insight for max pooling.

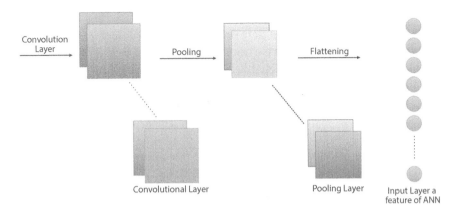

Figure 6.3 Max pooling.

• Flattening:

After the pooling process is finished, it gives the multiple pooled map function. Now, flattening our pooled feature map into a single column and fit this data as input nodes in the artificial neural network. After the flattening stage, there is a long vector that basically inputs data that passes through the artificial neural network which is input values for the ANN. Below cited Figure 6.4 gives the insight for flattening in convolution neural network.

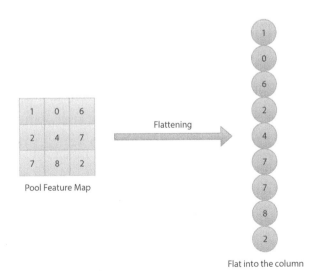

Figure 6.4 Flattening.

- Full Connection:

In this step, an artificial neural network is connected to a convolution neural network. Here, the input layer and fully connected output layer, which thus leads to the fully connected layer in the artificial neural network. It is called it fully connected because they are hidden layers but at the same time, they are more specific types of hidden layers that do not need to be fully connected in artificial neural networks. The whole column or output vector got after the flattening step is moved into the input layer. The artificial neural network combines function into more attributes that even better predict the classes in the model. There are two classes here cancer and non-cancer. Rendering it to a binary performance that is 1 - lung cancer found and 0 - long cancer not found. A prediction is made that 80% of patients have lung cancer and 20% of patients do not have lung cancer, and then, the error is calculated.

6.3.3.2   Model Optimization

Weight is modified and the feature detector matrix is also modified so it can boost next time. Whenever feature detectors are changed, weights are adjusted and this whole process happens again, and again, the errors spread back and on. This is how the network is optimized. This is how a neural network trains the data. But what is important here is that the data goes through the whole from the very beginning to the very end. The error is then measured so that the error is estimated and then propagated again. There is a various method for optimizing weights in the neural network to optimize the model.

- Gradient Descent:

The gradient descent algorithm is the algorithm for iterative optimization. This algorithm is used to find a differential function to the local optimum. To understand this definition, let us consider an analogy, assume a person is at the top of the hill and the goal is to reach the river downside the hill. Ideally, each time the person takes one step down to reach the goal person, it takes a downward step until it reaches the minimum point.

$$J(\Theta_0, \Theta_1) = \frac{1}{2m} \sum_{i=1}^{m} [h_\Theta(x_i) - y_i]^2$$

$$\Theta_j = \Theta_j - \alpha \frac{\partial}{\partial \Theta_j} J(\Theta_0, \Theta_1)$$

Now,

$$\frac{\partial}{\partial\Theta}J_{\Theta} = \frac{\partial}{\partial\Theta}\frac{1}{2m}\sum_{i=1}^{m}[h_{\Theta}(x_i)-y]^2$$

$$= \frac{1}{m}\sum_{i=1}^{m}(h_{\Theta}(x_i)-y)\frac{\partial}{\partial\Theta_j}(\Theta x_i - y)$$

$$= \frac{1}{m}(h_{\Theta}(x_i)-y)x_i$$

Therefore,

$$\Theta_j := \Theta_j - \frac{\alpha}{m}\sum_{i=1}^{m}[(h_{\Theta}(x_i)-y)x_i]$$

where α is learning rate, x_i is the predicted value, y_i true value.

Gradient descent comes under the picture when backpropagation phase is there. Here, measure the error delta and start backpropagation from the final layer for going back to the propagation stage. Measuring error to figure out how many changes is required so to take partial function derivative with respect to Θ.

Here, to add what the change is required with the learning rate. As part of the output, it is going to deduct it from the previous output value from which we get the updated value. If the dataset is very huge, we would not be able to use a reasonable gradient because it takes a lot of time and it will be stuck in the local optima.

- Stochastic Gradient Descent:

When a dataset is a very huge, stochastic gradient descent method is used. Stochastic method deals with a random probability. So, it deals with few instances of the huge dataset, rather than the entire dataset.

1. Input x: Set the corresponding activation a1 for the input layer.
2. Feedforward: For each l = 2,3....,L compute $z^l = w^l a^{l-1} + b^l$ and $a^l = \sigma(z^l)$

3. Output error δ^L : Compute the vector $\delta^L = \nabla_a C \odot \sigma'(z^L)$
4. Back propagate the error: For each l = L-1, L-2,...... compute
   $\delta^l = ((w^{l+1})^T \delta^{l+1}) \odot \sigma'(z^l)$
5. Output: The gradient of the cost function is given by
   $$\frac{\partial C}{\partial w'_{jk}} = a_k^{l-1} \delta_j^l \text{ and } \frac{\partial C}{\partial b'_j} = \delta_j^l$$

The stochastic gradient descent algorithm helps to find the cost function at each iteration for a single example, rather than the sum of the gradients of the cost function of all the examples in the gradient descent.

- Adam Optimizer:

Adam optimizer method of adaptive learning rate optimization is used instead of the stochastic gradient descent. It is essentially a combination of RMSprop and stochastic gradient descent with momentum. It is an adaptive learning rate approach since it measured individual learning rate for different parameters.

Adam optimizer makes use of the first and second gradient moments by which learning rates are adopted for each weight of the neural network. It has an adaptive learning rate approach so Adam optimizer is the best optimizer used to train the 3D CNN in this model.

6.4   Results and Discussion

Figure 6.5 gives the insights of basic system flow implementation, followed while preparing the proposed model. Dataset used in this study is the patient lung CT scan dataset from Kaggle Data Science Bowl (DSB) 2017. This dataset has details taken as low-dose CT images from high-risk patients. DICOM is standardly defined for medical imaging purposes. The header of a DICOM file contains all the necessary information regarding the patient such as patient id, patient's name, slice location, and slice thickness. The dataset contains data for 1,595 patients, which is divided into a training set that contains data of around 12,222 patients and a test set that contains data of 1,333 patients. Every patient's file contains about 100–400 images of 512×512 pixels. For each patient, the data is labeled as 0 and 1: 0 having a non-cancerous nodule (benign) and 1 for cancerous nodule (malignant). Firstly, pre-process CT scan lung cancer data and visualize the pre-processed data. Then, splitting data into train set, validation set, and test set. After splitting the dataset validate on validation set if the model fails, iterate to the splitting of data. Finally, evaluate the model on the test set

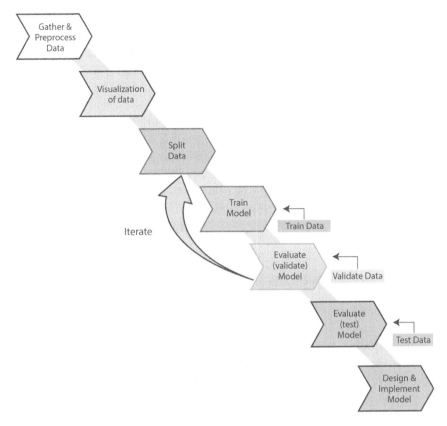

Figure 6.5 Basic flow for system implementation.

and implementation of the final model. In this model, the flatten layer is employed on top of it and followed by two layers that were fully connected. The activation function was relying upon throughout except the last layer where it was Sigmoid, as this is a problem of binary classification. Here, there is the use of Adam as a loss of optimizer and cross-entropy. Here, two classes of cancer and non-cancer are prepared and used for the evaluation purpose. Results are rendered as binary performance, i.e., 1 - lung cancer means not found and 0 - lung cancer as positive for lung cancer.

6.4.1 Gathering and Pre-Processing of Data

6.4.1.1 *Gathering and Handling Data*

First, we are trying to do some data handling that is essentially about loading the dataset and going through each section to catch a few details about our actual data. We have data of 2D slices, which is combined to produce a 3D rendering of the scan. We have CT scans of approximately 1,595 patients in our Kaggle dataset and within the folder of each patient, there is this label data in 0 and 1 which indicates whether it is cancerous(1) or non-cancerous(0). We have a list of patients identified by their unique ids and each has its corresponding label stored in the data frame. These scans are in DICOM format. We used the pydicom library to access those DICOM files or scans. Iterating through the file of each patient we tried figuring more about the label, we got the full path to patient's details. These details are the approx. 200 scans that were rendering to produce 3D scans. These scans contain information regarding patients like patient id, patients name, slice location, and slice thickness.

6.4.1.2   Pre-Processing of Data

Each scan is of size 512 × 512 pixels which quite a large size for a model to deal with. Keeping the scans of the same size and running will become computationally expensive for a model. Thus, reducing the 150 × 150 will be a better approach.

Above quoted image represents the code for setting up the required size of images for image evaluation and model training. Above cited code sets the size of to 150 pixels. Below cited Figure 6.6 and Figure 6.7 gives the insights of code snippet for data pre-processing and results of data pre-processing respectively.

```
In [6]:

import cv2
import numpy as np
import sys

IMG_PX_SIZE = 150

for patient in patients[:1]:
    label = labels_df.get_value(patient, 'cancer')
    path = data_dir + '/' + patient
    slices = [pydicom.read_file(path + '/' + s) for s in os.listdir(path)]
    slices.sort(key = lambda x: int(x.ImagePositionPatient[2]))
    fig = plt.figure()
    for num,each_slice in enumerate(slices[:12]):
        y = fig.add_subplot(3,4,num+1)
        new_img = cv2.resize(np.array(each_slice.pixel_array), (IMG_PX_SIZE,IMG_PX_SIZE))
        y.imshow(new_img, cmap=plt.cm.hot)
    plt.show()
```

Figure 6.6 Code snippet for data pre-processing.

```
C:\Users\sod._.p\Anaconda3\envs\panda\lib\site
t_value is deprecated and will be removed in a
accessors instead
```

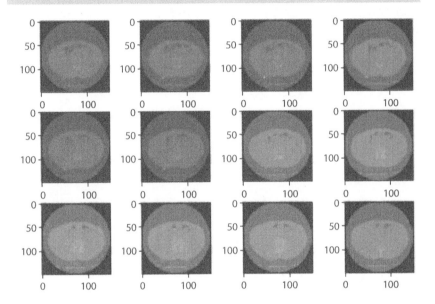

Figure 6.7 Results of data pre-processing.

6.4.2   Data Visualization

The dataset used is made up of numerous CT images of Patient in DICOM format.image has a set of multiple axial slices and a different number of chest cavities of 2D slices. To use the microdicom file viewer these images are in DICOM format. Microdicom lets convert .png, .bmp and .jpg format files in Dicom format. First, the classification is attempted by converting the images to .png format, but due to data loss, the accuracy is not satisfactory. Dicom is the main de-facto file of medical imagery. These files contain a lot of metadata (such as the pixel size, so how long in the real world there is one pixel in every dimension). Using python language we use the pydicom kit in the Jupyter notebook to work with photos in Dicom format. This scan pixel size/coarseness varies from scan to scan (for example, the distance between slices can differ), which can hurt CNN approach results. Below is code to load a scan, which consists of multiple slices.

In CT scans, the measuring unit is the Hounsfield Unit (HU), which is a radiodensity measurement. CT scanners are carefully calibrated to accurately measure this.

Some scanners have cylindrical boundaries for scanning but the output image is square. The pixels falling outside these boundaries get the fixed value −2,000. The first step is to set those values to 0, which corresponds to air at the moment. Below cited Figure 6.8 give the density of common substances on CT.

Substance	HU
Air	−1000
Lung	−500
Fat	−100 to −50
Water	0
CSF	15
Kidney	30
Blood	+30 to +45
Muscle	+10 to +40
Grey matter	+37 to +45
White matter	+20 to +30
Liver	+40 to +60
Soft Tissue, Contrast	+100 to +300
Bone	+700 (cancellous bone) to +3000 (cortical bone)

Figure 6.8 Density of common substances on CT.

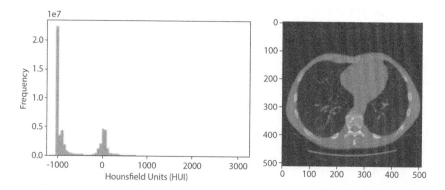

Figure 6.9 Distinguishing between pixels and air.

From the histogram and Figure 6.9, one can see which pixels are air and which are tissue. This would be used for lung segmentation.

6.4.2.1   Resampling

- A scan which has a pixel spacing of [2.5, 0.5, 0.5], indicating that the slice size is 2.5 mm. This could be [1.5, 0.725, 0.725] for a particular search, this may be troublesome for automated analysis (e.g., using ConvNets)
- A common method of addressing this is to resample the complete dataset to some isotropic resolution. If we want to resample anything to 1mm × 1mm × 1 mm pixels we can use 3D convnets without thinking about the invariance of zoom/slice thickness.

6.4.2.2   3D Plotting Scan

- It is helpful to be able to view a scan 3D image for visualization.
- Using marching cubes to create an approximate mesh for our 3D piece, and use matplotlib to plot that.
- Plot function takes up a threshold argument that can use to plot some structures, like all tissue or just the bones.

6.4.2.3   Lung Segmentation

- Segmentation of the lungs to (and usually some tissue around it) reduces space for the problem.
- For the visualization of the 3D image of the CT scan, there is a marching cubes graph which will create an approximated mesh of the 3D CT scan image and that can be plot using matplotlib.
- Here, plot function has a threshold argument which is used to plot certain structures by conveyance of the Hounsfield unit table in Figure 6.6, 400 is a good threshold for showing bones only.
- Here, the segmented lung is plotted by keeping threshold of −320 Hounsfield unit, by determining the label of air around person fill it with 1s in binary image and for every axial slice of scan find largest solid connected component, setting others (like body and air around the person) to 0 for a binary

image. This will eventually fill structures in the lungs by keeping the largest air pocket. Figure 6.10 give the insights bone structure of lungs.

- To visualize structures within the lungs, there is a need to include structures such as lung nodules which are solid, not including the segmented air in the lungs. This segmentation can be failed for some edges due to noise in CT scan and fact there can be air outside the patient which is not connected to air in lungs. Figure 6.11 give the insights of segmented lungs.

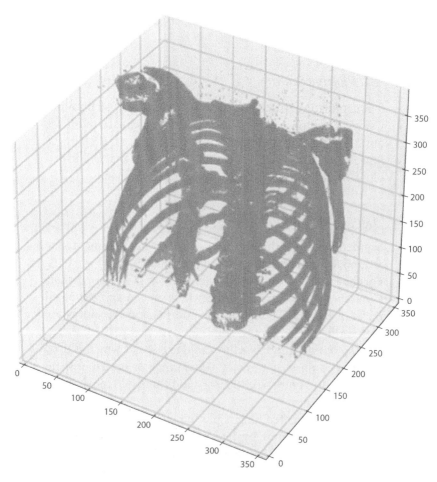

Figure 6.10 Bone structure.

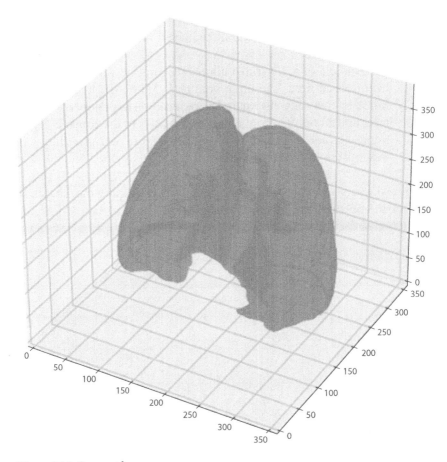

Figure 6.11 Segment lungs.

6.4.3 Training and Testing of Data in 3D Architecture

- After the data pre-processed, and compressed, now, feed it over 3D convolution network.
- In reality, the data is 3D data, not 2D data.
- It uses a 3D CNN as a linear classifier. It uses weighted cross-entropy loss softmax (weight for a label is the reverse of label frequency in the training set) and Adam Optimizer, and the CNNs use ReLU activation and dropout after each convolutionary layer during training. For relatively small Kaggle dataset, the network is shrunken to avoid parameter overload.

- CNN is made up of several convolutionary layers, followed by one or more completely linked layers and finally a layer of production.
- An example of a 3D convolutionary neural network architecture used here. The input volume is 3D on the left, followed by two convolutionary layers, a completely connected layer and an output layer. Filter (or channel) in the convolutionary layers is defined by a volumes. Figure 6.12 give the insights bone structure of lungs.

Figure 6.13 gives the insight of code employed for passing the dataset as an input and obtained model fitting results.

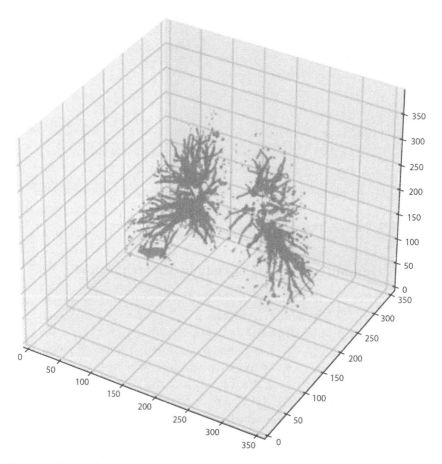

Figure 6.12 Inner lungs structure.

```
        print('Epoch', epoch+1, 'completed out of',hm_epochs,'loss:',epoch_loss)

        correct = tf.equal(tf.argmax(prediction, 1), tf.argmax(y, 1))
        accuracy = tf.reduce_mean(tf.cast(correct, 'float'))

        print('Accuracy:',accuracy.eval({x:[i[0] for i in validation_data], y:[i[1] for i in va
lidation_data]}))

        print('Done. Finishing accuracy:')
        print('Accuracy:',accuracy.eval({x:[i[0] for i in validation_data], y:[i[1] for i in validat
ion_data]}))

        print('fitment percent:',successful_runs/total_runs)

train_neural_network(x)
```

Figure 6.13 Code snippet for training and testing the dataset.

```
WARNING:tensorflow:From C:\Users\sod._.p\Anaconda3\envs\panda\lib\site-
packages\tensorflow_core\python\util\tf_should_use.py:198: initialize_all_variables (from
tensorflow.python.ops.variables) is deprecated and will be removed after 2017-03-02.
Instructions for updating:
Use `tf.global_variables_initializer` instead.
Epoch 1 completed out of 10 loss: 213404249516.0
Accuracy: 0.53
Epoch 2 completed out of 10 loss: 17541067383.625
Accuracy: 0.54
Epoch 3 completed out of 10 loss: 5666365127.125
Accuracy: 0.62
Epoch 4 completed out of 10 loss: 3274527343.2578125
Accuracy: 0.56
Epoch 5 completed out of 10 loss: 2188831547.0625
Accuracy: 0.62
Epoch 6 completed out of 10 loss: 1491843312.03125
Accuracy: 0.64
Epoch 7 completed out of 10 loss: 1027017956.65625
Accuracy: 0.61
Epoch 8 completed out of 10 loss: 674994728.6796875
Accuracy: 0.56
Epoch 9 completed out of 10 loss: 300458776.36821765
Accuracy: 0.58
Epoch 10 completed out of 10 loss: 130963502.74585728
Accuracy: 0.57
Done. Finishing accuracy:
Accuracy: 0.61
fitment percent: 0.9992289899768697
```

Figure 6.14 Training results.

Once the above-cited code is successfully executed following results are obtained. Figure 6.14 gives the insights of the training results obtained.

For testing the proposed model, data of 100 patients are employed and from obtained results claims that 72 patients do not have lung cancer and 28 patients do have lung cancer, as shown in Figure 6.15.

```
In [47]:

labels_df.ix[-100:].cancer.value_counts()
```

```
Out[47]:

0    72
1    28
Name: cancer, dtype: int64
```

Figure 6.15 Final output.

6.5   Conclusion

Lung cancer is the most deadly disease around the globe. Thousands of people lost their lives every year. This is either due to late lung cancer diagnosis or due to insufficient treatment. In this manuscript, we tried to find an optimal way to do early diagnosis. We have used deep CNNs to detect nodules in patients. The model's accuracy turns out to be quite well. Concluding it all, the project will accurately and efficiently predict the probability of a person having lung cancer or not. In this project, we had to apply extensive pre-processing techniques to get the accurate nodules to enhance the accuracy of detection of lung cancer. Our job is to predict % chance of cancer; thus, our model is 61% accurate. In future, we cannot just do early diagnosis but be able to find the exact location of a lung nodule in the lungs.

References

1. Malik, P.S. and Raina, V., Lung cancer: Prevalent trends & emerging concepts. *Indian J. Med. Res., 141*, 1, 5, 2015.
2. Sathishkumar, K., Vaitheeswaran, K., Stephen, S., Sathya, N., Impact of New Standardized Population for Estimating Cancer Incidence in Indian Context-an Analysis from the National Cancer Registry Programme (NCRP). *Asian Pac. J. Cancer Prev.: APJCP, 21*, 2, 371, 2020.
3. Bray, F., Ferlay, J., Soerjomataram, I., Siegel, R.L., Torre, L.A., Jemal, A., Global cancer statistics 2018: GLOBOCAN estimates of incidence and mortality worldwide for 36 cancers in 185 countries. *CA Cancer J. Clin., 68*, 394–424, 2018.
4. Noronha, V., Pinninti, R., Patil, V.M., Joshi, A., Prabhash, K., Lung cancer in the Indian subcontinent. *South Asian J. Cancer, 5*, 3, 95, 2016.
5. Russakovsky, O., Deng, J., Su, H., Krause, J., Satheesh, S., Ma, S., Berg, A.C., Imagenet large scale visual recognition challenge. *Int. J. Comput. Vision, 115*, 3, 211–252, 2015.

6. LeCun, Y., Bottou, L., Bengio, Y., Haffner, P., Gradient-based learning applied to document recognition. *Proc. IEEE*, *86*, 11, 2278–2324, 1998.

7. Szegedy, C., Liu, W., Jia, Y., Sermanet, P., Reed, S., Anguelov, D., Rabinovich, A., Going deeper with convolutions, in: *Proceedings of the IEEE Conference on Computer Vision and Pattern Recognition*, pp. 1–9, 2015.

8. He, K., Zhang, X., Ren, S., Sun, J., Deep residual learning for image recognition, in: *Proceedings of the IEEE Conference on Computer Vision and Pattern Recognition*, pp. 770–778, 2016.

9. Simonyan, K. and Zisserman, A., Very deep convolutional networks for large-scale image recognition. arXiv 1409.1556, 2014.

10. Alakwaa, W., Nassef, M., Badr, A., Lung cancer detection and classification with 3D convolutional neural network (3D-CNN). *Lung Cancer*, *8*, 8, 409, 2017.

11. Badrinarayanan, V., Kendall, A., Cipolla, R., Segnet: A deep convolutional encoder-decoder architecture for image segmentation. *IEEE Trans. Pattern Anal. Mach. Intell.*, *39*, 12, 2481–2495, 2017.

12. Huang, G., Liu, Z., Van Der Maaten, L., Weinberger, K.Q., Densely connected convolutional networks, *2017 IEEE Conference on Computer Vision and Pattern Recognition (CVPR)*, Honolulu, HI, USA, pp. 2261–2269, 2017.

13. Bansal, A., Chen, X., Russell, B., Gupta, A., Ramanan, D., Pixelnet: Towards a general pixel-level architecture. arXiv preprint arXiv:1609.06694, 2016.

14. Noh, H., Hong, S., Han, B., Learning the deconvolution network for semantic segmentation, in: *Proceedings of the IEEE International Conference on Computer Vision*, pp. 1520–1528, 2015.

15. Sasikala, S., Bharathi, M., Sowmiya, B.R., Lung cancer detection and classification using deep CNN. *IJITEE*, *8*, 2S, 2018.

16. Tekade, R. and Rajeswari, K., Lung cancer detection and classification using deep learning, in: *2018 Fourth International Conference on Computing Communication Control and Automation (ICCUBEA)*, 2018, August, IEEE, pp. 1–5.

17. Monkam, P., Qi, S., Ma, H., Gao, W., Yao, Y., Qian, W., Detection and classification of pulmonary nodules using convolutional neural networks: A survey. *IEEE Access*, *7*, 78075–78091, 2019.

18. Song, Q., Zhao, L., Luo, X., Dou, X. Using deep learning for classification of lung nodules on computed tomography images. *J. Healthc. Eng.*, *2017*, 2017.

19. Yadav, S. and Sharma, N., Homogenous ensemble of time-series models for Indian stock market, in: *International Conference on Big Data Analytics*, 2018, December, Springer, Cham, pp. 100–114.

20. Yadav, S. and Sharma, N., Forecasting of Indian stock market using time-series models, in: *Computing and Network Sustainability*, pp. 405–412, Springer, Singapore, 2019.

21. Yadav, S. and Sharma, K.P., Statistical analysis and forecasting models for stock market, in: *2018 First International Conference on Secure Cyber Computing and Communication (ICSCCC)*, 2018, December, IEEE, pp. 117–121.

22. Sultana, N. and Sharma, N., Statistical models for predicting swine flu incidences in India, in: *2018 First International Conference on Secure Cyber Computing and Communication (ICSCCC)*, 2018, December, IEEE, pp. 134–138.

23. Chauhan, P., Sharma, N., Sikka, G., The emergence of social media data and sentiment analysis in election prediction. *J. Ambient Intell. Hum. Comput.*, 1–27, 2020.

24. Singh, B., Kumar, P., Sharma, N., Sharma, K.P., Sales forecast for amazon sales with time series modeling, in: *2020 First International Conference on Power, Control and Computing Technologies (ICPC2T)*, 2020, January, IEEE, pp. 38–43.

25. Mahajan, A., Rastogi, A., Sharma, N., Annual rainfall prediction using time series forecasting, in: *Soft Computing: Theories and Applications*, pp. 69–79, Springer, Singapore, 2020.

26. Verma, S. and Sharma, N., Statistical models for predicting chikungunya incidences in india, in: *2018 First International Conference on Secure Cyber Computing and Communication (ICSCCC)*, 2018, December, IEEE, pp. 139–142.

27. Verma, S., Sharma, N., Sharma, K.P., Comparative analysis of time series models for the prediction of conjunctivitis disease. *Proceedings of the International Conference on Advances in Electronics, Electrical & Computational Intelligence (ICAEEC) 2019*, Available at SSRN: https://ssrn.com/abstract=3572573 or http://dx.doi.org/10.2139/ssrn.3572573, 2020.

28. Sultana, N., Sharma, N., Sharma, K.P., Ensemble model based on NNAR and SVR for predicting influenza incidences. *Proceedings of the International Conference on Advances in Electronics, Electrical & Computational Intelligence (ICAEEC) 2019*. Available at SSRN: https://ssrn.com/abstract=3574620 or http://dx.doi.org/10.2139/ssrn.3574620, 2020.

29. Singh, N., Sharma, N., Sharma, A.K., Juneja, A., Sentiment score analysis and topic modelling for gst implementation in India, in: *Soft Computing for Problem Solving*, pp. 243–254, Springer, Singapore, 2019.

30. Sharma, S., Juneja, A., Sharma, N., Using deep convolutional neural network in computer vision for real-world scene classification, in: *2018 IEEE 8th International Advance Computing Conference (IACC)*, 2018, December, IEEE, pp. 284–289.

7

Pneumonia Detection Using CNN and ANN Based on Deep Learning Approach

Priyanka Bhartiya*, Sourabh Yadav, Ayush Gupta and Divesh Gupta

Gautam Buddha University, Greater Noida, Uttar Pradesh, India

Abstract

Pneumonia is a sort of disease that is caused by microscopic organisms, infections in our one or both lungs. The organisms that are answerable for pneumonia are transmittable that implies it tends to be move from one individual to the next one. Pneumonia remains a top infectious disease and the major cause of childhood death under age 5. Microbiology testing, for example, sputum or endotracheal suction societies, might be dishonestly negative or, as frequently happens in the constantly ventilated patient, can be erroneously sure because of incessant respiratory plot colonization with microorganisms. This manuscript proposes a model that was trained by the convolutional neural network (CNN) and Keras that classify or detect whether the person is suffering from pneumonia or not by chest x-ray images. For classification, binary classification is employed, and datasets are consumed of two classes: normal and pneumonia. The basic idea is to build a CNN that can extract features from chest x-ray images and classifies it. This model can assist to weaken the dependability and understandability challenges regularly confronted when managing clinical symbolism. Additionally, proposed model displays the performance of the model on test data by generating f1Score, precision, and accuracy which make it different from deep learning models.

Keywords: Convolutional layer, neural network, feature detector, pooling filters, RELU, down sampling, flattening, deep learning

*Corresponding author: bhartiyapriyanka123@gmail.com

Monika Mangla, Nonita Sharma, Poonam Mittal, Vaishali Mehta Wadhwa, Thirunavukkarasu K. and Shahnawaz Khan (eds.) Emerging Technologies for Healthcare: Internet of Things and Deep Learning Models, (181–202) © 2021 Scrivener Publishing LLC

7.1   Introduction

Pneumonia is a type of disease that people may face at any time of their lifespan. Microscopic organisms and viruses are the basic reason for the cause of pneumonia. Nearly 200 million population of the world are affected by pneumonia in which 100 million are in adults and around 100 million are under the age of 5. According to WHO, annually, around 4 million immature deaths occur due to air pollution diseases like pneumonia and 1 million deaths occur in the USA. In India, one in three deaths occurs due to pneumonia.

Pneumonia is a type of disease that happens in the lungs and the early diagnosis is the only consideration for a wealthy treatment procedure. Generally, chest x-ray images are utilized for diagnosis purposes. Pneumonia is a higher weight in low-income nations where it is the main source of death, where there is restricted admittance to demonstrative and therapeutic offices.

Sometimes, the diagnosis cannot be very effective for several reasons such that unclear presentation of x-ray images or confused with other diseases. On the other side, study of x-ray images can be monotonous, time taking, and require expert knowledge that may not be available in small cities. So, we need some computer-based diagnosis systems that make work easier for radiologists. Therefore, CAD comes into the picture. CAD stands for computer-aided diagnosis. CAD becomes the most convincing system for the detection of breast cancer, lung cancer detection, pneumonia detection, etc. Based on recent research deep learning, especially convolutional neural network (CNN) becomes the most admired algorithm for image classification. Specialists, researchers, and companies all around the world are turning out deep learning for image classification that can examine 100 of x-ray and CT images. Medical images examine is one of the most prominent research areas for diagnosis and decision making for several infectious diseases. Deep learning can restructure disease diagnosis by building a classification model that has the potential to classify images that is a strenuous task even for experts' radiologist.

This study proposed a model that classifies pneumonia using chest x-ray images. The model is based on a CNN. Few artificial CNNs were prepared to classify several chest x-ray images into two classes, labeled normal and pneumonia. The dataset has been collected from the healthcare department. Training of CNNs involves splitting the dataset into train, test, and validation phase. The training dataset consists of 5,216 chest x-ray images, the test consists of 624 images, and validation consists of 16 images. Machine learning encounters different types of classifiers but in our research, we are using binary classifiers. The binary classifier belongs to two class labels 0 (normal) and 1 (abnormal). In this manuscript, class 0 belongs to normal and 1 belongs to pneumonia patients. We aim to train a deep learning classifier model to classify images that we are feeding as the input images and the classifier are responsible to differentiate the images once our model is trained, and then, we perform the validation and testing part. Our ensemble model arrived with an accuracy of 86% and an F1 score of 86.

7.2   Literature Review

A timely diagnosis of pneumonia is an important factor. Clinical choices have been reviewed as the highest quality for diagnosis, but it is not ideal in all situations. Therefore, in this study, the author developed a CNN classifier model which makes the diagnosis process faster, accurate, and structured. In this project, the author trained the model on 4,099 images, tested on 1,757 images, and the accuracy rate is 96.18% and lastly compared the proposed model with others model [1]. In this research, the author tries to explain the model overfitting. While building a model for the classification of images feature abstraction is performed. These features are slighter sensitive toward orientation and positions of images which leads to a lack of inaccuracy. This paper presents the residual structure to avoid overfitting and dilated convolutional to avoid loss feature problem caused by the depth of the model. In data training, to avoid problem caused by inadequate data, author applied transfer learning method [2]. A convolutional artificial neural network (ANN) model is developed from scratch by extraction feature to classify chest x-ray images whether a person is infected from pneumonia or not. As we know, the collection of a large number of datasets is a strenuous task. So, to overcome this problem, author applied different data augmentation techniques to upgrade accuracy [3]. Detection of pneumonia in children from chest radiograph images by computer-aided diagnosis. This article presents a model framework, titled pneumo-CAD, which was developed to distinguish images [4]. Nowadays, companies, researchers, and specialists all over the world are turning out deep learning and image handling-based frameworks that can deal with maximum numbers of images and CT (computed tomography) to classify pneumonia disease. This study presents a correlation between deep CNNs. The proposed model is tested on 5,856 chest x-ray images and provides validation and training accuracy of more than 96% [5]. While deep learning model architectures are pledge in classifying disease using x-ray images, model based on the state-of-the-art CNN has shown some performance loss due to the shifting of data. Models trained on the dataset gathered from one hospital results in a good performance when tested on the dataset collected from the same hospital but lacks when dataset collected from another hospital. To overcome, this we developed a classifier model with the concept of adversarial optimization [6]. In deep learning model, it is trained by extracting feature on a large amount of dataset. We calculate the functionality of the model and the results shows that pre-trained CNN models utilized supervised learning classifier algorithm can be extremely useful in examining chest X-beam images of pneumonia [7]. Few factors like patient positioning and inspiration depth can change the presentation of chest x-ray images. This article proposed a Mask-RCNN, a deep neural network model that focuses on local features and the global features pixel-wise analysis. This model achieved better performance when evaluated on chest radiography images [8]. The medical treatment might not be appropriate for each case of pneumonia. This case study approach toward Siamese convolutional network (SCN) to distinguish images between three labels first one is the normal condition, second is viral pneumonia, the third label is bacterial pneumonia. SCN gives accuracy of 80.03% and f1 score of 79.59% [9]. This article proposed a classifier model to detect pneumonia disease using dataset chest X-Ray images and labeled optical coherence tomography (OCT). The total dataset presents 5,863 with two labels. K fold method is used to generalize the capacity of the model [10]. In this article, researchers present an idea of the automatic detection of pneumonia by pattern recognition and ultrasound of lung images. Analysis of brightness distribution patterns present in characteristic vectors methodology is to be preferred from the digital ultrasound images. Firstly, detection and elimination of skin, fat, and muscle in an ultrasound frame are to be done and characteristic vectors are examined by the neural network [11]. CNNs were applied to extract features, and models like AlexNet, VGG-16, and VGG-19 were used to appreciate the specific task [12]. CAD helped analysis frameworks indicated the potential for improving demonstrative precision. In this work, researchers build up the computational methodology for pneumonia districts discovery dependent on single-shot identifiers, press and-termination profound convolution neural organizations, increases and perform multiple tasks learning. The approach was assessed with regards to the Radiological Society of North America Pneumonia Detection Challenge, accomplishing perhaps the best outcome in the test [13]. By grouping two CNN named Mask R-CNN and RetinaNet, we can detect the pneumonia disease. For training and evaluating the model, another thing that needs to be taken care of is dataset. Properly defined and cleaned dataset must be employed for efficient learning [14–17]. Moreover, playing with dataset comes under machine learning. Depending upon the dataset, the accuracy of algorithms is improved and enhanced. But recent machine learning researches are more focused on enhancing the accuracy whereas validating the dataset is ignored somewhere [18]. In the present scenario also, dataset importance is quite visible from the fact that every forecasting starts with prediction based on historical dataset [19–23]. Sentiment analysis is considered a widely acceptable branch of computer science, which always results in the enhancement of the efficiency of prediction model [24]. Moreover, current ongoing research in the field of computer vision is experiencing drastic changes and improved results quality due to the introduction of the machine and deep learning [25].

7.3   Proposed Methodology

Figure 7.1 depicts the system architecture of the proposed model.

7.3.1   Data Gathering

7.3.1.1   Data Collection

Data collection is a strategy for collecting data from countless multiple sources. We gather data to build practical machine learning and

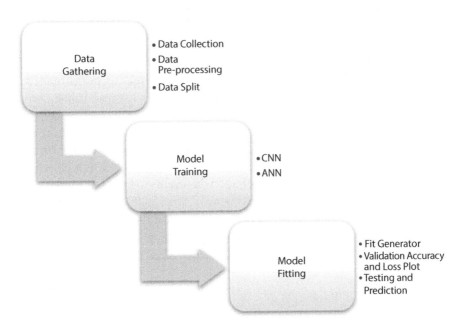

Figure 7.1 Proposed methodology.

artificial intelligence models. It must be collected from the relevant sources. Gathering data helps us to catch documentation of previous occasions so that we can utilize it for data analysis purposes to discover recurring patterns and from those designs and patterns develop predictive models using machine learning algorithms that analyze trends and predict the future. Predictive models perform efficiently when they are built with quality data. So, the high-performance model requires good data collection. The data must be garbage-free and contain structure information. Data can be an assortment of images, text, audios, videos, etc. We can collect fresh information either from different trustworthy sources or use currently available sources to train the model. Data plays a crucial role in artificial intelligence, data analytics, and machine learning. Even with the help of data researchers and big enterprises, it can make better decisions for the future and business. So, without data training of the model is impossible. Without legitimate information, ML models are much the same as bodies without soul.

7.3.1.2   Data Pre-Processing

Data pre-processing is a tool used to prepare raw data and render it suitable for model. Always use clean and structured data when operating on a plan. The phase of pre-processing renders the data ready for further use. Generally, the actual data is not so structured. It which contain bugs, garbage values, missing values, and multiple errors much of the time, making data unfit to feed models. This involves the pre-processing phase to make data about the point to be used in the model, thus increasing performance. Most of the pre-processing steps are used to identify missing value, conflicting value and redundant values.

Image is represented by bunch of pixels everything around us is relatively digital. To represent an image like gray scale image is divided into bunch of pixels and each of these pixels contains a value where 0 represents black and 255 represents white color and whatever is in between represents gray color. Binary system uses digits 0 and 1 where 00000000 is for black and 11111111 for white. This is only for grayscale, and if desire to represent color image, then we need three channels: red, green, and blue (i.e., R, G, and B).

7.3.1.3   Data Split

In data splitting, for the sole purpose of doing cross-validation, the available data set is split into two parts. While one component is used as a predictive model the other is used to measure the model's performance. The dividing ratio normally is 70:30, i.e., 70% for the preparation and 30% for the exam. You may adjust these splitting ratios depending on the size of the dataset and model used.

- *Training Dataset*: In this, a series of examples are used to fit the ended model training parameter on the training dataset. It consists of the vector of input which corresponds to the output vector. Model is derived from data set for the training. Here, it is learning and it is trying to change its parameters.
- *Testing Dataset*: It is used for model evaluation. This data set is used to provide an impartial contribution to our model that operates on the training dataset. This dataset is usually never used for training and data set cross-validation.

7.3.2   Model Training

Libraries play an important role in model training. Python libraries have become the most likely libraries for deep learning applications. It makes our work more trouble-free in visualization, solving a mathematical equation, division of train and test, etc. Libraries used for manufacturing the proposed model are listed in Figure 7.2.

- *NumPy*: NumPy is a library that is available in python to perform scientific computing. It contains a powerful n-dimensional array object. It provides tools for integrating with C, C++, and useful in linear algebra, Fourier transform, and random number capabilities. NumPy can also be used as

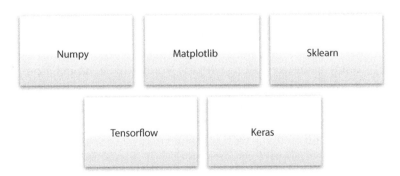

Figure 7.2 Different libraries employed for development of proposed model.

an efficient multi-dimensional container for generic data. NumPy is more preferred over list because it occupies less memory and very fast as compared to the list and found more convenient in working. Some of the basic computational operations of NumPy used in deep learning is to find dimensions of the array whether it is a 1D or 2D array, the byte size of each element, datatypes of the element that are stored in the array, shape, size of an array and performing reshaping and slicing operations. Sine functions, cosine functions, exponential, and logarithmic functions are special functions of NumPy.

- *Matplotlib*: Matplotlib is a free open-source library used for data visualization. It is a python package used for visualization of 2D graphics. Data visualization is the presentation of data in a pictorial or graphical format and allows us to quickly interpret the data and adjust different variables to see their effects. Visualization involves the study of data. Understand what type of data by visualizing in graphical and pictorial format. With the help of matplotlib, we can plot the bar graph, histograms, scatter plot, pie plot, hexagonal bin plot, and area plot. Analysis of data is a process for collecting raw data and transform it into useful information for making decisions by clients. After analysis, we make a document of data like which country percentage of employment youth is increased, decreased, or stable (i.e., no change in percentage). A transform dataset is a process of removing certain fields from the dataset that is not necessary or adding relevant fields to the dataset that are required.

- *Sklearn*: Sklearn is an open-source library which is used to perform machine learning task. An easier and efficient tool for data analysis and data mining. It is developed on NumPy, scipy, and matplotlib library and licensed under BSD. Additionally, the best part of scikit learn is that many tuning parameters along with the wonderful documentation and the support functions.

- *TensorFlow*: TensorFlow is a machine learning framework developed by the google brain team. TensorFlow is an open-source library used for mathematical calculations and provides high-performance models. It is used for machine learning applications such as a neural network. TensorFlow is generally preferred for the large dataset and provides the ease of the process of procuring data, model training, make predictions, and refining future results. Data science teams utilize TensorFlow for object detection and classify images. TensorFlow provides multi-level abstraction and high-level as well as low-level Application programming interfaces. Build on complicated and for beginners difficult to use. Debugging is difficult because of complicated networks. TensorFlow binds together machine learning models and deep learning models with their algorithm and makes them convenient. Airbnb, PayPal, coco-cola, etc., are the companies using TensorFlow.

- *Keras*: Keras is a free, open-source, and user-friendly library used to develop a neural network. It has the capability to run on top of the Theano, TensorFlow, and Microsoft CNTK. It was developed for fast experimentation and architecture is simple to understand which makes it more readable and concise. Keras is recommended for small dataset because of its slow speed, simple networks less frequently need to debug. Keras model has the ability to run on both GPU as well as CPU and provides high-level application programming interfaces. If compared to speed Keras is slower than TensorFlow and PyTorch. While implementing the Keras model, sequential function is used to define the sequence of layers in ANNs. Flatten is used to convert a 2D array into a 1D array. Dense is used to add a new layer of neurons. RELU and softmax are the most preferred activation function to be used in training the model.

7.3.2.1   Training of Convolutional Neural Network

Artificial intelligence in general is the information processing model that tries to the mimic human brain. A CNN is a special type of feed-forward ANN which inspired by the visual cortex. It is a type of neural network that has one or two layers and are utilized for image processing, characterization, and division. While directly feeding images to fully connected neurons, we may face problems. To overcome that problem, we need to perform pre-processing by adding convolutional layers. CNN has layers such as convolution, RELU, pooling, and flattening. Figure 7.3 comprises of CNN layer to overcome overfitting problem.

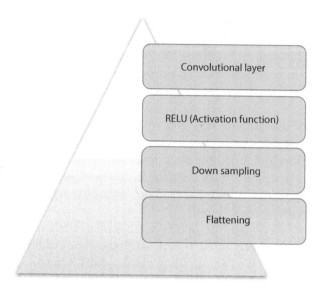

Figure 7.3 CNN layers.

- *Convolutional layer*: This is also known as feature detector or feature extraction. Convolutional uses a kernel matrix to scan a given image and apply filters to obtain a certain effect. Image kernel is a framework used to apply impacts, for example, obscuring, honing, and so forth. Portions are utilized in AI for include extraction to choose the most significant pixels of a picture. Pick pictures at that point apply parts or highlight identifiers to create include maps. Highlight maps are essentially various varieties of the pictures. Along these lines, convolutional is essential since it moderates the spatial connection between pixels.
- *RELU*: RELU stands for rectified linear units. RELU layers are required to add non-linearity in the feature map. It also increases the sparsity of feature maps, i.e., how distributed a feature map is. If the values within the feature map lesser than 0, are set to 0, however, for values greater than 0 then, the same value is passed. The gradient of the RELU does not vanish as we increase x compared to the sigmoid function.
- *Pooling*: Pooling is also known as downsampling. After the convolutional layer, pooling comes into the picture to decrease the dimensions of the feature map. Pooling causes the model to sum up by abstaining from overfitting and

improves computational effectiveness while saving the highlights. It is expected that human face is gone to one side or left side; then without applying the maximum pooling position of face matters, however, on the off chance that we apply max pooling, at that point, moving of the face does not make a difference since it focusses on the most important pixels. In the event that one pixel is moved, the pooling that includes guide will, at present, be the equivalent. Max pooling works by holding the most extreme component reaction inside a given example size in an element map

- *Flattening*: Flattening is a technique of changing all the resultant 2D exhibits started from highlighted pooled maps into a 1D cluster. The included pooled map is a straightening section like structure and is at long last connected with a completely associated layer. The reason behind this is to take care of the information directly to the ANN. In simple words, arrange all the pixels in a straight line. Figure 7.4 incorporates the basic flow of CNN.

7.3.2.2 Training of Artificial Neural Network

Neurons are the basic unit of our brain that is the smallest and individual unit. The brains have over 100 million neurons communicating through electrical and chemical signals. Neurons communicate with each other and help us to see, think, and generate ideas. Human brains learn by connections among these neurons. In human brains, neurons take input from sensory organs such as eyes, ears, and skin, and then, neurons process, interpret, and generate output to take appropriate actions at a given instance. This process is achieved artificially then it is called an ANN.

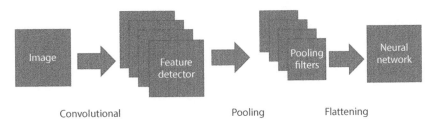

Figure 7.4 CNN basic flow.

Figure 7.5 represents the procedure to train the ANN model which comprises the input layer, hidden layer and, output layer.

- *Single neuron model:* The neurons collect signals from input channels named dendrites, process information in its nucleus, and then generate an output in a long thin branch called an axon.

Algorithm for ANN
STEP 1. Bunch of inputs are P1, P2, and P3.
STEP 2. Bunch of weights are W1, W2, and W3.
STEP 3. Multiply inputs with their respective weights.
STEP 4. Add the bias signal.
STEP 5. Lastly, apply activation function to generate the output.

$$Y = f(P1W1 + P2W2 + P3W3 + b)$$

where $X1 = X2 = X3 =$ Inputs; $W1 = W2 = W3 =$ Weights; $b =$ Bias; $f =$ Activation function.

Figure 7.6 gives the basic idea of working of ANN algorithm. Bias allows us to shift the activation function curve up or down. The number of adjustable parameters is four (i.e., 3 weights and 1 bias). The activation function generates a particular output for a given node based on the input provided.

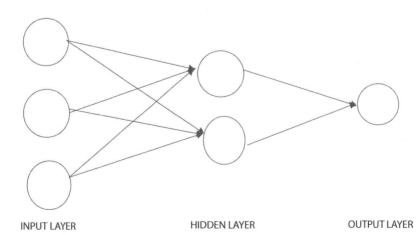

INPUT LAYER   HIDDEN LAYER   OUTPUT LAYER

Figure 7.5 ANN training.

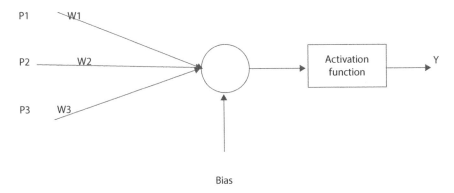

Figure 7.6 ANN working algorithms.

7.3.3   Model Fitting

7.3.3.1   Fit Generator

This part of module is designed for model fitting. It basically takes the training dataset and fit it into the model. There many predefined libraries which can be employed and fit_generator() can be called. This function generally takes multiple arguments such as training dataset, epochs, validation dataset, and callbacks like checkpoints.

7.3.3.2   Validation of Accuracy and Loss Plot

Once the data is fitted in the model, it is validated by passed validation dataset. So, this validation prepares few graphs, i.e., accuracy and loss plot. These plots indicate the accuracy of the fitted model with passed dataset, whereas loss plot indicates about the data points lost during model training.

7.3.3.3   Testing and Prediction

This part of model building requires some testing data. Testing data is passed to the fitted model, and model processes the dataset and results with prediction. After which, confusion matrix is prepared to analyze the results obtained.

- *Confusion Matrix:* Confusion matrix defines how many samples have been classified and misclassified from the given dataset. It is a better way to evaluate the performance of the model.

$$Classification\ Accuracy = \frac{(TP + TN)}{(TP + TN + FP + FN)}$$

$$Misclassification\ rate = \frac{(FP + FN)}{(TP + TN + FP + FN)}$$

$$Precision = \frac{TP}{(TP + FP)}$$

$$Recall = \frac{TP}{(TP + FN)}$$

TP stands for the true positive. Classifier model forecasts true and the actual class is also true.

TN stands for true negative. Classifier model forecasts false and the actual class is also false.

FP stands for false positive. It is a TYPE 1 error in which the classifier model forecasts true but the actual class is false.

FN stands for false negative. It is a TYPE 2 error in which the classifier model forecasts false but the actual class is true.

Key performance indicators: In the confusion matrix, each column indicates a predicted class, and row indicates true class.

7.4 System Implementation

This research proposed to build a classifier model that can classify the given dataset images into two classes: label 0 or label 1. Our dataset consists of chest x-ray images, and with the help of these images, we are trying to predict that a particular person is suffering from pneumonia disease or not. So, 0 label indicates normal and 1 indicates pneumonia. Figure 7.7 comprises of steps involve in system implementation.

7.4.1 Data Gathering, Pre-Processing, and Split

7.4.1.1 Data Gathering

Initially, in proposed model, data gathering is performed. In data gathering, basically, data is collected from different verified sources. The dataset

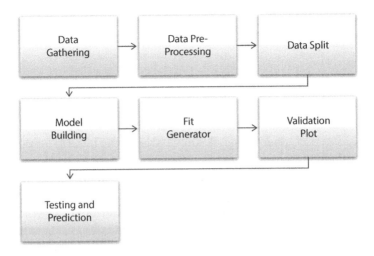

Figure 7.7 System implementation.

should carry clear chest x-ray images. Sometimes, it is difficult to collect large amounts of datasets. So, to solve that problem one can apply the data augmentation algorithm. Then, import the dataset for the training of the classifier.

7.4.1.2   Data Pre-Processing

Next, it involves data pre-processing. In data pre-processing, input dataset containing different images is processed. Each scan is of size 512 × 512 pixels which quite a large size for a model to deal with. Keeping the scans of the same size and running will become computationally expensive for a model. Thus, reducing the 150 × 150 will be a better approach. Figure 7.8

```
import cv2
import numpy as np
import sys

IMG_PX_SIZE = 150

for patient in patients[:1]:
    label = labels_df.get_value(patient, 'pneumonia')
    path = data_dir + '/' + patient
    slices = [pydicom.read_file(path + '/' + s) for s in os.listdir(path)]
    slices.sort(key = lambda x: int(x.ImagePositionPatient[2]))
    fig = plt.figure()
    for num,each_slice in enumerate(slices[:12]):
        y = fig.add_subplot(3,4,num+1)
        new_img = cv2.resize(np.array(each_slice.pixel_array),(IMG_PX_SIZE,IMG_PX_SIZE))
        y.imshow(new_img, cmap=plt.cm.hot)
    plt.show()
```

Figure 7.8 Code snippet for data pre-processing.

cited code helps in processing the images and converting them into gray-scaled images.

7.4.1.3 Data Split

Next step is to split the dataset into training, testing, and validation. Moreover, in this step, remaining images are resized and adjusted if in case any image is not fit model input. Below cited code can be used for data split.

Figure 7.9 represents the data splitting and then applying data augmentation on the training set. The training dataset comprises of maximum numbers of chest x-ray images as compared to the testing and validation part. Once the dataset is separated into the train, test, and validation phase, then for training, we need to perform data augmentation. Data augmentation is a process of transforming images such as rotation, shearing, rescaling, translation, and horizontal. Generally, data augmentation is used to achieve new training samples from the existing one. It increases the generalization of the model. So, data augmentation can be applied on the training, testing, and validation phase.

7.4.2 Model Building

CNN and ANN: Once the dataset pre-processing things are over, dataset is ready for usage. For that, next step involves model building. It is similar to building machine where dataset will be passed as an input. Before passing the dataset directly the model, dataset is passed to CNN builder, performing tasks like feature detection. CNN network makes the dataset ready for artificial neural network. First layer is the convolutional layer; chest x-ray

```
In [5]: train_datagen = ImageDataGenerator(
                        rescale=1./255,
                        validation_split=0.1,
                        shear_range=0.05,
                        horizontal_flip=True,
                        rotation_range=30,
                        zoom_range=0.20,
                        zca_whitening=True,
                        fill_mode="nearest"
                        )

C:\Users\Dell\anaconda3\envs\Tensorflow\lib\site-packages\keras_preprocessing\image\image_data_generator.py:336: UserWarning: T
his ImageDataGenerator specifies `zca_whitening`, which overrides setting of `featurewise_center`.
  warnings.warn('This ImageDataGenerator specifies '

In [6]: validation_datagen = ImageDataGenerator(
                        rescale=1./255,
                        shear_range=0.05,
                        horizontal_flip=True,
                        rotation_range=30,
                        zoom_range=0.20,
                        zca_whitening=True,
                        fill_mode="nearest"
                        )

In [7]: test_datagen = ImageDataGenerator(rescale=1./255)
```

Figure 7.9 Data split.

```
model = Sequential()

model.add(Conv2D(100, kernel_size = (5, 5), activation=activationFunction, input_shape=(img_rows, img_cols, numOfChannels)))
model.add(Dropout(0.1))
model.add(MaxPooling2D(pool_size=(2,2)))

model.add(Conv2D(50, kernel_size=(3,3), activation=activationFunction))
model.add(Dropout(0.1))
model.add(MaxPooling2D(pool_size=(2,2)))

model.add(Conv2D(50, kernel_size=(3,3), activation=activationFunction))
model.add(Dropout(0.1))
model.add(MaxPooling2D(pool_size=(2,2)))

model.add(Flatten())
model.add(Dense(100, activation=activationFunction))
model.add(Dropout(0.1))
model.add(Dense(50, activation=activationFunction))
model.add(Dense(2, activation = 'softmax'))
model.compile(optimizer='adam', loss='binary_crossentropy', metrics=['accuracy'])

return model

model = getModel()
```

Figure 7.10 Model training.

images are initially fed to the feature detector, after that, apply RELU activation function, and next images are handover to the max-pooling layer to figure out the decisive pixels and then to the flattening layer to flatten the pixels, and lastly, model fitting is performed in which dataset is fitted into the prepared model. Figure 7.10 refers to code snippet that is employed for preparing model.

7.4.3   Model Fitting

7.4.3.1   Fit Generator

Next step involved is model fitting. Dataset prepared after performing pre-processing is passed to the model prepared using CNN and ANN layers. Depending upon epochs, passed model is rendered and it results into matrix of accuracy and loss in the data points. Figure 7.11 gives the insights of how fit_generator() is utilized for model fitting.

7.4.3.2   Validation of Accuracy and Loss Plot

Once the model fitting is completed, accuracy and loss plot is prepared. Figures 7.12 and 7.13 give the insights of accuracy and loss plot for the dataset employed for model training and validation.

```
In [11]:  # fit model
          history=model.fit_generator(train_generator,
                                      epochs=epoch,
                                      validation_data=validation_generator,
                                      callbacks=[checkpoint, early_stopping])
```

Figure 7.11 Model fitting.

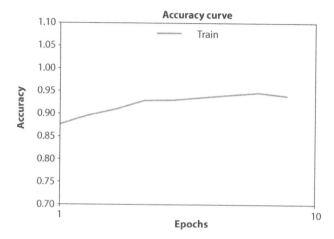

Figure 7.12 Accuracy curve.

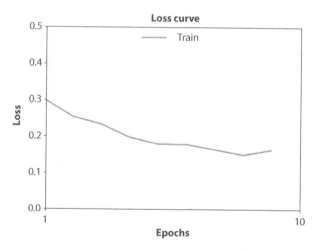

Figure 7.13 Loss curve.

7.4.3.3 Testing and Prediction

Last step involves the testing and prediction based on the prepared model. Figure 7.14 states the accuracy and precision of the trained model. Figure 7.14 shows the accuracy, precision and, f1Score of the implemented model.

```
Accuracy  : 0.8621794871794872
Precision : 0.8619814651368048
f1Score  : 0.8601822682268226
[[177  57]
 [ 29 361]]
```

Figure 7.14 Accuracy and precision matrix.

7.5   Conclusion

Deep learning is most widely used for image classification. In the field of medical, deep learning plays a crucial role in the detection of diseases like lung cancer, pneumonia, and breast cancer. Our project goal is to detect pneumonia from chest x-ray images. So, firstly, we imported all the necessary libraries like TensorFlow, Keras, NumPy, Matplotlib, and Sklearn. Secondly, the dataset is divided into train, test, and validation portion. Comparatively, training dataset portions contain a large amount of data. As to avoid over-fitting, there is a requirement of performing pre-processing before training the neural network. Firstly, perform a feature detector using a convolutional layer for generating different effects like sharpening and blurring and feature map. Secondly, apply RELU activation function for converting values lesser than 0 to 1 and greater than 0 to 1. Now, apply the pooling layer also known as down sampling to decrease the dimension of the feature map by extracting important pixels then perform flattening to convert pixels on the 2D array to 1D, and now, the images are ready to feed to a fully connected ANN.

References

1. Bhatt, R., Yadav, S., Sarvaiya, J.N., Convolutional neural network based chest X-ray image classification for pneumonia diagnosis, in: *International Conference on Emerging Technology Trends in Electronics Communication and Networking*, 2020, February, Springer, Singapore, pp. 254–266.
2. Liang, G. and Zheng, L., A transfer learning method with deep residual network for pediatric pneumonia diagnosis. *Comput. Methods Programs Biomed.*, 187, 104964, 2020.
3. Stephen, O., Sain, M., Maduh, U. J., & Jeong, D. U. An efficient deep learning approach to pneumonia classification in healthcare. *Journal of healthcare engineering*, 1–7, 2019.
4. Oliveira, L.L.G., e Silva, S.A., Ribeiro, L.H.V., de Oliveira, R.M., Coelho, C.J., Andrade, A.L.S., Computer-aided diagnosis in chest radiography for detection of childhood pneumonia. *Int. J. Med. Inf.*, 77, 8, 555–564, 2008.

5. Asnaoui, K.E., Chawki, Y., Idri, A., Automated methods for detection and classification pneumonia based on x-ray images using deep learning, *Electrical, Computer and Communication Technologies (ICECCT)*, IEEE, 1–7. 2020.
6. Janizek, J.D., Erion, G., DeGrave, A.J., Lee, S., II, An adversarial approach for the robust classification of pneumonia from chest radiographs, in: *Proceedings of the ACM Conference on Health, Inference, and Learning*, 2020, April, pp. 69–79.
7. Varshni, D., Thakral, K., Agarwal, L., Nijhawan, R., Mittal, A., Pneumonia detection using CNN based feature extraction, in: *2019 IEEE International Conference on Electrical, Computer and Communication Technologies (ICECCT)*, 2019, February, IEEE, pp. 1–7.
8. Jaiswal, A.K., Tiwari, P., Kumar, S., Gupta, D., Khanna, A., Rodrigues, J.J., Identifying pneumonia in chest X-rays: A deep learning approach. *Measurement*, 145, 511–518, 2019.
9. Prayogo, K. A., Suryadibraya, A., & Young, J. C. Classification of pneumonia from X-ray images using siamese convolutional network. *Telkomnika*, 18, 3, 1302–1309, 2020.
10. Saraiva, A.A., Ferreira, N.M.F., de Sousa, L.L., Costa, N.J.C., Sousa, J.V.M., Santos, D.B.S., Soares, S., Classification of images of childhood pneumonia using convolutional neural networks, in: *Bioimaging*, pp. 112–119, 2019.
11. Correa, M., Zimic, M., Barrientos, F., Barrientos, R., Román-Gonzalez, A., Pajuelo, M.J., Figueroa, D.A., Automatic classification of pediatric pneumonia based on lung ultrasound pattern recognition. *PloS One*, 13, 12, e0206410, 2018.
12. Toğaçar, M., Ergen, B., Cömert, Z., Özyurt, F., A deep feature learning model for pneumonia detection applying a combination of mRMR feature selection and machine learning models. *IRBM*, 41, 4, 212–222, 2020.
13. Gabruseva, T., Poplavskiy, D., Kalinin, A., Deep learning for automatic pneumonia detection, in: *Proceedings of the IEEE/CVF Conference on Computer Vision and Pattern Recognition Workshops*, pp. 350–351, 2020.
14. Gabruseva, T., Poplavskiy, D., Kalinin, A., Deep learning for automatic pneumonia detection, in: *Proceedings of the IEEE/CVF Conference on Computer Vision and Pattern Recognition Workshops*, pp. 350–351, 2020.
15. Yadav, S. and Sharma, N., Homogenous ensemble of time-series models for Indian stock market, in: *International Conference on Big Data Analytics*, Springer, Cham, pp. 100–114, 2018 December.
16. Yadav, S. and Sharma, N., Forecasting of Indian stock market using time-series models, in: *Computing and Network Sustainability*, pp. 405–412, Springer, Singapore, 2019.
17. Yadav, S. and Sharma, K.P., Statistical analysis and forecasting models for stock market, in: *2018 First International Conference on Secure Cyber Computing and Communication (ICSCCC)*, 2018, December, IEEE, pp. 117–121.

18. Sultana, N. and Sharma, N., Statistical models for predicting swine flu incidences in India, in: *2018 First international conference on secure cyber computing and communication (ICSCCC)*, 2018, December, IEEE, pp. 134–138.

19. Chauhan, P., Sharma, N., Sikka, G., The emergence of social media data and sentiment analysis in election prediction. *J. Ambient Intell. Hum. Comput.*, 1, 1–27, 2020.

20. Singh, B., Kumar, P., Sharma, N., Sharma, K.P., Sales forecast for Amazon Sales with time series modeling, in: *2020 First International Conference on Power, Control and Computing Technologies (ICPC2T)*, 2020, January, IEEE, pp. 38–43.

21. Mahajan, A., Rastogi, A., Sharma, N., Annual rainfall prediction using time series forecasting, in: *Soft Computing: Theories and Applications*, pp. 69–79, Springer, Singapore, 2020.

22. Verma, S. and Sharma, N., Statistical models for predicting chikungunya incidences in India, in: *2018 First International Conference on Secure Cyber Computing and Communication (ICSCCC)*, 2018, December, IEEE, pp. 139–142.

23. Verma, S., Sharma, N., Sharma, K.P., Comparative analysis of time series models for the prediction of conjunctivitis disease. Available at SSRN 3572573, 1–8, 2020.

24. Sultana, N., Sharma, N., & Sharma, K. P. Ensemble model based on NNAR and SVR for predicting influenza incidences. Available at SSRN 3574620, *Proceedings of the International Conference on Advances in Electronics, Electrical & Computational Intelligence (ICAEEC)* 2019, 1, 1–9, 2020.

25. Singh, N., Sharma, N., Sharma, A.K., Juneja, A., Sentiment score analysis and topic modelling for gst implementation in India, in: *Soft Computing for Problem Solving*, pp. 243–254, Springer, Singapore, 2019.

26. Sharma, S., Juneja, A., & Sharma, N. Using deep convolutional neural network in computer vision for real-world scene classification. In 2018 *IEEE 8th International Advance Computing Conference (IACC)*, 1, 284-289, IEEE, December, 2018.

8

Personality Prediction and Handwriting Recognition Using Machine Learning

Vishal Patil* and Harsh Mathur

Madhyanchal Professional University, Bhopal, M.P., India

Abstract

Personality analysis and identification of writer depend on handwriting samples that were in place of graphologist online tool that can be useful. Graphology is the subconscious thinking of the human brain that is expressed by handwriting. Machine learning algorithms will be given input as handwritten samples from the dataset. Various features from the handwritten samples have been used to find the pattern and strokes in the given samples by using image processing. An analysis of the personality of the person and identification of the handwriting has been done using various personality traits like baseline, size, zones, and the height of "t" bar. The source of information and handwriting style is difficult to model mathematically. This paper mentions the different features used for the detection of personality traits and describes the writer and algorithms for the identification of the writer. Here, a note has been made of the steps taken to perform the necessary functions using the tool.

Keywords: K-NN, random forest classifier, support vector machine, artificial neural network, personality prediction, handwriting recognition

Motivation

We have been educated to write particularly when we were children in school but it is evident that nobody keeps on writing exactly the way they are taught and everyone's penance seems peculiar. When anyone may write, he or she gradually modifies letter types and sizes according to specific tastes and dislikes. The explanation is that our personalities

---

*Corresponding author: vp0106@gmail.com

Monika Mangla, Nonita Sharma, Poonam Mittal, Vaishali Mehta Wadhwa, Thirunavukkarasu K. and Shahnawaz Khan (eds.) Emerging Technologies for Healthcare: Internet of Things and Deep Learning Models, (203–236) © 2021 Scrivener Publishing LLC

affect how our penance comes after we have been told to write. This is because of the degree of penetration that is the example of our brain research conveyed through pictures on the website, and these images are like our particular DNA. If you get to know the penmanship of a man, you interpret his substance, just as if it was a notable painting or image. Graphology relies on the rule that every person's penmanship has its own specific character, and that is complete due to the personality of the author. It is therefore the essayist's differences from copybooks that enable master graphologists to assess the character and skill of the writer with the highest precision. In reality, graphologists are exceedingly blessed in what they see before them, in stark contrast, in a representative form of the whole mental profile of an author. By ambiguity, psychoanalysts and psychotherapists all over the world must make their conclusions solely dependent on what the client is told about over a period of time. It is ideal for evaluating individuals in all fields of human activity.

For example, it is ideal in the following areas:

1) Recruitment where it is a very useful guide because an experienced graphician can quickly and easily pick the best applicants.
2) Selection in commercial and industrial managers where psychometric testing is used.
3) Corporate preparation in which worker's strengths and limitations, ability, and motivation may be stressed.
4) Safety checks and honesty and integrity assessments.
5) Guidance to occupations or change of course for those looking for jobs.

8.1 Introduction to the System

A person's handwriting is useful for telling much more about the person. By finding patterns in the samples and strokes in the handwriting, personality features can easily find out [13]. This method of finding patterns and strokes is popularly known as graphology [9]. There are many samples of handwritten text that is stored in the database which can be provided as input to the online tool developed using the Django framework. There are two sections provided in the online tool. One is for personality analysis and the second one is handwriting recognition [7]. Handwritten samples consist of English language sentences that can be of cursive writing or simple handwritten without cursive. Hence, personality analysis can be useful in many areas; like for interview selection, we can check whether the person will useful for the company; it can be useful for marriage purpose on matrimonial websites to check whether two persons will be compatible with each other or not by their handwriting. So, online tool can be useful because graphologist takes more time for the analysis if the document size is bigger. So, the effectiveness of the online tool will be more than graphologists and graphologists are more expensive [5]. The strokes in the handwriting samples are beneficial for searching the corresponding features [10].

This paper identifies the method for the personality of the human from the extracted features [11]. The extracted features are baseline, size of the left margin, size of the right margin, spaces between the words, and the height of the bar in character "t" [12]. The routine adopted for deriving the feature from the baseline is called polygonization. Python programming language has been utilized for execution of the task and the Django system has been utilized for the web improvement [13]. For the writer identification process, we have extracted traits from the handwritten samples and can be useful for identifying the person [13]. Writer identification has many useful applications like forensic; hence, it gained immense popularity nowadays. With the extracted features from the handwritten samples specification of the author can be effortlessly by the tool [13]. We have utilized the examples from the IAM dataset for the training and testing of AI calculations like help vector machine irregular forest, K-nearest neighbor counterfeit neural network, and multilayer perceptron.

This paper discusses graphology assisted by machine, i.e., the study of the personality and the distinction of the writer in the light of manually written contents in which the structure is prepared rather than the graphologist to perform the investigation without much human mediation. A certifiable dataset of manually written content examples is maintained and given a few highlights, such as edges, gauge, estimate, and zones. An approximate analysis of the identity of the essayist will be done. You should dissect or someone else's the penmanship. The best way to get an example of "typical" handwriting is to write handwriting [1], which is not exceptionally compiled to be broken. If you receive an example from another person, do not tell them why you need it until they have finished the writing process. They would not recognize their written work along these lines, which may alter their qualities.

Scope: The device uses a handwritten text in the form of a scanned image of an A4-sized user document. The machine then tests the sample characteristics and compares it with the characteristics stored in the database [25]. The personality characteristics are established and the author's identity is seen as a production dependent on similarity.

1. Popular people can use this work to evaluate their handwriting.
2. The device can be hosted online (the architecture of the client server).
3. The device can also be used for other ends or in other fields (employee recruitment)

8.1.1 Assumptions and Limitations

8.1.1.1 Assumptions

The text/scanned image must be in English only. The text should be put on a blank page.

8.1.1.2 Limitations

1. The only Web-App was made. No desktop and mobile apps are available.
2. During the uploading of the samples, continuous Internet connection should be available.

8.1.2 Practical Needs

1. In the provided format, the device takes a picture of handwriting samples (.jpeg and .png).
2. The framework will classify authors from existing data.
3. The system recognizes personality attributes.

8.1.3 Non-Functional Needs

1. The framework should work with Google Chrome, the most popular web browser.
2. The device should be simple to run and navigate.

3. It will, in future, be scalable to a wider user base.
4. The server should be stable and error-tolerant so that during deployment it does not crash.

8.1.4   Specifications for Hardware

1. When the user uploads a picture, the device should have an uninterrupted Internet connection.
2. The scanner that is used to scan upload images should be 1200 dpi.

8.1.5   Specifications for Applications

1. The tool should be compatible with all new browser versions.
2. Proper and continuous network connection should be available for scanned images to be uploaded.
3. Any OS, such as Windows, Mac OSX, and Ubuntu, is supported.

8.1.6   Targets

1) Create an examination tool that can predict personality traits automatically without human intervention.
2) Defining an individual by handwriting.
3) Include a comprehensive report on a specific manuscript sample, including the author's name and the characteristics of personality extracted.

8.1.7   Outcomes

1) The method may take a picture as an input for handwriting analysis.
2) The tool shall include an accurate and specific report showing the writer's personality.
3) The tool can also provide handwritten sample writer information, the details of which are already in the database.
4) The user can use the tool at any time when the user has a continuous Internet connection.
5) The tool shall serve as an alternative to the previous handwriting analysis manual method.

8.2 Literature Survey

8.2.1 Computerized Human Behavior Identification Through Handwriting Samples [5]

The parameters utilized in this paper were the tallness of the bar on the stem of the letter t. The stature shows the fearlessness of the author, i.e., a lower bar demonstrates low confidence/certainty while a higher bar demonstrates the inverse. The method used to calculate the height is template matching. The baseline of the words: the baseline indicates openness, i.e., a forward baseline indicates that the writer is more open to others and is welcoming of judgment whereas a backward baseline means the writer is closed off to the outside world. The method used to calculate the orientation is polyganization method. The pen pressure indicates how much residual anger the writer has, i.e., when the pressure is low it indicates that the writer is a person with little to none residual anger from past experiences, whereas when the pressure is high that means a writer is a person who is angry about something that is either going on in his life or has happened before.

The pen pressure is calculated using the threshold value. At the bottom loop of the letters y and g, the width of the loop indicates a lot of different things but primarily a loop with a large width indicates the writer has a lot of friends/company around him, whereas a small width means the writer has either few or none friends/company. The width of the loop is determined utilizing summed up Hough transform. The inclination of the composing demonstrates a somewhat strange quality, i.e., a left inclination shows that the individual appreciates being separated from everyone else. A vertical slant indicates that the person is very organized and a left slant indicates that the person is very outgoing and trusting of other people. The slant is calculated via template matching. The accuracy of the methods proposed in the paper is as follows, the "t" bar which uses template matching has an accuracy of 85% (manual) and 88% (automated). The baseline which uses the polyganization method has an accuracy of 84% (manual) and 80% (automated). The pen pressure utilizing dark level limit esteem has a precision of 95% (manual) and 95% (automated). The lower part of the letter "y" utilizing summed up though change has a precision of 83% (manual) and 86% (computerized). The inclination of composing utilizing format coordinating has a precision of 82% (manual) and 87% (automated).

8.2.2   Behavior Prediction Through Handwriting Analysis [14]

The parameters used in this paper are the baseline of words; a forward baseline means that the person is an extrovert and likes to open up to other people, and a horizontal baseline means the person is very careful of who is around him and what he does every time. A backward baseline means the person is resentful and is holding back emotions and is introvert as well. Letter slants: slants indicate a variety of things about someone. A left slant means the person is very untrusting of others. A vertical slant indicates a rather balanced person who thinks with his head the whole time and a right slant indicates a very outgoing and trusting person. Pen pressure indicates anger within the person, if a person writes lightly, it means that the person can go through trauma and not reveal any telling signs. A medium writer means someone who is not severely traumatized but needs help now and then, whereas a heavy writer means that the person is very traumatized and is holding back a lot of anger. The formation of f indicates a lot of things but the main thing that the graphologists look at is the creation of the upper body of f which indicates the reaction of the writer upon interference by someone. The formation of i indicates whether the writer is a massive dreamer or a subtle thinker.

The algorithm used in this paper is artificial neural network (ANN) architecture. Methods used for individual parameters The baseline and letter slants are calculated using the polyganization method. The pen pressure is calculated using a grey level threshold value. Lastly, the formations of letter f and i are calculated using template matching. The tool used is Matlab.

8.2.3   Handwriting Sample Analysis for a Finding of Personality Using Machine Learning Algorithms [15]

This paper uses the KNN algorithm with incremental learning. The tool used for this paper is MATLAB. The parameters used by this team are rather very similar to the parameters that have been used in previous papers for eg, baseline, slant, creation of loops, the position of the bar on t, and the only new parameter is the page margin. A wide left page margin tells us that the person is courageous, a wide right margin is someone who is trying to avoid the future and is overall a very reserved person, someone who writes with no margin is Insecure and devotes oneself completely. On the contrary, someone with even margins indicates that the person is well organized and balanced. The methods used for individual parameters are the Polygonization method, Template matching, and Vertical scanning for page margin.

8.2.4   Personality Detection Using Handwriting Analysis [16]

The algorithm used in this paper is ANN. The features that were used after extraction (parameters) are zones, baseline, slant, letter size, pen pressure, word spacing, and margin. Pre-processing is done to enhance the image data as input and also some image features quality is improved for further processing. Image pre-processing includes noise removal, binarization, and normalization. Classification is done using a rule-based system or classifier.

8.2.5   Automatic Predict Personality Based on Structure of Handwriting [17]

The algorithm used in this paper is SVM. The personality of this paper was analyzed based on five features: page margin, word spacing, line spacing, vertical zone domain, and baseline. The process specified in the paper is as follows: We take the handwriting sample and do some pre-processing on it like grayscale, thresholding, noise reduction, and cleanup. After the pre-processing comes to the extraction of features which is followed by classification which itself is followed by measurement and finally the personality is deduced. The paper proposes a mathematical model that is np-complete. The only disadvantage from the paper seems to be that if the database is huge, the time consumed will be a lot which is very inefficient.

8.2.6   Personality Identification Through Handwriting Analysis: A Review [6]

ANNs are used to build the classifiers in this approach. The features used for classifying are baseline, slant, size of alphabets, margins, pen pressure, speed (flow of writing), spacing, zones, print writing and cursive writings, connecting strokes, and signature. The method follows these steps: 1) scanning the images of handwritten text or using a clean dataset with handwritten text and scanning that database; 2) pre-processing of the dataset and images to remove any unwanted noise; 3) extraction of features; and 4) classification using ANN. The accuracy is stated to be more than 90%.

8.2.7   Text Independent Writer Identification Using Convolutional Neural Network [18]

The paper proposes a new way to identify text-independent writers. The paper proposes to use the deep learning approach to end and extract the features via a Convolutional Neural Network (CNN) that are then combined to preserve writer features while minimizing character-specific features. It uses the CNN. JEITA-HP, the fire maker, and the IAM are the datasets used to create the data. Local characteristics and their sub-regions are taken from the overall character pattern. Then, these are combined with three separate methods into global functions. Random samples are used for the creation of several limited CNN sample training patterns. CNN automatically learned the writing features independently of the text by the end-to-end training. The JEITA-HP database achieved an identifying rate of 99.97% for the Japanese manuscript character. It was 92.80% precise when only 50 characters for 100 writers and 91.81% were trained to classify writers by one manuscript English text page.

8.2.8 Writer Identification Using Machine Learning Approaches [19]

The datasets used in this proposed paper are CEDAR-letter, IAM, and many other Arabic language-based datasets. CNN is used for the proposed process. Hidden Markov Models (HMM), Cosine similitude, Gaussian Mixture Model (GMM), Fourier Transformation approach, Euclidean distances, Bayesian classification, and neural networks approaches are the methods used in the literature of authors recognition. Distance-based classification is divided into three categories: classification based on conventional maker learning models and classification based on a deep learning model. Conventional models required adequate samples of training and produced results that were efficient and appropriate to the distance classification. The conventional probabilistic and statistic models are the Bayesian, Hidden Markov (HMM), Gaussian, Mixed Network (NN), Decision Tree Learning (KNN), Support Vector Machine (SVM), and Random Forest. The most common models are the Bayesian model.

8.2.9 Writer Identification from Handwritten Text Lines [20]

This study proposes disconnected content free and programmed writer ID from the pictures in the dataset. The highlights will be tried with KIAN, GMM, and typical thickness discriminant work (NDDF) Bayes classifiers. The proposed highlights were tried on a d 4 arrangement of 100 scholars from the IAM dataset and a right ID pace of 98.76% was accomplished. Two unique arrangements of analyses were done to test the highlights. In the primary investigation, the highlights are tried with various classifiers for assessment of the commitment to improve the distinguishing proof rates. The classifiers utilized in the principal set of distinguishing proof stage are KNN, GMM, and NDDF Bayes classifiers. The second gathering of investigations was intended to break down the exhibition of the highlights concerning the number of journalists in the question. The precision rates are as per the following:

1. For global features with 6 dimensions, KNN yields a 13% rate, GMM yields 27.61, and NDDF yields 35.23%.
2. For Local features with 6 dimensions, KNN yields 32.03%, GMM yields 43.65%, and NDDF yields 56.46%
3. For local features and global features with 30 dimensions, KNN yields 92.43%, GMM yields 92.47%, and NDDF yields 97.1%.

8.3   Theory

8.3.1   Pre-Processing

Pre-processing involves the removal from the sample of impurities. Images have been read with OpenCV and grayscale converted picture can be seen with different methods such as RGB and Grayscale (black color intensity). The photos have been translated into grayscale for review of this paper with a theoretical black value of 256, where 0 represents the black color and 255 represents the white color. The data was subsequently standardized.

A) **Polygonization:** Polygonization is a process to break the aircraft into polygons. This is the vital technique used to detect the benchmark's inclination. In Figure 8.1 polygonization process for the given text is performed.

B) **Thresholding Algorithm:** This image survey is a kind of image division objects by turning grayscale images into parallel images as shown in the Figure 8.2. This image study is a form of division of pictures by turning grey images into parallel pictures [8]. Python OpenCv library for thresholding images is used. When we use all the 0 to 255 values for the test, a

Figure 8.1 Polygonization [11].

Original Image

Result

Figure 8.2 Thresholding [6].

model can be very slow and overly large. Therefore, we have used global thresholds to improve our model's accuracy.

C) Binarization Algorithm: This image analytical algorithm is a kind of picture division that questions by turning grey images into double images. Figure 8.3 shows the process of binarization.

D) Gray scaling: It is a process that transforms a picture that has red, green, and blue channels into a light intensity representation as shown in Figure 8.4. The image output is 1 tube. Each pixel is 0 to 255, 0 is black, and 255 is white [21] as shown in the Figure 8.4.

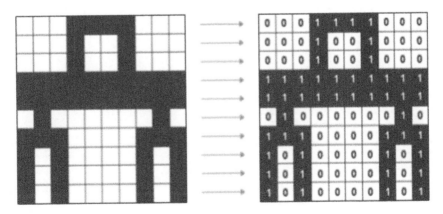

Figure 8.3 Binarization [24].

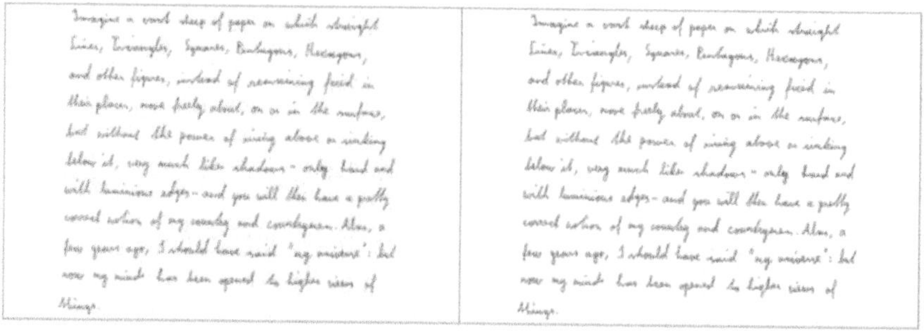

Figure 8.4 Gray scaling [10].

E) Noise Reduction: When minimizing noise, we have glued the picture taken as an input using the Gaussian blurs technique [22]. Most of the denoising approaches are used to minimize noise from blurring and non-local means. We used the denoising method for the removal of noise completely. Figure 8.5 shows the process of noise reduction.

F) Image Inversion: We have inverted the image in Image Inversion so that the inverted pixel strength transforms black to white pixels for background isolation from the text [23]. Figure 8.6 shows the process of image inversion.

G) Image Dilation: In dilating pictures, we extended the pictures to grey images and finished grids for the first time. It uses an element structuring the shapes in the input image to be examined and expanded [24]. Since we are using handwritten images, some text is typically less noticeable. Besides, the images may still contain a few remaining noises. Therefore, first, we used an erosion approach to solve this problem. Figure 8.7 shows the process of image dilation.

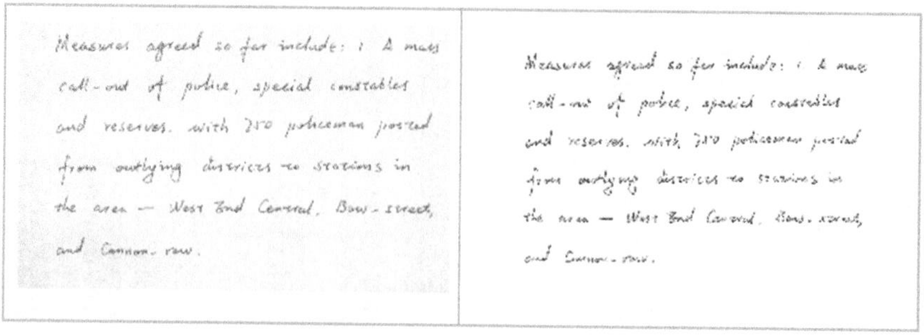

Figure 8.5 Noise reduction [10].

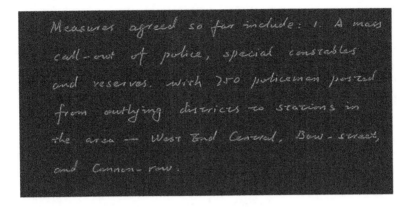

Figure 8.6 Image inversion [10].

Figure 8.7 Image dilation [10].

8.3.2   Personality Analysis

Segmentation (Separation): Several investigations of examination show that division is vital to extricate the right attributes [27]. For instance, a danger open-minded individual should have the ideal medium-size content, for example from 2 to 5 mm. Segmenting will decide the satisfactory size and utilize the equivalent for the ID of character in the penmanship messages. It assists in estimating the character's size.

Thresholding Algorithm: In this technique, the division is performed by changing dark scale pictures into nonexistent pictures [3]. It works successfully for pictures with elevated levels of difference. Hence, we can utilize this calculation for a transcribed example on a white sheet utilizing dark ink pen [3].

Hamming Distance: The Hamming distance between two one-dimensional arrays of the same length is the number of places where each element is different in a sequence of the two arrays. This is the least substitute for both arrays to be equal [4].

Consider two arrays of one dimension A and B. Let ham be the distance from the hamming.

$$Ham = 0 \; Ham$$

For each a, b in arrays A and B: If a! = b: = b:

$$Ham = Ham+1$$

Projection Profile: It is used to display a 2D image in a 1D image. They have two types: vertical and horizontal. With the support of projection profiles, the handwriting density distribution can be interpreted [27]. The horizontal projection profile involves calculating the number of foreground pixels on each pixel column of the image, while the number of foreground pixels per row is calculated on the vertical projection profile [8].

8.3.3   Personality Characteristics

Baseline: The baseline is a kind of line that lies on the penmanship. It indicates the inclination of penance. It is possible to obtain correct information about the essayist by using the norm [26]. There are three groups of the norm based on their text propensity as shown in Table 8.1. To discover a bookline pattern, the text line is turned around to cover a number of points and each has a flat projection profile. The edge is the one with the intense projection profile.

Letter Slant: The characteristics are solved based on the tendency of the letters. The pattern is observed using the horizontal projection profile of

Table 8.1 Personality characteristics for corresponding baseline level [5].

Baseline	Characteristics
Ascending	Optimistic
Level	Balanced
Descending	Pessimistic

Table 8.2 Personality characteristics for writing slant [5].

Writing slant	Personality characteristics
Left slant	Enjoy alone life: cannot express emotions
Vertical slant	Judgment rules: ruled by head, not heart
Right slant	Extrovert: emotional highs and lows

each text line. In order to locate the letter of a text line, a text line picture is inclined for a scope of points and a vertical projection profile is defined for each. The point with the largest projection profile are considered for analysis purpose. Attributes for the composing incline appear in Table 8.2.

Height of t bar: The lower case letter "t" indicates the author's exact detail. In several ways, the letter "t" can be written. There are various methods to make the bar t, each showing a particular characteristic [5]. We provide templates for the identification of t that fit the respective personalities [7]. The determination of the necessary characteristic requires measurement of the sample distance from the dataset. A maximum similarity with the minimum distance can be defined. Table 8.3 shows personality traits for the corresponding position of "t" bar [5].

Space Between Words: The space between words helps distinguish features such as the writer's proximity to other people and the intellect [6].

Margins: The margin is determined by the handwritten text structure. When handwritten text is written on an empty white paper, the writer leaves room for a new line [28]. If you see a handwritten page, you can find space on the left. Margin may describe intellect, adjustment, truth, and speed [6].

8.3.4   Writer Identification

Pre-processing Contours: A contour is a curve which joins all points along the border which are continuous with the same color or intensity. They help to analyze shapes, detect, and recognize image objects.

Image Dilation: Dilation is a mathematical morphology operator. It is used in binary images to stretch the area boundaries of the front pixels. This leads to wider areas of the front pixels and smaller gaps.

Table 8.3 Position of t bar and traits.

Position of t bar	Personality trait
Crossed very high (not above the stem, but in a very high region)	High confidence: This uncovers certainty, aspiration, and the capacity to prepare, significant standards, high close to home desires, and a general decent mental self-portrait. This is the key to individual favorable luck.
Crossed above the middle zone but not at the loop	Moderate confidence: This individual is handy. This is a positive quality and basic among effective individuals.
Crossed very low on the stem	Low confidence: This individual apprehensions disappointment and opposes change. He regularly stays in awful circumstances and connections for a long time and discovers blemishes with himself. He is seldom fruitful enough in his own eyes notwithstanding his achievements.
Crossed above the stem	Dreamer: This persons goals and Dreamer: This persons goals and Dreamer: This persons goals and Visionary: These people's objectives and dreams put some distance between the real world. These individuals regularly talk about what they will do as opposed to doing it.

Table 8.4 shows the personality traits for the corresponding space between words. It shows the personality traits based on the spacing between the words.

Table 8.5 shows the personality traits for the person by considering the margin size of the letters with respect to the page size.

Table 8.4 Personality traits for corresponding space between words [6].

Space between words	Personality trait
Wide Spacing	The individual shows qualities of separation, great taste, freedom, restrictiveness, segregation, depression, pretentiousness, and pride.
Narrow Spacing	The individual has warmth, compassion, gregariousness, obstructiveness, helpless taste, and in-capacity to be distant from everyone else.

Table 8.5 Personality traits for corresponding space between words [6].

Margin size	Trait
Less than 10% of the width of the paper	Sense of saving economy, caution, shyness, introversion, attachment to family. Bad taste, selfish and possessive conduct, problematic social contact.
15% of the width of the paper	Equilibrium, good esthetic sense, normal and simple life. Conscious order, harmony in tendencies. Excessive self-control
15% to 25% of the width of the paper	Generosity and extraversion, sociability, the amplitude of criteria, initiative, and decision, exceeds his budget, ostentation, scarce reflection
Over 25% of the width of the paper	Ignorance of the sense of the measures, chaos, extroversion, exhibitionism. Generosity, audacity, Waste of money, time and energy.

Zone Detection: A handwritten text line is divided into three areas: the higher, middle, and lower regions. In Figure 8.8 the image is divided in to the zones. This technique was described in [10]. In the Figure 8.9 the process of zone detection for the given text is explained.

Circle Hough Transform: It is a technique used to detect circles in an image during image processing. Figure 8.10 indicates the word detection using contours. This method is a specialization of Hough transform to discover circular objects in an image. Figure 8.11 shows the detection of enclosed space using Hough circle transform.

8.3.5 Features Used

Mean Space Between Words: When a writer writes a letter, there are gaps between sentences. These areas are a significant feature in the identification of a writer. The approach used to locate the spaces is by word detection by means of image threshold, picture dilation, and contour detection. After

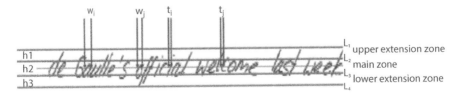

Figure 8.8 Division of the image into zones [11].

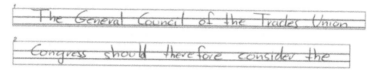

Figure 8.9 Zones detected in handwritten text [5].

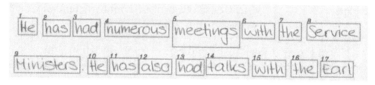

Figure 8.10 Word detection using contours [5].

worked out by the Ohiofs

Figure 8.11 Detected enclosed space using Hough circle transform [5].

the word contours is found, a space is determined between successive contours and the mean of all values is determined [30].

Mean Area of Enclosed Space: For each text line, the area of enclosed handwriting spaces is determined. The spaces included are spaces which appear in letters such as a, b, d, and e. The Hough circle transform here is used for circle detection [29].

Height of Each Zone: Here, the middle zone and lower zone are measured and used as a feature in the training model by means of zone detection height in the upper zone.

Height of Text Line: The height of a handwritten text line is measured using contour detection.

8.4 Algorithm To Be Used

Artificial Neural Network
Perceptron: The basic building block of an ANN is perceptron, as shown in Figure 8.12.

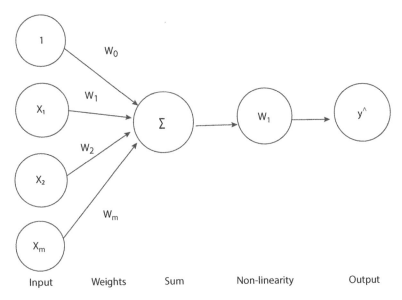

Figure 8.12 The perceptron network [8].

In the above diagram x_1, x_2, and x_3 are the inputs for the perceptron and w_1, w_2, and w_3 represents the weights along with the inputs whereas "w_0" represents the bias value which is 1. The summation adds the input by multiplying with the values of the weights shown in the above-given formula. In the given formula, "y" represents the output for the given formula; "g" is a non-linear activation function.

Artificial Neural Network
The ANN with an input layer, two hidden layers, and the output layer [2]. We can have more than two hidden layers present in the neural network. An integral part of the deep learning process lies in ANNs. It is inspired by the human brain's neural structure. According to AI LabPage, ANNs are "complex computer code written with the number of simple, highly interconnected processing elements which is inspired by human biological brain structure for simulating human brain working and processing data (Information) models."

Training of Artificial Neural Network Algorithm:

Step 1: Initialize weights and learning rate (take some small random values).
Step 2: Perform Steps 2–9 when stopping condition is false.
Step 3: Perform Steps 3–8 for training pair.

Feed forward phase:

Step 4: Each input unit receives input signal xi and sends it to the hidden unit (i = 1 to n).

Step 5: Each hidden unit Zj (j = 1 to p) sums its weighted input signals to calculate net input:

$$Z_{inj} = v_{0j} + \sum_{i=1}^{n} x_i v_{ij}$$

Step 6: Calculate output of the hidden unit by applying its activation functions over Z_{inj} (binary or bipolar sigmoidal activation function).

$Z_j = f(Z_{inj})$ and send the output signal from the hidden unit to the input of output layer units.

Step 7: For each output unit y_k (k = 1 to m), calculate the net input:

$$y_{ink} = W_{0k} + \sum_{j=1}^{p} Z_j W_{jk}$$

and apply the activation function to compute output signal

$$y_k = f(y_{ink})$$

Back-propagation of error (Phase ll):

Step 8: Each output unit y_k (k=1 to m) receives a target pattern corresponding to the input training pattern and computes the error correction term:

$$\partial k = (t_k - y_k) f'(y_{ink})$$

$$\partial$$

The derivative $f'(y_{ink})$ can be calculated and On the basis of the calculated error correction term, update the change in weights and bias:

$$\Delta w_{jk} = \alpha \, \partial_k \, z_j \qquad\qquad \Delta w_{0k} = \alpha \, \partial_k$$

Also, send ∂_k to the hidden layer backwards.

Step 9: Each hidden unit (zj, j = 1 to p) sums its delta inputs from the output units:

$$\partial_{inj} \sum_{k=1}^{m} \partial_k w_j k$$

The term ∂_{inj} gets multiplied with the derivative of $f(Z_{inj})$ to calculate the error term:

$$\partial j = \partial\ inj\ f'(z_{inj})$$

The derivative $f'(z_{inj})$ can be calculated and depending on whether binary or bipolar sigmoidal function is used. On the basis of the calculated ∂j,

Step 10: Update the change in weights and bias.
Step 11: Check for the stopping condition after several epochs when the actual output is equal to the predicted output.

ANNs define a particular class of machine-learning algorithms to obtain their knowledge by using useful patterns. The ANNs are approximating functions, mapping inputs and are made up of several processing units associated, called neurons. However, when many neurons cohesively function together, their combined efficacy is remarkable in learning performance. When each neuron is intrinsically limited for providing the exact information brain. In the Figure 8.13 ANN has three layers like input layer,hidden layer and output layer.

Comman Activation Functions
1) Sigmoid Function: A sigmoid-function is a small, differentiable, and real function that is defined for all real input values and which at all points

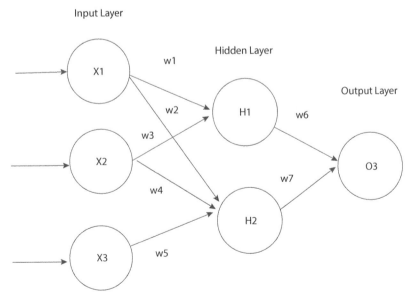

Figure 8.13 Artificial neural network [12].

contains a non-negative derivative. The same entity is referred to by the sigmoid "shape" and the sigmoid "curve."

2) Hyperbolic Tangent Function: Hyperbolic tangent function can be used as an alternative to sigmoid function in neural networks. If your back page, derivatives of the activation function are included in the weight mistake calculation. Hyperbolic tangent function derivatives have a basic shape much like a sigmoid function. This explains why neural networks have hyperbolic tangent common.

3) ReLU Function: Rectified linear unit is the most widely used deep learning tool. The function returns 0 if it gets any negative input, but returns the value back for any positive value xx. So, it can be written as f(x) = max(0,x) f(x) = max(0,x).

8.5   Proposed Methodology

The model is developed using the IAM database/datasets. Dataset images are analyzed in the dark scale at 300 dpi, 8 bits/pixel. Once the dataset is prepared, it is difficult to identify attributes compared to another example. The Vector Matrix for another penetration test is rendered and its similarity with the prepared dataset is then determined using a similarity system technique.

ANN classifier is used to classify the class that is ideally suited for the penetration test given the similarity context. This distinguishes penmanship in a class that delineates penmanship with its comparative attribute. In the Figure 8.14 the system architecture has been given. We need to provide the sample text from the web interface then it goes to processing server for

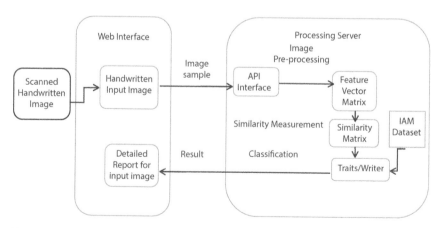

Figure 8.14 System architecture [13].

further processing. Once the processing has been done then it gives back the output to the interface. After the results are generated, they are placed in the prepared dataset. By placing the new example into the class to which it is mapped, you will be able to update the incremental machine learning. It is intended to extend precision without bounds.

8.5.1 System Flow

The proposed structure explores the writer's identity and makes the author more successful. The frame stream (Figure 8.15) displays the control stream. The customer then move the image tests and then the system distinguishes highlights from examples such as pattern, flat line tallness in "t," letter inclination, margin introduction and recognizes identity consistency. On the other hand, the test by the writer is separated by order calculations from the actual knowledge in the database.

In Figure 8.16, the steps for personality prediction have been given. The first step is capturing the image from the A4 size paper and store in the dataset. After that, we do the pre-processing of the image in which we remove the noise from the image. The next step is character recognition in which the algorithm identifies the character from the handwritten sample. The next step is feature extraction in which an ANN extracts the important features from the dataset. Using various classifiers we can predict the personality of the person.

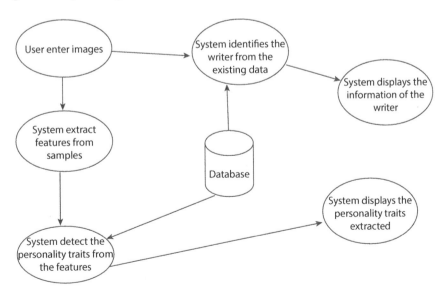

Figure 8.15 System flow [14].

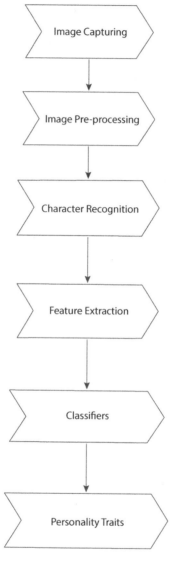

Figure 8.16 Flowchart for personality prediction [15].

8.6   Algorithms *vs.* Accuracy

The following diagram demonstrates the accuracy of each algorithm used for training and checking 50 to 100 handwritten lines with 650 authors. The samples from the IAM database were used. The following figure shows that ANN is an effective algorithm with an exactness of 86% for this specific

Table 8.6 Comparison table for personality analysis using various machine learning techniques [16].

Sr. no.	Work/year	Method (Algorithm used)	Tool used	Dataset	Parameters used	Prediction accuracy
1	H.N Champa & Anandakumar [2010] [5]	Rule-based classifiers	MATLAB	120 handwritten samples	baseline, slant, pen pressure, letter "t", a lower loop of "y"	68%
2	U.-V. Marti, R. Messerli, and H. Bunke [2001] [9]	k-closest neighbor	MATLAB	Multiple samples	baseline, the letter slant, pen pressure, letter "i" and letter "f"	87.8%
3	Prof. Seema Kedar, Ms. VaishnaviNair [2015] [6]	Artificial Neural Network	-	-	baseline, slant, size, spacing,	90%
4	Current Work	Support Vector Machine	Jupyter notebook, Django	IAM, 650 samples	Baseline, letter "t", slope, slant	70%
5	Current Work	K-Nearest Neighbor	Jupyter notebook, Django	IAM, 650 samples	Baseline, letter "t", slope, slant	68%
6	Current Work	Mpl-Neural	Jupyter notebook, Django	IAM, 650 samples	Baseline, letter "t", slope, slant	72%
7	Current Work	Artificial neural network	Jupyter notebook, Django	IAM, 650 samples	Baseline, letter "t", slope, slant	86%

application. Table 8.6 shows the comparison table for personality analysis using various machine learning techniques and their results for the same.

8.6.1   Implementation

Dataset

Hand-written images for training and research were derived from the hand-written images of the IAM database. It has 1,539 handwritten pages with 650 contributors. The features were extracted from text lines to implement the mathematical models [12].

The hand-written images for training and testing were collected for hand-written images from the IAM database. There are 1,017 lines of handwritten text of 650 authors. For each writer, the number of text lines ranges from 50 to 100. The features were extracted from text lines to implement mathematical models. We took 70% of the data for training model for writer recognition, which remained 30% to test.

In Figure 8.17, we have plotted the bar chart for various machine learning algorithms like Random Forest, K-NN algorithm, SVM algorithm, MPL_ Neural, and ANN. The accuracy of the ANN is highest among all the machine learning algorithms. So, we can conclude that the deep learning method is far better than the machine learning algorithms. For writer identification, 10 features are extracted and fed to the ANN with a single hidden layer which gave us an accuracy of 86%. ANNs or neural networks are computer algorithms. It simulates the conduct of biological systems composed of neurons.

Programming Language: The tool was built in version 3.4 of python. The Django Framework was used to create the website for downloading analytical images. The tensor flow was used for the development of ANN.

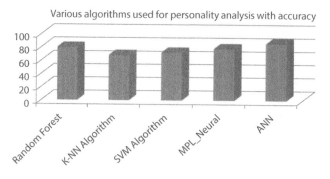

Figure 8.17 Graph of the algorithm used for personality analysis versus its accuracy [23].

Steps for Personality Analysis:

Step 1: Insert the writer's name.

Step 2: Pick your handwritten sample scanned image.

Step 3: Upload the study picture.

Step 4: The personality characteristics detected are shown.

Writer Identification

The writer identification process in the proposed method is given in the below framework. We take the handwritten sample from the dataset then we perform the feature extraction process in which we filter the important features from the dataset. After feature extraction, we calculate the similarity index for each sample from the dataset for which we want to check the handwriting.

The sample with the highest similarity index will be the result for the given input handwritten sample from the IAM dataset. Figure 8.18 shows the process of writer identification.

In Figure 8.16, we have handwritten samples from the IAM dataset from the dataset we extract the various important features that will play a crucial role in the identification of the writer [1]. We have evaluated several handwritten data samples for which we have calculated the similarity values and the sample with the highest similarity is the performance of the given entry.

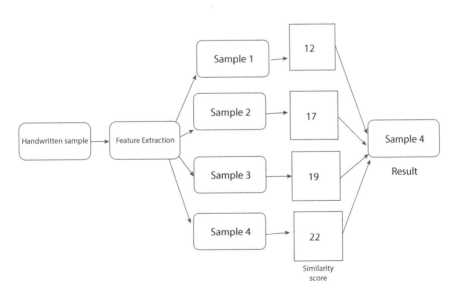

Figure 8.18 Writer identification framework [18].

Table 8.7 shows the comparison of various writer identification using various machine learning techniques with the various tools used for the implementation.

Table 8.7 Comparison table for writer identification using various machine learning techniques [20].

Sr. no.	Work/year	Method (Algorithm used)	Tool used	Dataset	Parameters used	Prediction accuracy
1	Hung Thuan Nguyena [2019] [18]	Convolutional Neural Network	-	IAM,JETIA-HP, Fire Maker (100 Samples)	Local features	91.81%
2	Onder Kirliand M. Bilginer [2018] [20]	KNN, Normal Density Discriminant function(NDDF)	-	IAM-Dataset (100 Writers)	-	98.76
3	Garg et al. [2018] [69]	Naive Bayes	-	Gurmukhi dataset (49,000 samples)	Statistical	70.10
4	Chahi et al. [2018] [43]	KNN with hamming distance	-	IAM, IFN/ENIT AHTID/ MW, CVL	Structural	88.99
5	Venugopal and Sundaram [2017] [182]	SVM	-	IAM online	Statistical	97.81
3	**Current Work**	Support Vector Machine	**Anaconda (Python)**	**IAM-Dataset (200 Samples)**	**Thickness, width, and slant information**	80.76%
4	**Current Work**	**Random Forest**	**Anaconda (Python)**	**IAM-Dataset (200 Samples)**	**Thickness, width, and slant information**	88.46%
5	**Current Work**	K-NN	**Anaconda (Python)**	**IAM-Dataset (200 Samples)**	**Thickness, width, and slant information.**	57.69%

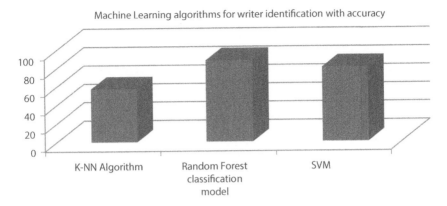

Figure 8.19 Writer identification with a machine learning algorithm [25].

Features are extracted from the image after pre-processing [2]. Global features include visual attributes such as thickness, width and slant details. Local characteristics are derived from areas such as the medium radius of the enclosed area and the medium enclosed area. When the data set has removed features, classification algorithms are used to classify them according to specified parameters and the sample with the highest score gives the most similarity. The sample with the highest score is the sample editor. In the Figure 8.19 comparison of various algorithm has been done. The random forest algorithm gives better accuracy as compared to K-NN and Support vector machine.

Figure 8.18 shows the writer's web framework identification component. We may upload the manuscript picture we want to look for.

Writer Identification using various machine learning algorithms:
Training:
1. Choose add writer.
2. Add a new name and image if not previously uploaded.
3. Features in the database are uploaded.

Testing:
1. Upload the file.
2. The name of the writer is shown as stored in the database.

8.7 Experimental Results

For personality analysis, the system uses extracted features to more effectively evaluate personalities. Features such as the base line and the text slant are extracted and the output is the personality characteristics based on the features described. On the basis of graphology, each function defines the personality characteristics. Parameters such as space between words are used for the writer's identity to identify the individual writer. The writer's information is stored here in advance and can only be remembered based on the specific information stored. The handwritten sample submitted by the user will check the degree of similarity between the features of the specified sample and the samples stored in the database and will give the handwriting the maximal similarity. An online tool for users to add a new author is created to find the personality of the writer from the handwritten text image. After training 50 to 100 handwritten lines of 650 authors, it can be concluded that the ANN is a good 86% accurate algorithm for this application.

8.8   Conclusion

The tool takes a picture for interpretation and thus produces an accurate and accurate report that defines the author's personality. Our system may also include information on the handwritten sample author whose details are already stored in the database. It is always open to the user as long as the user has a continuous internet connection that acts as an alternative to the previous manual handwriting analysis method. The system will have a comprehensive report stating the personality and the author. It is open to the consumer at all times as long as the user has an uninterrupted Internet link and is an alternative to the previous manual handwriting analysis method.

8.9   Conclusion and Future Scope

This system has a set of attributes used to identify the identity and character of the writer through hand written text. In addition, we will include more features in our system ensuring that time complexity is kept low and that less processing is required. The analyses of the personality can be achieved by using handwriting samples to predict the gender power of the individual and to verify the financial conduct of the individual by eliminating different features from the data collection.

Acknowledgment

Presentation, encouragement, and inspiration have always been crucial to the success of every undertaking. I am profoundly grateful to my guide

Dr. Harsh Mathur who has given me valuable guidance and kind supervision in this entire paper which has influenced the present work. Last but not least, I am inspired by my parents as well. I therefore express my gratitude to them with due respect.

References

1. Pervouchine, V. and Leedham, G., Extraction and analysis of forensic document examiner feature used for writer identification. *Pattern Recognit.*, 12, 117, 2007.
2. Champa, H.N. and AnandaKumar, K.R., Artificial neural network for human behavior prediction through handwriting analysis. *Int. J. Comput. Appl.* (0975 8887), 2, 2, 446–467, May 2011.
3. Devi, H., Thresholding: A Pixel-Level Image Processing Methodology Pre-processing Technique for an OCR System for the Brahmi Script. *Ancient Asia J.*, 1, 190–198, Dec 2006.
4. Tian, H. and Shen, H., Hamming Distance and Hop Count Based Classification for Multicast Network Topology Inference. *Proceedings of the 19th International Conference on Advanced Information Networking and Applications (AINA05)*.
5. Champa, H.N. and AnandaKumar, K.R., Automated Human Behavior Prediction through Handwriting Analysis. *First International Conference on Integrated Intelligent Computing*, 2010.
6. Kedar, S., Nair, V., Kulkarni, S., Personality Identification through Handwriting Analysis: A Review. *Int. J. Adv. Res. Comput. Sci. Software Eng.*, 5, 1, 889–899, January 2015.
7. Champa, H.N. and AnandaKumar, K.R., Handwriting Analysis for Writers Personality Prediction. *International Conference on Biometric Technologies and Applications- the Indian perspective, Under the Aegis of Biometrics India Expo*, 2008.
8. Ptak, R., Zygado, B., Un- Old, O., Projection-Based Text Line Segmentation with a variable threshold. *Int. J. Appl. Math. Comput. Sci.*, 27, 1, 195206, 2017.
9. Margins, G., Graphology Analysis: Margins. What Margins Say. Handwriting and graphology. Available at: http://www.handwriting-graphology.com/graphology- analysis-margins/ [Accessed 8 Apr. 2018], *Personality Analysis Using Machine Learning Algorithms*, 20, 788–789, 2018.
10. Marti, U.-V., Messerli, R., Bunke, H., Writer identification using text line based features. *Proc. Sixth Intl. Conf. Document Analysis and Recognition (ICDAR)*, pp. 101–105, 2001.
11. Kirlinder, and Bilginer Glmezolu, M., Writer identification from handwriting text lines. Innovations in Intelligent Systems and Applications (INISTA). *2011 International Symposium on IEEE*, 2011.

12. Marti, U.-V. and Bunke, H., The IAM-Database: an English sentence database for offline handwriting recognition. *Int. J. Doc. Anal. Recognit.*, 5, 1, 39–46, 2002.
13. Patil, V. and Mathur, H., A survey: Machine learning approach for Personality Analysis and writer Identification through Handwriting. *2020 International Conference on Inventive Computation Technologies (ICICT)*, 2020.
14. Grewal, P.K. and Prashar, D., Behavior "Prediction Through Handwriting Analysis. *IJCST*, 3, 2, 556–578, April - June 2012.
15. Joshi, P., Agarwal, A., Dhavale, A., Suryavanshi, R., Kodolikar, S., Handwriting Analysis for Detection of Personality Traits using Machine Learning Approach. *Int. J. Comput. Appl.* (0975 – 8887), 130, 15, 900–967 November 2015.
16. Hemlata, Sachan, M., Singh, S.K., Personality Detection using Handwriting Analysis. *Proc. of The Seventh International Conference on Advances in Computing, Electronics and Communication – ACE 2018.*
17. Shaikh, N., Kumar, R., Tidke, D., Borude, R., Badodekar, R., Automatic Predict Personality Based on Structure of Handwriting. *Automatic Predict Personality Based on Structure of Handwriting*, 25, 6, 2, 677–689, February 2018.
18. Nguyena, H.T., Nguyena, C.T., Inoa, T., Indurkhyab, B., Nakagawa, M., *Text Independent Writer Identification using Convolutional Neural Network*, 36, 122–156, 2019.
19. Rehman, A., Naz, S., Razzak, M., II, Writer identification using machine learning approaches. *Multimed. Tools Appl.*, 14, 189–195, Sep. 2018.
20. Kırlıand, O. and Bilginer Gülmezoğlu, M., WriterIdentification from Handwritten Text Lines. *IEEE*, 18, 200–224, 2011.
21. Garg, N.K., Kumar, M. *et al.*, Writer identification system for handwritten Gurmukhi characters: Study of different feature-classifier combinations, in: *Proceedings of International Conference on Computational Intelligence and Data Engineering*, Springer, pp. 12, pp. 125–131, 2018.
22. Chahi, A., Ruichek, Y., Touahni, R. *et al.*, Block wise local binary count for offline text-independent writer identification. *Expert Syst. Appl.*, 93, 1–14, 2018.
23. Venugopal, V. and Sundaram, S., An online writer identification system using regression-based feature normalization and codebook descriptors. *Expert Syst. Appl.*, 72, 196–206, 2017.
24. Gupta, S., *Automatic Person Identification, and Verification using Online Handwriting*, IIIT, Hyderabad, March 2008.
25. Jadhav, Y., Patil, V., Parasar, D., Machine Learning Approach to Classify Birds on the Basis of Their Sound. *2020 International Conference on Inventive Computation Technologies (ICICT)*, pp. 69–73, 2020.
26. Chaudhari, K. and Thakkar, A., Survey on handwriting-based personality trait identification. *Expert Syst. Appl.*, 124, 282–308, 2019.

27. Giannini, M., Pellegrini, P., Gori, A., Loscalzo, Y., Is Graphology Useful in Assessing Major Depression? *Psychol. Rep.*, 122, 2, 398–410, 2019.

28. Prasad, S., Singh, V.K., Sapre, A., Handwriting Analysis based on Segmentation Method for Prediction of Human Personality using Support Vector Machine. *Int. J. Comput. Appl.*, 8, 12, 25–29, 2010.

29. Duvernoy, J., Charraut, D., Baures, P.Y., Hybrid optical/digital image processing applied to handwriting recognition and aerial photograph clustering. *Opt. Acta (Lond)*, 24, 8, 795–810, 1977.

30. Wang, T., Wu, D.J., Coates, A., Ng, A.Y., End-to-end text recognition with convolutional neural networks. *Proceedings of the 21st International Conference on Pattern Recognition (ICPR2012)*, Tsukuba, pp. 3304–3308, 2012.

9

Risk Mitigation in Children With Autism Spectrum Disorder Using Brain Source Localization

Joy Karan Singh*, Deepti Kakkar and Tanu Wadhera

Department of Electronics and Communication Engineering, Dr. B.R. Ambedkar National Institute of Technology, Jalandhar, India

Abstract

Countless opportunities are provided by recent advances in technology for supporting individuals with autism spectrum disorder (ASD). There has been a great need to deal with risks associated with ASD. Despite a great amount of work has been done in this regard, several other risks are still needed to be addressed, and there is great amount of improvement required in this regard. To address these gaps, this chapter aims to address the challenges for improving the technology for ASD. In this chapter, we propose a tool sLORETA to assist clinicians for risk mitigation in ASD.

Methods: 20 normal (typically developing individuals) and 20 individuals diagnosed with ASD are considered in this chapter. A standard 10-20 electrode system is used.

Results: The activations were observed for autistic individuals. One of the major findings was observed in frontal, temporal, and parietal regions which showed decreased activity.

Discussion: sLORETA, a new software, has been used as a tool for risk mitigation in this chapter. This software has the potential of diagnosing ASD at an early stage. The altered functional connectivity is different regions of the brain can prove to be a biomarker for diagnosis at an early stage.

Keywords: Autism spectrum disorder, sLORETA, eye tracker, EEG, augumented reality, brain source localization, typically developing individuals

---

Corresponding author: joysachar@gmail.com

Monika Mangla, Nonita Sharma, Poonam Mittal, Vaishali Mehta Wadhwa, Thirunavukkarasu K. and Shahnawaz Khan (eds.) Emerging Technologies for Healthcare: Internet of Things and Deep Learning Models, (237–250) © 2021 Scrivener Publishing LLC

9.1 Introduction

Autism spectrum disorder (ASD) is a neurodevelopmental condition that has variable impact on different individuals. This disorder results in impairment in social interaction, restricted patterns, and behavior. ASD is characterized by restricted and repetitive behaviors and also language impairments [6]. The symptoms of ASD begin to appear at the age of 18–24 months which distinguish them from typically developing individuals and individuals with other developmental disorders.

The use of technology in our lives has become very practical and it has various benefits in real life but because of uncontrolled use in day to day life it results in many risks. In this chapter, the main focus is providing environment which is safe for autistic individuals and which helps in making their life better [26].

In order to support individuals in social life, IT has played a great role since the beginning. As time is changing technology has supported research and other clinical practices. In this chapter, we focus on the technologies that are used to treat ASD. One of the major deficits of people suffering from ASD is lack of social communication and interaction skills. The individuals with autism have deficiency in social interaction. The autistic individuals suffer from repetitive behavior patterns and have difficulty in daily life interaction [34]. IT-enabled systems have completely changed the life of autistic individuals by helping in overall development of individual by not causing any burden.

The new advances in technologies are of great support for social interaction aspect for autistic individuals. New studies hold great promise for enhancing the life of individuals with ASD and also for caretakers of individuals with ASD. Various studies have been conducted to assist individuals with ASD. In one of the studies computer assisted technologies are used to improve social interaction capabilities of persons suffering from ASD [29]. There are various technologies that have been applied to improve the quality of people with ASD these include virtual reality, robotics and computer training [11]. This chapter focuses on the risks involved and applying technology for dealing with individuals suffering from ASD.

In the earlier research done in this regard, the scientists identified the region of the brain or genetic factors that can explain autism in an effective way. This research lead to the discovery of risk factors which can identify autism at any stage. These risk factors include genetic as well as non-genetic factors [1]. There are various risk factors that are involved which identified and have been categorized into three categories: genetic factors, neurological factors, and atypical connectivity.

Experts have demonstrated various screening tools such as scales, interview methods, and observational methods for the diagnosis of the disorder [27]. These techniques are used for risk mitigation in autistic individuals. There are certain limitations regarding the use of these techniques:

1. The techniques are very age specific as different age scales are required for infants, child, and adults.
2. The process is very time consuming as the experts need a great amount of time to design questionnaires for taking responses from children and parents.
3. The process is dependent on clinical observation and is very subjective in nature.
4. Proper training of tools is required on the part of administrator before applying them to patients which poses a restriction.

In literature, various kinds of techniques have been proposed and introduced to diagnose ASD. In case of ASD, the impairments become very complex so screening of the brain activity is required. These mitigation techniques play a major role after the onset of disorder [4]. These techniques have proved to be inappropriate for the early diagnosis of this disorder. This highlights a greater need for developing systems that can prove to be biomarkers for early detection of ASD at an early stage of diagnosis [25]. The screening of sources of brain activity known as brain source localization is very helpful in keeping the track of the impairments. Recent research has pointed out faulty neural connectivity as one of the major symptoms of ASD [3].

sLORETA can be used as a biomarker for diagnosis of various diseases at an early stage. sLORETA a newer version of LORETA software is a tool that can be used for analyzing the functional connectivity in patients suffering from neurodevelopmental disorders [13]. This is one of the most advanced neuroimaging technique and has various advantages such as high temporal resolution and greater accuracy as compared to other tools [24]. It can be used to treat a wide variety of cognitive, neurobehavioral, and neuropsychiatric disorders [2]. Currently, there are very limited studies for diagnosis at an early stage but sLORETA can prove to be a tool for identifying children with risk of neurodevelopmental disorders.

9.2 Risk Factors Related to Autism

There are various risk factors that are involved whose onset occurs at various stages of development these include genetic factors, parental health

Table 9.1 Risk factors involved in ASD.

Risk factor	Explanation
Genetic factors	1. Alterations in DNA greatly increase the risk of autism 2. Family history of autism
Maternal health factors	1. History of autoimmune disease
Neurological factors	1. One of the major risk factors involved include birth injury or trauma 2. Birth complications

factors, and neurological factors. There are various risk factors involved in the individuals with ASD which have been discussed in Table 9.1.

9.2.1   Assistive Technologies for Autism

There are various assistive technologies that are available for early intervention in case of autistic patients as shown in Tables 9.2 and 9.3.

Table 9.2 Technological interventions for autism.

Advanced technology	Area of application
Virtual reality	One of the major advantages of using virtual reality is that it improves the learning skills of the individuals with ASD. ASD improves the social interaction capabilities of the persons suffering from ASD [5].
IoT and other wearable technology	IoT-enabled technologies provide the user feedback by using advanced technologies. It helps in improving social and cognitive skills for persons suffering with ASD [8].
Augmented reality	Helps in monitoring the behavior of individuals with ASD by the use of 3D graphics.
VSM	VSM is a technique of modeling that uses video to demonstrate appropriate behavior by considering the user as a model. VSM has helped autistic individuals in improving their interaction and behavior.
Mobile technology	The use of mobile technology has been demonstrated in the individuals who suffer from speech problems portable speech generating devices are examples of this technology [10].

(Continued)

Table 9.2 Technological interventions for autism. (*Continued*)

Advanced technology	Purpose
Eye tracker	Gaze patterns of ASD individuals can be identified using this technology and it also helps in diagnosing social interaction defects in children with autism [14].
Robotics	Use of robots to assist patients with ASD.
Use of biofeedback	Use of feedback to improve behavioral deficits in patients with ASD.
Gamification	Use of games to improve motor patterns in individuals with ASD [15].

Table 9.3 Sensitivity of various assistive technologies.

Assessment technique used	Average age of individual	Sensitivity of the technique
ML-based technique	2.5	92%
EEG-based technique	10	85%
MRI-based techniques	5	57%
Neurofeedback techniques	24	91%
Tracker-based techniques	5	80%
Gamification	4	84%
Questionnaire	2	85%

9.2.2 Functional Connectivity as a Biomarker for Autism

Different brain regions are connected through anatomical links known as functional connectivity. Anatomical connectivity is measured with the help of EEG/MEG [23]. Connectivity has become increasingly popular for identification of brain abnormalities. Atypical connectivity in brain usually appears at a very early stage which later on develops into autism [33]. Over connectivity or hyperconnectivity refers to excessive communication between various regions of the brain [7]. Overconnectivity in the frontal lobes of the brain has led to disruptions in information (emotional, language, and sensory). Autism is known to cause disruptions in frontal lobes and can result in excessive connectivity in frontal lobes of the brain [3]. Studies of infants that are diagnosed with ASD have shown that features of ASD are present at the age of 12 months [35]. However, many children show symptoms at the age of 4 years [18]. This highlights a greater need for developing systems that can prove to be biomarkers for early detection of ASD at an early stage of diagnosis.

The various patterns observed in case of autistic patients include deficiency in social interaction and repetitive behavior [19]. The deficiency in language processing is one of the other patterns observed in patients with ASD [20]. Functional connectivity can be used to evaluate alterations in brain activity and brain disorders at an early stage of development.

9.2.3 Early Intervention and Diagnosis

In literature, various kinds of techniques have been proposed and introduced to diagnose ASD. In case of ASD, the impairments become very complex so screening of the brain activity is required [9]. These mitigation and screening techniques play their role after the onset of the disorder. These techniques have proved to be inappropriate for the early diagnosis of this disorder. This highlights a greater need for developing systems that can prove to be biomarkers for early detection of ASD at an early stage of diagnosis [4]. The screening of sources of brain activity known as brain source localization is very helpful in keeping the track of the impairments. Various commercial and academic softwares are available for brain source localization as shown in Table 9.4.

This highlights a greater need for developing systems that can prove to be biomarkers for early detection of ASD at an early stage of diagnosis.

Table 9.4 Softwares available for diagnosis.

Software name	Category
Brainstorm	Academic software
Cartool	Academic software
EEG lab	Academic software
Fieldtrip	Academic software
Loreta	Academic software
BESA	Commercial software
Brain vision	Commercial software

sLORETA can be used as a biomarker for diagnosis of various diseases at an early stage [28]. sLORETA, a newer version of LORETA sofware, is a tool that can be used for analyzing the functional connectivity in patients suffering from neurodevelopmental disorders. This is one of the most advanced neuroimaging technique and has various advantages such as high temporal resolution and greater accuracy as compared to other tools [5]. It can be used to treat a wide variety of cognitive, neurobehavioral, and neuropsychiatric disorders [22]. Currently, there are very limited studies for diagnosis at an early stage but sLORETA can prove to be a tool for identifying children with risk of neurodevelopmental disorders.

9.3   Materials and Methodology

9.3.1   Subjects

In this study, two groups of participants have been considered. Two groups including 20 patients with ASD and 20 typically developing individuals are considered in this experiment.

9.3.2   Methods

All the typically developing individuals considered in this experiment had no history of any neurodevelopmental disorder. ASD individuals were recruited by taking permission from parents and caretakers from special schools from Jalandhar. Various diagnostic criteria including (ADI-R) and diagnostic and statistical manual criteria (DSM-IV) was followed in this regard. TD individuals were recruited from schools and were not taking any medication.

9.3.3   Data Acquisition and Processing

Step1: The first step involves conversion from ".txt" to ".sxyz" (text file to Talairach electrode coordinates at a sampling frequency of 102.4 Hz) (Figure 9.1).
Step 2: The transformation matrix and EEG files (.asc) are entered into the software and (.sxyz) file is selected from the utility window.
Step 3: After proceeding with the transformation, the file is entered into the explorer utility of the software.
Step 4: In the last step, the results are visualized in the software which includes 3D cortex map, slice viewer, and scalp map. The various regions which show activation are visualized in the software (Figure 9.2).

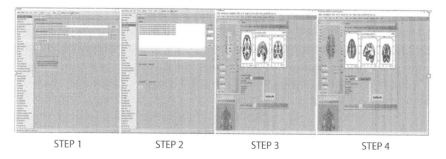

STEP 1   STEP 2   STEP 3   STEP 4

Figure 9.1 Steps for data acquisition and processing.

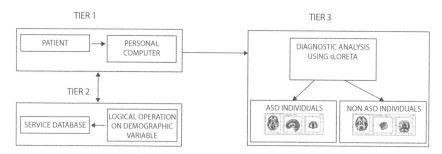

Figure 9.2 Proposed system for risk mitigation in ASD individuals.

9.3.4   sLORETA as a Diagnostic Tool

For early diagnosis of individuals with ASD a system has been proposed. There have been very limited systems that have been proposed for early

Table 9.5 Categorization of activation in different regions of brain.

Type	Lobe of brain	Activation	Type	Lobe	Activation
Healthy	Frontal lobe	Increased activity	ASD	Frontal lobe	Decreased activity
Healthy	Temporal lobe	Increased activity	ASD	Temporal lobe	Decreased activity
Healthy	Parietal lobe	Increased activity	ASD	Parietal lobe	Decreased activity
Healthy	Occipital	Decreased activity	ASD	Occipital	Increased activity

Table 9.6 Type of activity and color coding.

Category	Color coding
Least	Aqua Blue
Moderate	Royal Blue
Moderate	Red
Maximum	Yellow

diagnosis of ASD, so there is a great need for developing such systems. The system proposed takes input from EEG dataset. The system is a three tier system (Tables 9.5 and 9.6).

a) For real-time monitoring a patient interface.
b) A database consisting of EEG recordings of patients.
c) sLORETA software system for diagnosis of various nuero-developmental disorders.

9.4   Results and Discussion

This is a first of its kind study which has been used to identify the functional connectivity in ASD individuals using the software sLORETA [21]. The findings in this chapter indicate decrease in activity in individuals with ASD (8). Reduced connectivity along with increase in activity in some

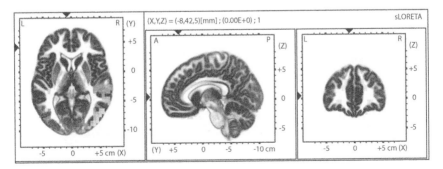

Figure 9.3 Activations in parietal, temporal, and frontal regions showing decreased activity for ASD individuals.

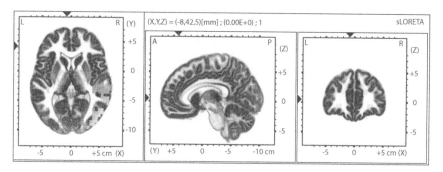

Figure 9.4 Activations in frontal and temporal lobes showing reduced activity for ASD individuals.

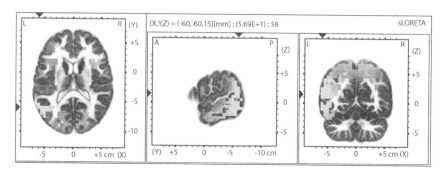

Figure 9.5 sLORETA images of young individuals showing increase in activity in frontal and parietal lobes.

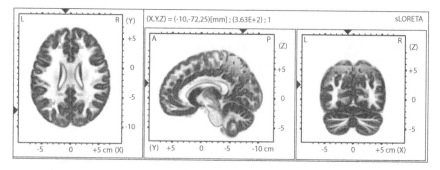

Figure 9.6 sLORETA images of young patients showing increase in activity in frontal and parietal lobes.

regions shows aberrant connectivity in various regions of the brain. High disconnectivity in various regions of the brain is in agreement with the literature [16, 17, 32]. Recent studies have shown underconnectivity in frontal and temporal regions of the brain [30, 31]. A number of studies have shown that fMRI can be used to identify individuals with ASD [28]. One of the studies also showed increase in grey matter in individuals with ASD. Neuroinflammation has also been reported in patients with ASD which has resulted in inability to transmit information to various regions of the brain [12]. The inability to transmit information has resulted in various other disorders of the brain including speech and language problems [23]. Localization of deep brain sources can be done using sLORETA which has resulted in great accuracy (Figures 9.3–9.6).

9.5   Conclusion and Future Scope

This chapter helps in providing a roadmap for safe autism dedicated systems. sLORETA as a potential tool for EEG-based brain source localization has been introduced in this chapter. The interactive system demonstrated can help in early diagnosis of autism. This chapter aims to mitigate the risks involved in ASD at an early stage.

In the future of healthcare, IoT can provide various applications including real-time health monitoring. Use of sensors and other medical devices constitute a major part of IoT. IoT provides a solution for efficient scheduling of resources by providing best service to patients living in remote areas.

References

1. Sarkar, B.K., Big data for secure healthcare system:a conceptual design. *Int. J. Complex Intell. Syst.*, 3, 2, 6–11, 2017.
2. Dimitrios, Athanasios, Andreas, Deep neural architectures for prediction in healthcare. *Int. J. Complex Intell. Syst.*, 4, 1, 8–12, 2017.
3. Luxmi, Sangeet, Negi, An intelligent noninvasive model for coronary artery disease detection. *Int. J. Complex Intell. Syst.*, 6, 1, 9–13, 2018.
4. Munsif, Nidal, Aamir, EEG based brain source localization comparison of sLORETA and eLORETA. *Int. J. Australas. Phys. Eng. Sci.*, 7, 2, 10–15, 2014.
5. Munsif, and Nidal, Brain source localization using reduced EEG sensors. *Int. J. Signal Image Video Process.*, 10, 2, 258–260, 2018.

6. Plamen, and Petar, Quantitative EEG comparative analysis between autism spectrum disorder and attention deficit hyperactivity disorder. *J. Int. Med. Assoc. Bulg.*, 9, 2, 268–270, 2017.

7. Nidal, and Muhammad, Low resolution brain source localization using EEG signals. *Int. J. Signal Process. Image Process. Image Recognit.*, 10, 3, 268–271, 2017.

8. Aitana, and Antonio, Evaluating functional connectivity in autism spectrum disorder using network based statistics, *Int. J. Enviromental Research and Public Health,17,19,pp281-284 Control* 2018, doi: 10.1155/2012/649609.

9. Lamb, G.V. and Green, R.J., Tracking epilepsy and autism. *Egypt. J. Neurol. Physchiatr. Neurosurg.*, 3, 2, 5–7, 2019.

10. Munsif, and Nidal, A survey of methods used for used for source localization using EEG signals. *Int. J. Biomed. Signal Process. Control*, 16, 18, pp. 256–261, 2014.

11. Daniele, and Vera, Brain Connectivity impairments and categorization disabilities in autism: A theoretical approach via artificial neural networks. *International Conference on Autism*, 2012.

12. Wendel, K., Väisänen, O., Malmivuo, J., Gencer, N.G., Vanrumste, B., Durka, P., Magjarević, R., Supek, S., Pascu, M.L., Fontenelle, H., Grave de Peralta Menendez, R., EEG/MEG source imaging: Methods, challenges, and open issues. *Comput. Intell. Neurosci.*, 18, 20, pp. 286–290, 2009.

13. Jatoi, M.A., Kamel, N., Malik, A.S., Faye, I., Begum, T., A survey of methods used for source localization using EEG signals. *Biomed. Signal Process. Control*, 11, 42–52, Elsevier, 2014.

14. Javed, E., Faye, I., Malik, A.S., Reduction of ballistocardio- gram artifact using EMD-AF, in: *Neural information processing*, M. Lee, A. Hirose, Z.-G. Hou, R.M. Kil (Eds.), Springer, Berlin Heidelberg, 2013.

15. Javed, E., Faye, I., Malik, A.S., Abdullah, J.M., Reference-free reduction of ballistocardiogram artifact from EEG data using EMD-PCA. *5th International Conference on Intelligent and Advanced Systems (ICIAS)*, pp. 1–6, 2014.

16. Soomro, M.H., Badruddin, N., Yusoff, M.Z., Jatoi, M.A., Automatic eyeblink artifact removal method based on EMD-CCA, Complex Medical Engineering (CME). *2013 ICME International Conference on*, pp. 186–190, 25–28, 2013.

17. Tanu, T. and Kakkar, D., Strengthening risk prediction using statistical learning in children with autism spectrum disorder. *Adv. Autism*, pp. 198–202, 14, 16, 2018.

18. Tanu, and Kakkar, D., A study on machine learning based generalized automated seizure detection system, in: *2018 '8th International Conference on Cloud Computing, Data Science and Engineering (Confluence)*, IEEE, pp. 769–774, 2018.

19. Tanu, and Kakkar, D., Accounting for order-frame length tradeoff of savitzky-golay smoothing filters. *5th International Conference on Signal Processing and Integrated Networks (SPIN)*, IEEE, pp. 805–810, 2018.

20. Tanu, and Kakkar, D., Eye tracker: An assistive tool in diagnosis of autism spectrum disorder, in: *Emerging Trends in the Diagnosis and Intervention of Neurodevelopmental Disorders*, IGI, USA, 2018.

21. Wadhera, T. and Kakkar, D., Influence of emotional imagery on risk perception and decision making in autism spectrum disorder. *Neurophysiology*, 51, 4, 281–292, 2019.

22. Wadhera, T. and Kakkar, D., Multiplex temporal measures reflecting neural underpinnings of brain functional connectivity under cognitive load in Autism Spectrum Disorder. *Neurol. Res.*, 42, 4, 327–328, 2020.

23. Wadhera, T. and Kakkar, D., Diagnostic assessment techniques and non-invasive biomarkers for autism spectrum disorder. *Int. J. E-Health Med. Commun. (IJEHMC)*, 10, 3, 79–95, 2019.

24. Wadhera, T., Kakkar, D., Wadhwa, G., Raj, B., Recent advances and progress in development of the field effect transistor biosensor: A review. *J. Electron. Mater.*, 48, 12, 7635–46, 2019.

25. Singh, A.K., Kakkar, D., Wadhera, T., Rani, R., Adaptive neuro-fuzzy based attention deficit/hyperactivity disorder diagnostic system. *Int. J. Med. Eng. Inf.*, 12, 5,6-11, 2020. In Press.

26. Tanu, and Kakkar, D., A study on machine learning based generalized automated seizure detection system, in: *2018 '8th International Conference on Cloud Computing, Data Science and Engineering (Confluence)*, IEEE, pp. 769–774, 2018.

27. Tanu, and Kakkar, D., Accounting for order-frame length tradeoff of savitzky-golay smoothing filters. *5th International Conference on Signal Processing and Integrated Networks (SPIN)*, IEEE, pp. 805–810, 2018.

28. Kakkar, D., Automatic detection of autism spectrum disorder by tracing the disorder co-morbidities, in: *2019 9th Annual Information Technology, Electromechanical Engineering and Microelectronics Conference (IEMECON)*, 2019, March, IEEE, pp. 132–136.

29. Tanu, T. and Kakkar, D., Drift-diffusion model parameters underlying cognitive mechanism and perceptual learning in autism spectrum disorder. *3rd International Conference on Soft Computing: Theories and Applications*, 2020.

30. Tanu, T. and Kakkar, D., Analysis of weighted visibility graphs in evaluation of austim spectrum disorder. *International Conference ICTESM*, Kuala Lumpur, Malaysia, pp. 37–43, 2020.

31. Wadhera, T., Kakkar, D., Singh, J.K., Design and analysis of field effect transistor-based biosensor to assist screening and detection of autism spectrum disorder. International behavior. *3rd BMI International Autism Conference*, Hyderabad, 2020, 2020.

32. Wadhera, T. and Kakkar, D., Eye tracker: An assistive tool in diagnosis of autism spectrum disorder, in: *Emerging Trends in the Diagnosis and Intervention of Neurodevelopmental Disorders*, pp. 125–152, IGI Global, 2019.

33. Kakkar, D., Drift-diffusion model parameters underlying cognitive mechanism and perceptual learning in autism spectrum disorder, in: *Soft Computing: Theories and Applications*, pp. 847–857, Springer, Singapore, 2020.

34. Wadhera, T., Kakkar, D., Kaur, G., Menia, V., Pre-Clinical ASD screening using multi-biometrics-based systems, in: *Design and Implementation of Healthcare Biometric Systems*, pp. 185–211, IGI Global,USA, 2019.

35. Wadhera, T. and Kakkar, D., Big data-based system: A supportive tool in autism spectrum disorder analysis, in: *Interdisciplinary Approaches to Altering Neurodevelopmental Disorders*, pp. 303–319, IGI Global, USA, 2020.

10

Predicting Chronic Kidney Disease Using Machine Learning

Monika Gupta* and Parul Gupta†

Computer Science, J.C. Bose University of Science and Technology, YMCA, Faridabad, India

Abstract

The kidney is a vital organ of the body. The function of kidney is to filter the blood in the body. When the kidneys filter blood, urine is made from excess and excess fluid in the body. The kidneys process waste, excess salt, and urea (nitrogenous wastes produced during the body's metabolic processes), regulate body fluids, blood pressure, and blood levels, and also regulate salt *levels, maintaining* the concentration of sodium, potassium, and phosphorus in the blood cells and minerals such as blood. Kidney failure occurs when the kidneys are not functioning properly. Kidney failure can have a profound effect on body health. Chronic kidney failure is a progressive kidney loss that includes uremia (urea and other nitrogenous residues in the blood) and can be fatal and cause other problems if there is no dialysis or kidney transplantation. An effort to determine the symptoms of kidney failure as early as possible is needed by a decision support system that can make decisions of chronic kidney disease. Large data can be used to explore patterns or knowledge using data mining methods. Machine learning techniques, for example, clustering, classification, and so on, are utilized to discover examples and information connections among an enormous arrangement of components and to manufacture dependable prediction models dependent on information input gave. These machine learning processes are carried out to produce valuable knowledge which will then be implemented into a decision support system application. In the field of health, machine learning has been used for diagnosis and prognosis of disease as well as for predicting the results of medical procedures.

*Corresponding author: monika.mittal167@gmail.com
†*Corresponding author*: parulgupta_gem@yahoo.com

Monika Mangla, Nonita Sharma, Poonam Mittal, Vaishali Mehta Wadhwa, Thirunavukkarasu K. and Shahnawaz Khan (eds.) Emerging Technologies for Healthcare: Internet of Things and Deep Learning Models, (251–278) © 2021 Scrivener Publishing LLC

Keywords: Kidney, disease, chronic disease, logistic regression

10.1 Introduction

Health has a very significant position in every human activity. Every human being is perfect, from infancy to old age. In the development of human life, humans are always looking for a healthy lifestyle or looking for a cure for an illness. Keeping your health from various diseases is very important to do. At current, many diseases are injurious to individual's health. One of the diseases that are harmful to human health is kidney failure. The kidneys have a very important role in the body's approval with body fluids, electrolyte balance, and approval of logistical results [1]. Kidney failure is a disease that has a huge impact on medical, economic, and social problems for patients and families in developed or developing countries [2]. An increase in incidence, prevalence, and the level of morbidity causes kidney disease that represents health problems in the world. Every year people with kidney failure increase by 20%–25% based on data in the United States Renal Data System (USRDS Annual Data Report, 2016). Patients with kidney failure in India are estimated to increase every year, and according to a WHO survey in India by 46% from 1955 to 2025, there will be an increase in the number of people with chronic kidney disease (CKD) [3].

Health problems related to chronic kidney failure occur when the kidneys are no longer able to function optimally. If the glomerular filtration rate (GFR) is less than 60 ml/min or 1.73 m^2 for 3 months or more, the person will experience chronic kidney failure [4]. Chronic kidney failure is generally caused by diffuse and chronic intrinsic kidney disease. About 60% of CKD is caused by Glomerulonephritis, essential hypertension, and pyelonephritis [5]. Many factors that cause kidney failure include age, sex, and a history of diseases such as diabetes, hypertension, and other metabolic disorders that can cause a decrease in kidney function [6]. Patients with kidney failure have a risk of developing complications including hypertension, anemia, bone disease, heart failure, and decreased excretion [6]. Symptoms arising from chronic kidney failure do not appear directly but appear gradually; the initial symptoms that are not clear make a decrease in kidney function is not felt, at a stage that is already severe and difficult to treat is only known [7]. In addition to the symptoms that are caused, other problems for patients with kidney failure are expensive treatment costs with results that cannot ascertain the total recovery [8]. Symptoms of kidney failure need to be known as early as possible so as not to continue at a severe stage and difficult to treat, patients can get help to change their lifestyle to better maintain their health [9].

A kidney is an organ that functions to regulate blood composition by accumulating waste and balancing the fluid that is in the body [10]. Maintaining kidney health is very important because the kidneys are one of the important organs in maintaining a healthy body. Kidney disease (CKD) is damage to the kidneys which causes the kidneys to not be able to release toxins and blood residual products, marked by the presence of protein in the urine and decreased GFR that lasts more than 3 months [11, 12]. Delay in handling and detecting this disease led to the prevalence of death from CKD. Early detection was needed to increase the prevalence rate due to CKD.

10.2   Machine Learning Techniques for Prediction of Kidney Failure

Efforts to determine the symptoms of kidney failure as early as possible are needed by a decision support system that can make decisions of CKD [13, 14]. Large data can be used to explore patterns or knowledge using data mining methods [15]. Machine learning techniques, for example, clustering, classification, and so on, are utilized to discover examples and information connections among an enormous arrangement of components and to manufacture dependable prediction models dependent on information input gave. These machine learning processes are carried out to produce valuable knowledge which will then be implemented into a decision support system application [16]. In the field of health, machine learning has been used for the diagnosis and prognosis of disease as well as for predicting the results of medical procedures [17]. In previous studies conducted using data mining methods and kidney disease dataset by several researchers, C4.5 algorithm method was used to get an accuracy of 91.50% [18]. The research is included in the classification of machine learning techniques. For this research, we will analyze a dataset of CKD using Multi-Variate Linear Regression and Logistic Regression method, under these conditions, the researchers conducted a study with the title "Prediction of Chronic Kidney Failure Using Multi-Variate Linear Regression, and Logistic Regression". This system hopes to be able to classify patients suffering from CKD [20] or not suffering from kidney failure. The results of this system can be used for early detection of chronic kidney failure.

10.2.1   Analysis and Empirical Learning

The learning assignments can be characterized into various measurements [29]. One significant measurement is the contrast between empirical learning and analysis. Empirical learning will be discovering that depends on some type of outer experience, though expository learning does not need outside info. For instance, tic-tac-toe. Assume a developer has given encoding rules to a game as a capacity that demonstrates whether the proposed development is lawful or unlawful, and different capacities that show winning, losing, or drawing. By taking a gander at the two capacities above, it is not hard to compose a program that will consistently play the tic-tac-toe game without anyone else. Assume that this program recalls each progression it has taken. For every last position (i.e., where it is resolved who wins, loses, or draws), he will recall the outcome. As more games are played, the program will recollect which steps made him lose, and which steps made the enemy to win. Moreover, he can recollect which steps made him experience triumph, and which steps made the foe lose. Subsequent to playing very some games [21], in the end, the program can decide the means that cause triumph or annihilation and play tic-tac-toe impeccably. The conversation above is a type of learning investigation on the grounds that no outer info is required. This program can improve execution just by breaking down issues. The program will figure out which steps can be taken and a specialist will show which are legitimate and unlawful advances and places that will cause triumph, destruction, or draw. The program can recall this experience. Subsequent to attempting each conceivable position and attempting each conceivable advance, the program will have total information on the standards of the game. This is called experimental learning, on the grounds that the program cannot close the principles of the game in investigation, the program must connect with a specialist to give learning. The isolating line among explanatory and observational learning [22] can be obscured. Assume a program definitely knows the standards of the tic-tac-toe game. In any case, if in the past body of evidence the program played against itself, this time the program would be against people. By considering the guidelines, the program will recall the means that have been taken and realize the means expected to acquire triumph, thrashing, or arrangement. The capacity of the program to play tic-tac-toe [23] will increment quickly when playing against educated players (not by attempting different irregular positions when playing with himself). Along these lines, during the learning cycle, the program will show better execution. Yet, for this situation the program need not bother with a specialist or other outside information, since he finishes up the game strides in an

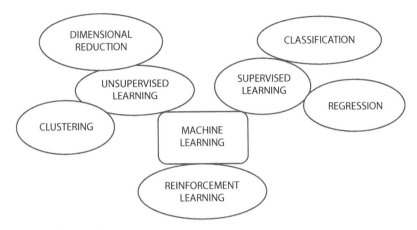

Figure 10.1 Machine learning ecosystem.

explanatory manner. In the above issue, the entire learning task did by the program is a learning investigation, on the grounds that the learning program examines the means he has ever done; however, the program takes care of the issue experimentally, in light of the fact that the program has to realize which steps are commonly utilized by people. Contrasts in investigation and experimental learning did not have all the earmarks of being excessively noteworthy in tic-tac-toe. In any case, in chess, both of these exercises will give totally different outcomes.

Machine learning techniques, for example, classification and clustering, as appeared in Figure 10.1 are utilized to discover patterns and information connections among an enormous arrangement of variables and to manufacture dependable forecast models dependent on information input gave.

10.2.2 Supervised Learning

Assume we need to make a program that when given an image of somebody, can decide if the individual in the image is male or female. The program that we made is known as a classifier, on the grounds that the program attempts to allot a class (for example, male or female) to an item (picture). The undertaking of managed learning [30] is to assemble a classifier by giving a bunch of classed preparing models (for this situation, models are pictures that have been placed into the correct class). The fundamental test in administered learning is a speculation. After breaking down a few example pictures, directed learning must create a classifier that can be utilized appropriately on all images [24]. The article pair and the class that focuses to the item are examples that have been named. The arrangement of models that have been named will deliver a learning calculation called a preparation set. Assume we give a preparation set to a learning calculation, and the calculation produces yield as a classifier. How would you measure the nature of this classifier? The arrangement usually utilized is to utilize a bunch of other named models called test sets. We can gauge the level of models that are accurately arranged or the level of models that have been misclassified. The methodology taken to figure rates expects that every order is autonomous, and every arrangement is similarly significant.

This assumption is often forgotten. The suspicion that each class is free is regularly disregarded if there is a transitory reliance on information. For instance, a specialist at a facility realizes that a plague is occurring. Subsequently, in the wake of seeing a few patients every one of whom have this season's virus, there is a high chance that the specialist will think about the following patient to have a similar infection, regardless of whether the patient does not show side effects as unmistakably as the patient's past sickness. Model: the classifier must decide if a patient has malignancy or not founded on research facility estimations. There are two sorts of errors. The first is known as a bogus positive mistake, which is a blunder that emerges when the classifier groups a solid individual as an individual with malignancy. Bogus negatives show up when the classifier groups individuals with malignancy as solid individuals. By and large, bogus negatives are more regularly in danger than bogus positives, so we should utilize a learning calculation that can cause less bogus negatives, despite the fact that the outcomes will cause all the more bogus positives. Administered learning learns the classifier, yet in addition examines capacities that can foresee a mathematical worth. For instance: when given a photograph of somebody, we need to anticipate the age, tallness, and weight of individuals in the photograph. This errand is frequently alluded to as relapse. For this situation, each preparation model that has been named contains an article and its worth. The nature of the expectation function [25] is generally estimated as the square of the distinction in the anticipated worth. There are many taking in calculations created from managed learning. These calculations are choice trees, fake neural organizations, and uphold vector machines.

10.2.3   Unsupervised Learning

Unsupervised learning is a machine learning technique that is used to gain knowledge by examining data whose output is unknown. The system will be given an input pattern and will be instructed to look for regular patterns. Deep Belief Networks (DBNs) [31] and sparse coding are models of unsupervised learning that are often used. Following the development of algorithms, these models have been applied to some machine learning applications, including computer vision, text modeling, and collaborative filtering [26]. This model is suitable for problems with high dimensions. When applied to images, the model can produce millions of parameters; these parameters can be processed using millions of training examples that have not been labeled as input. Unfortunately, with the current algorithm, learning parameters can take a very long time, even weeks if only using one CPU. Therefore, to examine DBNs and sparse coding, we must use inputs that have few parameters or by dividing existing parameters. The following are the tasks that can be completed using unsupervised learning.

10.2.3.1 Understanding and Visualization

Most unsupervised learning calculations make a similar various leveled game plan. The assignment of various leveled bunching is to sort out a gathering of items into an order so that protests that have similitudes can be made into one gathering. As a rule, this is finished by deciding the size of the similitude between two items and afterward searching for an assortment of articles that are more like each other than they are to objects in different gatherings. Non-progressive bunching endeavors to segment information into a few groups that have been depicted. Another way to deal with comprehension and picturing information is to mastermind objects in low elements of room (for instance, in a two-dimensional plane) so comparative articles become near one another. For instance, an item is spoken to by five genuine qualities with credits: tallness, width, length, weight, shading, and thickness. We can gauge the likeness of two items by taking a gander at the Euclidean distance [27] (the separation of two focuses that can be determined with the estimating instrument and the Pythagorean recipe) in their five-dimensional plane. Each item is given two new measurements (x and y) with the goal that the Euclidean separation between objects in the two-dimensional plane gets corresponding to the Euclidean separation in the five-dimensional plane. We can place each protest as a point in a two-dimensional plane, and see the comparability of items.

10.2.3.2 Odd Detection

The second task of unsupervised learning is distinguishing peculiarities. Model: to distinguish fake utilization of credit cards [28], we should initially gather an assortment of legitimate credit card exchanges, and decide the estimation of P (t) for exchanges t. At that point, another exchange named t' is given, on the off chance that the estimation of P (t') is exceptionally little, at that point it very well may be inferred that t' is a bizarre exchange, and should be accounted for to the specialists. In an assembling plant, one of the quality control techniques is to give a notice each time an unordinary object is created by the get together cycle.

10.2.3.3   Object Completion

Humans have an extraordinary ability to provide fragmental descriptions of an object or situation. For example, just by looking at the back of a car, we can determine accurately what the car is like. Object completion aims to predict the missing part of an object by using a partial description of the object.

10.2.3.4   Information Acquisition

The fourth task of unsupervised learning is to acquire applicable articles (reports, drawings, and fingerprints) from a gathering/gathering of items. Getting data is normally done by giving an incomplete portrayal of an item, at that point utilizing it to figure out which objects in a gathering have likenesses with the depiction that has been given.

10.2.3.5   Data Compression

In certain situations, we do not want to save or send an object full of details. For example, pictures taken by a camera require 3 megabytes of space. By using data compression, the image can be reduced to 50 kilobytes (60 times smaller) without reducing image quality. Data compression includes the acknowledgment, and disposal of angles that are not applicable to information (or perceive, and take significant parts of the information). Most information compression techniques work by distinguishing sub pictures, and substrings that frequently show up, and placing them in a "word reference". Each sub picture, and substring can be supplanted by an a lot littler reference found in the "word reference".

10.2.3.6   Capital Market

In the world of capital markets, stock movements are essential for investors and analysts to consider. To benefit from investments that are invested, investors must have the ability to analyze future stock price movements. Before we discuss further about stock movements, it helps us to understand

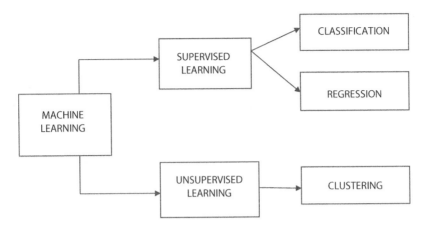

Figure 10.2 Supervised and unsupervised learning models.

in advance the notion of the capital market. According to [19], the capital market is a market for a variety of long-term financial instruments that can trade, both in the form of debt or own capital. The capital market in Indonesia is managed by Bapepam under the control of the finance minister of the Republic of Indonesia. The capital market has a major part in the economy of a nation in light of the fact that the capital market performs two capacities immediately, in particular the monetary capacity and money related capacity. The capital market is said to have financial capacities on the grounds that the capital market gives offices that unite two premiums, to be specific the individuals who have overabundance reserves (speculators) and the individuals who need reserves (backers). The capital market is said to have a budgetary capacity in light of the fact that the capital market gives the chance and chance to acquire a (return) for the proprietor of the store.

Figure 10.2 shows that machine learning utilizes two sorts of procedures: supervised learning, which prepares a model on known information and yield information so it can anticipate future yields, and unsupervised learning, which finds concealed examples or inherent structures in input information.

10.2.4   Classification

Classification can be defined in detail as a job that conducts training/ learning of the target function f which maps each vector x into one of several class labels y available. The training is conducted to produce a model which is then stored as a memory. Clustering is the way toward finding a model or capacity that clarifies or recognizes information ideas or classes, to have the option to assess the class of an item whose mark is obscure.

In characterization, there are target variable classifications. To arrange an article in a choice tree do not utilize separation vectors. Regularly observational information has credits that are of ostensible worth. Assume the article is a gathering of creatures that can be recognized dependent on the properties of shape, shading, size, and number of legs. The shape, shading, size, and number of feet are ostensible amounts. With the estimations of these properties, a choice tree is then made to decide an article including what sort of creature if the estimation of each trait is given [32]. In the standard characterization measure, two cycles must be completed, to be specific:

(i) Training Process
(ii) Testing Process

10.2.4.1   Training Process

In this process, training data sets or sample data that are known to the labels or attributes of the sample data are used to build the model.

10.2.4.2   Testing Process

In the testing process, a test is conducted to determine the accuracy of the model that has been made in the training process so that data is built called data testing to classify the labels. The model in the classification has the same meaning as the black box, where there is a model that can receive input and then conduct an analysis using the model to provide answers as the output of the results of his thinking.

New data for which class labels are unknown can be predicted using a model built during training. In developing the model during the training process, an algorithm is used to build a model called the training algorithm. In the classification process shown in Figure 10.3, the data that is imported is a data record or sample data. Each record is known as a case or case indicated by a tuple (x, y) where x is the arrangement of characteristics and y is the attribute announced as a class label. The primary segments of the characterization cycle include the following:

1. Class: Class is a label of the classification results are not independent variables. For example: customer loyalty class, storm class, kidney failure class, and others.
2. Predictors: Predictors are independent variables of a model based on the characteristics of the classified data attributes, for example smoking, drinking alcoholic beverages, and so on.

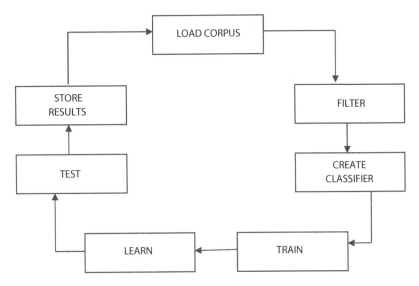

Figure 10.3 Classification process.

3. Training Data Set: The training data set is a complete set of data that contains classes and predictors to be trained to get a model in order to group data into the right class.
4. Test Data Set: Test data sets, containing new data, are used to test a model by grouping data based on a particular model to determine the accuracy of the model that has been made.

10.2.5   Decision Tree

Decision tree is a tree that is utilized as a thinking methodology to find a solution to the issue entered. Trees that are shaped are not generally parallel. In the event that the element in the informational index utilizes two sorts of all out qualities, the subsequent tree is a twofold tree. In the event that it contains multiple sorts of straight out qualities or utilizations numeric sorts, the state of the decision tree delivered is normally not a paired tree [33].

Decision tree is a stream diagram that has a tree-like structure in which each interior node expressing the trial of a trait, each branch expresses the yield of the test and the leaf hub expresses the classes or class dissemina-tions. The earliest node is known as the root node. A root node has a few leave edges however does not have an approaching edge. Inward hubs will have one passage edge and a few leave edges, while a leaf hub will just have one section edge and a few leave edges, while the leaf hub will just have one passage edge without having an edge.

To order an example of information that is obscure to its group, a decision tree strategy can be utilized to be known to go into existing classes. The primary information testing way is through the root node lastly through the leaf node which will finish up the class expectation for the information. The attribute data used must be in the form of categorical data, if the data is continuous then the attribute must be discredited in advance [33]. Flexibility makes this technique alluring, on the grounds that it can give benefits as perception of recommendations (as a choice tree) that makes the expectation system effectively discernible. Decision tree is regularly used to determine instances of dynamic, for example, in medication (conclusion of patient's illness), software engineering (information structure), brain research (dynamic hypothesis), etc [33].

A decision tree is a predictive model technique that can be used for classification and prediction of tasks. The technique used in the decision tree is the technique of dividing and conquering to divide the problem search space into a set of problems [33]. The process in the decision tree is to change the data in the form of tables into a model tree that can be used to conclude. The tree model will produce rules and be simplified [33]. The basic concept of a decision tree is shown in Figure 10.4.

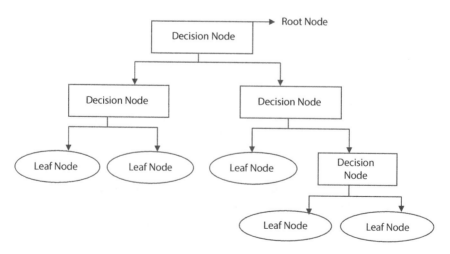

Figure 10.4 Decision tree example.

The characteristics of the decision tree as shown in Figure 10.4 are formed by the following elements:

a) Root node: The root node has no input arm and has zero or more output arms.
b) Internal nodes: Each non-leaf node that has exactly one input arm and two or more output arms. This node states that testing is based on feature values.
c) Arm: Each branch states the value of the test results in nodes not leaves.
d) Leaf nodes: Leaf nodes are the nodes that have exactly one input arm, and do not have an output arm. This node states the class label (decision).

10.2.6   Regression Analysis

Sir Francis Galton first used regression as a statistical concept. Regression analysis is used to estimate the value of a variable against one other variable associated with that variable [34]. To form a regression equation that must meet the basic principle between the response variable with the independent variable related to the causal relationship, the relationship either based on theory, previous research, or based on certain logical explanations. Regression analysis in general is about the response of one variable with one or more independent variables, which is to estimate the average participation or average value of the response variable based on the value of the independent variable owned. The results obtained from the regression analysis consist of regression for each independent variable and how the coefficients are obtained by predicting the response value [34].

10.2.6.1   Logistic Regression

Regression analysis in statistics is one method for determining the causal relationship between one variable with another variable. Cause variables are referred to by various terms, such as explanatory variables, explanatory variables, independent variables, or X variables (because they are often described in graphs as abscissa, or X-axis) [35]. The affected variables are known as the dependent variable or the Y variable. Both of these variables can be random variables, but the affected variable must always be a random variable. Regression analysis is one of the most popular and widely used analysis. Almost all fields of science that require causal analysis are certain to be familiar with this analysis. Logistic regression is one part of the regression analysis used to predict the probability of an event occurring by matching the data to the logic curve logistic function. This method is a general linear model used for binomial regression. Like a regression analysis in general, this method uses one or several independent variables with one independent variable as dichotomous freedom. Logistic regression is also used in medicine, social science, and even in the field of marketing, such as market predictions to buy products or stop buying. Logistic regression does not require the assumption of normality, heteroscedasticity, and autocorrelation because the variables required in logistic regression are dummy variables (0 and 1), so the residuals do not need to be tested properly. To assume multicollinearity, because it only requires independent variables, it still needs to be tested. For multicollinearity testing, a suitability test (goodness of fit test) can be used which is then solved by testing the hypothesis to see which independent variables are significant and can be used in research. Furthermore, among the independent variables that are highly interrelated, framework can be designed. It can be undeniably related to multicollinearity in the research model [36]. Logistic regression is one of the nonparametric statistical methods to obtain hypotheses. The Logistic regression method is a mathematical method that describes the relationship between one or more independent variables with one dichotomous independent variable whose variables are considered to have only two possible values, 0 and 1, which may be interpreted as multiple. In general, regression analysis forms an equation to predict the dependent variable based on the independent variable. The multiple logistic regression models are a logistic regression model with more than one independent variable. The probability function for each observation is as follows:

$$fy = \pi^y(1 - \pi)^{1-y} \text{ With y=0; 1} \tag{10.1}$$

where if $y = 0$ then $f(y) = 1-\pi$ and if $y = 1$ then $f(y) = \pi$. Function Logistic regression can be written as follows:

$$fz = \frac{1}{1+e^{-z}} \quad equivalent\ to \quad fz = \frac{e^z}{1+e^{-z}} \tag{10.2}$$

where

$$Z = \beta_0 + \beta_1 x_1 + \beta_2 x_2 + \cdots + \beta_k x_k \tag{10.3}$$

where k = the number of independent variables The z value is between $-\infty$ and $+\infty$ so the value f (z) lies between 0 and 1 for every z given. This shows that the logistics model describes the probability or risk of an object. Model Logistic regression can be written as follows:

$$nx = \frac{e^{\beta 0 + \beta 1 x 1 + \beta 2 x 2 + \cdots + \beta kxk}}{1 + e^{\beta 0 + \beta 1 x 1 + \beta 2 x 2 + \cdots + \beta kxk}} \qquad (10.4)$$

10.2.6.2 *Ordinal Logistic Regression*

Logistic regression is a regression model used when variables responses are qualitative. This model consists of a simple logistic regression dichotomous which requires that the response variable consists of two categories and polytomous logistic regression [37] with response variables of more than two categories. Polytomous logistic regression with multilevel response variables is known as ordinal logistic regression. Predictor variables can be included in the model in the form of continuous and categorical data consisting of two or more variables [13].

- Proportional Odd Model

An ordinal scale response variable can consist of $K + 1$ and expressed as $0,1,2,\ldots, K$. General expression of conditional opportunity $Y = k$ on vector x of p the predictor variable is $Pr\ [Y = k \mid x] = \phi k\ (x)$. For example $\phi k\ (x) = \pi k\ (x)$, then for $K = 0,1,2$, the model formed is explained by the following equation:

$$P(Y = 0|x) = \frac{1}{1 + e^{g1(x)} + e^{g2(x)}} = {}_0(x)$$

$$P(Y = 1|x) = \frac{e^{g1(x)}}{1 + e^{g1(x)} + e^{g2(x)}} = {}_1(x)$$

$$P(Y = 2|x) = \frac{e^{g2(x)}}{1 + e^{g1(x)} + e^{g2(x)}} = {}_2(x)$$

so, the form of the equation is as follows:

$$P(Y = k|x) = \frac{e^{gk(x)}}{\sum_{i=1}^{k} + e^{gi(x)}}$$ (10.5)

where g0 $(x) = 0$, and $k = 0.1, ..., K$. The base line logit model has a $K (p + 1)$ coefficient, this form emerges from the fact that the model is usually parameterized [38], so the log efficient odds compare the category $y = k$ with the basic category $y = 0$.

$$g_k(x) = \text{In}\left[\frac{\phi_k(x)}{\phi_o(x)}\right]$$ (10.6)

$$= \text{In}\left[\frac{P(Y = K|x)}{P(Y = 0|x)}\right]$$

$$= \beta_{k0} + x'\beta_k, k = 0,1,2,...,K,$$ (10.7)

equation is called the baseline logistic model, with β_{k0} as an intercept. In ordinal logistic regression, the model can be obtained with the odds model proportional (proportional odds model). This logit model is a model obtained by comparing cumulative opportunities, i.e., opportunities less than or the same as the response category on the is stated expressed predictor variable in vectors x, $P (Y \leq k | x)$, with greater opportunity than categories ke, $P (Y> k | x)$ responses are defined as follows:

$$\text{logit } P(Y \leq k|x) = c_k(x) = \text{In}\left[\frac{P(Y \leq k|x)}{P(Y > k|x)}\right]$$

$$= \text{In}\left[\frac{\phi_0(x)+\phi_1(x)+...+\phi_k(x)}{\phi_{k+1}(x)+\phi_{k+2}(x)+...\phi_k(x)}\right]$$ (10.8)

$$= \tau_k - x'\beta, \text{ for } = 0,1,2,..., K-1$$

10.2.6.3   Estimating Parameters

The most commonly used method for estimating parameters on the Logistic Regression model is the maximum likelihood method (method of maximum likelihood). The initial step to applying the maximum likelihood method is by forming a function called the likelihood function. This function describes the opportunity function of the data observed as a function of parameter estimator [39]. In general, the likelihood function is defined as a joint probability function of random variables formed by the sample. Especially for samples of size n with observations $(y_1, y_2, ..., y_n)$ corresponds to a random variable $(Y_1, Y_2, ..., Y_n)$. As long as Y_i is considered independent, then the probability density function with it is as follows:

$$g(Y_1, Y_2, ..., Y_n) = \prod_{i=1}^{n} f(Y_i) \qquad (10.9)$$

The method used to match each model is based on adjustments to multinomial likelihood. The general form of the likelihood for samples from n independent observations (z_i, x_i), $i = 1, 2, ..., n$; is as following:

$$(\beta) = \prod_{i=1}^{n} [\phi0(xi)^{z0i} \times \phi1(xi)^{z1i} \times ... \times \phi K(xi)^{zKi}], \qquad (10.10)$$

where $\phi k (x)$ is a function of unknown parameters and $z' = (z_0, z_1, ... z_k)$ is formed from an ordinal response. The maximum likelihood method gives the estimator value of the vector $\beta_k' = (\beta_{0k}, \beta_1, ... \beta_{pk})$ by maximizing the joint possible function in equation. The logarithm of the possibility function with it can be written as follows:

$$(\beta) = \sum_{i=0}^{n} z0i \ln[\phi_0(xi)] + \cdots + z_{Ki} \ln[\phi_{Ki}(xi)]. \qquad (10.11)$$

To get the estimator value of $\beta_k' = (\beta_{0k}, \beta_1, ... \beta_{pk})$ which maximizing $L(\beta)$, obtained by deriving the equated equation with zero [], equations obtained are as follows:

$$\frac{\partial L(\beta)}{\partial \beta_{jk}} = \sum_{i=1}^{n} (z_{ji} - \phi_{ji}) = 0 \qquad (10.12)$$

where $j = 1, 2, ..., J - 1$ and $k = 0, 1, 2, ..., p$ with $x_{0i} = 1$ for each subject. Variance estimation methods and coefficient of estimator coefficients are obtained based on the maximum estimation theory. Estimator variety and charter obtained is a matrix derived from the second partial derivative of the general form of elements in the second partial derivative matrix as following:

$$\frac{\partial^2 L(\beta)}{\partial \beta_{jk} \, \partial \beta_{jk'}} = \sum_{i=1}^{n} x_{k'}(z_{ji} - \phi_{ji}) = 0 \qquad (10.13)$$

for j and $j' = 1,2$ and k and $k' = 0,1,2,\ldots, p$. Next is defined $I(\beta)$ a matrix of size $2(p + 1) \times 2(p + 1)$ whose elements are negative values. The matrix is called an information matrix. Correlation matrix of maximum likelihood estimators is the inverse of the information matrix, $\Sigma(\beta) = I(\beta)$ -1. Estimator of the matrix information and corrections are obtained by replacing parameters with values guessed.

10.2.6.4   Multivariate Regression

Multivariate regression models are linear regression models with more than one dependent variable Y correlated with one or more independent variables X. In the analysis of the regression model, a multivariate selection of the best model is an important thing. This is due to the best model selection on a multivariate regression model and depends on how many independent variables are involved in the model [40]. The purpose of this study is to determine what factors affect the degree of health in Indonesia and can determine the best multivariate regression model based on factors that affect the degree of health in Indonesia. Based on the results of the model selection using Method *AICC* obtained [35], factors that influence the degree of health in India are percentage births performed by medical personnel, the percentage of complete immunizations, and the percentage of households use your clinical facility.

Multivariate linear regression model is a linear regression model with more than one dependent variable Y are correlated with and one or more independent variables X. With the following models:

$$Y_{(n \times p)} = X_{(n \times (q+1))} \, \beta_{((q+1) \times p)} + \varepsilon_{(n \times p)} \qquad (10.14)$$

where $E(\varepsilon_{(i)}) = 0$ and $Cov(\varepsilon_{(i)}, \varepsilon_{(k)}) = \sigma_{ik} I$ where $i, k = 1,2, \ldots m$. Additional assumptions regarding the model are as follows: $E(Y) = X\beta$ or $E(\varepsilon) = 0$ *cov* $(\ ) = \Sigma$ for all $i = 1,2, \ldots, n$ where yi^T is the i row of the Y matrix *cov* $(yi, yj) = 0$ for all $i \neq j$.

Correlation Coefficient Between Dependent Variables: Correlation coefficient is a value that shows whether a linear relationship is strong or not between two variables, which can be used by calculating the intercellular correlation matrix variable. With the following equation:

$$r_{ik} = \frac{1}{n-1} \sum_{r=1}^{n} \left(\frac{x_{ir} - \bar{x}_i}{\sqrt{s_{ii}}} \right) \left(\frac{x_{kr} - \bar{x}_k}{\sqrt{s_{kk}}} \right) \qquad (10.15)$$

where i = 1,2, ... p and k = 1,2 ... p score r_{ik} is between $-1 \leq r_{ik} = 1$, when $r_{ik} = 0$ means there is no relationship between variables, perfect relationship when $r_{ik} = \pm 1$, +1 means the relationship is unidirectional and −1 when opposite.

10.3   Data Sources

In this study, the dataset used was obtained from a data provider site, the UCI repository. The data used are secondary data of 400 records consisting of 24 attributes and one label. Secondary data is the data which is not obtained from data collected directly by researchers.

Data attributes used are:

1) *Age*
   It is the unit of time that measures the time of existence of an object or creature, both living and dead. The range used is 0–30 years is young, 31–45 years is adult, and 46 years and so is the elderly.
2) *Blood pressure*
   This is the pressure that occurs in arteries when blood is pumped by the heart to flow to all members of the body. Normal blood pressure is in the range of 60–80 mm/Hg.
3) *Specific gravity of urine*
   This shows the relative proportion of components dissolved in the overall volume of urine specimens. Knowledge of specific gravity is needed in interpreting the results of tests in urine analysis.
4) *Albumin*
   This is a type of protein monomer that is soluble in water or salt and experiences coagulation when exposed to heat.

Its function is to maintain the osmotic pressure caused by albumin to maintain kidney function.

5) *Blood sugar*

This is the level of glucose in the blood. If the blood sugar level is too low it will cause hypokalemia, the symptoms are feeling tired, losing consciousness. If the blood sugar level is too high, hyperchloremia will occur. In the long run, it can cause diabetes, kidney disease, eye damage, and nerves.

6) *Status of red blood cells*

Red blood cells are blood cells that function to carry oxygen to body tissues through the blood. Lack of red blood cells can trigger the existence of anemia, the symptoms are easily tired and the immune system is getting weaker. Excess red blood cells can cause blood clots, kidney damage, spleen, and eyes. The status of red blood cells is divided into two, namely normal or abnormal.

7) *Status of pus cells*

This is a collection of fluids, white blood cells, microorganisms, and cellular material that shows an infected wound or abscess. Pus cell clumps are white blood cells that gather in urine tests, usually one of the signs of an infection.

8) *Bacterial presence status*

Bacteria that enter through the urethra and travel to the bladder cause bladder infections. Usually, the body can get rid of bacteria by watering the bacteria to come out when urinating.

9) *Glucose levels in the blood*

High glucose can indicate diabetes, but many diseases and other conditions can also be caused by glucose in the blood. Glucose levels in the blood are normal in the range of 70–130 mgs/dl.

10) *Blood urea nitrogen*

Nitrogen level in blood is the amount of nitrogen content in blood. If there is a problem with the ability of the kidneys to work, the amount of concentration in the blood will also be disturbed. Normal blood urea nitrogen is in the range of 15–40 mgs/dl.

11) *Creatinine serum levels*

Creatinine levels are another waste from the processing of muscle formation. When there is a problem with kidney function, the creatinine levels in the blood will increase. Normal creatinine levels are in the range 0.4–1.4 mgs/dl.

12) *Sodium blood test*

Sodium test is utilized to identify strange groupings of sodium, including low sodium and high sodium. It is regularly utilized as a feature of the electrolyte or fundamental metabolic board for routine wellbeing checks. Typical sodium levels are in the reach 135–145 mEq/l.

13) *Potassium test*

Potassium tests are used to detect abnormal concentrations of potassium. It is often used as part of the electrolyte or basic metabolic panel for routine health checks. Normal potassium levels are in the range of 3.5–5.0 mEq/l.

14) *Hemoglobin*

Hemoglobin levels are metalloproteins (proteins that contain iron) in red blood cells that function as carriers of oxygen from the lungs throughout the body. Normal hemoglobin levels are in the range of 10–18 gms.

15) *Packed cell volume*

This is the level of the volume of erythrocytes in the blood packed by turning at a specific speed and in a specific time. The motivation behind this test is to decide the convergence of erythrocytes in the blood. The typical condition of stuffed cell volume is 36 half.

16) *The number of white blood cells*

Which shows the increase and decrease that occurs in white blood cells. The number of normal white blood cells is 4,500–10,000 cells/cum.

17) *The number of red blood cells*

Which shows the increase and decrease that occurs in red blood cells. The number of normal red blood cells is 3.9–5.7 millions/cmm.

18) *History of hypertension*

Hypertension is a constant condition where the circulatory strain in the corridor dividers increments. Hypertension can make genuine harm the heart and different organs, for example, the kidneys, mind, and eyes.

19) *History of diabetes mellitus*

Diabetes mellitus is a disease characterized by high blood sugar levels caused by disorders of insulin secretion or impaired insulin action. High blood glucose levels make the screening process in the kidneys more severe. This can cause a number of acute and chronic health problems.

20) *History of coronary heart disease*
    Coronary heart disease is a disease in which a waxy substance called plaque builds up in the coronary arteries. These arteries supply oxygen-rich blood to the heart muscle.

21) *Level of appetite*
    Appetite is the desire to eat food, feel hungry.

22) *History of the edema pedal*
    Pedal edema is a disease in which there is an abnormal collection of fluid in the space between cells.

23) *History of anemia*
    Anemia is a condition that occurs when the amount of hemoglobin in a person's blood falls below normal.

24) *Categorical Class*
    Class is a variable that indicates whether a patient has kidney failure or not.

10.4   Data Analysis

Data analysis is also called data management and data interpretation. The purpose of data analysis is to simplify data in a form that is easier to read and interpret. Data analysis is intended to understand what is in the data by grouping it, summarizing it, and finding general patterns that arise from the data. Explanation of data attributes can be seen in Table 10.1. Data that has been collected is stored in tabular format in the CSV format available on Microsoft Excel. The data obtained are grouped to facilitate the process of entering data. Furthermore, the data that has been grouped is normalized so that nothing is empty.

After all, the normal data is divided into training data and testing data. Training data is used for the process of forming prediction models, training data taken from 66% of all data. Testing data is used to test the prediction model whether it is valid or not. The table given above depicts the same.

Table 10.1 Data attribute information.

No.	Attribute name	Data type and value
1	Age (age)	Numeric Age in Natural Number values
2	Numeric Blood Pressure (bp)	Bp in mm/Hg
3	Specfic Gravity (Sg)	Categorical 1005, 1010, 1015, 1020, 1025
4	Albumin (al)	Categorical 0, 1, 2, 3, 4, 5
5	Blood Sugar (su)	Categorical 0, 1, 2, 3, 4, 5
6	Status of RBCs)	Categorical Normal, not normal
7	Status Pus cell (pc)	Categorical Normal, not normal
8	Bacteria presence status (ba)	Categorical Yes, no
9	Blood glucose levels (BGR)	Numeric Bgr in mgs/dl
10	Blood Urea Nitrogen (bu)	Numeric Bu in mgs/dl
11	Serum creatinine (SC)	levels of Numeric SC in mgs/dl
12	Results of Sodium blood test (sod)	Numerical Sod in mEq/l
13	Results of Potassium Test (pot)	of Numerical Pot in mEq/l
14	Levels of Hemoglobin (hemo)	Numerical Hemo in gms
15	Packed cell volume (pcv)	Numerical Pcv in%
16	Number of white blood cells (wc)	Numeric Wc in cells/cum
17	Rc numeric red blood cell (rc)	in illions/cmm
18	History of Hypertension (htn)	Categorical Yes, no
19	History of diabetes mellitus (dm)	Categorical Yes, no
20	History of Heart Disease Coronary (CAD)	Categorical Yes, no
21	Levels of appetite ()	Categorical Good, deficient
22	History of Pedal edema (pe)	Categorical Yes, no
23	History of Anemia (ane)	Categorical Yes, no
24	Categorical Classes ()	Ckd, not ckd

10.5   Conclusion

Based on the results of calculations and trials of Multi-Variate Linear Regression and Logistic Regression that have been carried out for the prediction of chronic kidney failure, it can be concluded that:

1. The prediction model obtained from the calculation of the value of the Ratio of Curve with Multi-Variate Linear Regression and Logistic Regression is a rule formed from the Gradient and Loss function.
2. The attributes of the regression analysis are formed using a history of hypertension, red blood cell status, blood pressure, history of diabetes mellitus, pus cell status, and packed cell volume. Attributes that are not in the decision model do not affect the decision making. Therefore, based on the Multi-Variate Linear Regression and Logistic Regression, the confusion matrix obtained can be used to make predictions of chronic kidney failure.

10.6   Future Scope

Research on the prediction of chronic kidney failure using Multi-Variate Linear Regression and Logistic Regression is still lacking. Thus, several things can be suggested as a material for future improvement, including comparing with any other classification methods to find out what classification method is best for CKD prediction.

References

1. Sultana, N. and Sharma, N., Statistical models for predicting swine flu incidences in India, in: *2018 First international conference on secure cyber computing and communication (ICSCCC)*, 2018, December, IEEE, pp. 134–138.
2. Singh, N., Sharma, N., Sharma, A.K., Juneja, A., Sentiment score analysis and topic modelling for gst implementation in India, in: *Soft Computing for Problem Solving*, pp. 243–254, Springer, Singapore, 2019.
3. Wang, X., Bonventre, J., Parrish, A., The aging kidney: Increased susceptibility to nephrotoxicity. *Int. J. Mol. Sci.*, 15, 15358–15376, 2018.
4. Mangla, M., Akhare, R., Ambarkar, S., Context-aware automation based energy conservation techniques for IoT ecosystem, in: *Energy Conservation for IoT Devices*, pp. 129–153, Springer, Singapore, 2019.

5. Brod, J., Chronic pyelonephritis. *Lancet*, 267, 6930, 1956, 973–981, 2017, https://doi.org/10.1016/S0140-6736(56)91798-6. (http://www.sciencedirect. com/science/article/pii/S0140673656917986.

6. Sharma, S., Juneja, A., Sharma, N., Using deep convolutional neural network in computer vision for real-world scene classification, in: *2018 IEEE 8th International Advance Computing Conference (IACC)*, 2018, December, IEEE, pp. 284–289.

7. Arya, P., Maurya, N., Sengar, N., Kumari, S., A review: Nutrition in chronic kidney disease patients. *Int. J. Adv. Innov. Res.*, 5, 97–108, 2018, 10.5281/ zenodo.1423081.

8. Zhang, H., Zhang, C., Zhu, S. *et al.*, Direct medical costs of end-stage kidney disease and renal replacement therapy: A cohort study in Guangzhou City, southern China. *BMC Health Serv. Res.*, 20, 122, 2020, https://doi.org/ 10.1186/s12913-020- 4960-x.

9. Verma, S. and Sharma, N., Statistical models for predicting Chikungunya incidences in India, in: *2018 First International Conference on Secure Cyber Computing and Communication (ICSCCC)*, 2018, December, IEEE, pp. 139–142.

10. Verma, S., Sharma, N., Sharma, K.P., Comparative analysis of time series models for the prediction of conjunctivitis disease (April 10, 2020). *Proceedings of the International Conference on Advances in Electronics, Electrical & Computational Intelligence (ICAEEC) 2019*, Available at SSRN: https://ssrn. com/abstract=3572573.

11. Sultana, N., Sharma, N., Sharma, K.P. Ensemble model based on NNAR and SVR for predicting influenza incidences (April 13, 2020). *Proceedings of the International Conference on Advances in Electronics, Electrical & Computational Intelligence (ICAEEC) 2019*, Available at SSRN: https://ssrn. com/abstract=3574620.

12. Sharma, N., Sharma, A.K., Shashvat, K., H-SIR: Heterogeneous source initiated reactive protocol for wireless sensor network. *Int. J. Comput. Appl.*, 975, 8887, 2019.

13. Stephenson, M. and Bradshaw, W., Shared decision making in chronic kidney disease. *Ren. Soc Australas. J.*, 14, 26–32, 2018.

14. Sharma, S., Juneja, A., Sharma, N., Using deep convolutional neural network in computer vision for real-world scene classification, in: *2018 IEEE 8th International Advance Computing Conference (IACC)*, 2018, December, IEEE, pp. 284–289.

15. Haripriya, P. and Porkodi, R., A survey paper on data mining techniques and challenges in distributed DICOM. *IJARCCE*, 5, 741–747, 2016.

16. Akhare, R., Mangla, M., Deokar, S., Wadhwa, V., Proposed framework for fog computing to improve quality-of-service in IoT applications, in: *Fog Data Analytics for IoT Applications*, pp. 123–143, Springer, Singapore, 2020.

17. Li, Y., Wu, B., Shen, B., Diagnosis and differential diagnosis of crohn's disease of the ileal pouch. *Current Gastroenterology Reports*, 14, 5, 406–413, 2012.

18. Cahyani, N. and Muslim, M., Increasing Accuracy of C4.5 Algorithm by applying discretization and correlation-based feature selection for chronic kidney disease diagnosis. *J. Telecommun.*, 12, 25–32, 2020.

19. Kumar, R., Hill, C.M., McGeown, M.G., Acute renal failure in the elderly. *Lancet*, 1, 90–91, 1973.

20. Yang, L., Humphreys, B.D., Bonventre, J.V., Pathophysiology of acute kidney injury to chronic kidney disease: Maladaptive repair. *Contrib. Nephrol.*, 174, 149–155, 2011.

21. Nichols, L.A., Slusarz, A., Grunz-Borgmann, E.A., Parrish, A.R., Alpha(e)-catenin regulates bmp-7 expression and migration in renal epithelial cells. *Am. J. Nephrol.*, 39, 409–417, 2014.

22. Thakar, C.V., Zahedi, K., Revelo, M.P., Wang, Z., Burnham, C.E., Barone, S., Bevans, S., Lentsch, A.B., Rabb, H., Soleimani, M. Identification of thrombospondin 1 (tsp-1) as a novel mediator of cell injury in kidney ischemia. *J. Clin. Investig.*, 115, 3451–3459, 2005.

23. Li, Z., Chen, X., Xie, Y., Shi, S., Feng, Z., Fu, B., Zhang, X., Cai, G., Wu, C., Wu, D., *et al.*, Expression and significance of integrin-linked kinase in cultured cells, normal tissue, and diseased tissue of aging rat kidneys. *J. Gerontol. A Biol. Sci. Med. Sci.*, 59, 984–996, 2004.

24. Advances in Social Science, Education and Humanities Research, volume 205, *The 2nd International Conference on Culture, Education and Economic Development of Modern Society (ICCESE 2018)*, pp no. 318–322.

25. Kang, D.H., Anderson, S., Kim, Y.G., Mazzalli M., Suga S., Jefferson J.A., Gordon K.L., Oyama T.T., Hughes J., Hugo, C., *et al.*, Impaired angiogenesis in the aging kidney: Vascular endothelial growth factor and thrombospondin-1 in renal disease. *Am. J. Kidney Dis.*, 37, 601–611, 2001.

26. Deokar, S., Mangla, M., Akhare, R., A secure fog computing architecture for continuous health monitoring, in: *Fog Computing for Healthcare 4.0 Environments*, pp. 269–290, Springer, Cham, 2019.

27. Barbara, B., Schindler, R.M.: Internet forums as influential sources of consumer information. *J. Interact. Mark.*, 15, 3, 31–40, 2001. http://dx.doi.org/10.1002/dir.1014.

28. Yu, Y., Duan, W., Cao, Q., The impact of social and conventional media on firm equity value: a sentiment analysis approach. *Decis. Support Syst.*, 55, 4, 919–926, 2013. http://dx.doi.org/10.1016/j.dss.2012.12.028.

29. Hiroshi, K., Tetsuya, N., Hideo, W., Deeper sentiment analysis using machine translation technology. In: *Proceedings of the 20th International Conference on Computational Linguistics (COLING 2004)*, pp. 494–500. Geneva, Switzerland, 23–27 Aug 2004.

30. Coresh, J., Astor, B.C., Greene, T., Eknoyan, G., Levey, A.S., Prevalence of chronic kidney disease and decreased kidney function in the adult us

population: Third national health and nutrition examination survey. *Am. J. Kidney Dis.,* 41, 1–12, 2003.

31. Webb, S., Dobb, G. Arf, atn or aki? It's now acute kidney injury. *Anaesth. Intensive Care.,* 35, 843–844, 2007.

32. https://news.vidyaacademy.ac.in/wp- content/uploads/2018/10/NotesOn MachineLearningForBTech-1.pdf

33. Kellum, J.A., Bellomo, R., Ronco, C., Definition and classification of acute kidney injury. *Nephron Clin. Pract.,* 109, c182–c187, 2008.

34. Bellomo, R., Kellum, J.A., Ronco, C., Acute kidney injury. *Lancet.* 380, 756–766, 2012.

35. Van den Noortgate, N., Mouton, V., Lamot, C., van Nooten, G., Dhondt, A., Vanholder, R., Afschrift, M., Lameire, N., Outcome in a post-cardiac surgery population with acute renal failure requiring dialysis: Does age make a difference? *Nephrol. Dial. Transplant.,* 18, 732–736, 2003.

36. Xue, J.L., Daniels, F., Star, R.A., Kimmel, P.L., Eggers, P.W., Molitoris, B.A., Himmelfarb, J., Collins, A.J., Incidence and mortality of acute renal failure in medicare beneficiaries, 1992 to 2001. *J. Am. Soc. Nephrol.,* 17, 1135–1142, 2006.

37. Koletsi, D. and Pandis, N., Ordinal logistic regression. *Am. J. Orthod. Dentofacial Orthop.: Off. Publ. Am. Assoc. Orthodontists, its constituent societies, Am. Board Orthodontics,* 153, 157–158, 2018, 10.1016/j.ajodo. 2017.11.011.

38. Melk, A., Ramassar, V., Helms, L.M., Moore, R., Rayner, D., Solez, K., Halloran, P.F., Telomere shortening in kidneys with age. *J. Am. Soc. Nephrol.,* 11, 444–453, 2000.

39. Farman, M., A control of logistic model of bladder cancer with dimensionless estimate parameters, in: *Experimental Techniques in Urology & Nephrology,* vol. 2, 2019, 10.31031/ETUN.2019.02.000544.

40. Stott, R.B., Cameron, J.S., Ogg, C.S., Bewick, M., Why the persistently high mortality in acute renal failure. *Lancet.,* 2, 75–79, 1972.

Part III

ADVANCED APPLICATIONS
OF MACHINE LEARNING
IN HEALTHCARE

11

Behavioral Modeling Using Deep Neural Network Framework for ASD Diagnosis and Prognosis

Tanu Wadhera[1]*, Deepti Kakkar[1] and Rajneesh Rani[2]

[1]Department of Electronics and Communication Engineering, NIT Jalandhar, Punjab, India
[2]Department of Computer Science, NIT Jalandhar, Punjab, India

Abstract

The algorithms based on Machine Learning (ML) demand handcrafted features for data recognition and classification. Deep learning, on the other hand, directly extracts the features from the raw data through tuning of different convolutional and pooling layers and then perform classification. In deep learning context, the theory of transfer learning is quite useful while analyzing the biomedical signals. The primary objective of present chapter is to detect Autism Spectrum Disorder (ASD) by utilizing pre-trained frameworks based on transfer learning approach for brain signal classification. An experimental paradigm is designed to acquire the neural patterns from ASD and comparative Typically Developing (TD) groups. The brain activation signals related to risk-perception, cognition and working memory are targeted to detect ASD. Different pre-trained models such as EEGNet and DeepconNet were utilized as initial layers and the last few layers are replaced to accommodate EEG signals for our classification purpose. The models were trained on the self-collected data with 70:30 as training and testing ratio. On validation of the models, it is found that DeepConvnet exhibited best performance compared to EEGNet. This is additionally generic as it worked without any call for of handcrafted features and achieved an accuracy of 92.3%. Other performance measures sensitivity (95.4%), specificity (90.5%), F-score (93.2%), and area under the curve (0.963). Thus, transfer learning approach proved good in modeling behavior for ASD identification and prediction.

Keywords: Autism, deep learning, EEG, transfer, perception, risk, SVM

---

*Corresponding author: tanu1991libra@gmail.com

Monika Mangla, Nonita Sharma, Poonam Mittal, Vaishali Mehta Wadhwa, Thirunavukkarasu K. and Shahnawaz Khan (eds.) Emerging Technologies for Healthcare: Internet of Things and Deep Learning Models, (281–298) © 2021 Scrivener Publishing LLC

11.1   Introduction

Autism is a persistent developmental disability shown by atypical behavior of the children at the birth time or with the growth [1]. Autism is a brain handicap which makes the children disabled ones [2]. The disorder is not embarked by any unique symptom but it is a spectrum of symptoms broadly summed under three domains: (i) sparsity of social interaction, relations, and enormous aloofness (ii) unable to communicate and share emotions, motor impairments and qualitative and quantitative language disability, (iii) repetitive activities, distressed behavior and constrained interests [1–6]. The uncertainty of symptoms can vary from individual to individual more or less and cannot be limited to any particular extent [7]. Various other deficits present along with the disorder are: obsessed with their daily activities, movements, and verbal recitations and would not welcome any change [3, 4], poor dealing with the context and circumstance-based information [8]. The communicative deficit extends not only to verbal signals such as never development of speech signals nor partial development but also to non-verbal signals such as fixation of eyes, facial images during interaction, hand signs and societal interactions [4, 5, 9]. They are very much sensitive and respond very resolutely to some particular environmental sound, daily routine disturbances and loud noises such as mechanical toys, elevators sound, food processors sound with which the normal developing children are comfortable [3, 10, 11]. This complex behavior of the children can be pooled under clinical syndrome called Autism Spectrum Disorder (ASD) [12, 13].

ASD is a disorder in the children present at birth time not any disease described by the triad of disorders: autism condition, Pervasive Developmental Disorder - Not Otherwise Specified (PDD-NOS) and Asperger condition [13, 14]. Rett's syndrome and childhood degenerative disorder are also found in children but less frequently as compared to the triad of disorders [15]. The disorders under ASD have similarity of symptoms with each other [16]. The symptoms of AS appears in a child at near about 2.5 years of his age [17] and can be clubbed with children suffering from high functioning autism [18]. AS cannot be considered as autism directly but can be marked as its variant [19]. Asperger's have less qualitative communication impairments, language delay, and obsession for materialistic things as compared to the children with autism but like autistic children they have deficits in interchangeable social conversations. Also in children with autism, language development is delayed and level of intelligence ranges from intellectual disability to better level of intelligence, while criteria for the asperger's exclude cognitive impairment. The developmental disorders discussed can be differentiated on the basis of their symptoms and impairments in different parts of body: gaze pattern, response to gestures, vocal processing and speech development [9], body posture, level of intelligence, and routine development.

The initial evidence of autism was reported by a child psychiatrist in 1943 [3] and then in 1944 by Asperger. The children reported with autism were 11 (8 boys and 3 girls) in number in 1940s [3]. After that, number suddenly rises from 1970 where 1 to 5 children per 10,000 are affected in U.S. to 1990, where 6–70 children per 10,000 are affected, and in 2000–2012, the number has changed to 1 in 161 children [20]. Autism is more common in boys as compared to the girls [7]. The ratio in which the boys are affected as compared to girls is 2:1 in the severe cases rather than 3–4:1 (Rutter, 1985), but in 2006, the author quoted that the ratio between boys and girls to be 3–4:1 or nearly four times in males as compared with girls [6]. The presence of autism in females is observed by severe-brain damage and mental retardation along with impairments of imagination, social, and communication, whereas in males, it is often because of genetic factors. The disability percentage in seeing is 18.8, in hearing is 18.9, in speech is 7.5, in movement is 20.3, mental retardation is 5.6, mental illness is 2.7, any other which includes autism also is 18.4 and multiple disabilities is 7.9. Autism is not only a brain disorder but is an entire body disorder which requires early detection. The early revelation leads to medication at early stages which will be beneficial for both children and parents. The early intervention resolves the issues of autistic children at the beginning of the disorder and resolves to such an extent that the affected children behave more like a normal individual [15]. The variety in the criterion for diagnosis of autism increased awareness among practitioners and families, and accuracy of detection methods and professionals has reported cases of many undiagnosed children [20]. This has sharply increased the number of autistic children and as per Center for Disease Control and Prevention (CDC), that is 1 in 50 children in U.S. as per the latest record [20].

The gold-standard diagnostic methods adopted by clinicians, for example, the Autism Diagnostic Observation Schedule 2nd Edition (ADOS-2), indicated noteworthy advancement in expanding ASD detection accuracy. Notwithstanding, effectively directing ADOS-2 requires broad and expensive preparing to make exact conduct evaluations and cautious perceptions of regularly unpretentious meaningful gestures and behavior happening within a restricted time-frame. As of now, a minimum age of 1.5 years is the requirement to administer ADOS-2. In any case, there is a basic requirement for more achievable methodologies that can recognize ASD as right on time as could be expected under the circumstances, for example, in infancy. This is a remarkable confront for distinguishing ASD early marker that is lined up with current social behavior in ASD.

One methodology is to develop affordable, objective, and efficient framework for diagnosing ASD that depends on neuro-physiological information and maps the biomarkers as per current demonstrative measures. Such framework would diminish the intense work and significant expense of current analytic methodologies limit the prospective for misdiagnosis because of subjective and complex tools. One promising neuro-physiological technique is electroencephalography (EEG). The high temporal resolution, non-invasive nature, low noise, and easy setup makes it an principle choice for analyzing neuro-physiological traits of ASD.

EEG technique measures electrical signals from the brain using different positioned scalp-electrodes. The electrical signals result from the postsynaptic activity and can be utilized to investigate complex neuropsychiatric conditions. EEG signals can be analyzed in the domain in which they are captured, i.e., time-domain or can be converted into five frequency bands. The bands involve "delta (0–4 Hz)", "theta (4–8 Hz)", "alpha (8–13 Hz)", "beta (13–30 Hz)", and "gamma (>30 Hz)". EEG is complex, non-linear, and non-stationary method which traces significant information and depicts the variations of one person to another.

11.2   Automated Diagnosis of ASD

In ASD investigation, the studies have shown the potential of EEG by providing significant biomarkers. Most of the diagnostic frameworks have implied advances Machine Learning (ML) based approaches with EEG for detecting ASD. Additionally, the signals and data optimization techniques are also utilized to bring out the significant features crucial for diagnosis. The different methodologies based on EEG signal analysis for ASD detection are described in Table 11.1.

From the tabular summary, it is very much clear that comparative methods and statistical measures can analyze the results for the automated detection. These methods made it possible to detect the features extracted from the brain signals that specifically distinguishes EEG signals of Typically Developing (TD) individuals from those with ASD. The pattern recognition and classification approach have paved potential steps in ASD recognition by separating their brain signals from TDs.

Table 11.1 Summary of automated ASD investigation techniques based on EEG signal analysis.

Year published	Subjects	Database	Description
[21]	ASD:10 TD:9 (6–11 years)	Self-recorded (19 channels)	A classification accuracy of 89.5% is achieved to distinguish ASD and TD. Coherence is measured for different rhythms (alpha, beta, and gamma) between total pairs (171 pairs) reflected more connectivity abnormalities within left hemisphere as well as of right temporal lobe with other lobes.
[22]	ASD: 49 TD: 33 (3–36 months)	Self-recorded (19 channels)	The study computed 192 features comprising Low, high, and mean Modified MultiScale Entropy (mMSE). A multi-class Support Vector Machine acquired an accuracy of 90%.
[23]	ASD: 463 TD: 571 (2–12 year)	Self-collected (32 channels)	Reduced short-range and enhanced long-range coherences found in ASD compared to TDs. A classification accuracy of 98.1% (2 to 4 years) 99.1% (4 to 6 years) and 93.9% (6 to 12 years) is achieved in separating ASD from TD group.
[24]	ASD: 20	PhysioNet and Swartz Center for Computational Neuroscience	Utilized discrete wavelet transform + ICA and computed regression and correlation coefficient. Average correlation coefficient: 0.75 Regression: 0.69 were found on cleaned EEG data which can enhance ASD diagnostic accuracy.

(Continued)

Table 11.1 Summary of automated ASD investigation techniques based on EEG signal analysis. (*Continued*)

Year published	Subjects	Database	Description
[25]	TD: 30 ASD: 19	Experiment based data collection	Study collected the data using oddball paradigm to collect event related potential and compared different classifiers (SVM, Logistic Regression, and Naïve Bayes) The study reported that Naïve Bayes outperformed all in ASD diagnosis by achieving an accuracy: 79%
[26]	TD: 10 (9–16 y) ASD: 9; (10–16 y)	King Abdulaziz University Brain Computer Interface	Applied Discrete wavelet transform and computed Shannon entropy. The study achieved an accuracy of 99.71%.
[27]	TD: 10; (age:7–12y) ASD: 15 (age7–14y)	Villa Santa Maria Institute	The study proposed I-FAST technique and acquired Multi-scale entropy. A Leave-one-out random forest classifier is utilized for ASD detection. An accuracy of 92.8% is achieved in automated ASD diagnosis.
[28]	TD: 89 ASD: 99	Boston Children's Hospital/ Harvard Medical School	A wavelet transform is utilized and non-linear measures are fetched from EEG data. The statistical models acquired a specificity of 100% and sensitivity: 100%.

(Continued)

Table 11.1 Summary of automated ASD investigation techniques based on EEG signal analysis. (*Continued*)

Year published	Subjects	Database	Description
[29]	TD: 7 (age: 2–6 y) ASD: 7 (age: 2–6 y)	Self-collected dataset	Features based on recurrence quantification analysis are extracted; the Principal component analysis, 10-fold validation and SVM classifier are utilized which provided an accuracy of 92.9%, sensitivity of 100%, and specificity 85.7%.
[30]		Self-collected Dataset based on emotions	Power spectral density is computed from EEG signals. The classifiers-SVM and ANN achieved an accuracy of 90.5%.
[31]	TD: 10 ASD: 10 age: 4–13 y	Self-collected (64 channel cap)	Computed empirical mode decomposition to find point-to-point pulsations of extracted Intrinsic Mode Functions. A 3D mapping technique is utilized to visualize and mark abnormal brain activities. The stability of local pulsation pathways detected ASD.
[32]	34 participants	Self-collected	The eye movements are coupled with EEG signals. Different statistical features, entropy, & FFT values were extracted and fed to different classifiers, namely SVM, logistic regression DNN, naïve Bayes. The Naïve Bayes and Regression classifiers have provided 100% accuracy.

(*Continued*)

Table 11.1 Summary of automated ASD investigation techniques based on EEG signal analysis. (*Continued*)

Year published	Subjects	Database	Description
[33]	ASD: 99 (3–36 mo) TD: 89	Self-collected	Computed non-linear features from EEG signals and fed it to statistical analysis methods. SVM classifier was applied that gave 100% accuracy.
[34]	TD: 5 ASD: 10 age: 5–17y	Self-collected	Performed DWT and computed correlation-based feature which were fed to logistic, SVM, naïve Bayes, and random forest classifiers. A possibility to use minimum EEG channels is provided through this study. Among different classifiers, the random forest classifier acquired an accuracy of 93% in detecting ASD.
[35]	TD: 37 ASD: 40	Self-collected	The texture-based parameters are extracted from EEG signals and local sensitivity discriminant analysis is carried out. A t-test is performed to compare the means and PNN classifier utilized for classification which achieved an accuracy of 98.7%.

11.2.1 Deep Learning

The development of artificial intelligence (AI), specifically, deep learning neural systems, is quite possible for the neurologists to examine the neural information gathered from ASD and perform early diagnosis of ASD. The deep learning method is an information driven technique which can discover crucial information covered in the data. Such learning-based models and methods are profoundly inclined for the detection of neurological disorders such as ASD.

As of late, deep learning methods like Convolutional Neural Networks (CNNs) got predominant in the area of AI. CNN can consequently extract the signal features highlights by synchronizing the convolutional ("conv") as well as pooling ("pool") layers. In the biomedical field, the CNN models have been effectively applied to diagnose various neurological and brain pathology conditions. The vital part of CNNs is that the features required for classification or identification need not to be extracted beforehand. The CNN algorithm consequently extract mainly distinctive features without any optimization or propagation requirement. It is presented conceivable without utilizing any feature extractor because of data training within CNN calculation. Deep learning, especially CNN, is applied because of the capacity of the calculation to really perceive remarkable features of brainwaves from EEG data. Numerous reports have demonstrated achievement in incorporating EEG signal into CNN calculation. Since EEG is mind boggling and non-straight in nature, numerous direct classifier techniques could not precisely distinguish this sign as EEG. Subsequently, CNN has gotten progressively well known and is turning into an exceptionally favored new procedure in signal location and order.

The CNN hypothesis is primarily persuaded by the human brain. It is a neural system comprising Multilayer Perceptron (MLP) such that each MLP provides its unique service with a proper execution arrangement. In all MLPs, the input layer is required that originates from the input information, at least one hidden layer and then an output layer. There are a few layers that are generally referred to in CNN, for example, (i) convolution layer: which put different learnable filters called as "kernel" and provide output features for next layer; (ii) activation layer which improves the back-propagation and lessen redundancy; this layer is much needed for hidden and output layer. Some of the words—ReLu, dropout, and flatten—are the activation functions which subsist in CNN algorithms [24–26]. The ReLu is used in each CNN model, dropout prevents data overfitting among fully connected layers and flatten layer flattens the data to a 1-D array. (iii) Pooling layer which diminishes amount of highlights from convolutional layer; (iv) completely associated layer or thick layer which has to predict the output; and finally, (v) softmax layer, i.e., an activation function which discovers mean square error. In CNN framework, all these layers are executed in a cascading manner. The addition of more layers can provide better learning which causes better classification and thus, improves detection accuracy. Next is the training process in deep learning which include determination of different parameters such as feature mapping, learning weights, size of sample, optimization methods, and decision on epoch size.

Deep learning algorithms carry forward the classification one step further compared to strict supervised techniques. The algorithms utilize complex information from the models. Deep learning methodology requires negligible human association for extracting the features via unsupervised learning. The recognition of the data using the unsupervised criteria will allow research for neural patterns in identification of the psychiatric disorders. It is less reliant in assuming the hypothesis for feature selection due to which deep learning algorithms are less vulnerable to classification errors. In the supervised algorithms, the prior assumed labels are utilized to model the classifier and discover the brain patterns linked to the different psychiatric conditions. In the unsupervised methodologies, the classifier identifies the relationship between the provided patterns of data such as brain signals without any requirement of a prior tag or label. The unsupervised methods involve less subjectivity compared to the supervised methods. Similarly, the deep learning algorithms are less subjective and more unrestrained in application of ML based techniques to the large datasets from numerous repositories.

11.2.2 Deep Learning in ASD

A study applied deep learning algorithms based on a combination of supervised and unsupervised learning to identify ASD symptoms from the brain connectivity patterns (Heinsfeld *et al.*, 2018). The study utilized multi-site brain-imaging database called ABIDE (Autism Brain Imaging Data Exchange). The study investigated multiple patterns of brain functional connectivity to quantitatively detect ASD by unveiling the neural metrics emerging from classification. The findings enhanced the state-of-the-art by attaining 70% classification accuracy in distinguishing ASD and TD individuals. The classification patterns revealed an anticorrelation between anterior and posterior brain areas which corroborates anterior-posterior brain disturbance in ASD.

11.2.3 Transfer Learning Approach

In context of deep learning algorithms, the transfer learning method speeds the rate at which the models converge. In this approach, the features attained by training model on one dataset can be reutilized to boost the convergence when training some other model on a smaller/other dataset. The characterization ability of CNN is profoundly dependent on the dataset size utilized for training. If the dataset size is little, then after few epochs overfitting begins in the CNN model. In this situation, the exceptional area of deep learning, recognized as transfer learning gets developed as a compelling technique in clinical diagnosis. For transfer learning method, the "conv" layer weights from already trained models are utilized, but the final dense layers are trained using the novice data. For example, Talo et al. [31] utilized the pre-prepared ResNet-34 model in classification of brain abnormality data. The author proposed a few adjustments in final layers and then tuned and trained the model.

In ASD, a study utilized autoencoder and transfer learning method to recognize traits of ASD from the fMRI images of dataset ABIDE II. The results concluded that transfer learning strategy has brought better classifiers which provide enhanced accuracy and exactness in ASD identification [36]. Another model utilized a MLP with two hidden layers and synthetic minority over sampling to generate artificial data, prevent overfitting and consequently enhance the classification accuracy [26]. Further, SVM classifier is utilized to investigate the classification power of the extracted features. An auto tune model was utilized to re-arrange the hyper-parameters of SVM classifier and find the best-fit value. The proposed methodology acquired 80% accuracy in detecting ASD. The authors reported that the proposed schema has improved classification performance (SVM:26%; MLP 16%) and consequently ASD classification (by 14%) [26]. Recently, a study proposed a deep transfer learning–neural network (DTL-NN) model for analysis of entire neural connectivity [37]. Basically, the Stacked Sparse Autoencoder (SSAE) is trained offline to acquire normal functional connectivity. The prepared SSAE prototype is transferred to DTL-NN framework for ASD recognition. The model is validated by applying on MRI data from ABIDE dataset with ASD as a target task. In contrast to existing deep learning–based methods, the proposed approach acquired improved accuracy (71%), sensitivity (73%), specificity (75%), and area under characteristic curve (0.72) [37].

As the literature has shown that deep learning and transfer learning, approaches have been used for image dataset in classification of ASD and TD individuals. However, there is no study that has conducted analysis and classification of ASD using EEG dataset. Some of the deep learning–based studies on EEG datasets provided some pre-trained models such as [38] (i) EEGNet which is a dense CNN architecture improvised for EEG analysis; (ii) DeepConvNet which is a discriminative spectral–spatial input to present variety in patterns of brain signals.

11.3   Purpose of the Chapter

The purpose of the chapter is to provide a quantitative measure of neural markers corresponding to activation of risk-perception related regions. A risk-sense model as proposed in [39] to study the risk information in ASD is utilized in the present chapter. To study about the risk development, the risk-sense and action prediction ability for choosing the efficient path is studied in a risk-involving situation. The factors related to modeling of risk-perception are shown diagramatically in Figure 11.1.

The deep insights into the objective contribution of the model parameters is provided in Figure 11.2. The different parameters are determined by statistically computing the number of trials correctly identified as danger and safe signals from the total number of provided trials.

The detailed explanation of the parameters is given in [39]. The knowledge of each individual after every trial is investigated and the weights of the model parameters increases if a correct response is given by the participants. The flowchart of model working in upgrading the model parameters is shown in Figure 11.3. The weights will keep on upgrading with the repetition of trials if there is addition of new information in autistic individuals mind and if not then their weights will remains same. The weight up-gradation simply follows a step function.

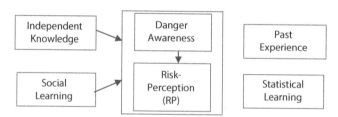

Figure 11.1 Factors modeled in risk-perception model.

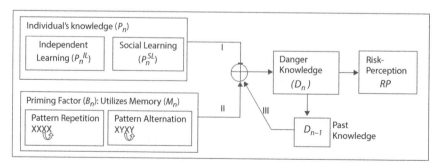

Figure 11.2 Schematic representation of the modeled parameters.

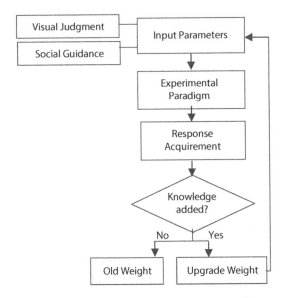

Figure 11.3 Flowchart representing the weight up-gradation in risk assessment.

Our EEG data was tested and optimized using the pre-trained models, namely, EEGnet and DeeoConvnet architecture as proposed by Lawhern (2018) and Kwon (2019) [40, 41]. The performance of the system is computed through different parameters, namely, sensitivity, specificity, accuracy, area under the curve, and F-score.

11.4   Proposed Diagnosis System

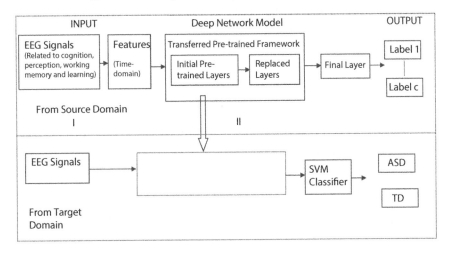

Table 11.2 Comparison of performance of the pre-trained deep learning–based networks.

Pre-trained model	Accuracy	Sensitivity	Specificity	AUC	F-score
EEGNet	89.6%	92%	89.3%	0.943	90.2%
DeepConvNet	92.3%	95.4%	90.5%	0.963	93.2%

While performing the experiment, the EEG signals were recorded from the participants. The parameters modeled for risk-perception needs to be extracted from EEG. The steps performed in the classification of ASD participants from TD are given below:

Step 1: Use the EEG signals comprising both the normal (TD) and ASD signals. Place signals in data/train directory.
Step 2: Prepare the data to read the signals. Labelize the signals according to the folder name and include different sub-folders within directory.
Step 3: Reduce input signal size to show consistency with input layer size containing pre-trained network model.
Step 4: Partition the data and give 60% to training and 40% to test set.
Step 5: Analyze network architecture and swap the final layers.
Step 6: Train the constructed network.
Step 7: Afterward, investigate model performance on the testing dataset,
Step 8: Compute the performance metrics.

The performance of using different pre-trained classifiers is shown in a tabular form in Table 11.2. It is very clear that both pre-trained networks performed very well in comparison to the existing ML–based automated diagnosis methods.

11.5   Conclusion

Early diagnosis is a noteworthy confront for neurodevelopmental disorders, especially ASD where analyzing large cohorts is mandatory. The investigators have undertaken combining EEG signals with advanced ML to unveil unseen pathological brain patterns and reveal diagnostic markers. The state-of-the-art techniques, such as deep learning, are outperforming conventional ML methods. The insufficiency of biomedical signals has hindered the whole brain classification by using deep learning methods. Therefore, inspired by the transfer learning approach, we utilized EEGNet and DeepConvnet for analyzing EEG signals. The knowledge of the pre-trained models is transferred for ASD classification tasks. Among both the models, DeepConvnet outperformed EEGNet by achieving 92.3% accuracy in detecting ASD using behavioral influenced EEG data signals. In future, there is a need to develop more such models which can help in automated diagnosis and prognosis of ASD clinically.

References

1. Tanu, T. and Kakkar, D., Strengthening risk prediction using statistical learning in children with autism spectrum disorder. *Adv. Autism*, 4, 3, 141–152, 2018.

2. Kakkar, D., Diagnostic Assessment Techniques and Non-Invasive Biomarkers for Autism Spectrum Disorder. *Int. J. E-Health Med. Commun. (IJEHMC)*, 10, 3, 79–95, 2019a.

3. Kanner, L., Autistic disturbances of affective contact. *Nerv. Child*, 2, 3, 217–250, 1943.

4. Tas, A., Yagiz, R., Tas, M., Esme, M., Uzun, C., Karasalihoglu, A.R., Evaluation of hearing in children with autism by using TEOAE and ABR. *Autism*, 11, 1, 73–79, 2007.

5. Elhabashy, H., Raafat, O., Afifi, L., Raafat, H., Abdullah, K., Quantitative EEG in autistic children. *Egypt. J. Neurol. Psychiatr. Neurosurg.*, 52, 3, 176–182, 2015.

6. Kakkar, D., Automatic Detection of Autism Spectrum Disorder by Tracing the Disorder Co-morbidities, in: *2019 9th Annual Information Technology, Electromechanical Engineering and Microelectronics Conference (IEMECON)*, 2019b, March, IEEE, pp. 132–136.

7. Tanu, T. and Kakkar, D., Strengthening risk prediction using statistical learning in children with autism spectrum disorder. *Adv. Autism*, 4, 3, 141–152, 2018.

8. Tanu, T. and Kakkar, D., Drift-Diffusion Model Parameters Underlying Cognitive Mechanism and Perceptual Learning in Autism Spectrum Disorder. *3rd International Conference on Soft Computing: Theories and Applications*, 2020.

9. Tanu, T. and Kakkar, D., Analysis of Weighted Visibility Graphs in Evaluation of Austim Spectrum Disorder. *International Conference ICTESM*, Kuala Lumpur, Malaysia, pp. 37–43, 2020.

10. Tanu, and Kakkar, D., A Study on Machine Learning Based Generalized Automated Seizure Detection System, in: *2018 '8th International Conference on Cloud Computing, Data Science and Engineering (Confluence)'*, IEEE, pp. 769–774, 2018.

11. Tanu, and Kakkar, D., Accounting For Order-Frame Length Tradeoff of Savitzky-Golay Smoothing Filters. *5th International Conference on Signal Processing and Integrated Networks (SPIN)*, IEEE, pp. 805–810, 2018.

12. Wadhera, T. and Kakkar, D., Influence of Emotional Imagery on Risk Perception and Decision Making in Autism Spectrum Disorder. *Neurophysiology, 51*, 4, 281–292, 2019.

13. Wadhera, T. and Kakkar, D., Multiplex temporal measures reflecting neural underpinnings of brain functional connectivity under cognitive load in Autism Spectrum Disorder. *Neurol. Res., 42*, 4, 327–339, 2020a.

14. Wadhera, T. and Kakkar, D., Conditional entropy approach to analyze cognitive dynamics in autism spectrum disorder. *Neurol. Res., 42*, 8, 1–10, 2020c.

15. Wadhera, T., Kakkar, D., Singh, J.K., Design and Analysis of Field Effect Transistor-based Biosensor to assist Screening and Detection of Autism Spectrum Disorder. *International Behavior. 3rd BMI International Autism Conference*, Hyderabad, 2020, 2020.

16. Wadhera, T. and Kakkar, D., *Interdisciplinary approaches to altering Neurodevelopmental disorders*, IGI Global, Hershey, Pennsylvania, 2020.

17. Wadhera, T. and Kakkar, D., Eye Tracker: An Assistive Tool in Diagnosis of Autism Spectrum Disorder, in: *Emerging Trends in the Diagnosis and Intervention of Neurodevelopmental Disorders*, pp. 125–152, IGI Global, Hershey, Pennsylvania, 2019.

18. Wadhera, T. and Kakkar, D., Big Data-Based System: A Supportive Tool in Autism Spectrum Disorder Analysis, in: *Interdisciplinary Approaches to Altering Neurodevelopmental Disorders*, pp. 303–319, IGI Global, Hershey, Pennsylvania, 2020.

19. Wing, L., Asperger's syndrome: a clinical account. *Psychol. Med.*, 11, 01, 115–129, 1981.

20. Dillenburger, K., Jordan, J.A., McKerr, L., Devine, P., Keenan, M., Awareness and knowledge of autism and autism interventions: A general population survey. *Res. Autism Spectr. Disord.*, 7, 12, 1558–1567, 2013.

21. Behnam, H., Sheikhani, A., Mohammadi, M.R., Noroozian, M., Abnormalities in connectivity of quantitative electroencephalogram background activity in autism disorders especially in left hemisphere and right temporal, in: *tenth international conference on computer modeling and simulation (uksim 2008)*, 2008, April, IEEE, pp. 82–87.

22. Bosl, W.J., Tager-Flusberg, H., Nelson, C.A., EEG analytics for early detection of autism spectrum disorder: a data-driven approach. *Sci. Rep.*, 8, 1, 1–20, 2018.

23. Duffy, F.H. and Als, H., A stable pattern of EEG spectral coherence distinguishes children with autism from neuro-typical controls-a large case control study. *BMC Med.*, 10, 1, 64, 2012.

24. Jadhav, P.N., Shanamugan, D., Chourasia, A., Ghole, A.R., Acharyya, A., Naik, G., Automated detection and correction of eye blink and muscular artefacts

in EEG signal for analysis of Autism Spectrum Disorder, in: *Proceedings of the 36th Annual International Conference of the IEEE Engineering in Medicine and Biology Society*, Chicago, IL, USA, 26–30 August 2014, IEEE, Chicago, IL, USA, pp. 1881–1884.

25. Eldridge, J., Lane, A.E., Belkin, M., Dennis, S., Robust features for the automatic identification of autism spectrum disorder in children. *J. Neurodev. Disord.*, 6, 1–12, 2014.

26. Djemal, R., Al Sharabi, K., Ibrahim, S., Alsuwailem, A., EEG-Based computer aided diagnosis of autism spectrum disorder using wavelet, entropy, and ANN. *Biomed. Res. Int.*, 2017, 1–9, 2017.

26. Eslami, T. and Saeed, F., Auto-ASD-network: A technique based on deep learning and support vector machines for diagnosing autism spectrum disorder using fMRI data, in: *Proceedings of the 10th ACM International Conference on Bioinformatics, Computational Biology and Health Informatics*, 2019, September, pp. 646–651.

27. Grossi, E., Olivieri, C., Buscema, M., Diagnosis of autism through EEG processed by advanced computational algorithms: A pilot study. *Comput. Methods Programs Biomed.*, 142, 73–79, 2017.

29. Heunis, T., Aldrich, C., Peters, J.M., Jeste, S.S., Sahin, M., Scheffer, C., Vries, P.J., Recurrence quantification analysis of resting state EEG signals in autism spectrum disorder—A systematic methodological exploration of technical and demographic confounders in the search for biomarkers. *BMC Med.*, 16, 1–17, 2018.

30. Harun, N.H., Hamzah, N., Zaini, N., Sani, M.M., Norhazman, H., Yassin, I.M., EEG classification analysis for diagnosing autism spectrum disorder based on emotions. *J. Telecommun. Electron. Comput. Eng.*, 10, 87–93, 2018.

31. Abdulhay, E., Alafeef, M., Hadoush, H., Alomari, N., Bashayreh, M.A., Frequency 3D mapping and inter-channel stability of EEG intrinsic function pulsation: Indicators towards autism spectrum diagnosis, in: *2017 10th Jordanian International Electrical and Electronics Engineering Conference (JIEEEC)*, 2017, May, IEEE, pp. 1–6.

32. Thapaliya, S., Jayarathna, S., Jaime, M., Evaluating the EEG and eye movements for autism spectrum disorder, in: *2018 IEEE international conference on big data (Big Data)*, 2018, December, IEEE, pp. 2328–2336.

33. Bosl, W.J., Tager-Flusberg, H., Nelson, C.A., EEG analytics for early detection of autism spectrum disorder: A data-driven approach. *Sci. Rep.*, 8, 1, 1–20, 2018.

34. Haputhanthri, D., Brihadiswaran, G., Gunathilaka, S., Meedeniya, D., Jayawardena, Y., Jayarathna, S., Jaime, M., An EEG based channel optimized classification approach for autism spectrum disorder. *Proceedings of 2019 Moratuwa Engineering Research Conference (MERCon), Moratuwa, Sri Lanka*, 3–5 July 2019, IEEE, Chicago, IL, USA, 2019.

35. Vicnesh, J., Wei, J.K.E., Oh, S.L., Arunkumar, N., Abdulhay, E.W., Ciaccio, E.J., Acharya, U.R., Autism Spectrum Disorder Diagnostic System Using

HOS Bispectrum with EEG Signals. *Int. J. Environ. Res. Public Health*, 17, 3, 971, 2020.

36. Vaijayanthi R, P., Gunturu, A., Krishna, V., Identification of Autism Spectrum Disorder (ASD) using Autoencoder. *Int. J. Innov. Technol. Exploring Eng. (IJITEE)*, 9, 4, 945–948, 2020.

37. Li, H., Parikh, N.A., He, L., A novel transfer learning approach to enhance deep neural network classification of brain functional connectomes. *Front. Neurosci.*, 12, 491, 2018.

38. Ju, C., Gao, D., Mane, R., Tan, B., Liu, Y., Guan, C., Federated Transfer Learning for EEG Signal Classification. In *2020 42nd Annual International Conference of the IEEE Engineering in Medicine & Biology Society (EMBC)*, pp. 3040-3045, IEEE, 2020.

39. Wadhera, T. and Kakkar, D., Modeling Risk Perception Using Independent and Social Learning: Application to Individuals with Autism Spectrum Disorder. *J. Math. Sociol.*, 44, 1–23, 2020.

40. Lawhern, V.J., Solon, A.J., Waytowich, N.R., Gordon, S.M., Hung, C.P., Lance, B.J., EEGNet: A compact convolutional neural network for EEG-based brain–computer interfaces. *J. Neural Eng.*, 15, 5, 056013, 2018.

41. Kwon, O.Y., Lee, M.H., Guan, C., Lee, S.W., Subject-independent brain-computer interfaces based on deep convolutional neural networks. *IEEE Trans. Neural Networks Learn. Syst.*, 31, 10, 3839–3852, 2019.

Random Forest Application of Twitter Data Sentiment Analysis in Online Social Network Prediction

Arnav Munshi[1*], M. Arvindhan[1†] and Thirunavukkarasu K.[2]

*[1]School of Computer Science and Engineering, Galgotias University,
Greater Noida, UP, India*
*[2]Unitedworld School of Computational Intelligence (USCI) Karnavati University,
Uvarsad, Gandhinagar, Gujarat*

Abstract

In today's world, we, humans, have been communicating with each other through calls and social media applications like WhatsApp, Facebook, and Twitter. From the social media apps, we get social media data from those applications and check what sentences are positive and negative sentiment using Sentiment Analysis and use deep learning methods like deep neural networks for classifying them under positive or negative sentiment polarity from twitter accounts. The data that we get from these social sites are being used for many social problems and used in government to analyze the opinion about social media users. This technique is called Sentiment Analysis. The main purpose of this Sentiment Analysis for this project will be to comparatively determine the writings made by the user and check if they are going toward positive or negative. Only one technique will be used here—Machine Learning Algorithm–Random Forest. This paper uses the Machine Learning Algorithm and Random Forest. The scope of this project will be widely used in classifying the text in terms of positive and negative polarity and help the government to handle social and threats due to the text classification.

Keywords: Sentiment analysis, random forest, Hindi tweets

*Corresponding author: munshiarnav@gmail.com
†Corresponding author: m.arvindhan@galgotiasuniversity.edu.in

Monika Mangla, Nonita Sharma, Poonam Mittal, Vaishali Mehta Wadhwa, Thirunavukkarasu K. and Shahnawaz Khan (eds.) Emerging Technologies for Healthcare: Internet of Things and Deep Learning Models, (299–314) © 2021 Scrivener Publishing LLC

12.1   Introduction

12.1.1   Motivation

The motivation behind using Twitter Sentiment Analysis for my project was to observe a large number of tweets made in public and analyze them regarding their native languages. As for Indian native language, Hindi, I chose to do the Sentiment Analysis based on the Hindi Tweets made by various people which I will be showing in later topics.

Other than this, I found this project motivating because I found that the dataset is larger in twitter as compared to other sites. Secondly, not only Sentiment Analysis is used for text analysis or tweets analysis but also being used in various fields like: Various companies are selling their product online and promoting their products and services in social media platforms also. Now, the customers might view those ads and click it to see about the product and if it looks interesting, then they go for check-out and order the product as per their interest. Now, the company uses this Sentiment Analysis for analyzing the customer opinions about their product by seeing their comments or filling a Q&A, reviews, and so on and that is how they can know about the customer's likes and dislikes and that is how the companies grow. Now, if I move on with my topic which is doing Sentiment Analysis on Twitter Data, then it means looking for positive and negative tweets. This kind of work goes well in English but I am using Hindi Tweets dataset for this finding of this positive and negative tweets and using of Random Forest to find the score of my implementation which helps me to understand that how well this concept of Sentiment Analysis works on Twitter Data which may help in analyzing social threats by seeing over customer tweets and so on which may help the government to work on the issues. Although this kind of work has been done by many of the authors before me and I am also performing this project with only Random Forest and using only NLTK and see how my result stands out among the authors.

12.1.2   Domain Introduction

Now, before this, we talked about the motivation and slight introduction toward Sentiment Analysis on Twitter Data. In this subtopic, I will talk somewhat a brief introduction about Twitter Sentiment Analysis.

Sentiment Analysis is a concept that falls under "Pattern Classification" and Data Mining. But if we go toward performing toward Sentiment Analysis on Text Analysis like in Twitter data for analyzing tweets, then we also approach toward Text Mining and also in a more advanced concept called Natural Language Processing (NLP).

NLP is defined as a field/concept in AI giving the machine to read, understand, and derive meaning from human native languages and in simpler means handles human's natural language like speech/text [5].

The main application of NLP corresponds to predictive of diseases, acting like a cognitive assistant, stopping spam mails by identifying the mails, helping in identifying fake news, and also used in finance to generate massive reports.

For mainly to keep in concise, NLP also helps in Sentiment Analysis by identifying and extracting information from social media and provide a lot of information about customer choice and decision drivers.

Now, we will talk about NLTK which we are using as an NLP library in this project. NLTK is one of the powerful NLP libraries and is mainly used in Python to work with human language data. The NLTK provides a suite of text processing libraries for classification, tokenization, stemming, tagging, parsing, and semantic reasoning, wrappers for industrial-strength NLP libraries with the NLTK, we can do simple things, tokenization and tagging of text, naming entities, and displaying parse trees [6].

There are about more than 100 microblogging sites in today's world being used by millions of users across the globes through short messages and posts. Like other micro-blogging sites, Twitter is also one of them where users daily post and share messages which are about millions of posts daily on an average and also comment about positive or negative views on a post made by someone. This kind of nature of humans making positive and negative comments are being supervised by many of the manufacturing companies where they see this as a way of earning profit regarding the products and services and how the customer interacts with their products and services and this is how positive and negative comments and sentences or words got differentiated and studied leading to a new concept called Sentiment Analysis (SA) [7–9].

Sentiment Analysis is a study of the positive and negative comments, sentences, or even words, and these techniques are now being used by many of the companies to know about their product well like Amazon, Google, etc., and so the list goes on. For this particular paper, I have used Sentiment Analysis on the Hindi tweets dataset and checked that how are the sentences being classified into positive, negative, or neutral sentiment.

This can be achieved by using the method—Machine Learning (ML)—The best Machine Learning Algorithms for text classification will be Random Forest.

Random Forest or Random Decision Forest are the algorithms used for classification and regression consist of a large number of individual decision trees and each tree comes out with a class prediction.

Random Forest Classifier—Random Forest is defined as a large number of decision trees acting as a multiple machine learning algorithm to get better predictive performance as compared to using one decision tree algorithm. There will be more than one Decision Tree acting as a class prediction on an individual level and the class prediction's output generated individually to make up the model prediction output for the Random Forest. The best part of the Random Forest Classifier is that it can be used for classification and regression [10].

12.2 Literature Survey

Sentiment analysis on Twitter Data has been done and executed successfully by many authors which help us in getting more information about what the previous authors did is explained below:

1. Apoorva Aggrawaal presented Sentiment Analysis of Twitter Data, used two combinations of models like:
    a. Unigram Model
    b. Tree Kernel Model
    c. 100 Sentiment features model, etc.
    The author used Support Vector Machine and report averaged five-fold cross-validation test results and also used a binary classification task with positive and negative polarity and the chance of baseline occurred to be 50%. He also investigated two kinds of models: tree kernel and feature-based models and founded that these two models outperform the unigram model.
2. Duyu Tang and Furu Wei (2014) developed a Deep Learning System, called "Coooll" which is a deep learning model that builds sentiment classifiers from Tweets and manually annotated sentiment polarity.
    The author used two kinds of features which are: SSWE feature and STATE features.
    As proposed by the author, the SSWE feature learned from 10 Million Tweets consisting of positive and negative emotions and been verified in the positive and negative classification of Tweets.
3. Varsha Sahayak and Vijaya Shete (January 2015) have proposed Sentiment Analysis on Twitter Data where the author

uses the Maximum Entropy method, Naïve Bayes Classifier, and Support Vector Machine for Sentiment Analysis and did the following steps:

a. Retrieval of Tweets
b. Pre-Processing
c. Parallel Processing
d. Sentiment Scoring
e. Module Output Sentiment

The author concluded that three Machine Learning Algorithms used by him outperform the model, namely, unigram, feature-based model, and Kernel model using WEKA. He also concluded the difficulty increases with nuance and complexity of opinion expressed [11].

4. Dimitris Effrosynidis (21st Conference on Theory and Practice of Digital Libraries) which used pre-processing techniques like:

a. Removing numbers
b. Replacing repetition of punctuation
c. Handling capitalized words
d. Lower casing
e. Replace slang and abbreviation
f. Replace elongated word
g. Replace contraction
h. Replace negation
i. Removing stop words
   And using an advanced method like:
a. Stemming
b. Lemmatizing
c. Replace URLs and user mentions
d. Spelling correction
e. Remove punctuations

5. Kalaivani A and Thenmozhi D (International Journal of Recent Technology, April 2019) only described that Sentiment Analysis has two categories of techniques which are the Machine Learning Approach and Deep Learning Approach [12].

The Machine Learning approach comprises of four stages:

Data collection Pre-processing Training data Classification as well as plotting result

The features of the Machine Learning approach are unigram, bigram, and trigram, and used algorithms like Support Vector Machine and Naïve Bayes.

The Deep Learning approach on Sentiment Analysis is very much efficient because they deliver impressive performance in NLP application and they do not need to be handpicked by doing the work themselves.

Every single unit in Neural Network is simple and by stacking layer of NN units of one competent to learn highly sophisticated decision boundaries and algorithms like RNN is also competent in Sentiment Analysis.

6. Adyen Narendra Ramdhani (2017) proposed Twitter Sentiment Analysis using a Deep learning method where the author used Deep Neural Network with including the specification of the ReLU activation function, three Hidden Layers, Feed-forward Neural Network and using Mean Square Unit and Stochastic Gradient and pre-processing techniques as I mentioned earlier.

The author concluded that Deep Neural Network achieved the result of 75.03% and 77.45% and for MLP accuracy got 67.45% for train data and 52.05% on test data [13].

12.3   Proposed Methodology

In the previous topic, we looked at various methods used by authors ranging from Random Forest to Neural Network, and now, we have seen the existing models used by existing authors, Support Vector Machine was the Machine Learning algorithm mostly used and for this, we will be using Random Forest so that we can compare our result among other existing results.

Table 12.1 shows comparison for the results for existing models which we specified earlier in the previous topic.

Now, below are the steps for the proposed system that we are using in this project and will also some explanation about each step.

Step 1: Downloading Hindi Tweets and Translating to English Tweets Dataset:

In this step, we are using the Github link to download the dataset in the Hindi tweet dataset. Later on, we convert add another column of Translated English tweet from Hindi Tweets and then import using the Pandas library [14].

Table 12.1 Summary of results by previous authors.

Author and year	Method applied	Purpose	Dataset used	Result
Apoorv Aggrawal [2]	Support Vector Machine	Sentiment Analysis	Twitter Data	60.50%
Duyu Tang, Furu Wei (2014) [3]	Developed "Cooll" Deep Learning System	Sentiment Analysis	Twitter Data	70.14%
Varsha Sahayak, Vijaya Shete (Jan 2015) [4]	Maximum Entropy Method, Support Vector Machine, Naïve Bayes Classifier	Sentiment Analysis	Twitter Data	Sentiment classified into positive, negative, and neutral
Kalaivani A, Thenmozhi D- [1]	SVM, KNN, and DBN	Sentiment Analysis	Twitter Data	SVM(0.72 accuracy with n = 0 and 0.62 with n = 10), KNN(0.64 accuracy with n = 0 and 0.63 with n = 10), DBN(0.6 with n = 0, 0.73 with n = 10)
Andreyan Ramdhani (2017) [6]	Deep Neural Network, MLP	Sentiment Analysis	Twitter Data	Deep Neural Network -75.03% and MLP - 52.03%

Step 2: Data visualization and Analysis:
Data visualization will be done on the dataset using the matplotlib library in Python and analyze the data by cleaning by removing noisiness in them Figure 12.1.

Step 3: Removing Usernames, Stop-words, Punctuations, and Symbols:
In this step, after we have visualized the data in the graph using matplotlib and seaborn library in python [15, 16], we will be now doing the pre-processing of the dataset by removing user name, stop-words, punctuations, symbols, etc., to use the dataset in proper format and also using methods like stemming, lemmatization, and tokenization which are techniques used in NLTK Figure 12.2.

Step 4: Using Features extraction methods—BOW and TF-IDF:
These methods—Bag of Words and TF-IDF—will be used for creating features from text and will help in splitting the dataset into train and test dataset Figure 12.3.

Step 5: Model Building—Random Forest Classifier:
In this step, after we have preprocessed the data in the proper format, we will be building the model using Random Forest Classifier. Random Forest Classifier is being defined as a large number of decision trees acting as a multiple machine learning algorithm to get better predictive performance as compared to using one decision tree algorithm acting as a class

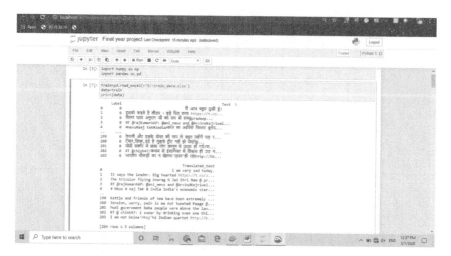

Figure 12.1 Importing of Pandas and Matplotlib and displaying the dataset.

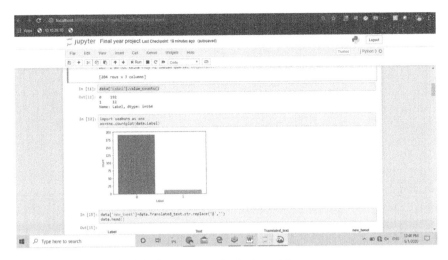

Figure 12.2 Bar graph of the dataset using the Seaborn Library.

Figure 12.3 Replacing usernames and punctuations.

prediction on an individual level and class prediction's O/P individually make upvotes and most votes with output make the model prediction O/P for Random Forest. The best part of Random Forest is that it can be used for Regression and Classification problem.

Below is the architecture for the Random Forest Classifier [16–18]:

The above diagram displayed shows the general architecture of the Random Forest Classifier Figure 12.4.

Figure 12.4 Using common words and tokenizing.

In this architecture, there is a large dataset D consisting of m rows and d columns and since we are using Random Forest means, that there will multiple models of individual decision trees using the concept of Bagging, which means of using multiple machine learning algorithms.

To use the new records in Decision Trees from D1 to D5, Row Sampling and Column Sampling will be done for each tree Figures 12.5 and 12.6.

Though with the Row Sampling and Column Sampling, there will be some rows and columns which will be the same among (RS + FS) taken into other Decision Trees models Figure 12.7.

Figure 12.5 Using stemming and lemmatization.

Figure 12.6 Using Bag of Words and TF-IDF count vectorizer and splitting the train and test dataset.

Figure 12.7 Calculating result using accuracy score and f1 score.

Decision Tree D will give prediction now and now the Test Data will be used in Decision Trees.

For example—binary classifiers and similarly, the same test data will be used for other Decision Trees. These Decision Trees will produce output for Binary Classifier as 1,0,1,1,1 and from which majority vote will be taken as 1.

In the case of Regression Situation, each tree will produce continuous data, and the result of the Random forest will be considered by taking the Mean of the Individual tree's output or using the Median method. Another thing to note about Random Forest is that the decision trees consist of two properties—Low Bias and High Variance.

Low Bias is defined as a concept where if the decision tree created, is being completed to the end, the result will be more accurate and the training error will be very less Figure 12.8.

As compared to Low Bias, High Variance is defined when we get new test data and apply on the decision tree, the decision tree has more tendency to give more error.

Now, the Random Forest works well by deciding that each Decision Tree will have a high variance, as having new test data but when each of these Trees will be combined and the vote will be for the majority, the high variance for Decision Trees will be converted to Low Variance.

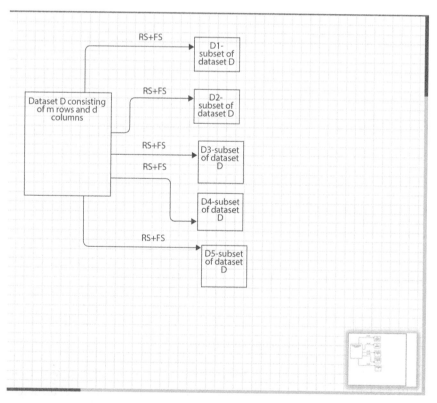

Figure 12.8 Architecture of random forest.

If we have 1,000 records, in a dataset and if we change 200 records, then also with the help of combined Decision Trees, the result will be in Low Variance resulting in good accuracy [19].

Step 6: Result With Accuracy Score and f1 Score:
After the model is being fit using Random Forest Classifier and testing for prediction, we will use the accuracy score and f1 score.

With this, we have explained the proposed system and explained some concepts [20].

12.4   Implementation

In this previous section, we explained about the proposed model and the steps involved in it. Now, in this section, we have shown the screenshot of each stop in Jupyter Notebook.

12.5   Conclusion

The implementation of the project concludes that the f1 score is achieved by 0.66354 by using Random Forest Algorithm for building and testing the model. This proves that the Hindi Tweets dataset implemented by Random Forest has an f1 score of 0.66354 and an accuracy score of 90.24. The future enhancements of this Sentiment Analysis are that automatic sentiment analysis has a fair way to go before it can replace human coding of sentiment—though even human coding will have problems, as my idea of negative or somewhat negative may well be different from yours. More and more, I am convinced that machine learning techniques and sophisticated text analytics algorithms will be needed to improve the accuracy of automatic Sentiment Analysis. Having said that, I believe that Sentiment Analysis will only increase in importance as more and more people use online channels to communicate, both directly and indirectly, with corporations.

References

1. Dos Santos, C.N. and Gatti, M., Deep convolutionalneural networks for sentiment analysis of short texts, in: *Proc. COLING 2014, the 25th Int. Conf. Computational Linguistics: Technical Paper*, Dublin, Ireland, pp. 69–78, 2014.

2. Hasan, M., Rundensteiner, E., Agu, E., EMOTEX: Detecting emotions in twitter messages, in: *Proc. 2014ASE Bigdata/Socialcom/Cybersecurity Conf*, Stanford University, CA, USA, 2014.

3. Liu, S.J., Yang, N., Li, M., Zhou, M., A recursive recurrent neural network for statistical machine translation, in: *Proc. 52nd Annual Meeting of the Association for Computational Linguistics*, Baltimore, MD, USA, pp. 1491–1500, 2014.

4. Tellez, E.S., Miranda-Jiménez, S., Graff, M., Moctezuma, D., Siordia, O.S., Villaseñor, E.A., A case study of Spanish text transformations for twitter sentiment analysis. *Expert Syst. Appl.*, 81, 457–471, 2017.

5. Neethu, M.S. and Rajasree, R., Sentiment analysis in twitter using machine learning techniques. *Computing, Communications and Networking Technologies (ICCCNT), 2013 Fourth International Conference on. IEEE*, 2013.

6. Amolik, A. *et al.*, Twitter sentiment analysis of movie reviews using machine learning techniques. *Int. J. Eng. Technol.*, 7, 6, 1–7, 2016.

7. Taketomi, A. and Hisano, M., Twitter users' characteristics and their emotional expressions in the tweets, IEICE Technical Report, NLC2014-34, vol. 114, No. 366, 1–4, 2014, (in Japanese).

8. Kwak, H., Lee, C., Park, H., Moon, S., What is twitter, a social network or a news media?, in: *Proc. 19th Int. Conf. World Wide Web*, Raleigh, North Carolina, USA, pp. 591–600, 2010.

9. Gupta, B. *et al.*, Study of Twitter Sentiment Analysis using Machine Learning Algorithms on Python. *Int. J. Comput. Appl.*, 165, 9, 29–34, 2017.

10. Jagdale, R.S., Shirsat, V.S., Deshmukh, S.N., Sentiment Analysis of Events from Twitter Using Open Source Tool, *International Journal of Computer Science and Mobile Computing (IJCSMC)*, 5, 4, 475–485, 2016.

11. Bahrainian, S.-A. and Dengel, A., Sentiment analysis and summarization of twitter data. *Computational Science and Engineering (CSE), 2013 IEEE 16th International Conference on. IEEE*, 2013.

12. Gurkhe, D. and Bhatia, R., Effective Sentiment Analysis of Social Media Datasets using Naive Bayesian Classification, 2014.

13. Yoo, S.Y., Song, J., II, Jeong, O.R., Social media contents based sentiment analysis and prediction system. *Expert Syst. Appl.*, 105, 102–111, 2018.

14. Laksito, A.D. *et al.*, A Comparison Study of Search Strategy on Collecting Twitter Data for Drug Adverse Reaction. *2018 Int. Semin. Appl. Technol. Inf. Commun*, pp. 356–360, 2018.

15. Chaturvedi, I., Cambria, E., Welsch, R.E., Herrera, F., Distinguishing between facts and opinions for sentiment analysis: Survey and challenges. *Inf. Fusion*, 44, 65–77, 2018.

16. Bandana, R., Sentiment Analysis of Movie Reviews Using Heterogeneous Features. *2018 2nd Int. Conf. Electron. Mater. Eng. Nano-Technology*, pp. 1–4, 2018.

17. Kanakaraj, M., Mohana, R., Guddeti, R., Performance Analysis of Ensemble Methods on Twitter Sentiment Analysis using NLP Techniques,

in: *Proceedings of the 2015 IEEE 9th Computing (IEEE ICSC 2015) Perforr*

18. Thanaki, J., *Python Natural Language* 2017.

19. Wagh, R., Survey on Sentiment Anal *Int. Conf. Electron. Commun. Aerosp.*

20. Medhat, W., Hassan, A., Korashy, F applications: A survey. *Ain Shams En*

in: *Proceedings of the 2015 IEEE 9th International Conference on Semantic Computing (IEEE ICSC 2015) Performance*, pp. 169–170, 2015.

18. Thanaki, J., *Python Natural Language Processing*, no. July, Packt, Birmingham, 2017.

19. Wagh, R., Survey on Sentiment Analysis using Twitter Dataset. *2018 Second Int. Conf. Electron. Commun. Aerosp. Technol.*, no. Iceca, pp. 208–211, 2018.

20. Medhat, W., Hassan, A., Korashy, H., Sentiment analysis algorithms and applications: A survey. *Ain Shams Eng. J.*, 5, 4, 1093–1113, 2014.

13

Remedy to COVID-19: Social Distancing Analyzer

Sourabh Yadav

Gautam Buddha University, Greater Noida, India

Abstract

In the current scenario of the pandemic, social distancing can act as a remedy to the widely spreading COVID-19, as it can slow down the spread of the virus. This is the reason why government officials are imposing lots of social distancing norms in the current scenario. But maintaining social distancing by the physical appointment of officials in the particular area may risk the life of that official. In the era of technology, finding a technical solution to this problem may not be a difficult task. With the advancement in deep learning algorithms, object detections are quite an easy job. The proposed manuscript initially tries to build a relationship between social distancing and an increase in new cases of COVID-19 and then targets build a social distancing analyzer using deep learning approaches. This social distancing analyzer may be utilized to remotely monitor the area where social distancing norms may breach by the general public or to monitor social events. Various deep learning and machine learning algorithms are employed to build to the model.

Keywords: COVID-19, deep learning, object detection, social distancing, TensorFLow

13.1 Introduction

On December 31, 2019, the entire world unexpectedly encountered an unknown disease in Wuhan, China that threatened human life like never before. The illness was later diagnosed as a kind of unknown pneumonia. It brought the wheel of life to a general standstill. It has grown so

Email: sourabhy1797@gmail.com

Monika Mangla, Nonita Sharma, Poonam Mittal, Vaishali Mehta Wadhwa, Thirunavukkarasu K. and Shahnawaz Khan (eds.) Emerging Technologies for Healthcare: Internet of Things and Deep Learning Models, (315–336) © 2021 Scrivener Publishing LLC

exponentially since its inception, crossing territorial borders and entering a range of countries and continents. It has been declared a world-class health crisis since World War II, given its spread effects. Furthermore, it has turned out to be significantly different from previous health emergencies such as Spanish flu, HIV, SARS, MERS, and Ebola, the extreme health emergencies during their time. Considering the severity and scale of its spread, on March 11, 2020 the World Health Organization (WHO) also declared the emergency as a pandemic. Coronavirus is defined as an RNA virus, which belongs to the subfamily of Orthocoronavirinae. Its exact origination is still not confirmed but it is said that it has been originated from the Seafood market of Wuhan, China. It is declared as a communicable disease, which communicates person-to-person, who came in contact with an infected person. Moreover, it communicates through the environment also. If a person is infected, he/she may remain infected for 12 to 13 days, i.e., a minimum of two weeks. It is considered as pathogens that directly attack the respiratory system of the human body. The person with week immunity, may not able to fight with the virus and the respiratory system will continuously deteriorate. That's why it is said that persons below 20 and above 60 are more prone to this virus. During these crucial times, each country strives hard to control this virus through various governing policies such as quarantine, social distancing, and rescheduling important events such as sports, results, and schools. However, it is very tragic that the disease continually spreads like a tsunami, despite implementing all policies. This uncontrollable propagation of the virus is adverse from different angles to humanity. In addition to affecting physical health, due to limitations imposed, the disease also affects psychological wellbeing, social relationships, and financial stability.

One of the best and majorly employed solutions to COVID-19 is social distancing. Effective remedy and appropriate vaccination are still not available for this virus. In the current scenario, the major spread of COVID-19 is due to person-to-person interaction, in which one person is COVID positive and another is COVID negative. It takes a minimum of 2 to 3 days for the proper deduction, whether the person is COVID positive or not. In all these situations, social distancing comes out to be the only remedy of COVID-19. Social distancing breaks the chain of spread. Social distancing only means maintaining physical distance among different mostly touched entities and maintaining a considerable gap with another person, whether he/she is COVID positive or not. In general, avoid touching commonly touched places and coming in contact with another person is quite difficult in the current routine. This is the only reason why government officials of different countries imposed lockdown among the different sectors of the countries. Due to this lockdown, physical distance is maintained among the general public.

World organizations have proposed stringency index to measure the lockdown scenario of different countries. The stringency index, in general, represents the measurable count of closed sectors with other correlating factors. The rise of the index represents the increase in closed sectors of the country. This is calculated in percentage, so the full lockdown scenario results in 100% in the index. When this index is analyzed with the number of COVID-19 patients per day, it shows that the stringency index is highly proportional to the COVID-19 cases, indirectly.

Figure 13.1 conveys that, with the rise of the stringency index, count of COVID patient comes down. This directly proves that social distancing acts as a useful remedy for COVID-19.

In the present scenario, maintaining social distancing is becoming quite a difficult job for government officials as lockdown is being lifted in a staged manner. Since life is getting to the normal pace, the general public unknowingly disrupts the rules of social distancing. Moreover, to maintain social distancing, government authorities require lots of officials. These officials become more prone to COVID-19. So there must be a way out, using which officials can monitor the general public and alert them to maintain social distancing. This brings the concept of a social distancing analyzer. In the era of technology, it is not a difficult task to build or propose a model that detects the distance among the public on a real-time basis. This brings the role of machine learning for building the analyzer.

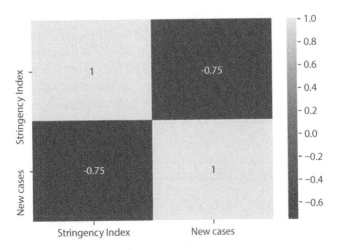

Figure 13.1 Correlation between COVID-19 new cases and stringency index.

The machine learning approach will figure out the different persons in the frame and further computations will calculate the distance among those persons. So, if the threshold is not maintained, the model will alert the official for breach of social distancing. In this way, Social Distancing Analyzer will support the front line corona warriors, i.e., government officials for maintaining social distancing among the general public. Moreover, the analyzer can be employed for other use cases also, like for performing contact tracing of COVID-19 positive patient with other non–COVID-19 public. It will lower down the risk of spread, and eventually, it will break the chain of spread.

This manuscript centers around building Social Distancing Analyzer using a deep learning approach. Deep learning approaches are widely used techniques for build project which requires live monitoring. Moreover, Deep Neural Network may work best for building Analyzer. Open CV library is one of the libraries which can be employed for building the model. These libraries incorporate predefined functions which help in model building and training. Other than the deep learning approach, there are some other computational requirements for building an effective social distancing analyzer. It requires simple mathematical logic for determining the distance among the persons. It requires effective graphic support to trace the person in the frame and its effective matching. Moreover, for building analyzers, a deep learning-based YOLO model is another option that can be employed for building and training the proposed model.

This research article contains a literature review section in which all the previously implemented and reviewed research is incorporated which gives the insight for building an efficient model. Following literature review, the proposed methodology section gives the insight of methodology employed to build and train the proposed model and some useful computations required for the efficient working of the model. All the implementation part of the proposed model is discussed in the system implementation section of the manuscript. Here, all the results obtained during the development of models are quoted. The last section is the conclusion, which brings out the main key features of this research and proposed model.

13.2 Literature Review

In the current period, the whole world is facing a very severe and unavoidable health emergency because of a pandemic caused by the novel Corona Virus which is also names COVID-19. Due to the lethal virus world facing lots of economic, social, and mental crises, which is not going to end soon.

Millions of lives are being affected by this virus. Big developed countries are facing huge economic crises and are not able to handle this situation. Undeveloped and developing countries are just somehow managing their living and existence. According to reputed researchers and available data of infected people, more than 7 billion people are infected and more than 40 million people have died this year, globally [1]. According to the research performed across the world, researchers are saying the poverty level will face an extreme increase by more than 400 million [2]. It is quite obvious, as many people who were living quite settled life with a secured job, their companies had made them resign. Moreover, fresh recruitment is also at hold, for maximum companies. Many sectors are facing an all-time low production rate, as their product is not reaching the market due to the pandemic situation. This pandemic has knocked on the door of the stock market of almost all the countries. The previous pandemic has not affected stock markets, like Spanish flu, it has just record small traces of downfall at American Stock Market, other than that, there is no market affected by the Spanish Flu. But this COVID-19 is creating a huge impact on the world market. Since markets are facing downfall; therefore, the whole country's economy is also facing big crises [3]. For overcoming this pandemic, many governments of many countries are taking respective steps, depending upon the situation in their area or boundaries. Most common step as imposing a lockdown. They just tried to predict the range of expected cases and imposed lockdown to overcome them. The period of lockdown was decided depending upon the geographical conditions and population of that zone. There are both pros and cons of imposing lockdown. An imposing lockdown has somewhere increased the doubling rate, it decreased the growth rate [4]. Lockdown has brought mental illness to the common people. No one in today's era wants to be bounded inside their houses. An imposing lockdown has increased the patients of depression by more than 17% [5]. There is no particular remedy for treating coronavirus patients. So, in that scenario, people are avoiding situations where they are prone to the virus. Almost every governing body is also requesting the general public to maintain a distance of at least 5 feet, which is generally known as Social Distancing. By following social distancing, one can protect them from being exposed to the infected person. Many medical experts are giving huge stress on making people aware of the positive impacts of social distancing during this pandemic situation, as according to their research, social distancing may break the chain of the spread of the novel coronavirus [6]. In the current period, almost all government officials are trying to make people aware of social distancing, and its positive impacts on lowering the rate of spread. Many researchers are on the note, in the absence of proper medication for COVID-19, strict enforcement of social distancing norms will break the chain of virus and will help to fight with this pandemic situation [7]. According to recent research, one of the worst affected countries, America, is giving stress on social distancing, as they consider the rate of spread can be controlled or decreased [8]. But people are not following the norms of socials distancing. Due to this, government is trying to enforce social distancing norms forcefully. Moreover, many government officials are monitoring the public places by assigning a few of their officers, for keeping check that social distancing is being followed or not. But this step is also equivalent to put the life of officers in danger, as they become prone to COVID-19 environment. So, there must be a way to figure out that social distancing is being followed in that particular area or not, without the actual presence of officials. In the era of technology, it is not a hard task to build a social distancing analyzer. Deep learning algorithms can help to build an effective and efficient analyzer. A deep learning algorithm plays a vital role in machine learning-based object detection. A deep learning algorithm plays a vital role in image and video processing [9]. Recent years have experienced lots of development in the field of Deep learning for image and video classification and processing [10]. The latest developments in deep learning algorithms for image processing and video analysis brought more powerful tools and training algorithms for specialized learning and enhanced performance [11]. Computer vision and deep learning go hand in hand. Computer vision is highly dependent upon deep learning algorithms. The latest deep learning approaches help in extracting more refined features from the input and helps in efficient training of the model. Moreover, detecting real-time objects is a very pivotal task in computer vision, which is highly dependent upon deep learning libraries and algorithms [12]. Due to the enhancement of deep learning packages, it has improved the object detection techniques and efficiency [13]. In the current scenario, systems are not just analyzing frames of video and images, but they are also trying to learn the behavior of performing objects [14]. For training and evaluating the model, another thing that needs to be taken care of is dataset. Properly defined and cleaned dataset must be employed for efficient learning [15–17]. Moreover, playing with the dataset comes under machine learning. Depending upon the dataset, the accuracy of algorithms is improved and enhanced. But recent machine learning researches are more focused on enhancing the accuracy whereas validating the dataset is ignored somewhere [18, 19]. In the present scenario also, dataset importance is quite visible from the fact that every forecasting starts with prediction based on historical dataset [20, 21].

13.3   Proposed Methodology

The proposed methodology is greatly dependent upon the OpenCV and Tensorflow library of Deep Learning. Figure 13.2 gives an insight into the glimpses of the architecture of the proposed model.

The development of the proposed model is cleaved two different types of development, i.e., Person Detection and Distance calculation among different detected persons.

13.3.1   Person Detection

This part of the proposed model aims to identify the person form the live feed. This module of the proposed model takes the live feed as an input, generates its frames, defines the contours, matches with the COCO model employed as a trained model, and final object deduced. This module is further bifurcated in three different parts, i.e., Frame Creation, Contour Detection, Mapping, and matching with the COCO model, and generating the final prediction of the object. This module of the proposed model

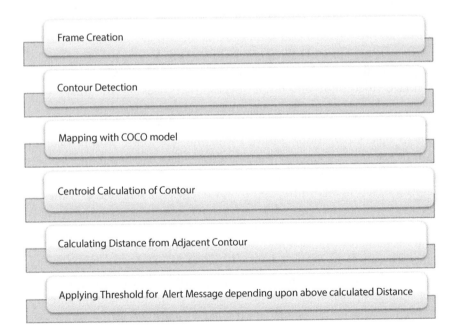

Frame Creation

Contour Detection

Mapping with COCO model

Centroid Calculation of Contour

Calculating Distance from Adjacent Contour

Applying Threshold for Alert Message depending upon above calculated Distance

Figure 13.2 Proposed modules to build analyzer.

is heavily dependent upon two well-known libraries, i.e., OpenCV and Tensorflow.

OpenCV is an open-source library that contains hundreds of algorithm based on computer vision, image and video processing, and machine learning. This library is most commonly used for operation dependent upon real-time actions. Real-time image and video processing are the most widely researched topics in the present era. Application-based on Real-time operations are required in almost every field/sector, like military operations to determine the movement of weaponized vehicles, police operations for monitoring the thieves movement, or detecting face and matching of the face from the predefined database, healthcare operation for reports (image) processing, and many other. In short, using OpenCV one can process the image and videos, and one can trace the handwriting. Other than real-time usage of OpenCV, it is also used with many other predefined libraries like Numpy. OpenCV generates the processing results of image and videos and saves them in the array, and that array can be utilized for performing other computations, like mathematical operations. OpenCV is a BSD license based library; therefore, it can be utilized commercially and academically. This library is mainly written for c, c++, java, and python. It is supported by a range of operating systems, like Ubuntu, Windows, MAC OS, Android, and IOS. OpenCV is mainly working on multi-core processing as all the codes of this library are mainly written in c/c++. The main and foremost aim of the development of the OpenCV library is to target real-time optimizations. OpenCV is mainly employed for image/video input and output operation, processing the image/video inputs, and presenting the image/video with some optimization. Other than image and video processing, it is employed for numerous use-cases, such as object detection, feature extraction, computer vision, machine learning, or CUDA acceleration. OpenCV takes the input image/video frame, normalizes the input, applies to boost (if required), applies the feature extraction algorithm, and finally applies the required classifier for detecting the object. Figure 13.3 gives the insights of work flow of OpenCV.

For deep learning approaches and algorithms, the most widely used library is named as TensorFlow, which is developed by Google. As known before, Google has great relation with machine learning, as they simulate their search algorithms around deep learning, their translations are dependent upon deep learning, and moreover, their recommendation and captioning model is highly dependent upon deep learning. Moreover, Google not just stores a huge amount of data but also it has installed the world's best and massive data storing computer. So, to utilize that large amount of data and to boost their research on deep learning, they have created a

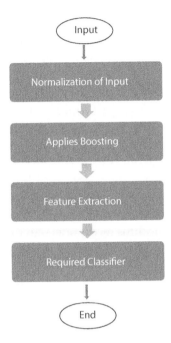

Figure 13.3 Working flow of OpenCV.

library to incorporate all the basic functions of deep and machine learning, named as TensorFlow. This library is platform-independent. Moreover, it can be utilized on more than one GPUs and CPUs. This library provides the AI researcher of the world to boost their research. Its basic implementation is dependent upon architecture cited in Figure 13.4.

Google has given the name TensorFlow, as multi-dimensional arrays are passed as an input, technically pronounced as Tensors. These Tensors are passed as input from one end of the model, and flowcharts are received from

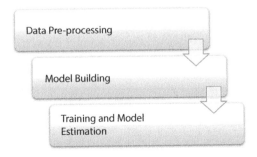

Figure 13.4 Basic architecture of TensorFlow.

another end known as Graphs. TensorFlow models are generally trained on desktop and can be utilized on multiple platforms, such as Desktops, Mobile Devices, and Cloud Services. Two basic components of TensorFlow are Tensors and Graphs. Tensors are arrays of n-dimensions, which illustrates almost all kinds of data. Graphs are the components that collect and arrange a series of computations performed while model training. Due to the Graph framework, TensorFlow is platform-independent. Moreover, it also maintains a ledger of computations for future validation. The main reason for the popularity of TensorFlow is wide acceptability by the users. TensorFlow library maintains a wide range of APIs for boosting deep learning approaches. Moreover, it offers a large number of algorithms for program debugging. Linear Regression, Linear Classifier, and DNN Classifier are the few prominent algorithms incorporated in the TensorFlow library.

Figure 13.5 gives the insights of the bifurcated parts of this module are discussed below.

13.3.1.1   Frame Creation

For real-time object detection, the live feed is passed as an input for the trained model. But this live feed is converted to frames. Frames are nothing just snapshot from the live feed at a particular time instant. Frames are used in different places in the world of computers. Frames are used in HTML. All the websites are divided into chunks of areas, and each chuck represents a different set of the webpage. Frames in the HTML domain allow more than one web page on the same screen. In the domain of graphics, frames play a major role. In programs of graphic designing, rectangular areas are defined as frames, which allows incorporating text and images in particular defined areas. In the domain of images, videos, and animations, frames are the chain of snapshots. It is generally measured in FPS, i.e., Frames per Second. Three-dimensional games have a big role in frames, in providing real-time experience to the users. Every live video feed needs to be converted into frames for its evaluation. Here, OpenCV library is one of the libraries which offers to convert video stream into frames without any hassle.

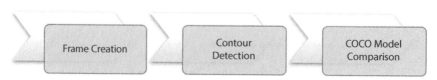

Figure 13.5 Sub-modules of person detection module.

Algorithm for Frame Creation
1. Object definition and creating instance for taking the video input.
2. Create the loop of video input till it ends for taking snapshots at each particular interval of time.
3. Passing it to frame()
4. Converting to grayscale image from BGR image for the further operations

13.3.1.2   Contour Detection

Contours are defined as an area or boundaries or a curve made by joining all the continuous boundary points, whose intensity matches with each other. These are the lines prepared by joining all the points at the boundaries that have the same intensity of colors in them. They are generally used to identify moving objects. Majorly, contours are employed to perform shape analysis, determining the object size, and identifying the object. In the medical domain, to study the shape of different body organs, it is very important to deduce correct body organs, as further analysis is highly dependent. To perform other deep learning approaches, the deduction of the body organ is really important. Deep learning approaches are highly dependent upon the probability of object detected and object detection is dependent upon contour detection. In the field of AI, bots will identify the objects and obstacles only when if the bot can differentiate properly in multiple objects. Contour detection plays a vital role in almost every domain where object detection and image processing are key implementations.

Algorithm for Contour Tracing
1. Converting grayscale image to Gaussian Blur Image.
2. Load first_frame object/variable with very first frame from the feed. It is used for subtracting the other frames for getting final frame.
3. Subtract other frames of grayscales.
4. Imposing Threshold.
5. Dilating Threshold frame.
6. Store the contour in contour object.

13.3.1.3 Matching with COCO Model

COCO model is a dataset comprises of commonly identifiable images. COCO stands for Common Objects in Context. This dataset contains two different sequences of files, i.e., Images and Annotations. Images are the commonly observable and identifiable snapshots that give the visual insights into the basic structure of objects. Moreover, color intensity identification becomes easy for the trained model. These snapshots are directly mapped and compared with live feed and input snapshots and tried to deduce the probability of matching with the saved database. Another part is the Annotations. These are the descriptive files generally in XML format. These files contain detailed information about the images saved in the model. These are directly mapped with each image, and their descriptions about the structure, basic color coding, and other stuff are mentioned in those annots. These annots are utilized while calculating the probability of matching of objects. These annots have many distinct fields that give a detailed view of mapped images. The below-cited figure gives the insight of COCO annot.

13.3.2 Distance Calculation

This part of the proposed model mainly aims to find out the distance between the two detected persons and display an alert message on the out screen. This part mainly comprises mathematical computations that need to be done for calculating the distance among the objects. This module basically calculates the centroid of the contour; further, it deduces the distance between the two different centroids. This distance is further passed for validation of distance allowed for coming close to each other, depending upon which alert message will be printed.

This module is further bifurcated into two sub-modules, i.e., calculating centroid of the contour and distance among different centroids.

13.3.2.1 Calculation of Centroid

This part of the proposed model mainly targets to calculate the centroid of the contours. Basically, contours are the rectangular boxes, drawn around the detected object. The distance of any object is always measured from the center of that object. In the case of deep learning, distance measurement is always performed after determining the contour of the object. Basically, in deep learning, the object distance is not taken care of, but the contour distance is the one who makes the move. In deep learning libraries, there are a large number of pre-defined libraries which are used to calculate the

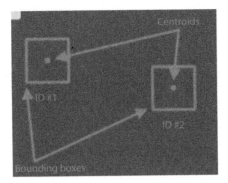

Figure 13.6 Bounding box with centroid point.

distance of the contours from the target object. OpenCV is one of the libraries which offers to calculate the center coordinates of the contour. These coordinates may help in calculating the centroid of the object. Libraries like NumPy are utilized to perform basic mathematical operations on the coordinates for further analysis. Figure 13.6 gives the basic idea of how centroid will be calculated using below-cited algorithm.

Algorithm for Centroid Calculation
1. For each contour, find the moment
2. Deduce the x and y coordinates from the moment
3. Pass it to cv2 circle function, to convert the analyse in the circular format
4. Pass it to cv2 putText() and highlight its centre, and output must be object defined for centroid.

13.3.2.2 Distance Among Adjacent Centroids

As discussed in earlier sections, distance is always measured from the center of the contour in deep learning approaches. This is purely mathematical computation. Distance between to coordinates is measured using Equation (13.1):

$$D = \sqrt{(x_1 - x_2)^2 + (y_1 - y_2)^2} \tag{13.1}$$

where x1 and x2 are x abscissa of two centroids and y1 and y2 ordinates of same centroids.

Algorithm for calculating distance among Centroid
1. Calculate the difference of abscissas of centroid coordinates
2. Calculate the difference of ordinates of centroid coordinates
3. Take the square root of the sum of squares of differences, i.e., abscissa difference and ordinate difference.

13.4 System Implementation

Figure 13.7 gives the insights of the basic implementation flow of the proposed Social Distancing Analyzer. This social distancing analyzer is built by using different deep learning algorithms and pre-defined libraries. Majorly, TensorFlow, and OpenCV are employed for identifying the person as an object, and the NumPy library is employed to perform basic mathematical computations in the proposed model. Other than that, the proposed model uses COCO model/dataset that is employed for efficient object detection. The proposed model is flexible with any sort of inputs, such as image, video, or live video feed. Figure 13.8 gives the structural view of work flow of proposed model.

Stage 1 of the proposed model is preparing the COCO model dataset. This dataset contains two types of files, i.e., image and XML file. Image files are the images of the object. These images will provide the color intensities or visual structure of the object in the image. Corresponding to the particular image, there will be one XML file, which contains all the required details of images, with whom they are mapped. This XML file contains the different fields like image field, max_boxes, output, min_score, and models. The image field is used to store the URL of the image or image location in the system. Max_ boxes field is used to store the number of maximum boxes need to define the

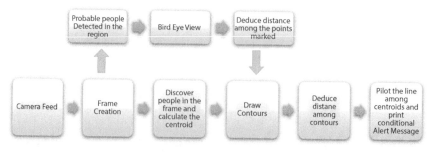

Figure 13.7 System implementation.

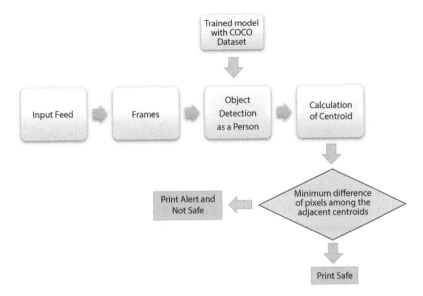

Figure 13.8 Work flow of proposed model.

contour of the image. Min_score contains the minimum annotated score, i.e., it is used to store the threshold probability of matching, if the threshold is passed, the image will be returned as an output. The output field is used to store the final score of the probability of matching. By defining all the attributes, the annotation file is prepared is ready for further computations.

Figure 13.9 is an annotated file which has a corresponding image mapped to it. The stage comprises of model input for the proposed model. As discussed earlier in the manuscript, the proposed model is flexible to take any sort of input, such as image, video, or live video feed. For taking images or videos as an input OpenCV library is employed. Pre-defined functions of OpenCV are used to import the video stored in the system database.

```
{
    "image": String,
    "output": String,
    "max_boxes": Integer,
    "min_score": Float,
    "model": String
}
```

Figure 13.9 Annotated file JSON representation.

For the proposed model, the VideoCapture() function of OpenCV is employed to import the video. Stage 2 comprises of fragmentation of video input into frames. This part is of the proposed model is done by using the same library named OpenCV. Fragmentation into frames means taking a snapshot of the videos at a particular instant of time and viewing them as a sequence of images. By using the above-cited algorithm of frames creation, a sequence of frames can be generated. The below-cited figure gives the insights of code snippets of frame creation from video input.

Figure 13.10 contains the code snippet when executed, will run the video input in a frame converted form. It will print a sequence of frames converted from video input using OpenCV. Stage 3 comprises of contour detection. Contour means joining the edges of images with the same intensities. Contours can be detected using the algorithm cited above. Here also, the OpenCV library will be utilized to define the rectangular boxes around the object detected. For the proposed model, contours are being defined depending upon the threshold area of the contours. Figure 13.11 gives the insight of code snippet for contour detection.

Stage 4 comprises of COCO model comparison. COCO model prepared in the first stage will be compared with the image frame, for validation of the object. The stage basically compares the image with the COCO model, gives the name of the object with its matching probability. The TensorFlow model is employed for making the prediction of the object. TensorFlow utilizes the COCO dataset for model training. The basic flow of the TensorFlow model is cited in Figure 13.12.

The trained model will take the image frame and performs model evaluations. Basically, it will make the object id with the COCO model's person label. If that id matches, the model will result in an object detected.

```
import cv2
import numpy as np

cap = cv2.VideoCapture(r'./test.avi')

while cap.isOpened():
    ret.frame = cap.read()

    cv2.imshow("inter", frame)

    if cv2.waitKey(40) == 27
        break

cv2.destroyAllWindows()
cap.release()
```

Figure 13.10 Code snippet for frame creation.

```
import cv2
import numpy as np

cap = cv2.VideoCapture(r'./test.avi')

ret.frame1 = cap.read()
ret.frame2 = cap.read()
]while cap.isOpened():
    diff = cv2.absdiff(frame1, frame2)
    gray = cv2.cvtColor(diff,cv2.COLOR_BGR2GRAY)
    blur = cv2.GaussianBlur(gray, (5,5), 0)
    _,thresh = cv2.dialte(thresh, None, iterations=3)
    dilated = cv2.dilate(thresh, None, iterations=3)
    contorus, _ = cv2.findContours(dilated, cv2.RETR_TREE, cv2.CHAIN_APPROX_SIMPLE)
    cv2.drawContours(frame1, contours, -1, (0,255,0), 2)

    cv2.imshow("feed", frame1)
    frame1 = frame2
    ret, frame2 = cap.read()

]   if cv2.waitKey(40) == 27
        break

cv2.destroyAllWindows()
cap.release()
```

Figure 13.11 Code snippet for contour detection.

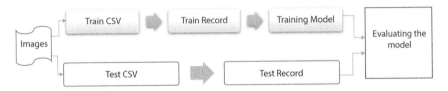

Figure 13.12 TensorFlow workflow for model training.

Figure 13.13 gives the insights of code prepared to compare the object id with the COCO model's person label.

Above cited code not only just determines the person in the frame but also calculates the center of the rectangular contour for calculating the distance among the different centroids. Moreover, the above-cited code not only matches the object ID with the person label but also calculates the probability of matching, which is quoted as confidence, in the above code. The next step will be to calculate the distance among the centroid and draw the line RGB color representing the distancing policy, like, if the line among the person appears as Red, then the corresponding message will be Alert Message, whereas if the line is green, then it indicates the safe distancing is being maintained. Below-cited code is prepared to print the required messages, with proper line among the centroid of the person contour detected.

```
for detection in output:

    scores = detection[5:]
    classID = np.argmax(scores)
    confidence = scores[classID]
    if LABELS[classID] == "person":

        if confidence > confid:
            box = detection[0:4] * np.array([W, H, W, H])
            (centerX, centerY, width, height) = box.astype("int")

            x = int(centerX - (width / 2))
            y = int(centerY - (height / 2))

            boxes.append([x, y, int(width), int(height)])
            confidences.append(float(confidence))
            classIDs.append(classID)
```

Figure 13.13 Code snippet for COCO model comparison.

```
cv2.rectangle(FR, (535, H+80), (1060, H+140+40), (100, 100, 100), 2)
cv2.putText(FR, "Bounding box shows the level of risk to the person.", (545, H+100),
            cv2.FONT_HERSHEY_SIMPLEX, 0.6, (100, 100, 0), 2)
cv2.putText(FR, "-- DARK RED: HIGH RISK", (565, H+90+40),
            cv2.FONT_HERSHEY_SIMPLEX, 0.5, (0, 0, 150), 2)
cv2.putText(FR, "--   ORANGE: LOW RISK", (565, H+150),
            cv2.FONT_HERSHEY_SIMPLEX, 0.5, (0, 120, 255), 2)

cv2.putText(FR, "--   GREEN: SAFE", (565, H+170),
            cv2.FONT_HERSHEY_SIMPLEX, 0.5, (0, 150, 0), 2)


tot_str = "TOTAL COUNT: " + str(total_p)
high_str = "HIGH RISK COUNT: " + str(high_risk_p)
low_str = "LOW RISK COUNT: " + str(low_risk_p)
safe_str = "SAFE COUNT: " + str(safe_p)

cv2.putText(FR, tot_str, (10, H +25),
            cv2.FONT_HERSHEY_SIMPLEX, 0.6, (0, 0, 0), 2)
cv2.putText(FR, safe_str, (200, H +25),
            cv2.FONT_HERSHEY_SIMPLEX, 0.6, (0, 170, 0), 2)
cv2.putText(FR, low_str, (380, H +25),
            cv2.FONT_HERSHEY_SIMPLEX, 0.6, (0, 120, 255), 2)
cv2.putText(FR, high_str, (630, H +25),
            cv2.FONT_HERSHEY_SIMPLEX, 0.6, (0, 0, 150), 2)
```

Figure 13.14 Code snippet for printing predictions.

By using the implementation cited in Figure 13.14, final model of the social distancing analyzer will give efficient judgment, whether people are following social distancing or not. The final model implementation is visible from below-cited figure.

TOTAL COUNT: 13   SAFE COUNT: 1   LOW RISK COUNT: 0   HIGH RISK COUNT: 12

Figure 13.15 Final model.

Figure 13.15 shows that it has detected a total of 13 people in the frame and 12 people are at high risk. This model can prove to be an effective model of usage by government authorities and police authorities, who stand on their toes to maintain social distancing among the people.

13.5   Conclusion

This manuscript targets to propose a deep learning-based social distancing analyzer, which can act as the remedy for treating the coronavirus without any medication. This model can utilize any government authority and police authorities to monitor the particular areas where they found difficulty in detecting whether people are following social distancing or not. Proposed manuscripts firstly prove why social distancing is a key to bring down the count of new COVID cases. Stringency index is employed to build the correlation between confirmed cases and social distancing norms. Manuscripts have proposed a pictorial representation correlation between stringency index and confirmed cases. Furthermore, the manuscript incorporates the full proof proposed methodology to build a social distancing analyzer. This analyzer uses OpenCV and TensorFlow libraries, which are counted as the most used libraries in the domain of deep learning algorithms in the present period. The proposed model takes live feed video stream as an input, which is further converted into the frames, and passed for contour detection. Once the region with people is detected, it is sent to the trained model, which uses the COCO model/dataset for validation of the object as a person. It is done by using the TensorFlow library. Once the object detected is identified as a person, the centroid of its contour is calculated, after which distance among adjacent centroid is calculated. Depending upon the threshold distance of 50 pixels, alert messages are defined, where the person is at high, moderate, and low risk. Moreover, a line joining the centroid of the contours also indicates the same message differently. This manuscript contains the code snippets of different modules, which are prepared to build the proposed model.

References

1. Walker, P., Whittaker, C., Watson, O., Baguelin, M., Ainslie, K., Bhatia, S., Cucunuba Perez, Z., Report 12: The global impact of COVID-19 and strategies for mitigation and suppression, Imperial College London MRC Centre for Global Infectious Disease Analysis, 2020.
2. Sumner, A., Hoy, C., Ortiz-Juarez, E., *Estimates of the Impact of COVID-19 on Global Poverty*. United Nations University World Institute for Development Economics Research, 800-809, 2020.
3. Baker, S.R., Bloom, N., Davis, S.J., Kost, K.J., Sammon, M.C., Viratyosin, T., *The unprecedented stock market impact of COVID-19 (No. w26945)*, National Bureau of Economic Research, Cambridge, 2020.
4. Lau, H., Khosrawipour, V., Kocbach, P., Mikolajczyk, A., Schubert, J., Bania, J., Khosrawipour, T., The positive impact of lockdown in Wuhan on containing the COVID-19 outbreak in China. *J. Travel Med.*, 27, 3, taaa037, 2020.
5. Rossi, R., Socci, V., Talevi, D., Mensi, S., Niolu, C., Pacitti, F., ... & Di Lorenzo, G., COVID-19 pandemic and lockdown measures impact on mental health among the general population in Italy. *Frontiers in Psychiatry*, 11, 790, 2020.
6. Simonov, A., Sacher, S.K., Dubé, J.P.H., Biswas, S., *The persuasive effect of fox news: non-compliance with social distancing during the covid-19 pandemic (No. w27237)*, National Bureau of Economic Research, Cambridge, 2020.
7. Wilder-Smith, A. and Freedman, D.O., Isolation, quarantine, social distancing and community containment: pivotal role for old-style public health measures in the novel coronavirus (2019-nCoV) outbreak. *J. Travel Med.*, 27, 2, taaa020, 2020.
8. Andersen, M. *Early evidence on social distancing in response to COVID-19 in the United States*. SSRN Working Paper No. 3569368. Amsterdam: Elsevier, 2020. Available at: https://ssrn.com/abstract=3569368.
9. Kim, J. and Pavlovic, V., A shape-based approach for salient object detection using deep learning, in: *European Conference on Computer Vision*, 2016, October, Springer, Cham, pp. 455–470.

10. Pathak, A.R., Pandey, M., Rautaray, S., Pawar, K., Assessment of object detection using deep convolutional neural networks, in: *Intelligent Computing and Information and Communication*, (pp. 457–466), Springer, Singapore, 2018.

11. Zhao, Z.Q., Zheng, P., Xu, S.T., Wu, X., Object detection with deep learning: A review. *IEEE Trans. Neural Networks Learn. Syst.*, 30, 11, 3212–3232, 2019.

12. Wei, W. and Hu, Y., Improve Real-time Object Detection with Feature Enhancement, in: *2019 IEEE 8th Joint International Information Technology and Artificial Intelligence Conference (ITAIC)*, 2019, May, IEEE, pp. 235–238.

13. Sabat, N.K., Pati, U.C., Das, S.K., A Short Survey on Real-Time Object Detection and its Challenges, in: *Advances in Systems Control and Automations*, pp. 93-100, Springer, Singapore, 2020.

14. Thakur, M., Real Time Object Detection in Surveillance Cameras with Distance Estimation using Parallel Implementation, in: *2020 International Conference on Emerging Trends in Information Technology and Engineering (ic-ETITE)*, 2020, February, IEEE, pp. 1–6.

15. Yadav, S. and Sharma, N., Homogenous ensemble of time-series models for indian stock market, in: *International Conference on Big Data Analytics*, 2018, December, Springer, Cham, pp. 100–114.

16. Yadav, S. and Sharma, N., Forecasting of Indian Stock Market Using Time-Series Models, in: *Computing and Network Sustainability*, pp. 405–412, Springer, Singapore, 2019.

17. Yadav, S. and Sharma, K.P., Statistical Analysis and Forecasting Models for Stock Market, in: *2018 First International Conference on Secure Cyber Computing and Communication (ICSCCC)*, 2018, December, IEEE, pp. 117–121.

18. Caveness, E., GC, P.S., Peng, Z., Polyzotis, N., Roy, S., Zinkevich, M., TensorFlow Data Validation: Data Analysis and Validation in Continuous ML Pipelines, in: *Proceedings of the 2020 ACM SIGMOD International Conference on Management of Data*, 2020, June, pp. 2793–2796.

19. Chauhan, P., Sharma, N., Sikka, G., The emergence of social media data and sentiment analysis in election prediction. *J. Ambient Intell. Hum. Comput.*, 1, 1–27, 2020.

20. Singh, B., Kumar, P., Sharma, N., Sharma, K.P., Sales Forecast for Amazon Sales with Time Series Modeling, in: *2020 First International Conference on Power, Control and Computing Technologies (ICPC2T)*, 2020, January, IEEE, pp. 38–43.

21. Mahajan, A., Rastogi, A., Sharma, N., Annual Rainfall Prediction Using Time Series Forecasting, in: *Soft Computing: Theories and Applications*, pp. 69–79, Springer, Singapore, 2020.

14

IoT-Enabled Vehicle Assistance System of Highway Resourcing for Smart Healthcare and Sustainability

Shubham Joshi* and Radha Krishna Rambola†

Computer Engineering SVKM's NMIMS MPSTME Shirpur, Shirpur, India

Abstract

Recently, the Internet of Things (IoT) has received strong scientific justification as a new research topic in several academic and industrial disciplines, particularly in healthcare. IoT revolution will transform the modern healthcare system, including technological, economic, and social perspectives. It develops a more personalized healthcare system than usual, where patients can be more easily diagnosed, treated, and monitored. New severe infectious respiratory syndrome the current global pandemic problem caused by COVID-19 represents the largest public health crisis in the world since the pandemic flu epidemic of 1918. From the beginning of the pandemic, the rapid efforts of different scientific communities can use many methods for countering this global issue, and many of the IoT technologies have been developed in this field. IoT is, predictably, the new wave of the internet that will change our lives. The internet was entrusted to people, and now it combines "things" to combine fluent information exchange and intelligence. IoT is a novel technology with a huge ability to change the world and our lives. Not so long ago, the idea of the IoT in automotive production was considered a theoretical concept, and today, we already have a lot of information about Parking, the environment, and the supply chain.

With the adoption of the IoT, vehicles can be transformed into an intelligent vehicle monitoring system; it monitors the situation, driver's health and prevents accidents to provide human support. This paper presents an IoT-enabled vehicle assistance system of highway resourcing for smart healthcare. The system

*Corresponding author: shubhamjoshi@ieee.org

†Corresponding author: dr.rambola@gmail.com

Monika Mangla, Nonita Sharma, Poonam Mittal, Vaishali Mehta Wadhwa, Thirunavukkarasu K. and Shahnawaz Khan (eds.) Emerging Technologies for Healthcare: Internet of Things and Deep Learning Models, (337–358) © 2021 Scrivener Publishing LLC

feels, investigates, predicts, and reacts to road conditions. The main objective of the research is to presents an IoT enabled vehicle assistance system of highway resourcing for smart healthcare, it performing tasks on the user side, and provides human support, allowing researchers to independently interact with the environment and participate in the development of context-conscious applications in distributed computing and Human-Computer Interaction (HCI).

Keywords: Internet of Things, adoption of IoT in automobiles, vehicle assistance system, smart healthcare, automotive industry

14.1 Introduction

Internet of Things (IoT) was first introduced in a presentation on the implementation of radio frequency identification (RFID) by Kevin Ashton, a supply chain management company [1]. IoT combines all networks and technology for human communication [2]. Any object or thing that is connected to the internet with a device capable of monitoring and data transmission is a possible device for those who are online [3]. Recently, IoT has pioneered compelling research as an interesting topic across different sectors, like healthcare. Health is an important factor in a person's life. We need to keep our health at its best. Some of the parameters of health are the glucose level, the temperature of the person, heart rate, etc. To measure these parameters need to use healthcare monitoring systems. IoT is becoming increasingly important in healthcare systems that can provide lower costs, a better quality of service, and an improved user experience with a wide range of features including tracking, identification, and authentication, and data collection. The greatest growth of the IoT in healthcare will be from $ 72 billion by 2020. It is expected to grow to $ 188 billion by 2025 [2, 4–8].

Road injuries are leading causes of death worldwide, based on WHO reports on the subject [9]. In developing countries, road injuries are on the rise. Medical institutions are serving useful services [10]. Training has been making recently to increase the provision of a necessary medical facility. There is a policy implemented for emergency services and a curriculum for suppliers of emergency services but there are some issues [11]. The countries face more issues, including weak training. But the developing world does not have a medical transport system.

Demand for smart and connected vehicles to the internet and smart devices is steadily growing in the era [12]. According to forecasts, by 2020, automakers will try to include built-in connections and IoT systems in vehicles [13, 14]. IoT has four-stage architecture, which is essentially a process stage (Figure 14.1). All phases store the data and processed the data and

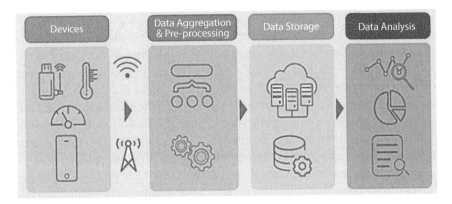

Figure 14.1 Steps of IoT solution [15].

sent output to the net stage. The combined value in the process gives input and offers an exciting chance for the business. The first step is to deploy interconnected devices, including sensors, monitors, etc. Typically, sensors or other devices collect data in analog format, and further data processing requires aggregating and converting to digital format. After that, the data is preprocessed and saved to storage. The final data will be processed and analyzed at the required level. Advanced analysis for applying this information provides practical business intelligence for effective decision-making.

Today, basically all cars are connected not only to homes, offices, and car factories. IoT has created a name in all fields to make life comfortable and safe. IoT ideas in the automotive industry are divided into three industries first is vehicle-to-vehicle communication, second is vehicle infrastructure communication, and third is a vehicle to devise communication [16, 17]. IoT connects to a device or things that are built into the software, a computer, and executive mechanisms, network connections that collect and share data [18]. IoT typically includes devices with technical capabilities and network connectivity, and these computer devices generate and consume information with little human input, and new IoT products such as exchange-enabled IoT devices, automotive automation components, and power management devices can provide greater comfort and safety for drivers on the road.

This chapter presents interest in developing a low-cost health monitoring vehicle assistance system (VAS) based on the IoT, regularly monitoring the health of patients in certain communities, and integrating additional measures to ensure the health of patients. In emerging markets, such as India, accidents on road because of illnesses of drivers, such as heart attack, stress because of constant work, etc. Also, due to heart attack during work, affects the driver's health and also the life of the passenger, since the vehicle is out of control of the driver. Therefore, if an intelligent health detection system is present at a low price, so it used by the driver, potentially reducing the number of road accidents. Wearable medical devices calculate certain parameters of the body, such as blood pressure, temperature, patient's pulse rate, and so on. This work uses sensors that touch his body and periodically check the health of the driver. If there are any deviations in health, the sensor sends information about the health condition to the vehicle office server through the internet. The health status received from the driver is updated in the database; the driver's photo is updated whenever he is in a state of drowsiness, and at the same time gives an alarm to the driver for alertness. The vehicle record is already available on the central server of the transport department. After that, the notification message is also forwarded to the transport office. If the transport office requires emergency services for the driver, the nearest ambulance is selected using GPS and notified to the ambulance unit.

The system also plays an important role in performing tasks and provides human support, allowing researchers to independently interact with the environment and participate in the development of context-conscious applications in distributed computing and Human-Computer Interaction (HCI). Thus, an IoT-enabled VAS system sense analyzes, predicts, and responds to road conditions, which are key characteristics of context-awareness. These studies show that information is collected: the road environment, the surrounding obstacles, the environment within the vehicle, often referred to as context.

The remaining chapters are as follows. (i) Section 14.2 describes related work of the IoT in medical applications. (ii) The research objectives and context is described in Section 14.3. (iii) Section 14.4 describes the technical background of the system. (iv) IoT infrastructural components for VAS are presented in Section 14.5. (v) Section 14.6 presents the implemented IoT-enabled VAS of highway resourcing for smart healthcare and its sustainability. (vi) Challenges in implementing the IoT-enabled VAS are described in Section 14.7. (vii) Section 14.8 is the conclusion.

14.2   Related Work

Analysis of road situations to help the driver and warnings about safety are among the activities that cover many areas of research, such as information technology, automotive technology, cognitive, and psychology. This chapter also conducts a comprehensive literature review of the use of IoT in medical applications.

14.2.1   Adoption of IoT in Vehicle to Ensure Driver Safety

Several middleware's ontology developed models are discussed mainly in navigation, infotainment programs, security aspects, etc. [19], which implements the project as a car and infrastructure, adaptive support middleware, ontology is intended for vehicles. The VMTL project [20] is a web-based database of mobile transport applications focused on navigation information, providing continuous location tracking and tracking of tourism data, while RT-Stream [21] focuses primarily on media access control and routing protocols, and is a platform for real-time communication. This real-time model did not discuss the presentation of data, compatibility issues, and the reasons for the situation. Cars connected-conscious speed selection Project [22] proposed an algorithm that focuses on package transmission to achieve rapid adaptation of data rate VANET. None of the above models discussed problems with middleware software. Prototype Context-Aware information Care Services [23] notice traffic problem and alerts on forecasts of overload, which are transmitted from peer to peer network JXTA, include a source message. This is again a middleware software type for publish-subscribe, where calls for this feature are required for server groups and storage servers [24].

14.2.2   IoT in Healthcare System

People do not perceive health seriously and drive constantly, without any rest for the body. Mainly drivers do not focus on their health and because of this there will be so many health problems, and to avoid this, there are some people who have given the solution to health.

Paper [25] highlights the improvement of the human health monitor was using the combined technology of IoT and cloud computing. In [26], it presents an IoT smart home platform for healthcare, which seamlessly combines intelligent sensors, feel human body for physiological analysis the daily management of medications, as well as offering a variety of medical applications for health with minor modifications. In [27], data is consolidated using a Rasberry Pi and a Docker container to show how to store data on a server and send information to users. In [28], it presents a patient monitoring system that uses in hospitals and homes, with parameters such as temperature and ECG, and an accurate detection system of abnormalities send warning messages to caretakers and doctors in case of any deviation. Adaptive learning of developed systems increases the accuracy of predictions and increases the effectiveness of decisions.

In [29], Smartphones and gadgets to control the health and custom electronic health sector are presented. They offer quick information at a bargain price that allows them to retain it for users. Materials and methods used for the detection of human activities using data mining methods that are necessary for applications in healthcare. There are different types of approaches to health monitoring, and one of them is that they used human data via a network, using an optimization method that is a colony of ants. Another approach is to take human values in real time using a sensor that is used as wearable devices or wired devices. In [30], parameters for route identification using ACO, and parameters for route length, route identification period, and local effective threshold, energy, time, and delay are used. These parameters are used to determine the shortest path in less time, which is more energy-intensive, and this optimization is used in medical services.

The wireless sensor network (WSN) allows the healthcare industry to measure important patient parameters using a medical sensor attached to their body to monitor the health parameters [31]. The acquisition of information on health and their transmission on different scales remains are an important task in the modern medical system [32]. In [33, 34], a non-invasive glucose sensor *in vivo* to measure blood sugar levels was developed. In [35], user experience and services are improving home healthcare services with wearable sensors, such as the latest IOT devices that integrate the platform. The data produced by the IoT systems and their availability in the medical field were discussed in [36, 37]. In [38], the authors propose an intelligent technology based on the IoT, it reduces the problems faced by urgent calls for providing automatic data that can incorporate from the patient in the emergency calls. These systems not only improve urgent help and save time but also decrease the capabilities of IoT, it contributes to the development of new applications. The work [39] represents the study of IoT in the medical field. This work describes a processing system for emergency medical use based on semantics and ontology when used in conjunction with large-scale medical data and data analysis. The study also introduced so-called indirect emergencies designed to ensure data availability. This can happen through medical records. In [40], the concept of experimental solutions to interoperability problems in IoT systems was presented. It is a barrier and a particularly main issue in the field of emergency medical care. In [41], an IoT-based blood donation analysis system was described. The system also helps you create a report file. A platform for remote analysis and management of medical data is presented.

14.2.3 The Technology Used in Assistance Systems

The following technologies have been studied to model intelligent driver assistance systems for safety warnings.

14.2.3.1 Adaptive Cruise Control (ACC)

ACC was developed by the launch of the Prometheus program in 1986. Today, the ACC is used in laser technology to follow vehicles and manage safe clearance. This allows the car to maintain speed, but adapt to an operating case that changes with automatic braking and acceleration [42, 43]. It decreases accelerations and decelerations, allows synchronize the speed of the vehicle, contributes to a smooth change in the behavior of the lane, and reduces the likelihood of accidents [44, 45]. If the situation gets out of control, the car slows down and stops for the driver's safety in the worst conditions.

14.2.3.2 Lane Departure Warning

It warns the drives if the car leaves the lane and the video camera in the rearview mirror allows the electronics to track the lane markings on the road ahead. It detects the car position on the lane and analyzes the position with input given from the steering angle sensor, brake position, and whether the indicator is being used [46]. When a car starts drifting off the lane, the driver warns by an audible warning.

14.2.3.3 Parking Assistance

The parking space measurement system [47, 48] is based on the supplier's Parking assistance system; it helps to avoid obstacles when parking. During operation, the sensor measures space if it is moving at a speed of up to 20 km/h. The assistant will alert the airbag to any obstacles, whether the gap in the car is large enough, narrow, or just too small.

14.2.3.4 Collision Avoidance System

The application of warning/collision avoidance functions in the system allows drivers to take action to prevent crash events [49]. Possible collision risks with the sensor include how close the vehicle is to other modes of transport, how close it is to the road, or if it needs to slow down when turning. The system uses sensors that signal and receive traffic from other vehicles; road obstacles [50]. For example, if the car is in a blind area when the driver tries to change his lane. The sensor detects that it is a vehicle and informs the driver to prevent an accident.

14.2.3.5   Driver Drowsiness Detection

A sleep-related road accident (SRVA) is more frequent in car accidents. The hypo-vigilance system warns the driver based on the intended state of hypo-driver vigilance and also the presumed risk in traffic. The system uses an airbag, a variety of modality acoustic, visual, and tactile output signals that warn the driver of his drowsiness, which prevents accidents [51].

14.2.3.6   Automotive Night Vision

Turning a night vision system into a system of interest includes many areas and components [52]. A system that makes it possible to recognize night vision in pedestrian systems is certainly an advantage. This increases the perception of the driver and distance vision in dark or bad weather to reach beyond the lights of the vehicle.

14.3   Objectives, Context, and Ethical Approval

Digital transformation has become the most important factor in the growth of several business lines at once. Companies are exploring new ways to work with customers and creating new digital and autonomous systems. This transition to digital transformation is even more important for urban mobility, especially to overcome the challenges associated with the development of COVID-19. IoT combines health goals with network connections from the digital and physical worlds. Also, personal health and IoT technologies can be combined to maximize the use of IoT for sharing user data, increasing awareness of the context. The main objective of the research is to presents an IoT-enabled VAS of highway resourcing for smart healthcare, it performing tasks on the user side, and provides human support, allowing researchers to independently interact with the environment and participate in the development of context-conscious applications in distributed computing and HCI.

In developing countries, in particular, IoT is being used to provide accurate and appropriate patient-centered information to emergency medical professionals and emergency medical centers autonomously and automatically in real-time, significantly reducing death rates. This study's goal is to explain the technology of vehicle underlying IoT and medical information of existing IoT data with various related system data. The problems and related solutions in this area will be also discussed. IoT-based devices made remote sensing possible in the healthcare sector, freeing up the potential to ensure patient safety and health, and empower doctors to provide superior medical care.

At this stage, the focus of the study is on improving the VAS for road accidents. Thus, developing countries and accidents on road present a research study. The primary reasons for selection are: (i) some problems of approach to healthcare that people face, (ii) problems facing emergency transport, (iii) absence of communication technology infrastructure, and the lack of medical care. Developed countries are also considered. The goal of the assessment is for participants in a cohort of simulation tests, assessments offered by various systems. We work with relevant hospitals to initiate patients using the snowman method. The interested person agrees to gather measure and store data. The data was gathered, measured, and stored anonymously.

14.4   Technical Background

14.4.1   IoT With Health

IoT connects healthcare institutions with a network connection. Also, it binds the IoT technology with health and IoT and fully exploits the IoT to expand opportunities, to share data, and to improve contextual awareness based on collected and analyzed data [53].

14.4.2   Machine-to-Machine (M2M) Communication

M2M is self-sufficient communication by cellular networks, such as GSM and LTE. Communication via the main network is carried out via the base station or access point of the M2M server (application server) [54].

14.4.3   Device-to-Device (D2D) Communication

D2D communication allows the devices to make a direct connection without interacting with the base station. It is designed for data sharing using many techniques like ultra-wideband (UWB), Wi-Fi, or LTE Direct [54].

14.4.4   Wireless Sensor Network

WSN mentions scattered and specialized sensors for track and documents environmental states. Sensors process the data, as well as communicate with each other. The WSNs designed effective and economical medical supervision/supervision to dispatch centers by ambulance so medical professionals can easily follow their inpatient, regardless of place and time, and gather relevant information about effective treatment.

14.4.5   Crowdsensing

Crowdsensing is an essential part of IoT [55]. Crowdsourcing data is a participatory or opportunistic crowdsensing paradigm that collects information using a participant's smartphone sensor smartphone sensors and sensor systems are increasingly used to measure ambient air quality [56] and temperature, as well as to detect biometric signals inside or outside the crowd. The crowdsensing system is either involved or strategic. Inclusive it wants the effective participation of participants: participants execute calculations, creates data entry systems, but opportunistic crowd sense does not require participants to participate: detection is more self-oriented, data is created automatically, and calculations are performed by participated sensors [57].

14.5   IoT Infrastructural Components for Vehicle Assistance System

This chapter briefly describes the IoT infrastructure components for implementing a smart VAS.

14.5.1   Communication Technology

- *Radio-Frequency Identification Device (RFID)*
  RFID-based conversation combines the use of electrostatic connections on wireless controlled parts for the unique recognition of objects, people, or animals [58]. It identifies elements, and makes a data file for a given item, and send the item via radio waves. Detection-tracking objects on the Internet by connecting to an RFID reader [59].
- *Global Positioning System (GPS)*
  GPS detects the places, also known as geolocation. Smartphones now also offer GPS systems to guides and monitoring equipment and products [60].

- *Global System for Mobile Communication (GSM)*
  GSM is creating and maintain conversation between devices. It sends input data through sensors or digitizes the device as an output message to the receiving device [61].
- *Wi-Fi*
  Wi-Fi is an IP based wireless network technology. Normally, you need a wireless adapter to receive the wireless network. Wi-Fi is a small range of wireless data transmission that connects PCs, mobile phones, and other portable gadgets [62].

14.5.2   Sensor Network

WSN is a set of sensors that track environmental and physical states and it is used in different applications, such as in home, medical research, road management, etc. [63]. The sensors are cooperating with an RFID system for state control products that provide data of location, temperature, and density, etc. [58]. The following are the number of sensors that can be used with VAS.

- *Eye Blink Sensor*
  The eye-link sensor shall consist of a relay, an IR sensor, and an eye-link frame and the driver shall use vibrating machines link to the IR transmitter (IR sends a beam to the driver's eye). The vibrator vibrates when the driver closes his eyes or there's an accident. The relay links with the microcontroller board to supply more power [64].
- *Acceleration Sensor*
  The sensor acceleration finds a small abrupt transition in speed in any direction or spin. It reads data while moving. A disaster alert can occur when the deceleration or acceleration reaches the limit value or when the sensor is tilted more than expected [65].
- *Gyroscope Sensor*
  A gyroscope is a sensor device that uses Earth's gravity to determine its direction. The gyroscope calculates the change rate of the angular rotational speed of time and issues, units of measurement MV/degree/second [66].
- *Impact Sensor*
  It detects collisions and is used for the immediate placement of airbags [65].

14.5.3   Infrastructural Component

- *Addressing System*
  The skill to identify a particular device in a group of devices is achieved by a processed system that is transmitted by each device over the Internet.
- *Middleware*
  Middleware plays an important role as a player between things and the application level, and its main purpose is abstract communication and device functionality [58]. Middleware is found in a diverse field of applications that collaborate on various interfaces [60].

14.5.4   Human Health Detection by Sensors

- *Heart Rate Monitor*
  A heart attack is usually caused by a blocked artery. The heart rate can be calculated with a heart rate monitor that shows your heart rate readings. Easily, high efficiency and low power micro board can measure blood pressure and heart rate. This microcontroller uses a heart rate sensor based on a plug and is designed to work by placing a finger on the sensor and issue a numerical output pulse [67].
- *Sugar Level Detector*
  Sugar and glucose are some of the important factors of human health and manage their level can lead to a minor imbalance in the human body, cause weakness, dizziness, etc. [68]. IoT-based systems can be deployed on vehicles to monitor the driver's sugar or glucose levels. The necessary sensors can be easily connected to the microcontroller. It also offers cloud Wi-Fi, which allows connecting this microcontroller. In this case, the controlled glucose value is obtained in analogs [69].
- *Blood Pressure Sensor*
  A blood pressure monitor uses an inflatable air bubble cuff or pressure sensor to measure blood pressure in arteries. High blood pressure likely to comes heart attack, stroke, or kidney disease. Their symptoms do not appear, so they need to be checked regularly.

14.6   IoT-Enabled Vehicle Assistance System of Highway Resourcing for Smart Healthcare and Sustainability

In recent years, digital transformation has become a major factor in the growth of several areas of the business. Companies are exploring new ways to work with customers and creating new digital and autonomous systems. This transition to digital transformation is even more important to urban mobility, especially to overcome the problems because of the COVID-19 pandemic. It is estimated that by 2050, almost half (more than $ 9,000 billion in total) of the mobility sector's revenue will come from digital services, including smart, digital finance, and general services [69]. The automotive industry has also adapted to this trend, and North American automakers have shifted from their role as traditional automakers to that of integrators of digital systems and service platforms. IoT-enabled VASs of highway resourcing could be one of the automotive industry's most transformative technologies. Fully self-driving cars can only be used with a combination of innovative digital technologies such as artificial intelligence (AI) and state-of-the-art hardware such as advanced sensors and high-performance processing units. Figure 14.2 shows a VAS system with an IoT, a combination of IoT to make decisions like a human leader in tasks such as perception, road planning, and control. It plays an important role in performing tasks and provides human support. Thus, an IoT-enabled VAS sense analyzes, predict, and respond to road conditions. The work has enabled us to achieve an accurate long-term forecast using the combined use of vehicle sensors, maps, and real-time traffic data.

Current autonomous vehicles cannot be partial autonomy under certain pre-defined conditions. While connectivity can extend the vehicle's information horizon beyond the range of on-board sensors, it provides additional useful information in near real-time. Therefore, the integration of IoT ensures that the vehicle will not be tied to work in a particular area, which can safely drive itself in any road conditions, any type of weather. Also, the emergence of smart cities [69] in the future will benefit from IoT-compatible VAS that can significantly connect driverless cars, trucks, and buses to the VAS ecosystem, reducing traffic congestion and making driving on the roads safer.

Also, with the latest trends in smart sensors and e-health devices powered by the IoT, the obtained data is becoming more complete and detailed. The rapid spread of smart devices opens opportunities for healthcare professionals to share medical information electronically. IoT is combined smart devices into the network. In healthcare systems, IoT is primarily used for rapid access

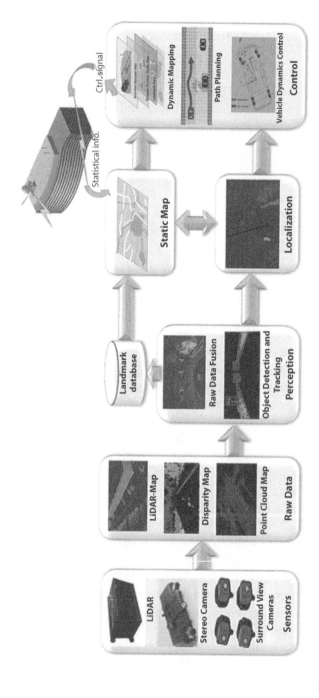

Figure 14.2 IoT-enabled VAS system.

to medical information. IoT is an interconnected network that connects different devices to make large amounts of information available to everyone.

In IoT-enabled VAS smart healthcare system, sensors are used by drivers who touch their bodies and regularly monitor the driver's health. If there are deviations in health, the VAS sends information about the driver's health status via Wi-Fi to the transport office server. The drivers' health status will be updated in the database, as well as a photo of the driver if they are in a state of drowsiness, at the same time, which will also alert the driver to be alert. The driver's original record is already available on the department of transport's centralized server. The notification is then also sent to the transport office. If the transport department needs emergency assistance to the driver, the nearest ambulance is chosen by GPS and reported to the emergency department.

Figure 14.3 shows the block diagram of the system. It monitors physiological parameters such as blood pressure and heart rate using various physiological sensors. The system consists of a healthcare sensor consisting of blood pressure and heart rate monitor sensors that together calculate the health status. This information is transmitted to the microcontroller device. The ARM7LPC2148 is used as an IC microcontroller to convert analog data to digital. The serial USB connector is used for data transfer. The following operations require MATLAB15 software. For cloud data transfer, the URL must be connected to the main program that runs in MATLAB. Also, to be able to perform the cloud-based work required for data transfer the ThingSpeak software is used. The main program must specify a specific key that is the user name and password of the ThingSpeak URL. Finally, the physiological data of the driver is available in the cloud, and use this data anywhere, anytime, and successfully receive the output.

The ARM7TDMI-S is a versatile 32-bit microprocessor that provides high performance and very low power consumption. It is based on the rules of the reduced computer instruction set (RISC). The pipeline method

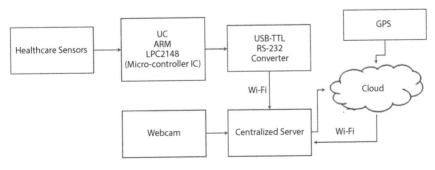

Figure 14.3 Block diagram of the smart healthcare system.

is used to ensure that all parts are work. THUMB is great for large applications with memory limitations or where code density is a problem. The key idea of THUMB is a much-shortened set of commands. One is the standard 32-bit ARM instruction set and the 16-bit THUMB instruction set. It operates an ARM7 processor configuration with a 128-bit wide interface/accelerator at high speeds of 60MHz. ThingSpeak is an open-source IoT that extracts data from things over the internet. It allows creating apps for registering sensors, a location tracking app, and a social network of things with status updates. IoT is deploying real robots that interact with people, such as VASs, which is crucial for ensuring the efficient operation and security of autonomous systems. With the help of our research, we intend to solve such research tasks to realize the vision of a future smart city that could increase safety, efficiency, and comfort for society.

In future, smart cities with numerous IoT enabling VAS an efficient IoT platform is essential to the best functioning of the connected vehicle ecosystem. Figure 14.4 shows a schematic diagram of such an ecosystem.

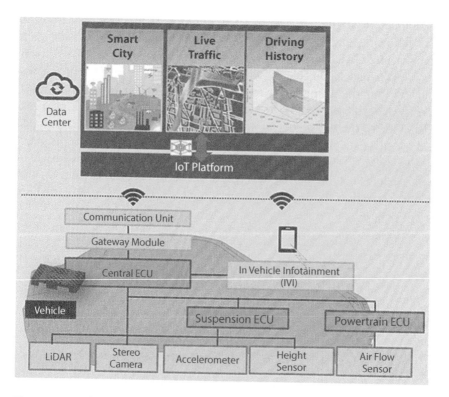

Figure 14.4 Architecture of the VAS ecosystem.

As shown in Figure 14.4, vehicle components such as sensors, in-vehicle infotainment (IVI) module, and separate electronic control units (ECUs) such as suspension and transmission, are all connected to a centralized ECU that collects and processes data and shares it with the IoT platform using gateways and communication modules. The IoT platform enables communication between the smart city data center and third-party partners to improve the customer experience.

14.7   Challenges in Implementation

There are significant issues that may arise and that need to be carefully considered when implementing IoT-based VASs: the data received from IoT devices is a variable term structure and is often achieved in real time. The entire routine of the connected application is highly dependent on the characteristics of managing service; we process this data in real time [70]. Device connectivity is useful when the vehicle is on a remote highway. The maintenance of the servers requires significant costs and investments to deal with the exchange of information [71]. Network protocol design is not easy, it must meet the overall system cost, ease of use, performance requirements network topology, and protocols must be carefully selected. Network topology has its strengths and weaknesses [72]. Accuracy of the delivery of data based on IoT and the accurate source is very important, especially for region requests based on emergency inspection, having several strict requirements [73]. There is no consideration when choosing communication devices and protocols, including human exposure delays. The selected devices and sensors should not harm the human body. There are no strong security and privacy features of any attempt to leak or hack [74, 75].

14.8   Conclusion

This paper describes progress in IoT in the vehicle industry, like connected car services/applications, auto communications, IoT smart shipping, auto management, supply chain management based on IoT, and the new generation of cars. As cars become smarter and more connected to other cars, smartphones, and other things, the corresponding analytical process can be applied to driving parameters, drivers, and road safety authorities. Currently, the main concern is the regular monitoring of people's health. This is easily done by implementing health systems in almost all areas, such as the automotive industry. Emergency medical care is also provided when people need it. Using this system, improve not only the health of the vehicle but also the people in it. Sensors collect the information necessary for analysis and take appropriate actions based on the results. Using this system, a healthy and comfortable environment can be provided for people who travel a lot by vehicle and can track their location or provide route details to people. The paper claims that IoT vehicles have several powerful and unique features based on driver safety and the interconnection of sensors in the car, which can be caused by driver health problems. After all, this paper also mentions significant issues that can be faced and must be taken into account when implementing an IoT-based VAS for smart healthcare.

References

1. Ashton, K. *et al.*, That Internet of Things thing. *RFID J.*, 22, 7, 97–114, 2009.
2. Ali, Z.H., Ali, H.A., Badawy, M.M., Intenet of Things (IoT): definitions, challenges and recent research directions. *Int. J. Comput. Appl.*, 128, 1, 37–47, 2015.
3. HaddadPajouh, H., Dehghantanha, A., Parizi, R.M., Aledhari, M., Karimipour, H., A survey on Internet of Things security: Requirements, challenges, and solutions. *Internet Things*, 90, 100129, 2019.
4. da Costa, C.A., Pasluosta, C.F., Eskofier, B., da Silva, D.B., da Rosa Righi, R., Internet of Health Things: Toward intelligent vital signs monitoring in hospital wards. *Artif. Intell. Med.*, 89, 61–69, 2018.
5. Islam, S.R., Kwak, D., Kabir, M.H., Hossain, M., Kwak, K.-S., The Internet of Things for healthcare: a comprehensive survey. *IEEE Access*, 3, 678–708, 2015.
6. Hu, F., Xie, D., Shen, S., On the application of the Internet of Things in the field of medical and healthcare, in: *2013 IEEE International Conference on Green Computing and Communications and IEEE Internet of Things and IEEE Cyber, Physical and Social Computing*, IEEE, pp. 2053–2058, 2013.
7. Qi, J., Yang, P., Min, G., Amft, O., Dong, F., Xu, L., Advanced Internet of Things for personalised healthcare systems: A survey. *Pervasive Mob. Comput.*, 41, 132–149, 2017.
8. IoT in healthcare market, https://www.marketsandmarkets.com/Market-Reports/iot-healthcare-market-160082804.html, 2020, Accessed June 29, 2020.
9. WHO, *Global status report on Road Safety: Time for Action*, World Health Organization, Geneva, 2009, Available from: www.who.int/violence_injury_prevention/road_ safety_status/2009.
10. Macharia, W., Njeru, E., Muli-Musiime, F., Nantulya, V., Severe road traffic injuries in Kenya, quality of care and access. *Afr. Health Sci.*, 9, 2, 118–124, 2009.
11. Nicholson, B., McCollough, C., Wachira, B., Mould-Millman, N.K., Emergency medical services (EMS) training in Kenya: Findings and

recommendations from an educational assessment. *Afr. J. Emerg. Med.*, 7, 4, 157–159, 2017.

12. Statista, *Number of vehicles in use worldwide 2015*, Statistic, 2015, [Online]. Available: https://www.statista.com/statistics/281134/number-ofvehicles-in-use-worldwide/. [Accessed: 25-Feb-2019].

13. Hassani, P., *Top 14 Advanced Car Technologies by 2020*, 2017, [Online]. Available: https://blogs.systweak.com/top-14-advanced-cartechnologies-by-2020/. [Accessed: 03-Jun-2019].

14. Fleisch, E., Weinberger, M., Wortmann, F., Business Models and the Internet of Things, 2014, LNCS 9001, pp. 6–10, 2015.

15. Kulkarni, D.D. and Jakkan, D.A., A Survey on Smart Healthcare System Implemented Using Internet of Things. *J. Commun. Eng. Innovations*, 5, 1, 2019, MAT Journals.

16. Dervojeda, K., Rouwmaat, E., Netherlands, P., Probst, L., Frideres, L., Luxembourg, P., Internet of Things Smart machines and tools Business Innovation Observatory, Gen. *Intern. Mark. Ind. Entrep. SMEs*, 2–16, 2015.

17. Cohen, A., Arce-Plevnik, L., Shor, T., IoT in automotive industry: Connecting cars. 10, 2116.6489, 2016.

18. Dhirani, L.L., Newe, T., Lewis, E., Nizamani, S., Cloud computing and Internet of Things fusion: Cost issues. *Proc. Int. Conf. Sens. Technol. ICST*, vol. 2017-Decem, no. December, pp. 1–6, 2018.

19. Weiss, E., Gehlen, G., Lukas, S., Rokitansky, C., MYCAREVENT- Vehicular Communication Gateway for Car Maintenance and Remote Diagnosis. *11th IEEE Symposium on Computers and Communications (ISCC'06)*, Cagliari, Italy, pp. 318–323, 2006, doi: 10.1109/ISCC.2006.106.

20. Gehlen, G. and Mavromatis, G., INVENT-VMTL A Web Service based middleware for Mobile Vehicular Applications, electronic and electrical systems, 111, 120–128, 2002, 2018.

21. Meier, *et al.*, *Towards real-time middleware for vehicular ad hoc networks*, in: *Proceedings of the 1st ACM international workshop on Vehicular ad hoc networks (VANET '04)*, vol 3543, pp. 95–96, LNCS, Springer, 2005.

22. Shankar, P., Nadeem, T., Rosca, J., Iftode, L., CARS: Context-Aware Rate Selection for vehicular networks. *2008 IEEE International Conference on Network Protocols*, Orlando, FL, pp. 1–12, 2008.

23. Santa, J. and Gomez-Skarmeta, A.F., Sharing context-aware road and safety information. *IEEE Pervasive Comput.*, 8, 3, 58–65, 2009.

24. Santa, J. *et al.*, A Multiplatform OSGi based Architecture for Developing Road Vehicle Services. *IEEE*, 17, 706–710, 2007.

25. Jayapradha, S. and Durai Raj Vincent, P.M., An IOT based Human healthcare system using Arduino Uno board. *2017 International Conference on Intelligent Computing, Instrumentation and Control Technologies (ICICICT)*, IEEE, 2017.

26. Lavanya, S., Lavanya, G., Divyabharathi, J., Remote prescription and I-Home healthcare based on IoT. *2017 International Conference on Innovations in Green Energy and Healthcare Technologies (IGEHT)*, IEEE, 2017.

27. Jaiswal, K. *et al.*, IoT-cloud based framework for patient's data collection in smart healthcare system using raspberry-pi. *2017 International Conference on Electrical and Computing Technologies and Applications (ICECTA)*, IEEE, 2017.

28. Mumtaj, S.Y. and Umamakeswari, A., Neuro fuzzy based healthcare system using iot. *2017 International Conference on Energy, Communication, Data Analytics and Soft Computing (ICECDS)*, IEEE, 2017.

29. Subasi, A. *et al.*, IoT based mobile healthcare system for human activity recognition. *2018 15th Learning and Technology Conference (L&T)*, IEEE, 2018.

30. Priyanka, P. and Kaur, J., Ant Colony Optimization Based Routing in IoT for Healthcare Services. *2018 Second International Conference on Intelligent Computing and Control Systems (ICICCS)*, IEEE, 2018.

31. Abed, A., Alkhatib, A., Baicher, G.S., Wireless sensor network architecture. *International Conference on Computer Networks and Communication Systems*, vol. 35(Cncs), pp. 11–15, 2012.

32. Yang, G., Xie, L., Mäntysalo, M., Zhou, X., Pang, Z., Da Xu, L., Kao-Walter, S., Chen, Q., Zheng, L.R., A health-IoT platform based on the integration of intelligent packaging, unobtrusive bio-sensor, and intelligent medicine box. *IEEE Trans. Ind. Inf*, 10, 4, 2180–2191, 2014.

33. Bandodkar, A.J., Jia, W., Yardımcı, C., Wang, X., Ramirez, J., Wang, J., Tattoo-based noninvasive glucose monitoring: A proof-of-concept study. *Anal. Chem.*, 87, 1, 394–398, 2015.

34. Liakat, S., Bors, K.A., Xu, L., Woods, C.M., Doyle, J., Gmachl, C.F., Noninvasive *in vivo* glucose sensing on human subjects using mid-infrared light. *Biomed. Opt. Express*, 5, 7, 2397, 2014.

35. On, R. and In, E., Editorial note on the processing. *Storage*, 14, 4, 895–896, 2010.

36. Rathore, M.M., Ahmad, A., Paul, A., The internet of things based medical emergency management using Hadoop ecosystem, in: *Xplore IEEE 2015 IEEE Sensors*, pp. 1–4, 2015.

37. Wan, J., Zou, C., Ullah, S., Lai, C.-F., Zhou, M., Wang, X., Cloud-enabled wireless body area networks for pervasive healthcare. *IEEE Network*, 27, 5, 56–61, 2013.

38. Bornheim, M., Fletcher, M., Al, E., Public Safety Digital Transformation the Internet of Things (IoT) and Emergency Services, in: *EENA Operations Document IoT and Emergency Services*, pp. 1–26, 2016.

39. Riazul Islam, S.M., Kwak, D., Humaun Kabir, M., Hossain, M., Kwak, K.-S., The internet of things for healthcare: A comprehensive survey. *IEEE Access*, 3, 678–708, 2015.

40. Ji, Z. and Anwen, Q., The application of internet of things (IOT) in emergency management system in China, in: *Xplore IEEE – 2010 IEEE Int. Conf. Technol. Homel. Secur. Xplore IEEE*, 2010.

41. Zhao, W., Wang, C., Nakahira, Y., Medical application on internet of things, in: *IET Conf. Publ. IET Int. Conf. Commun. Technol. Appl. ICCTA 2011*, vol. 2011, no. 586 CP, Elsevier, 2012.

42. Hella KGaA, Hueck & Co, *Electronics – Driver Assistance Systems*, Technical Information, 2005.
43. Lee, W.S., Sung, D.H., Lee, J.Y., Kim, Y.S., Cho, J.H., *Driving Simulation for Evaluation of Driver Assistance Systems and Driving Management Systems*, sponsored by the Korea Transportation Institute under the national project, Development of National Traffic Core Technology, 2007.
44. Henricksen, K. and Indulska, J., Software Engineering Framework for Context-Aware Pervasive Computing. *2nd IEEE Conference on Pervasive Computing and Communications (PerCom)*, 2004.
45. Iihoshi, A., Driver Assistance System (Lane Keep Assist System). *Presentation to WP-29 ITS Round Table Geneva*, 2004.
46. Saravanan, K., Thangavelu, A., Rameshbabu, A Middleware Architectural framework for Vehicular Safety over VANET (InVANET). *NETCOM 2009, First International Conference on Networks & Communications*, pp. 277–282, 2009.
47. Seiler, P., Song, B., Karl Hedrick, J., *Development of a Collision Avoidance System*, SAE Technical Papers, International Congress and Exposition - Detroit, MI, United States Society of Automotive Engineers, 1998.
48. Lasky, T.A., Yen, K.S., Ravani, B., *The advanced snowplow Driver Assistance system*, supported by Caltrans New technology and new Program through (AHMCT) program at UC-Devis under IA65X875- TO-96-9, Turin, Italy, 10, 2009, 2009.
49. Bekiaris, E., Nikolaou, S., Mousadakou, A., *System for effective Assessment of driver vigilance and Warning according to traffic risk Estimation*, National Center for Research and Technology, Hellas (CERTH) AWAKE Consortium, August 2004.
50. Kesseler, W., Kleinkes, M., Könning, T. Night vision systems developed for series production. ATZ Worldw, vol. 107, pp. 5–7, 2005.
51. Terry, N., Will the internet of health things disrupt healthcare? *SSRN Electron. J.*, 19, 2, 28–31, 2016.
52. Haus, M., Waqas, M., Ding, A.Y., Li, Y., Member, S., Security and privacy in device-todevice (D2D) communication: A review. *IEEE Commun. Surv. Tut.*, 19, 2, 1054–1079, 2016.
53. Liu, J., Shen, H., Zhang, X., A survey of mobile crowdsensing techniques: A critical component for the internet of things, in: *2016 25th International Conference on Computer Communication and Networks (ICCCN)*, Waikoloa, HI, USA, 2016.
54. Dutta, J., Gazi, F., Roy, S., Chowdhury, C., AirSense: Opportunistic crowd-sensing based air quality monitoring system for smart city, in: *Xplore IEEE 2015 Ieee Sensors*, 2016.
55. Chatzimilioudis, G., Konstantinidis, A., Laoudias, C., Zeinalipour-yazti, D., Crowdsourcing with smartphones. *IEEE Internet Comput.*, 16, 5, 36–44, 2012.
56. Botta, A., De Donato, W., Persico, V., Pescapé, A., Integration of Cloud Computing and Internet of Things: A Survey, Italy, 26, 684–700, 2015.

57. Evdokimov, X.S., Fabian, B., Günther, O., Ivantysynova, L., Ziekow, H., RFID and the Internet of Things: Technology, Applications, and Security Challenges, Foundation and Trends R in Technology. Information and Operations Management, 4, 2, 105–185, 2010.

58. Damani, A., Shah, H., Shah, K., Vala, M., Professor, A., Global Positioning System for Object Tracking. *Int. J. Comput. App.*, 109, 40–45, 2015.

59. Parab, A.S. and Joglekar, A., Implementation of Home Security System using GSM module and Microcontroller. *International Journal of Computer Science and Information Technologies*, 6, 3, 2950–2953, 2015.

60. Song, S. and Issac, B., Analysis of WiFi and WiMAX and Wireless Network Coexistence. *Int. J. Comput. Netw. Commun.*, 6, 6, 63–78, 2014.

61. F.A. and S.E., Wireless Sensor Networking in the Internet of Things and Cloud Computing Era. *EUROSENSORS 2014, XXVIII Ed. Conf. Ser.*, pp. 672–679, 2014.

62. K.K.B.M., Sethi, S., Kumar P, R., Kumar, N., Shankar, A., Detection of Driver Drowsiness using Eye Blink Sensor. *Int. J. Eng. Technol.*, 7, 499–504, 2018.

63. Mallidi, S.K.R. and Vineela, V.V., IoT Based Smart Vehicle Monitoring System. *Int. J. Adv. Res. Comput. Sci.*, 9, 2, 738–741, 2018.

64. Baker, B., *Accelerometer & Gyroscope Sensor Fusion*, Contrib. By Digi-Key's North Am. Ed., 2018.

65. Bandyopadhyay, S., Sengupta, M., Maiti, S., Dutta, S., Role Of Middleware For Internet Of Things: A Study. *Int. J. Comput. Sci. Eng. Surv.*, 2, 3, 94–105, 2011.

66. Patel, N., Patel, P., Patel, N., Heart Attack Detection and Heart Rate Monitoring Using IoT. *Int. J. Innov. Adv. Comput. Sci.*, 7, 4, 2018.

67. Goudjerkan, T. and Jayabalan, M., Predicting 30-Day Hospital Readmission for Diabetes Patients using Multilayer Perceptron. *Int. J. Adv. Comput. Sci. Appl. (IJACSA)*, 10, 2, 2019.

68. Vasanthakumar, R., Darsini, K.D., Subbaiah, S., Laxmi, K., IoT for monitoring diabetic patients. *International Journal of Advance Research, Ideas and Innovations in Technology*, 4, 2149–2157, 2018.

69. https://www.bvdw.org/fileadmin/user_upload/20180509_bvdw_accenture_studie_datadrivenbusinessmodels.pdf

70. Atlam, H.F., Walters, R.J., Wills, G.B., Internet of Things: State-of-the-art, Challenges, Applications, and Open Issues. *Int. J. Intell. Comput. Res.*, 9, 3, 2018.

71. Jindal, F., Jamar, R., Churi, P., Future and Challenges of Internet of Things. *Int. J. Comput. Sci. Inf. Technol.*, 10, 2, 2018.

72. Van Kranenburg, R. and Bassi, A., IoT Challenges, Communications-in-Mobile-Computing, Springer Open J. 1, 2, 2192–1121, 2012.

73. Helmi, O., Akbarpour Sokeh, M., Sepidnam, G., The Challenges Facing with the Internet of Things Challenges of Internet of Things. *Int. J. Sci. Study*, 527, 527, 26521–26544, 2017.

74. Baker, S.B., Xiang, W., Atkinson, I., Internet of Things for Smart Healthcare: Technologies, Challenges, and Opportunities. *IEEE*, 5, 26521–26544, 2017.

75. Sadiku, M.N.O., Tembely, M., Musa, S.M., Internet of Vehicles: An Introduction. *Int. J. Adv. Res. Comput. Sci. Software Eng.*, 8, 1, 11–13, 2018.

15

Aids of Machine Learning for Additively Manufactured Bone Scaffold

Nimisha Rahul Shirbhate[1] and Sanjay Bokade[2]

[1]Department of Mechanical Engineering, Lokmanya Tilak College of Engineering, Koparkhairane, University of Mumbai, India
[2]Department of Mechanical Engineering, Rajiv Gandhi Institute of Technology, Versova, University of Mumbai, India

Abstract

Bone scaffold is a three-dimensional porous construction that provides support to enhance natural cell growth in the injured or broken part of the bone. In recent years, investigators from various departments like biomedical, mechanical, and orthopedics have shown significant interest in accepting "bone scaffolds" as a promising treatment for bone injury. "Bone scaffold" is a porous architecture/ structure made up of bio-compatible material having grater advantages over the current grafting solution. To manufacture bone scaffold with additive manufacturing (AM) technology surely makes it easy with the aids of machine learning (ML).

ML, a subgroup of artificial intelligence (AI), has progressively become famous in AM research. For ML, algorithms, applications, and platforms are promoting AM practitioners to enhance product quality, optimize the manufacturing process.

The bone scaffold in the era of biomedical implants with 3D printing has compelling importance due to its advantage over grafting. This chapter tries to propose the new way of treating the bone defect at the same time padding the gap between theoretical and actual implementation of "bone scaffolds" by using aids of ML allowing upcoming opportunities for reinventing the new possibilities in the field of biomedical.

Keywords: 3D printing, additive manufacturing, biocompatible materials, bone scaffold, machine learning

*Corresponding author: nomotghare@gmail.com

Monika Mangla, Nonita Sharma, Poonam Mittal, Vaishali Mehta Wadhwa, Thirunavukkarasu K. and Shahnawaz Khan (eds.) Emerging Technologies for Healthcare: Internet of Things and Deep Learning Models, (359–380) © 2021 Scrivener Publishing LLC

15.1   Introduction

Bones in the human body are the most important architecture. The internal structure of the body is nothing but the framework made up of a bone that is why bones are so important. Bones are nothing but the honeycomb-like porous structure of tissues. Human life in its entire lifespan may come across different circumstances such as accidents, injury, or some kind of diseases which may directly or indirectly lead to damage of bone. In other words, it results in the degeneration of bone tissues in the individual anatomy. To facilitate the natural reworking of bones it is needed to repair the damaged tissues or facilitate the growth of tissues naturally [3]. This problem again can deal with replacing the tissues. Treatment commonly focuses on taking up the tissue from one section of the patient's body and replace to another part of the same patients which is called (an autograft) or tissues from one patient to another, this transplantation is called as (a transplanted or allograft) [2]. While these treatments are revolutionary and convenient in lifesaving, still there are some significant constraints to these treatments. Collecting tissues and transplant (auto-grafts) is costly and painful at the same time constrained by biological constraints which are correlated with taking sufficient quantity of tissue for one whom in requirement of while harvesting tissues from other body there is consistently chance of transmitting some type of infections from the donor's body to receiver body. This kind of problem can be treated with pours bone scaffolds which will promote the natural regrowth of the tissues. These scaffolds can be built with different bio adaptable materials and embedded in the human body. To compose bone scaffolds with porous structure is near about impractical with conventional manufacturing methods. Additive manufacturing (AM) technologies in the field of scaffolds bring out new hope. Three-dimensional printing (3DP) has an intense capability to manufacture bone scaffolds with different bio-compatible materials [1].

15.1.1   Bone Scaffold

A bone scaffold can be characterized as the support structure for the damaged or injured bone to facilitate natural cell growth to treat the bone defect. Bone Scaffold is a three-dimensional solid porous construction which contributes as support to promote natural cell growth in an injured or broken section of bone. In the last some years, researchers from various streams like biomedical, mechanical, and orthopedics have presented significant interest in adopting "bone scaffolds" as an upcoming treatment for bone injuries. "Bone scaffold" is a honeycomb-like architecture made up of bio-compatible material having grater advantages over ongoing grafting solution.

The internal supporting network of the body is nothing but central architecture made up of bones and which makes them so crucial. Human life in its entire lifetime may face various events such as accidents, injury, or some kind of diseases which may lead to bone damage. During lifetime, bones also undergo a process of degeneration. To enhance the natural reworking/regeneration of bones, it is necessary to repair the spoiled tissues or facilitate the growth of tissues naturally. The bone fractures are of two kinds first, in which it gets self-repair after fracture because of small in size. While in second type, larger fractures fall, they cannot heal perfectly by themselves and that is called a segmental bone defect.

"Bone scaffolding" is convenient treatment in the field of orthopedic section over "grafting". The process of bone repairing with the help of bone scaffold is as shown in Figure 15.1. It can be seen that bone scaffold is to implant in the damaged or injured section of the bone. Soon, cells start growing on it, and after some time, bone repairs completely.

The issues related to grafting can be removed or overcome with pours bone scaffolds, which will facilitate the regrowth of the tissues in the scaffold. These bone structures can be made with various bio suitable

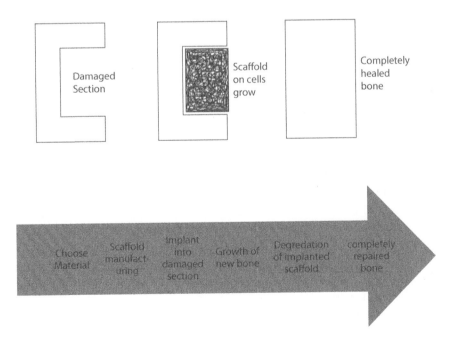

Figure 15.1 Bone repairing process [15].

materials and after words be implanted at the site of the cripple in the human body. To make bone scaffolds, with honeycomb-like structure, is a herculean task if pursued through traditional manufacturing techniques and the certainty of success remains doubtful. AM technologies have unbolted new possibilities like 3DP which could contribute to the ability to print bone substitute material [1]. The bone scaffold can be implanted in the human body as well as in animals [27], wherever the cells are damaged due to some disease or broken bone. In the field of biomedical [24], specifically in bone scaffolding one can recognize exceptional growth.

15.1.2   Bone Grafting

Bone grafting is a clinical technique that adopts transplanted bone to treat and repair a diseased or damaged section of bones. A bone grafting facilitates treatment almost anywhere in the human body for treating the bone defects. In bone grafting, doctors usually take bone from hips, legs, or ribs to perform the graft. The bone used in bone grafting is come from anywhere means from the patient's body or the donor's body. Bone grafting is possible because bone tissue can rejuvenate interlay if keep a suitable space to grow. As natural bone grows, it will generally replace the graft material completely, resulting in a fully integrated region of new bone. The biologic mechanisms that provide a rationale for bone grafting are osteoconduction, osteoinduction, and osteogenesis.

The practice of bone grafts is the standard to treat bone fractures or to recover and reconstruct badly injured bone, as indicated by the extensive number of bone graft operation observed globally. The most acceptable of these is the auto-graft; however, its adoption can result in complexity such as pain, infection, scarring, blood loss, and donor-site morbidity. The next option to treat is allografts, but they inadequate in the osteo-active capacity of auto-grafts and brings the risk of transferring infectious agents or immune rejection.

Bone grafting is accomplished for the below-mentioned reasons, including injury and disease. There are four important reasons for the use of bone grafts.

A bone graft usually used when the case is of multiple fractures or complex type of fractures or that kind of injury which do not heal thoroughly after the first treatment.

Fusion helps two bones heal together across a diseased joint. Fusion is most often done on the spine.

Reconstruction of tissues is used for bone loss due to disease, infection, or injury. This can involve using small amounts of bone in bone cavities or large sections of bones.

A graft can be used to help bone heal around surgically implanted devices, like joint replacements, plates, or screws.

All surgical conducts associate risks of bleeding, infection, and reactions to anesthesia. A bone graft brings these following types of risks and others [20]:

- Pain
- Swelling
- Nerve injury
- Rejection of the bone graft
- Inflammation
- Reabsorption of the graft

15.1.3   Comparison Bone Grafting and Bone Scaffold

Treatment of Bone defect can be serve by two methods Bone graft and Bone scaffold. The caparison of these two methods shown in Table 15.1.

Table 15.1 Comparison in between bone grafting and bone scaffold [2, 15].

Bone grafting	Bone scaffold
Take tissues from human body.	Bone scaffold provides the structure which facilitates natural cell growth.
Allo-grafting and auto-graft are two types of grafting.	It is framework made up of different biocompatible material.
Harvesting tissue from patient body is painful at the same time costly too.	This bone scaffold manufacturing by 3D printing and implanting in patient's body.
Always there is chance of rejection of cells by patient's immune system.	In bone scaffolds, there is always use of biocompatible and sometimes biodegradable materials.
Taking enough tissue from donors to patient is also challenge.	Bone scaffold can be implant in any section of body where cell growth stop due to injury or disease.

15.2   Research Background

From the literature review, it is seen that many researchers are working in the field of medical especially in the area of the bone scaffold to establish scaffold is more assuring treatment over allograft or autograft. The research articles included in this study, fabricated bone scaffold or reviewed bone scaffold adopting various biocompatible material and 3DP/RP as manufacturing techniques [20]. To evaluate and figure out the qualities and behavior of material used for the scaffold, some of the researchers carried out experimentation such as compression tests or tensile tests [7, 10, 13, 18]. Few of the researchers implanted the 3D printed scaffold into animals like rats or rabbits, to know about the cell growth on the implanted scaffold. Still, the research was limited to static analysis of the 3D printed bone scaffolds [28]. After implantation, bone scaffold would be an integral part of the human body. To make bone scaffold as a successful treatment to bone defect, it is so much required to be examined for dynamic conditions as well. How the used biocompatible material will behave in dynamic conditions needs to be figured out. Before going for the dynamic analysis researcher should know about the work which has been done in this same area. For this chapter, a systematic literature review of almost 35 papers in the same area which gives an idea about the number of manufacturing methods used by various researchers, the biocompatible material and the mechanical testing carried out by them [2]. After the systematic review, it clearly shows till the time study was limited to static analysis, so for further study to be carried out in this area this article will be expedient.

15.3   Statement of Problem

A research problem is a description of an area of interest, a situation to be enhanced, and adversity to be eradicated. This chapter is about discussing the topics of the area which are untouched and still needed betterment in the area of the bone scaffold. Scaffolds are intended to be used as an integral part of the human body. Since the bio-compatible material which is going to implant in the body should capable of withstanding all types of lodging and movement as well. So, static and dynamic analysis is essential. Static and dynamic analysis can be possible with the variation in the following:

- Biocompatible materials.
- Method of manufacturing.
- Porosity variation.

By which, better material can be suggested as a material for implant. This will be sustained in the body at any loading and movement. At the same time, this best material can be tested for cell growth in a controlled environment. Excluding the study of cell growth in this research, below are the listed research problems of the study:

- Comparative study of mechanical properties of the material used for the bone scaffold.
- Analysis of bone scaffold for static conditions.
- Analysis of bone scaffold for dynamic condition.

15.4 Research Gap

A research gap is a research question or problem which has not been defended appropriately or at all in a defined field of study. It mainly focuses on the area which remains untouched in a particular area of study. Based on the literature studied, it has been noticed that continuous efforts are being made to make bone scaffold useful for treating bone defects.

In the current medical world, bone tissue reparation is becoming an increasingly beneficial process. The technique most commonly used for this treatment is a bone graft, where specialist doctors place existing gathered bone mass from different origins and graft it to the area of bone being renovated. However, it is very difficult to amass the amount of bone necessary for such an execution of the operation.

Injury and diseases can result in damage and degeneration of tissues in the human body, which requires treatments to promote their regeneration.

According to the literature review, various researchers used many bio-compatible materials and manufacturing techniques as conventional and 3DP. Some of them moved towards testing, such as compression testing only but some of the areas still untouched to make scaffold as current treatment.

- Comparative study of mechanical properties of the bone scaffold can facilitate to choose between different bio-compatible materials.
- Static analysis of scaffold with different materials and porosity.
- Dynamic analysis of scaffold for some reparative motions.
- Check the material best in the static and dynamic test, for the cell growth in *VIVO* [26] and *VITRO* [6, 8].

15.5   Significance of Research

The research intends to inform action. Thus, the research study should explore to contextualize its discovery within the larger body of research. Research needs a consistent effort. It should always be of immense quality to produce awareness that is pertinent outside of the research context. Furthermore, the findings of your research may indicate policy and future project implementation.

The bone scaffold has greater advantages over bone grafting, bone scaffold made by 3DP will facilitate natural cell growth instead of harvesting from somewhere else [1]. This research will go to predict the behavior of different biocompatible material as a bone scaffold in various static and dynamic conditions.

The significance of this research is to overcome the limitations of bone grafting. This research will provide the various mechanical properties of the bone scaffold in static and dynamic conditions. So, its behavior according to material in the human body will be predicted and better treatment will be provided for treating the bone defect.

This research intended to the people who have to suffer from some kind of bone disease or accidents in which cells got damaged.

15.6   Outline of Research Methodology

Following are the proposed methodology of research work, as shows in Figure 15.2.

15.6.1   Customized Design of Bone Scaffold

Design is the first step in which the shape and size of the scaffold are to decide according to patients' requirements. 3D printing allows us to make it customized. Further, according to its volume a redesign of bone scaffold

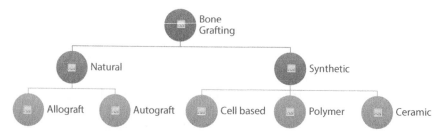

Figure 15.2 Bone substitute.

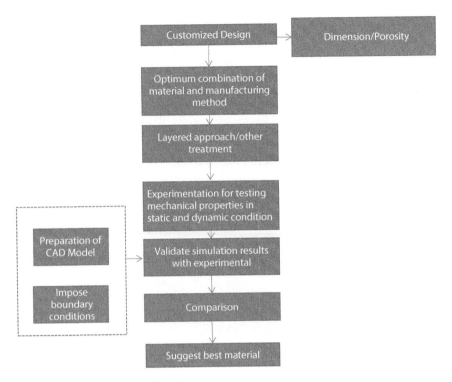

Figure 15.3 Methodology of work.

takes place for varying porosity [16]. To do this, any type of CAD software can be used. Figure 15.3 shows the methodology of work in which the customized 3D model is prepared and the same model is used for the simulation purpose and for conducting experiment as well, in order to understand the behavior of bio-compatible materials in static and dynamic conditions. A 3D mimic is a well-known software for the conversion of MRI into the 3D model shown in Figure 15.4, in which the MRI or CT scan image of the patient is taken, and from that, the 3D model gets prepared which then saves in an appropriate format so that it can send directly to the 3DP machine.

15.6.2   Manufacturing Methods and Biocompatible Material

About the previous step, the material and the manufacturing method will be selected. The material selection is the most important factor in bone scaffold because selected material should have desired qualities such as mechanical properties and porosity [4]. Mechanical properties are so meaningful that they can predict the behavior of bone scaffold inside the human body after implantation.

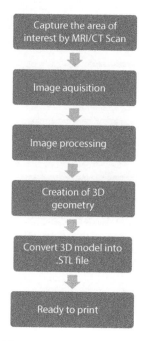

Figure 15.4 MRI to 3D model [6, 11].

The next important thing is porosity, which is nothing but the interconnected tiny holes. Porosity ensures cell growth. More is the porosity correlatively; higher will be cell growth, and at the same time, the more susceptible to fracture. So, to have a perfect balance in-between mechanical properties and the porosity, static and dynamic analysis are important for each type of material. Moreover, to take the advantage of the ceramic type of materials and metal combined, coting of one over another material can be done [21].

15.6.2.1 Conventional Scaffold Fabrication

Previously, when there was the unavailability of AM techniques, still, bone scaffolds got manufactured using different traditional or conventional methods such as solvent casting, salt leaching chemical or gas foaming, phase separation, freeze-drying, thermally comprised, and foam-gel are some of the methods used in previous research. Yet, using these conventional methods, it was difficult to control porosity, defined shape, internal architecture, and connectivity in-between [25]. To avoid all these kinds of difficulty in the fabrication of bone scaffold, AM plays a very important role. AM can produce intricate shapes at the same time internal architecture can be control. Porosity is an important factor to be focused while manufacturing specifically the bone scaffold [22]. Various techniques of AM and 3DP facilitate the controlled architecture, varying porosity, and interconnected internal structure [4]. In short by using AM, the bone scaffold can be manufacture easily, which will facilitate the natural cell growth in the damaged section of bone.

15.6.2.2 Additive Manufacturing

The AM technique is a convenient name to characterize the technologies or methods that able to produce 3D objects by adding layer-on-layer of the various materials as shown in Figure 15.5, whether the material can be plastic, metal, or even human tissue depending upon the need. AM also is known as 3DP, rapid prototyping, or freeform fabrication [19, 30]. Conventional manufacturing techniques are associated with a material to be shaped or finished up into the desired product by section of the material being removed in many numbers of ways. AM is exactly the reverse of conventional destructive manufacturing in which material gets remove layer by layer. AM facilitates the construction of complicated architecture like a honeycomb-like structure. AM work with computer-aided design (CAD) [12]. Using CAD or 3D object scanners, AM allows for the creation of objects with precise geometric shapes. Using different CAD software,

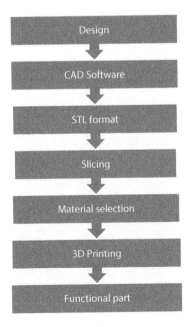

Figure 15.5 Process of additive manufacturing [11].

the intricate shapes can be made and using available slicer software the CAD design can be cut into the number of slices horizontally depending upon the layer thickness required by the 3D printer [13].

One of the most enormous assets of this more modern technology is that the greater range of shapes that can be produced or composed. Intricate Designs that cannot be manufactured in one entire piece with conventional means can easily be achieved. For example, a body with a scooped out or hollow in the center can be produced as a single part, without the involvement of weld or to attach individual components. This has the benefit of being stronger; with no weak spots that can be compromised or stressed.

The layer-by-layer deposition continues to the last layer to fabricate a complete 3D component. Various deposition methods are working on a different basis. However, these processes are similar in the thermal, chemical, and mechanical ways they fabricate parts. The most common processes are Stereo-Lithography (SLA), Liquid Polymerization (LP), Fused Deposition Modeling (FDM) [16], Selective Laser Sintering (SLS), and Binder Jet Printing (BJP). These entire AM methods can classify as solid, liquid, and powder-based techniques.

15.6.2.3   Application of Additive Manufacturing/3D Printing in Healthcare

Volume utilized by the medical field is one of the biggest end-users of AM techniques. This is one of the industries where AM advantages like tricky patterns and personalization can well utilize.

Hearing aids are one of the most appreciable illustrations in the case studies for 3DP where the demand for personalization meets the specification of patients the low volume have needed for each distinct item. The AM technique is idle for constituting the organic shapes precise to each user which then houses the stock electronic assembly.

One of the best utilization of AM techniques in the medical field which is already having an enormous impact is the ability to practice before the actual procedure. To treat critical operations, surgeons used to take data from CT scan and MR images of the particular patients to build 3D models of the patient's anatomy they will operate on. They then use this same 3D CAD data to develop 3D printed models, enabling them to practice critical surgery techniques on practical models to excellent technique. This methodology allows surgeons to be more precise and accurate about their work which again reduces the risk of getting wrong and allows operating faster.

The dentistry and orthodontics production is again one of the greatest technology users of 3DP. The medical market is without a doubt one of the most responsive to AM technologies. Compared to traditional applications, AM offers many customization advantages to this market. In terms of the dental market, the applications are very diverse, ranging from 3D printed implants, prostheses, crowns, etc. Using the same methodology as previous scans to be taken from the physically patient's mouth dentists and dental laboratories can easily manufacture accurate and tailored solutions to operate or treat the dental diseases or defects. Use cases incorporate 3D printed aligners which gradually move the teeth into the desired point as well as 3D printed crowns and spans. AM is the generous and developing player in the dental business and there are already several tools and elements built precisely for this mark.

Patient definite implants can be much costly and time-consuming to generate using conventional manufacturing techniques but AM can be executed rapidly and accurately in massively trimmed timelines. Especially for complicated biological architectures that conventional manufacturing techniques struggle with 3DP preserve its own. Two of the remarkable recognitions of 3DP for these operations are the capacity to use patient-specific data to manufacture the implants and the capacity to create matrix or lattice patterns on the area of the parts. These patterns reinforce Osseointegration and lower rejection.

3D printed surgical cutting and drill guides are a growing application in the medical field, specifically in dental. Similar to drill jigs for manufacturing which assures holes are in the appropriate place, surgeons commonly adopt jigs to ensure their operations are in the definite location. These have on the whole been off the shelf parts, and on the other hand, using 3DP it is now feasible to have bespoke guides erected to the patient's unique anatomy. This means more precise operations and greater postoperative outcomes.

Prosthetics are a few of the more leading case studies in 3DP for medical utilization. There have been many versions of companies setting up simple 3D printed prostheses for infants or people in progressing countries without approach to other options. This is just the surface and various associations are working on this in a very genuine way. AM provides the ability to manufacture patients' explicit prostheses without being overly expensive.

Some practices of 3DP outside traditional manufacturing incorporate the possibility of 3D print organs. This could be one of the most radical uses of 3DP and one with actual scope to develop the world as we know it. If it was desirable to print new body parts and organs by using our cells as the support, then millions of people who are desperate for transplant donors would no longer now have to wait for a suitable match.

Much 3D printed producer pharmaceuticals: Modern drug and medication manufacturing are on a mass scale and the medicines are not targeted but more catch-all explanations that work with modifying effectiveness and intensity for various people. AM launches the new prospect of printing designer medicines that are specific to you, your body, and your needs.

AM empowers not just personalization but also, particularly, cost reduction, and returns in success. There are sure to be countless more potential utilization. Not just of current technologies and materials but as new medical precise technologies are created and developed, 3DP will go on to change the face of the medical industry.

Stereo-Lithography Apparatus (SLA): Stereo-lithography is one of the most important and precise types of AM. Figure 15.6 shows the working of stereo-lithography apparatus. In stereo-lithography, the material used is in the form of liquid, and the LaserJet rays are used to solidify

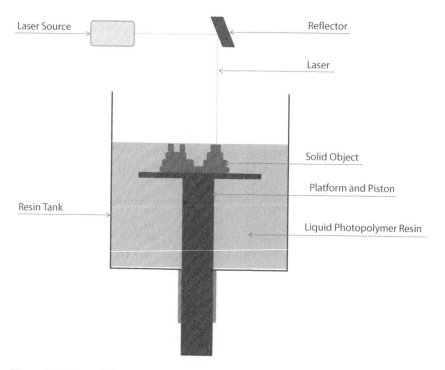

Figure 15.6 Stereo-lithography [20].

the topmost layer of material in the molten pool to print the part layer by layer. Stereo-lithography adopts the processes of the photochemical process. Each layer of molten metal gets solidifies with the help of a laser and goes down follows the bottom to top approach. 3D CAD model used the slicer software to cut out the entire 3D part. This slice information sends to the processor. In this way, the entire part gets fabricated.

Fused Deposition Modeling: FDM is a category of AM of polymer materials that do not employ laser. This system is provided with a computer-controlled nozzle head that amasses semisolid materials on a surface to develop a layer. This process is widely used in the deposition of hard polymer materials as they are in the semisolid form before to deposition [14].

The deposition materials get off the nozzle head in a filament tone with adjustable diameters and geometries building upon nozzle head position. The fabrication takes place in a layer-upon-layer fashion again. Subsequently, deposition of each layer, a milling head cuts the surface to conform surface finish and thickness of the layers.

Figure 15.7 shows the working of FDM in which the raw material is to feed in the wired form and it passes through the pair of rollers to continuous and proper supply of raw material. It then again passes through a hot chamber where the material gets melted and easily gets deposited in layers. To simplify material dismissal, the technique of FDM takes place at

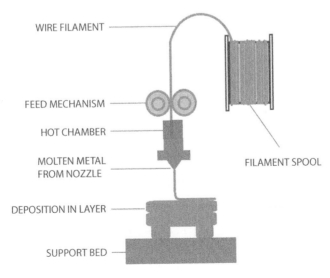

Figure 15.7 Fused deposition modeling [17].

a temperature near the melting point of the polymeric materials. Besides, a supporting nozzle can be added to the setup that can deposit inferior materials to have a composite and enhance the properties of the fabricated component [8]. A benefit of using this process is obtaining a finished part at the end without the need for post-processing and machining.

Selective Laser Sintering [21]: SLS is also one of the important laser-based systems shown in Figure 15.8, while its materials come in the form of powders but instead of binder laser is used in this type of technique [8]. A roller is also recognized as a coater, which helps to feed the metal powder materials into the place of fabrication [5]. A computer design file will provide the geometry of each layer and an integrated laser head will get the G-codes and move on the designated paths. After each pass of the laser, the materials that had interaction with the laser will melt and the rest of the powder particles remain untouched. That untouched powder itself works as a support and it can be reusable too. The basic principle of this technology is as in Figure 15.8. SLS uses a CO_2 laser beam to heat powder particles to the glass transition temperature, which is near their melting point, sintering the material directly from a solid model without entering the melting phase. Along with the workstation moving down layer by layer, the new powder is spread on the sintered object with a roller. The process repeats until the 3D part is complete.

Direct 3D Printing (3DP): One of the 3DP techniques is direct (straightforward) 3DP. Direct 3DP employs a jet technique. The direct 3DP is one of the powder bed technique in which the liquid binder is used to print the part. The material powder of desired thickness into the fabrication chamber with the help of roller gets spared. It uses an adhesive injector

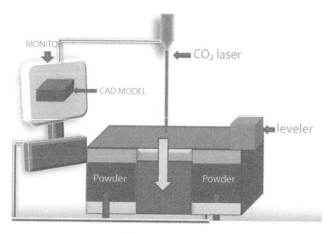

Figure 15.8 Schematic diagram of SLS [5, 24].

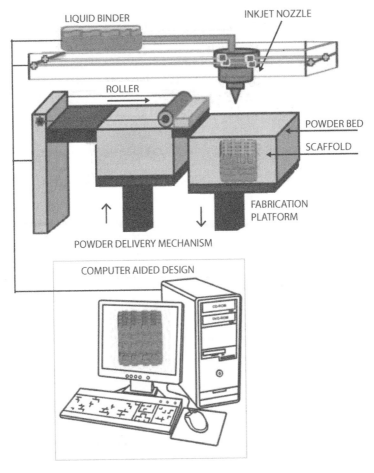

Figure 15.9 Direct 3D printing [8].

head to bond the materials. After all the layers are deposited and bonded with adhesives, the part is finished but not completed yet. The final step of fabricating parts is to cure them in a specific heat in a furnace. The curing temperature varies based on the adhesive and base materials used. Also its shown in Figure 15.9. The quality of the fabricated part depends on the particle size of the powder. The smaller is the particle size higher will be the density.

Mechanical Testing and Software Simulation: Once the bone scaffold gets manufactured, the next phase is testing and analysis. To know the behavior of bone scaffold after implanting in the human body, it is necessary to analyze it for various common movements of a human. To validate the result, software simulation also can be done.

15.6.2.4 Automated Process Monitoring in 3D Printing Using Supervised Machine Learning

In this article, a method has been proposed to monitor the 3DP process by pausing the printer at various checkpoints. This method used for the detection of possible defects and take proper corrective actions such as stopping the print if a potential defect is detected thereby reducing material wastage and time [32].

The process works in the following stages:

Stage 1 - Diagnose appropriate checkpoints for 3DP component according to its geometry.
Stage 2 - Take pictures of the semi-finished component at each checkpoint.
Stage 3 - Execute image processing and analysis.

Initially, the component required to be printed is performed by design software such as Solid-Works. After that, the STL file of the created model is secured. Then, checkpoints are pinpointed depending on the geometry of the part. The later step is to launch the printing process and it goes on until it attains a described checkpoint for the given print. When it reaches a checkpoint, the printing technique is interrupted for a while and the nozzle is boosted up to the specified height. Then, the bed moves entirely the whole way to the frontal end of the printer where the camera is located to take pictures. Then, the camera captures a picture after a small interruption. After that, the bed and the nozzle moved back to their initial position (where they lasted before the printer paused) and started printing again.

Support Vector Machine is the machine learning (ML) algorithm used in the process. SVM or Support Vector Machine is a linear model for classification and regression problems. It can solve linear and non-linear problems and work well for many practical problems. The idea of SVM is simple: The algorithm creates a line or a hyperplane which separates the data into classes. The most frequently used way to set up a non-linear classifier is the kernel trick. Kernel methods are essentially based on calculating the relationship between the unlabeled general inputs and the instruction inputs. Prediction for the unlabeled inputs, i.e., for the above-mentioned which are not in the instruction datasets, is done by the function of a similarity function k, called a kernel, among the unlabeled current input x' and each of the training inputs xi.

In the investigation, the section standards (of RGB values) of the images calculated at checkpoints are carried as input to the directions of training models. Two kinds of training models namely "good" (exact to the ideal parts) and "bad" (defective parts) have been carried into the system. Then, the SVM training algorithm has manufactured a model that classifies any new images loaded into the structure as either "good" or "bad" print. If a component is diagnosed as "bad" during the introductory stages of printing, suddenly a remedial measure to stop the printing process will be taken to prohibit further wastage of material and time and then reprint the part again.

15.7 Conclusion

In this chapter, the author tries to reevaluate the available literature on bone scaffold. This study aims to know about various 3D printing methods used for manufacturing scaffold, biomedical materials used, at the same time the properties of idle scaffold and ML employed in AM.

This research work analyses different work in the area of bone scaffold Material, method, and the behavior under different static loading conditions. For further research CAD model of the intended scaffold can be made using CAD software. The dimensions and shape of the scaffold may not be particular because the damaged section of bone always changes with the patient. Keeping the research objective focused on the dimensions and size can be appropriately chosen. Porosity is an important factor for the bone so, for different porosity different models can be made [12, 29, 23]. These models will be helpful while manufacturing scaffold by 3DP just by converting CAD files into .STL format. This bone scaffold can be then tested for various moving conditions (dynamic analysis). This will provide information on how it will behave in dynamic conditions.

Every research is intended toward modification, improvement, and betterment and so is this. This study focuses on improvement in the area of the bone scaffold by static as well as dynamic analysis of bone scaffolds that a better material can be suggested with probably all properties which an ideal scaffold should possess.

References

1. Leukers, B., Gülkan, H., Irsen, S.H., Milz, S., Tille, C., Schieker, M., Seitz, H., Hydroxyapatite scaffolds for bone tissue engineering made by 3D printing. *J. Mater. Sci.: Mater. Med.*, 16, 1121–1124, 2005.

2. Lipowiecki, M. and Brabazon, D., Design of Bone Scaffolds Structures for Rapid Prototyping with Increased Strength and Osteoconductivity. *Adv. Mat. Res.*, 83–86, 914–922, 2010.

3. Bose, S., Roy, M., Bandyopadhyay, A., Recent advances in bone tissue engineering scaffolds. *Trends Biotechnol.*, 30, 10, 546–554, 2012.

4. Bose, S., Vahabzadeh, S., Bandyopadhyay, A., Bone tissue engineering using 3D printing. *Mater. Today*, 16, 12, 496–504, 2013.

5. Feng, P., Wei., P., Shuai, C., Peng, S., Characterization of Mechanical and Biological Properties of 3-D Scaffolds Reinforced with Zinc Oxide for Bone Tissue Engineering. *PloS One*, 9, 1, e87755, 2014, doi: 10.1371/journal.

6. Jariwala, S.H., Lewis, G.S., Bushman, Z.J., Adair, J.H., Donahue, H.J., 3D Printing of Personalized Artificial Bone Scaffolds, Mary Ann Liebert, Inc., *Journal of 3D Printing and Additive Manufacturing*, 2, 2, 2015.

7. Robles-Vazquez, O., Orozco-Avila, I., Sánchez-Díaz, J.C., Hernandez, E., An Overview of Mechanical Tests for Polymeric Biomaterial Scaffolds Used in Tissue Engineering. *J. Res. Updates Polym. Sci.*, 4, 168–178, 2015.

8. An, J., Teoh, J.E.M., Suntornnond, R., Chua, C.K., Design and 3D Printing of Scaffolds and Tissues. *Engineering*, 1, 2, 261–268, 2015.

9. Aldemìr, B., Dıkıcı, S., Karaman, O., Oflaz, H., Development, 3D printing and characterization of calcium sulfate based scaffolds for bone tissue engineering. *2015 19th National Biomedical Engineering Meeting (BIYOMUT)*, Istanbul, pp. 1–4, 2015, doi: 10.1109/BIYOMUT.2015.7369434.

10. Senatovn, F.S., Niaza, K.V., Zadorozhnyy, M.Yu., Maksimkin, A.V., Kaloshkin, S.D., Estrin, Y.Z., Mechanical properties and shape memory effect of 3D-printed PLA-based porous scaffolds. *J. Mech. Behav. Biomed. Mater.*, 57, 139–148, 2016.

11. Munaz, A., Vadivelu, R.K., St. John, J., Barton, M., Kamble, H., Nguyen, N.-T., Three-dimensional printing of biological matters, *Journal of Science: Advanced Materials and Devices*, 1, 1, 1–17, 2016, https://doi.org/10.1016/j.jsamd.2016.04.001

12. Fradique R., Correia T.R., Miguel, S.P., de Sá, K.D., Figueira, D.R., Mendonça, G., Correia, I.J., Production of new 3D scaffolds for bone tissue regeneration by rapid prototyping, Biomaterials Synthesis And Characterization. 27, 69, 2016.

13. Jančař, J., Slovikova, A., Amler, E., Krupa, P., Kecova, H., Planka, L., Gal, P., Nečas, A., Mechanical response of porous scaffolds for cartilage engineering. *Physiol Res.*, 56 Suppl 1, S17-25, 2007.

14. Dong, L., Wang, S.J., Zhao, X.R. *et al.*, 3D- Printed Poly(ε-caprolactone) Scaffold Integrated with Cell-laden Chitosan Hydrogels for Bone Tissue Engineering. *Sci. Rep.*, 7, 13412, 2017. https://doi.org/10.1038/s41598-017-13838-7

15. Wu, T., Yu, S., Chen, D., Wang, Y., Bionic Design Materials and performance of Bone tissue Scaffold. *Mater. J.*, 10, 1187, 2017.

16. Gregor, A., Filova, E., Novak, M., Kronek, J., Chlup, H., Buzgo, M., Blahnova, V., Lukašova, V., Bartoš, M., Nečas, A., Hošek, J., Designing of PLA scaffolds for bone tissue replacement fabricated by ordinary commercial 3D printer. *J. Biol. Eng.*, 11, 31, 2017.

17. Konta, A., Garcia, M., Serrano, D., Personalised 3D Printed Medicines: Which Techniques and Polymers Are More Successful? *Bioengineering (Basel).* 4, 4, 79, 2017. doi: 10.3390/bioengineering4040079.

18. Naghieh, S., Karamooz-Ravari, M.R., Sarker, M.D., Karki, E., Chen, X., Influence of crosslinking on the mechanical behavior of 3D printed alginate scaffolds: Experimental and numerical approaches. *J. Mech. Behav. Biomed. Mater.*, 80, 111–118, 2018.

19. Wang, X., Wei, C., Cao, B., Jiang, L., Hou, Y., Chang, J., Fabrication of Multiple-Layered Hydrogel Scaffolds with Elaborate Structure and Good Mechanical Properties via 3D Printing and Ionic Reinforcement. *ACS Applied Materials & Interfaces*, 10, 21, 18338–18350, 2018.

20. Turnbull, G., Clarke, J., Picard, F., Riches, P., Jia, L., Han, F., Li, B., Shu, W., 3D bioactive composite scaffolds for bone tissue engineering. *Bioact. Mater.*, 3, 278e314, 2018.

21. Du, X., Fua, S., Zhu, Y., 3D printing of ceramic-based scaffolds for bone tissue engineering: an overview. *J. Mater. Chem. B*, 6, 4397–4412, 16th June 2018.

22. Ji, K., Wang, Y., Wei, Q., Zhang, K., Jiang, A., Rao, Y., Cai, X., Application of 3D printing technology in bone tissue engineering. *Bio-Des. Manuf.*, 1, 3, 203–210, 2018, doi: 10.1007/s42242-018-0021-2.

23. Bruyas, A., Lou, F., Stahl, A., Gardner, M., Maloney, W., Goodman, S., Yang, Y., Systematic characterization of 3D-printed PCL/β-TCP scaffolds for biomedical devices and bone tissue engineering: Influence of composition and porosity. *J. Mater. Res.*, 33, 14, 1948–1959, 2018, doi: 10.1557/jmr.2018.112.

24. Liu, J. and Yan, C., *3D Printing of Scaffolds for Tissue Engineering*, IntechOpen, London, IntechOpen Limited, UK, 2018.

25. Chocholata, P., Kulda, V., Babuska, V., Fabrication of Scaffolds for Bone-Tissue Regeneration. *Materials* (Basel). 12, 4, 568, 2019.

26. Zhang, Y., Wang, C., Fu, L., Ye, S., Wang, M., Zhou, Y., Fabrication and Application of Novel Porous Scaffold *in Situ*-Loaded Graphene Oxide and Osteogenic Peptide by Cryogenic 3D Printing for Repairing Critical-Sized Bone *Defect. Molecules.* 24, 9, 2019.

27. Qu, H., Fu, H., Hana, Z., Sun, Y., Biomaterials for bone tissue engineering scaffolds: a review. *RSC Adv.*, 9, 26252–26262, 2019.

28. Vazquez-Vazquez, F.C., Chanes-Cuevas, O.A., Masuoka, D., Biocompatibility of Developing 3D-Printed Tubular Scaffold Coated with Nanofibers for Bone Applications. *J. Nanomater.*, 2019, 6105818, 9th May 2019, https://doi.org/10.1155/2019/6105818

29. Ma, J., Lin, L., Zuo, Y., Zou, Q., Ren, X., Li, J., Li, Y., Modification of 3D printed PCL scaffolds by PVAc and HA to enhance cytocompatibility and osteogenesis. *R. Soc. Chem.*, *RSC Adv.*, 2019, 9, 5338–5346, 2019.

30. Wang, C., Huang, W., Zhou, Y., He, L., Hea, Z., Chen, Z., He, X., Tian, S., Liao, J., Lu, B., Wei, Y., Wang, M., 3D printing of bone tissue engineering scaffolds. *Bioact. Mater.*, 5, 1, 82–91, March 2020.

31. Zhao Yingchun, Hou Yue, Li Zhaoyu, Wang Ziyu, Yan Xinxin, Powder-Based 3D Printed Porous Structure and Its Application as Bone Scaffold, *Frontiers in Materials*, 7, 150, 2020, https://www.frontiersin.org/article/10.3389/fmats.2020.00150, 10.3389/fmats.2020.00150, ISSN=2296-8016

32. Delli, U. and Chang, S., Automated Process Monitoring in 3D Printing Using Supervised Machine Learning. *Proc. Manuf.*, 26, 865–870, 2018.

Index

3D plotting scan, 173
3DP, 359–377

ABE (attribute-based encryption), 115–117
ABIDE (autism brain imaging data exchange), 290
Accountability, 95, 114
Act, 93, 95, 96, 123
Actor(s), 94, 103–105, 122
Actuators, 25, 26, 29, 30, 33, 38, 55
Additive manufacturing, 359, 360, 369, 370
Adversary/adversarial, 104, 121, 120, 124
AES (advanced encryption standard), 109
Allograft, 360, 364, 366
Alzheimer's, 100
Anonymity, 114, 124
Anonymization, 93, 103, 104, 113, 123
Apps, 37, 40, 41, 43, 44
Arduino board, 27, 38
Artificial intelligence (AI), 6, 26, 94, 122, 359
Artificial neural network, 191–193, 210
Asperger condition, 282–283
Assistive technologies,
    IoT, 240
    virtual reality, 240
    VSM, 240

Autism diagnostic observation schedule 2nd edition (ADOS-2), 283–284
Autism spectrum disorder (ASD), 238, 282–283
    automated diagnosis of, 284, 289–291
    investigation techniques, 285–288
Autoencoder (AE), 47–49, 52, 54
Autograft, 360, 364, 366
Availability, 96, 103, 105, 114

BANs (body area networks),
    WBANs (wireless body area networks), 93, 94, 97–103, 105–109, 114
BCIs (brain computer interface), 99
BDL,
    BDL-IBS (blockchain and distributed ledger-based improved biomedical security), 120
Big data analytics, 93–95, 124
Biocompatible material, 359, 364
Bioimaging, 46, 49–51
Bioinformatics, 46, 49, 50
Biomedical, 97, 104, 120, 121, 125
Blockchain, 93, 95, 109, 119, 120–122
Body area network (BAN), 34
Bone scaffold, 359–377
BS (base station), 98–101, 104, 107, 109

Cell growth, 359–361, 363, 364
Centroid, 326–328
Cloud computing, 35–41, 93, 94, 103, 112–114, 116, 117, 119, 124
Cloud server, 30, 33–36
Confidentiality, 93, 96, 103, 114–116
COCO model, 321
Cognitive IoT, 26, 55
Compression test, 364
Computer vision, 320
Confusion matrix, 193–194
Convolutional layer, 190
Convolutional neural networks (CNNs), 47, 49–54, 93, 96, 103, 114–116, 189–191, 211, 289–290
Coooll, 302
COVID, 87, 337
Crowd sensing, 346
    blood pressure monitor, 349
    global positioning system (GPS), 346
    global system for mobile communication (GSM), 347
    middleware, 348
    wi-fi, 347
CUDA acceleration, 320

DaaS- data, 40
Data (databases), 93–125
Data acquisition, 26, 27, 38
Data analysis, 272–273
Data collection, 135–136, 185–186
Data gathering, 161, 185–187
Data preparation, 136–138
Data pre-processing, 162, 186
Data sources, 269–272
Data split, 162–163, 186–187
Data visualization, 162
DeepConvnet architecture, 293
Deep learning, 25, 26, 29, 40, 42, 44, 46, 49–55, 181, 289–290
Deep learning algorithms, 289–290

Deep learning models, 46–47, 53
Deep neural network (DNN), 41, 318
Deep transfer learning–neural network (DTL-NN) model, 291
DeepConvNet, 291
Descriptive analysis, 254
    multivariate analysis, 270–271
    multivariate regression analysis, 271–272
    regression analysis, 263–269
    standard deviation, 254
Diabetes, 82, 131–132
Diagnosis,
    medical diagnosis, 94, 97, 122
Differential,
    differential privacy, 105, 113, 123, 124
Direct 3D printing, 374
Distributed, 94, 119, 120
DMZs (de-militirized zone/peremiter network), 123
DNA (deoxyribonucleic acid), 111
DNNs (deep neural networks), 122, 125
Dropout, 77
Dynamic analysis, 364–366, 368, 377

Early intervention and diagnosis, 242
ECC (elyptic curve cryptography), 113, 123
ECG (electrocardiogram), 93, 97, 98, 109, 110, 123
EEG (electroencephlogram), 93, 97, 284
EEGNet, 291, 293
EELR (energy efficient location aided routing), 102
EHR (electronic health records), 95, 120, 121
Encryption, 96, 108, 109, 113, 115, 116, 118, 119, 123
Estimating parameters, 266–268
Exploratory data analysis, 171–173

Feature extraction, 306
Feature selection, 290
Feature(s), 98, 109, 111, 113, 119, 120,
    122
Feyn, 80
Field programmable gateway (FPGA),
    53
Flattening, 191
FOG, 17
Framework, 99, 122
FTPS (file transfer protocol secure),
    123
Function,
    hash function, 108
Fused deposition modeling, 373

Gait, 109–110
Gathering and handling data, 169–170
Geographic,
    GAF (geographic adaptive
        protocol), 102
GPRS (general packet radio service),
    97–98
Graphology, 204

Handwriting recognition, 203
Hardware,
    computing hardware, 112
    embedded hardware, 105
    hardware encryption, 109
    hardware manipulation attack, 106
    hardware security, 103
Health management system, 46, 53,
    54
Healthcare, 93–125
Hierarchical, 101, 107, 108
Highway resourcing, 338
Hindi tweets, 300, 304
HIPAA (Healthcare Insurance Privacy
    and Accountability Act), 93, 95,
    96, 112, 123, 124

Homomorphic,
    homomorphic encryption, 116, 118,
        119
HTTPS (hyper text transfer protocol
    secure), 123
Human-machine interface, 35, 37
Hybrid, 98, 113, 124

IaaS (infrastructure as a service), 21,
    25, 26, 29–33, 39–43, 55
IBE (identity based encryption), 115
ICU (intensive care unit), 93
Identity, 104, 108, 109, 114, 115
Implant, 361, 363, 364, 365
Implantable, 99, 100, 104, 106, 110, 123
Internet, 93–98, 100, 104, 106, 107,
    109, 112, 114
IoHT, 22
IoT (Internet of Things), 46, 50–53, 93,
    114, 337
IP (internet protocol), 100, 106, 109

Keras, 75
Kernel model, 303
Key, 105, 107–109, 115, 116, 119, 121

LEACH (low energy adaptive
    clustering hierarchy), 101
Linear regression, 255–256
Logistic regression, 262–265
Lung segmentation, 173–175

Machine learning [ML], 70, 93, 97,
    122, 133–134, 148–153, 359, 377
Machine learning algorithms, 303–304
    K nearest neighbor classification
        technique, 139–140
    logistic regression, 144–145
    random forest classifier, 142–143, 150
    support vector machine, 140–142,
        152

Machine learning methodology,
data accommodation, 135–138
model evaluation, 145
model training, 138–145
user interaction, 145–146
Machine learning techniques for
prediction of kidney failure, 253
analysis and empirical learning,
254–255
classification, 259–261
decision tree, 261–263
supervised learning, 255–256
unsupervised learning, 256–259
Malicious, 94, 103, 106, 108, 120, 122
Materials and methodology, 243, 244
Matplotlib library, 306
Maximum entropy method, 303
Medical imaging, 25, 46, 49–55
Microcontroller, 97, 101, 109
MIoT (medical Internet of Things), 94,
97, 100, 109
Model building, 196–197
Model lifecycle, 71
Model optimization, 166–168
Model training, 187–193
Monitoring, 74
Moodables, 9
MRI (medical resonance imaging), 122
MSNs (medical sensor networks),
WMSNs (wireless medical sensor
networks), 94, 97–99, 101–103,
107–109, 114
Multilayer perceptron (MLP), 289
Multivariate regression, 268–269

Naïve Bayes classifier, 303
Natural language processing (NLP),
301, 304
Network(s), 96–98, 100–103, 105–109,
112–113, 119–120
Next, 290
NLTK, 301, 306

Nodes, 98–99, 101–102, 104–109, 111,
120
Non-repudiation, 103, 104, 114

Obfuscation, 108
Ordinal logistic regression, 265–266
Oximeter,
pulse oximeter, 100

PaaS- platform, 35, 37
Pacemakers, 93, 97, 99, 105
Parameter, 72
Perceptron, 76
Person detection,
contour detection, 325
frame creation, 324–325
Personality prediction, 203
Pervasive developmental disorder - not
otherwise specified (PDD-NOS),
282–283
PKI (public key infrastructure), 107,
115
Pooling, 190–191
Porosity, 364, 365, 367, 368, 377
Pre-processing of data, 170–171
Privacy, 93–96, 101–104, 107–108,
113–116, 119–125
Proposed methodology, 161–168
Proposed system for risk mitigation in
ASD individuals, 244
Protocol, 100–103, 107, 120, 123
Python, 306

QGraphs, 81
QLattice, 80
QLattice workflow, 83
QoS (quality of service), 99, 102
Quantum,
post quantum cryptography, 119
quantum computers, 119
quantum encryption, 119
quantum mechanics, 119

Radio frequency identification (RFID), 338
Random forest classifier, 306–311
Random forest or random decision forest, 301–302
RELU, 190
ReLU activation function, 304
Resampling, 173
ResNet-34 model, 291
Results and discussion, 245–247
Risk-sense model, 292
Routing, 101–105, 107
RSA (algorithm), 123

SaaS- software, 35, 37
Security, 93–96, 99, 101–105, 107–109, 111, 113–116, 118–125
Sensitivity of various techniques, 241
  EEG-based, 241
  gamification, 241
  ML-based, 241
  MRI-based, 241
  neurofeedback, 241
Sensors, 25–27, 29–34, 38, 97–110, 114
Serial peripheral interface, 31
SLS, 370, 374
Smart connected vehicle, 338
Smart healthcare, 26, 27, 29, 31, 33, 34, 36
Smart hospitals, 40, 42, 43
Smart server, 34, 35
SSWE, 302
Stacked sparse autoencoder (SSAE), 291
Static, 364, 365, 366, 367, 377
Stereo-lithography, 372
Stringency index, 317
Supervised learning, 133
Support vector machine, 303
Sustainability, 349
  smart shipping, 353
  THUMB, 352

TCP (transmission control protocol), 106, 109
TEEN (threshold sensitive energy efficient sensor network protocol), 101
TLS (transport layer security), 109, 123
Training and testing of data in 3D architecture, 175–178
Training neural network, 163–166
Transaction, 103, 104, 120
Transfer learning, 73
Transfer learning approach, 290–291
Transmission, 101, 103, 107, 109
Tree kernel model, 302
Trust, 105, 107, 108, 120, 121, 124
TTDD (two tier data dissemination), 102
Twitter data sentiment analysis, domain introduction, 300–302
  implementation, 311
  literature survey, 302–304
  motivation, 300
  proposed methodology, 304, 306–311

Ubiquitous, 94, 112
Unigram model, 302

Vectors, 104, 107, 111
Vehicle assistance system (VAS), 339–341
  cognitive, 341
  healthcare system, 342
  human computer interaction, 340
  ontology, 341
  wearable medical devices, 340
Virtual assistants, 42
Visualization, 77
Vitro, 365
Vivo, 365
Vulnerabilities, 109

WBSNs (wireless biomedical sensor
    networks), 97, 103, 109, 111
Wearables, 42, 43, 45
WEKA, 303
Wireless body area networks, 4
Wireless sensor network, 342–345
    adaptive cruise control, 343
    automotive night vision, 345
    collision avoidance system, 344
    device to device, 345
    driver drowsiness detection, 344
    lane departure warning, 343
    machine to machine, 345

    parking assistance, 344
WMIoTs (wireless medical Internet of
    Things), 98, 99, 101–103, 107–109
WMSNs (wireless medical sensor
    networks), 97–99, 101–103,
    107–109, 114
Wormhole, 106–107
WSNs (wireless sensor networks), 97,
    101

YOLO model, 318

ZIGBEE (protocol), 97–100

Printed and bound by CPI Group (UK) Ltd, Croydon, CR0 4YY

Printed and bound by CPI Group (UK) Ltd, Croydon, CR0 4YY